A Construction Grammar of the English Language

Cognitive Linguistics in Practice (CLiP)
ISSN 1388-6231

A text book series which aims at introducing students of language and linguistics, and scholars from neighboring disciplines, to established and new fields in language research from a cognitive perspective. The books in the series are written in an attractive, reader-friendly and self-explanatory style. They include assignments and have been tested for undergraduate and graduate student use at university level.

Editors

Carita Paradis
Lund University

Stefanie Wulff
University of Florida

Editorial Board

Rosario Caballero
Universidad de Castilla-La Mancha

Ewa Dąbrowska
Northumbria University

Dagmar Divjak
University of Sheffield

Adele E. Goldberg
Princeton University

Stefan Th. Gries
University of California, Santa Barbara

Martin Hilpert
University of Neuchâtel

Suzanne Kemmer
Rice University

Todd Oakley
Case Western Reserve University

Klaus-Uwe Panther
University of Hamburg

Peter Robinson
Aoyama Gakuin University

Julio Santiago de Torres
Universidad de Granada

Marjolijn Verspoor
University of Groningen, Netherlands &
University of Pannonia, Hungary

Advisory Board

Günter Radden
Universität Hamburg

Volume 5

A Construction Grammar of the English Language
CASA – a Constructionist Approach to Syntactic Analysis
by Thomas Herbst and Thomas Hoffmann

A Construction Grammar of the English Language

CASA – a Constructionist Approach to Syntactic Analysis

Thomas Herbst
Friedrich-Alexander-Universität Erlangen-Nürnberg

Thomas Hoffmann
Catholic University Eichstätt-Ingolstadt

John Benjamins Publishing Company
Amsterdam / Philadelphia

The paper used in this publication meets the minimum requirements of the American National Standard for Information Sciences – Permanence of Paper for Printed Library Materials, ANSI z39.48-1984.

DOI 10.1075/clip.5

Cataloging-in-Publication Data available from Library of Congress:
LCCN 2024025667 (PRINT) / 2024025668 (E-BOOK)

ISBN 978 90 272 1498 0 (HB)
ISBN 978 90 272 1497 3 (PB)
ISBN 978 90 272 4676 9 (E-BOOK)

© 2024 – John Benjamins B.V.
No part of this book may be reproduced in any form, by print, photoprint, microfilm, or any other means, without written permission from the publisher.

John Benjamins Publishing Company · https://benjamins.com

Table of contents

Preface   XV

CHAPTER 1.

Introduction   1

1.1   Why Construction Grammar   1
1.2   What is Construction Grammar   2
1.3   What is a construction   4
     1.3.1   Definitions of construction   4
     1.3.2   Simple words as constructions   6
     1.3.3   Complex words as constructions   6
     1.3.4   Idioms as constructions   7
     1.3.5   Schematicity of constructions   8
     1.3.6   Collocations as constructions   10
     1.3.7   Lexico-grammatical space   11
1.4   How do we learn constructions   13
     1.4.1   Segmentation and pattern finding   13
     1.4.2   Entrenchment and pre-emption   14
1.5   How do constructions combine   15
1.6   Form and meaning in Construction Grammar   18
1.7   Construction Grammar as a model of linguistic description   20

CHAPTER 2.

Conventional wisdom: A chapter some readers might want to skip   22

2.1   The purpose of this chapter: Reminding you of things you already know   22
2.2   Word classes   22
2.3   Phrases, clauses and sentences   25
2.4   Clause constituents   27
2.5   Semantic roles   28

CHAPTER 3.

Sentence type constructions   30

3.1   Starting with children   30
3.2   From illocution to the semantic properties of different sentence types   30
3.3   Basic sentence type constructions   32
     3.3.1   Subject and predicate   32
     3.3.2   Declarative and interrogative constructions   33
     3.3.3   Imperative constructions   36
     3.3.4   Exclamative constructions   39
3.4   Sentence type fragments   39
3.5   The role of sentence type constructions in CASA   42

CHAPTER 4.
The roles of verbs 43
4.1 Introduction 43
    4.1.1 Language acquisition and adult language use 43
    4.1.2 A methodological question 45
4.2 Expressing different degrees of certainty 48
    4.2.1 Yes, no, possibly or perhaps 48
    4.2.2 The English modals 49
    4.2.3 Form and meaning of modal constructions 49
    4.2.4 Combining modal and other constructions 50
4.3 Using verbs to refer to time 51
    4.3.1 Problems of the morphological analysis of English verb forms 51
    4.3.2 Tense and person constructions 53
        4.3.2.1 Present and past-tense constructions 53
        4.3.2.2 Combining tense constructions with other constructions 57
    4.3.3 Referring to the future 58
        4.3.3.1 Referring to future time with the WILL CONSTRUCTION 58
        4.3.3.2 The BE-GOING-TO-V CONSTRUCTION 59
    4.3.4 Other multi-word constructions used to express 'time' 60
4.4 The PROGRESSIVE CONSTRUCTION 61
4.5 The PERFECTIVE CONSTRUCTION 62
    4.5.1 Form and meaning of the PERFECTIVE CONSTRUCTION 62
    4.5.2 Relating the PERFECTIVE CONSTRUCTION to other constructions 64
4.6 The PASSIVE CONSTRUCTION 64
    4.6.1 Active and passive 64
    4.6.2 Combining the passive construction with other constructions 66
4.7 More complex combinations 66
4.8 Subjunctive mood constructions 67
4.9 Negation and the DO-SUPPORT CONSTRUCTION 68

CHAPTER 5.
Who does what to whom? Argument structure constructions 70
5.1 General introduction 70
    5.1.1 Ways of looking at argument structure 70
    5.1.2 The emergence of argument structure constructions 70
    5.1.3 Argument structure constructions at different levels of abstraction 74
        5.1.3.1 Valency constructions and pre-emption 74
        5.1.3.2 Participant roles and argument roles 75
        5.1.3.3 Levels of knowledge associated with argument structure constructions 77

5.2	The CASA framework of argument structure constructions 80	
	5.2.1	Specification of argument structure constructions in CASA 80
	5.2.2	Specification of argument slots: Subj-, Obj- and Attr-arguments 81
	5.2.3	Why Subj does not automatically mean SUBJ 82
	5.2.4	Argument roles 84
	5.2.5	Names of constructions 84
	5.2.6	Subj-arguments 85
5.3	A one-argument construction: The English INTRANSITIVE CONSTRUCTION 86	
5.4	ÆFFECTOR and ÆFFECTED: Monotransitive constructions 86	
	5.4.1	Monotransitive constructions 86
		5.4.1.1 The MONOTRANSITIVE CONSTRUCTION with Obj$_{NP}$ 86
		5.4.1.2 Monotransitive constructions with clausal objects 88
	5.4.2	Introducing a RECIPIENT: Ditransitive constructions 88
		5.4.2.1 The DITRANSITIVE CONSTRUCTION with Obj$_{NP}$ 88
		5.4.2.2 Ditransitive constructions with clausal objects 90
5.5	Motion constructions 92	
	5.5.1	Self-motion and caused-motion 92
	5.5.2	CAUSED-MOTION and *TO*-RECIPIENT CONSTRUCTIONS 94
5.6	Attribute and resultative constructions 95	
	5.6.1	SUBJECT-ATTRIBUTE constructions 95
	5.6.2	OBJECT-ATTRIBUTE constructions 96
	5.6.3	A note on resultative constructions 97
5.7	Constructions with prepositional objects 99	
	5.7.1	General characterization 99
	5.7.2	CHANGE-OF-STATE and *INTO*-CAUSATIVE CONSTRUCTIONS 100
	5.7.3	FOCUS-AREA and REFERENCE-AREA: Obj$_{PP:about}$ and Obj$_{PP:on}$ 101
	5.7.4	Communication partners: *TO*-RECIPIENT/GOAL and *WITH*-PARTNER 103
	5.7.5	Instrument and emotion 104
	5.7.6	The English CONATIVE CONSTRUCTION 105
	5.7.7	DESIRED-THING constructions 106
	5.7.8	The nature of prepositional objects 108
5.8	Perspectivization of arguments 108	
	5.8.1	Actives and passives 108
	5.8.2	Discrepancies between active and passive expressions of arguments 109
	5.8.3	Perspectivization 110
	5.8.4	The mediopassive construction 111
5.9	Combining argument structure constructions with sentence type constructions 112	
5.10	Adjectival argument structure constructions 113	
	5.10.1	Argument structure constructions across word classes 113

5.10.2 General design of adjective argument structure constructions 114
5.10.3 Adjectival argument structure constructions with prepositional phrases 116
5.10.4 Adjectival argument structure constructions with *that-* and *wh*-clauses 117
5.10.5 Different types of infinitive constructions with adjectives: BE-ADJ-TO-V CONSTRUCTIONS 117

    5.10.5.1 *DIFFICULT*$_{ETC}$*-TO*-INFINITIVE *CONSTRUCTION* 118
    5.10.5.2 *WILLING*$_{ETC}$*-TO*-INFINITIVE CONSTRUCTION 119
    5.10.5.3 *BRAVE*$_{ETC}$*-TO*-INFINITIVE CONSTRUCTION 120
    5.10.5.4 The *SURPRISED*$_{ETC}$*-TO*-INFINITIVE CONSTRUCTION 120
    5.10.5.5 Adjective+infinitive constructions with quasi-modal meanings 121

5.10.6 Impersonal constructions with adjectives 123

    5.10.6.1 *IT-THAT*-CLAUSE CONSTRUCTION 123
    5.10.6.2 The IT-BE-*IMPORTANT*$_{ETC}$*-FOR*-X-*TO*-INFINITIVE CONSTRUCTION 124
    5.10.6.3 The IT-BE-*IMPORTANT*$_{ETC}$*-FOR*-BENEFICIARY-*TO*-INFINITIVE CONSTRUCTION 125
    5.10.6.4 The *NICE*$_{ETC}$*-OF*-X-*TO*-INFINITIVE CONSTRUCTION 125
    5.10.6.5 Impersonal adjective construction without PPs 126

5.11 Nominal argument structure constructions 126
5.12 A network of argument structure constructions 128
5.13 Argument structure in CASA and other approaches 130

CHAPTER 6.
Referring to, describing and evaluating things: Nominal constructions 132
6.1 Nouns and pronouns in language acquisition 132
6.2 Characteristics of NP-constructions 133

  6.2.1 NPs can fill the same slots 133
  6.2.2 NPs can be used to refer to 'things' 133

    6.2.2.1 Reference 133
    6.2.2.2 Grounding elements 137

  6.2.3 A family of NP-constructions 138
  6.2.4 Proper nouns, count and mass nouns 138

6.3 Indefinite NP-constructions 141
6.4 Definite NP-constructions 142

  6.4.1 *the* + nouns 142
  6.4.2 Personal pronoun constructions 143
  6.4.3 Reflexive NP-constructions 144
  6.4.4 Reciprocal constructions 145
  6.4.5 Genitive and possessive constructions 146

6.5 Demonstrative NP-constructions 147

6.6 Quantifying NP-constructions 148
    6.6.1 Numerical NP-constructions 148
    6.6.2 General quantifier NP-constructions 149
6.7 Ranking NP-constructions 151
6.8 Wh-NP-constructions 152
6.9 Name and title constructions 152
6.10 Noun phrases 154
    6.10.1 Basic NP-constructions 154
    6.10.2 Modifier-of-noun constructions 154
        6.10.2.1 Premodifier-of-noun constructions 154
        6.10.2.2 Postmodifier-of-noun constructions 155
        6.10.2.3 Discontinuous modifier-of-noun constructions 156
    6.10.3 A simplified, integrated view of NP-constructions 157
    6.10.4 Shortcut representations 159

CHAPTER 7.
Using adjectives to evaluate, describe and compare   162
7.1 Adjectives and adverbs 162
    7.1.1 Uses of adjectives 162
    7.1.2 The ADJECTIVE CONSTRUCTION 163
    7.1.3 The PREMODIFIER-OF-NOUN CONSTRUCTION 165
    7.1.4 Item-relatedness in attributive and predicative uses 165
7.2 Expressing degree 166
    7.2.1 Modifier-of-adjective constructions 166
        7.2.1.1 Premodifier constructions 166
        7.2.1.2 Postmodifier constructions 166
        7.2.1.3 Discontinuous modifier constructions 167
    7.2.2 Expressing maximum degree 167
7.3 Collocational parallels between adverb-adjective and adjective noun patterns 169
7.4 Comparing things 170
    7.4.1 The COMPARATIVE CONSTRUCTION 170
    7.4.2 The *MORE-THAN*-COMPARISON CONSTRUCTION 171
    7.4.3 Ways of expressing difference and likeness 174

CHAPTER 8.
Where, when and how: Specification of circumstances   176
8.1 Going beyond "who does what to whom" 176
8.2 Constructions situating an event with respect to location and time 176
    8.2.1 Different ways of expressing similar meanings 176
    8.2.2 Point of location 177
    8.2.3 Time 178
8.3 Constructions detailing the way the action described is carried out 179

x   A Construction Grammar of the English Language

8.4   Constructions that situate the event described within the domain of causation and interrelatedness of 'things'   180
8.5   Constructions that express an assessment of the event described by the speaker   181
8.6   Constructions that situate the event described within the text   182
8.7   The gradient character of these distinctions   182
8.8   The syntactic status of adjunct constructions   184
    8.8.1   Integration in sentences and utterances   184
    8.8.2   Adjunct constructions   185
    8.8.3   POINT IN TIME and POINT OF LOCATION as adjuncts or arguments   188
    8.8.4   CHANGE-OF-LOCATION constructions and multiple realization   189
    8.8.5   The (ir)relevance of the argument vs. adjunct distinction   191
    8.8.6   Vocatives   191

CHAPTER 9.
Joining ideas and clauses   192
9.1   Compression through blending   192
9.2   Coordination   192
    9.2.1   Asyndetic and syndetic coordination   192
    9.2.2   Levels of coordination   193
    9.2.3   Additive coordination constructions   193
9.3   Connectors and Connection Constructions in general   195
    9.3.1   Connectors as a word class   195
    9.3.2   Connection constructions   196
    9.3.3   Connection constructions with only one expressed CONNECTEE   197
9.4   Reasoning in discourse   197
    9.4.1   Discourse organization   197
        9.4.1.1   More on addition   197
        9.4.1.2   Sequence   198
    9.4.2   Contrast   198
    9.4.3   Why: Cause   199
    9.4.4   Conditions   199
    9.4.5   SCOPE
9.5   Linguistic implications   202

CHAPTER 10.
Information structure constructions   203
10.1   Information structure and construal   203
10.2   Reference: Which 'thing' are we exactly talking about?   204
10.3   Topic: What are we talking about? – Focus: What's new?   206
10.4   Summary   214

Table of contents   XI

CHAPTER 11.

Speaking idiomatically: Prefabricated chunks as low-level constructions   215

11.1   Idiomaticity   215
        11.1.1   The idiom principle   215
11.2   Idioms as constructions   216
11.3   Constructions involving particles   218
        11.3.1   Verb-particle constructions   218
        11.3.2   Constructions with two particles   223
11.4   Collocation   224
11.5   Small-scale constructions   225
        11.5.1   The *let-alone* construction   225
        11.5.2   The GOD-KNOWS CONSTRUCTION   227
        11.5.3   The COMPARATIVE-CORRELATIVE CONSTRUCTION   227
11.6   Outlook   230

CHAPTER 12.

Solving problems with construction grammar   231

12.1   Ligature   231
12.2   Reporting what other people have said   232
        12.2.1   The quotative construction   232
        12.2.2   REFERRING-TO-SOURCE CONSTRUCTION   233
        12.2.3   Indirect speech   234
12.3   Tag constructions   234
12.4   Constructions with *it* and *there*   235
        12.4.1   Existential *there*   235
        12.4.2   Other constructions with *there* and *here*   236
        12.4.3   Constructions with impersonal *it*   236
                12.4.3.1   Weather verbs   236
                12.4.3.2   Impersonal constructions with verbs, adjectives and nouns   237

CHAPTER 13.

Words as constructions in a constructional network   239

13.1   Words   239
        13.1.1   Word-lemmata and word-forms   239
        13.1.2   Words as nodes in networks   240
        13.1.3   A note on polysemy   241
13.2   From words to word classes: Similarities between words   243
        13.2.1   Aspects of word learning   243
        13.2.2   Plausibility   244
        13.2.3   Dual class membership   244

13.2.4 The CASA category of particles   245
    13.2.4.1 Particles and the traditional distinction between prepositions, adverbs and conjunctions   245
    13.2.4.2 Complex particles   248
13.2.5 Adverbs   249
13.2.6 Determiners and pronouns   250
13.2.7 *Wh*-words   251
13.2.8 The limits of classification   252
13.2.9 Summary   253
13.3 CASA word classes   255
13.3.1 Survey   255
13.3.2 Words that play a part in establishing reference to a 'thing'   255
    13.3.2.1 Nouns   255
    13.3.2.2 Pronouns   255
    13.3.2.3 Demonstratives   256
    13.3.2.4 Numerals   257
    13.3.2.5 Quantifiers   258
    13.3.2.6 Articles   258
13.3.3 Words that refer to relationships situated in time   259
    13.3.3.1 Verbs   259
    13.3.3.2 Modals   259
13.3.4 Words that have a descriptive or evaluation function   260
    13.3.4.1 Adjectives   260
    13.3.4.2 Adverbs   260
13.3.5 Words that refer to atemporal relationships   261
    13.3.5.1 Particles   261
    13.3.5.2 Connectors   262
13.3.6 Interjections   263
13.3.7 Items defying further classification   263
    13.3.7.1 Who, whose, whom, which, what, why, where, when, *and* how   263
    13.3.7.2 So   263
    13.3.7.3 As   264
    13.3.7.4 Not   264

CHAPTER 14.

Word order   265

14.1 The functions of word order in English   265
14.1.1 Meaning, textual organization, and processing   265
14.1.2 Word order in construction grammar   267

14.2 Word order and language processing   268
    14.2.1 Noun phrases   268
    14.2.2 Verbs in finite clauses   270
14.3 Word order in argument structure constructions   270
14.4 The position of adjunct constructions   271
14.5 Inversion   274

CHAPTER 15.
Putting it all together: Blending constructions   275
15.1 From constructions to constructs   275
15.2 Combining constructions   275
    15.2.1 Juxtaposition and superimposition   275
    15.2.2 Conceptual Blending as the cognitive process of construction   276
15.3 CASA construction grids   277
15.4 Sample analysis   278

References   287

APPENDIX I.
List of argument and other semantic roles   302

APPENDIX II.
Index of constructions (see www.constructicon.de)   304
II.1 Sentence type cxns   304
II.2 Modal, aspect, tense and voice constructions   304
II.3 Argument structure constructions   306
II.4 Noun phrase constructions   307
II.5 Adjective constructions   308
II.6 Adjunct constructions   309
II.7 Other constructions   309

Preface

This book originated from a coffee-break conversation between T.H. and T.H. back in 2017, in which we felt that the sorts of things we tested our students on in the finals examinations and, as a consequence, what we focused on in a considerable part of our teaching did not reflect the state-of-the-art in modern linguistics. Since we are absolutely convinced that the model of Construction Grammar has a lot to offer to future linguists and language teachers because it addresses issues of language description and language alike, we undertook the enterprise of developing a framework of syntactic analysis that would be easy to understand and apply, while at the same time incorporating current insights of usage-based research within constructionist frameworks.

We are extremely grateful to all colleagues with whom we had the opportunity to discuss the approach taken in this book, especially Adele E. Goldberg, Ewa Dąbrowska, Anatol Stefanowitsch, Mark Turner and Peter Uhrig. Furthermore, we would like to thank the editors of the series, Carita Paradis and Stefanie Wulff, as well as the two anonymous reviewers who commented in great detail on earlier manuscripts. We are very grateful for their feedback and the many useful suggestions they made. Furthermore, our thanks go to Thomas Brunner, Veronika Stampfer, Vladimir Buskin and Victoria Mußemann for their valuable suggestions on the first draft of the manuscript as well as to Armine Garibyan and Michael Klotz. Furthermore, we would like to thank Susan Hendriks and Ymke Verploegen from Benjamins, who supported us throughout the entire production process.

We hope that student and teachers alike will find CASA an insightful and helpful model that increases their understanding of Construction Grammar and raises their interest and curiosity in usage-based and cognitive research on language in general!

CHAPTER 1

Introduction

1.1 Why Construction Grammar

In this book, we attempt to introduce our readers to a model of linguistic analysis, namely Construction Grammar, and to show how a constructionist account can be applied to the analysis of English sentences and thus how it can further our understanding of how we produce and understand utterances. There are a number of reasons for doing this:

Linguistics, and especially syntactic theory, is perceived by many as being a very complicated, rather technical and formalistic kind of enterprise, which at best presents an intellectual challenge to the relatively small group of scholars who get paid for pursuing this rather obscure interest in various university departments all over the world. Linguistic theory is often seen as being far too difficult to understand and as being relatively useless for any practical purposes. We would like to demonstrate that, at the beginning of the 21st century, such a view of linguistics is totally misguided and perhaps even dangerous.

- Firstly, of course, developing a technical formalism is not at all a bad thing if it serves the purpose of making us understand the nature of the subject of investigation.
- Secondly, the theoretical approach that is currently being followed by a large number of linguists all over the world, which has become known under the label of Construction Grammar, is not just a theory of syntax but addresses the whole range of factors that determine how meaningful utterances can be created by speakers.
- Furthermore, the constructionist approach is deeply grounded in empirical research on first and second language learning (see also Chapter 3).
- Finally, as we will show, Construction Grammar offers future teachers of English a cognitively plausible theory of language that will inform and improve their teaching of the subject (De Knop & Gilquin 2016; Bierwiaczonek 2016; Boas 2022).

It is for these reasons that we decided to take a constructionist approach in our attempt to bridge the gap between linguistics and practical language teaching. Many teachers may envisage linguistics "as a system of arbitrary forms based on abstract principles unrelated to other aspects of cognition or human endeavor", as Langacker (2008:3) puts it. It is our aim to show that "it doesn't have to be that way" (Langacker 2008:3), that many insights concerning the learning and processing of human languages can be represented in a way that does not necessarily involve rigid formalism and formal operations, and in particular that Construction Grammar can easily be applied to language teaching methodology and the design of foreign language textbooks.[1]

---

1. We would like to add that this is not to deny the use of formalism in linguistic models per se. In fact, different models of Construction Grammar differ in the degree of formalization they employ, cf., eg., Fillmore (2013), Michaelis (2013); Steels (2013), and Boas (2013).

1.2 What is Construction Grammar

First of all, we have got to say that the term Construction Grammar must not be taken to refer to a single clearly defined model of grammar like the 1965 *Aspects*-model in generative linguistics, which was referred to as the Standard Theory within this strand of research. Rather, the term Construction Grammar is used for a number of approaches that are closely related so that it may be more appropriate to speak of **a constructionist approach to language**. The development of this approach began in the late 1980s and is inseparably linked to the work of Charles Fillmore (1929–2014), but also to scholars such as George Lakoff and Ronald Langacker.[2] In the decades that followed, a number of different strands of constructionist research developed, as documented in the *Oxford Handbook of Construction Grammar* (Hoffmann & Trousdale 2013),[3] one of the most influential ones being associated with the name of Adele Goldberg. Such constructionist approaches in the narrower sense are linked very closely not only to Cognitive Grammar (Langacker 2008a), but also to the usage-based approach in exemplar theory (Bybee 2010) and much work on language acquisition (Tomasello 2003; Ellis 2003; Behrens 2009a, 2009b; Dąbrowska & Lieven 2005; Lieven 2014; Dąbrowska 2014a).

What unites all these approaches is that they all share a set of insights and convictions such as the following:

i. Language can be seen as consisting of a network of **form-meaning pairings** referred to as **constructions.**
ii. Constructions range from very concrete units (such as *I, climate, climate change, person*) to units that are rather wide in scope and very abstract (such as words like *in, above* or *among*, or the ditransitive construction that underlies a sentence like *She gave him a book* and determines the relations holding between *she, him* and *a book*).
iii. Constructions can be very small (e.g., endings such as /z/ in *goes* or words such as *I, in, climate*) or extend over a number of words or phrases (such as the ditransitive construction or constructions determining sentence types).
iv. Constructions have varying degrees of fixedness and can have schematic slots (see below).
v. Constructions are learnt on the basis of exposure and knowledge of languages thus emerges as the result of language experience in usage events and processes of abstraction.
vi. The learning of a language is not seen as a process in which certain parts of an inborn Universal Grammar get activated by the child's analysis of the input they receive.

---

2. See, e.g., Lakoff (1987), Fillmore (1985, 1988), Fillmore, Kay, & O'Connor (1988), or Langacker (1987, 1991).

3. See also Ziem & Lasch (2013: 38–66) or, e.g., Felfe, Höllein & Welke (2024); for introductory texts to Construction Grammar see, e.g., Fischer & Stefanowitsch (2006); Herbst (2018a); Hilpert (2020) and Hoffmann (2022b).

Quite clearly, Construction Grammar is to be seen as an alternative theory to generative grammar. In the context of foreign language learning and teaching, CxG (Construction Grammar) has more to offer than the generative approach. To be fair, one should add that although generative grammar had dominated linguistic theory for much of the second half of the twentieth century, it focused on the principles underlying the so-called core-grammar (Chomsky 1986: 147), leaving aside aspects of language such as "irregular" morphological forms, collocations or idioms. In fact, Chomsky had made it clear very early on that he did not see any relevance of the theory to language teaching. In contrast, Construction Grammar considers idiomaticity, i.e., "usual ways of conveying certain notions" (Langacker 2008a: 19), to be a central characteristic of language and does not relegate it to some kind of periphery that lies outside the linguists' interest. As anyone who has ever learnt a foreign language knows, all languages have a huge number of idiomatic expressions. In English, if the doorbell rings and you want someone to else open the door, you can ask them *to answer the door* but not *to reply the door*. If you help someone with a difficult problem, you *give them a leg-up*, but you do not *give them a foot-up*. Or if someone tells you a secret, they have *spilled the beans*, but have not *spilled the peas*. Furthermore, *white coffee* is 'coffee with milk', *white wine* quite obviously is not 'wine with milk', but it would also be unusual to refer to tea with milk as *white tea*, although you can put *coffee whitener* into your tea. Any linguistic theory that wants to be a useful descriptive tool for foreign language learning and teaching must thus have a convincing explanation of idiomaticity (Herbst 2015) – and that is what constructionist approaches try to provide.

In some respects, constructionist approaches take up concepts and ideas of traditional linguistics and as such continue a line of thinking that had dominated linguistic research for many centuries. This is particularly apparent in the constructionist conviction that linguistic forms should always be analyzed together with linguistic meaning – hence the definition of constructions as form-meaning pairings. However, it differs from traditional grammar in that, like generative grammar, it takes a cognitive stance upon language and addresses questions such as what is going on in the minds of speakers when they use language or how human beings are able to learn language. Nevertheless, as far as syntactic analysis is concerned, it is probably fair to say that traditional descriptions such as the ones provided by the standard reference grammars, for example, *A Grammar of Contemporary English* by Quirk, Greenbaum, Leech and Svartvik (CGEL 1985) or the *Cambridge Grammar of the English Language* edited by Huddleston and Pullum (CAMG 2002), are more easily convertible into a constructionist than a generative framework.

Although all the various approaches within the constructionist paradigm are in agreement that the totality of language can be described in terms of constructions, it has to be said that much research puts the focus on isolated problems of description or on the learning of particular constructions. So far, there have been relatively few attempts to show how this can be done in a way that is both compatible with the depth of insight provided by the

A Construction Grammar of the English Language

research carried out and applicable to practical descriptive purposes (including foreign language teaching and learning). What we do find is approaches designing computational networks like FrameNet, Sign-Based CxG or Fluid CxG (which are too technical to be used in teaching) or analyses of texts (Fillmore 2014), which are exemplary rather than comprehensive in character. The model that we will present in this book – our Constructionist Approach to Syntactic Analysis (CASA) – is an attempt to close this gap and, in doing so, develop CxG further.

1.3 What is a construction?

1.3.1 Definitions of construction

Quite obviously, the term construction receives a special interpretation in Construction Grammar and arguably it is not the best term that could have been chosen to characterize the approach. In traditional grammar, the term is used for "the syntactic characterization of a sentence, or of any smaller unit that we can distinguish within it, grammarians use the equivalent Latin term 'construction'" (Matthews 1981: 1–2).[4]

As pointed out above, the Construction Grammar reading of the term construction requires formal units to be meaningful if they are to qualify as constructions. A sentence such as (1) is a construct (an authentic utterance) that consists of a large number of constructions:

(1) Tens of thousands of children skipped school in Belgium on Thursday to join demonstrations for action against climate change ... [5] NYT-31-Jan-2019

First of all, all the words in (1) have form and meaning and are thus classified as constructions in the Construction Grammar sense. But, of course, the meaning of (1) would not be described adequately if we just added up all the meanings of the words in it. It is obvious that (1) is a statement and not a question, so (1) is an instance of a DECLARATIVE-'STATEMENT' CONSTRUCTION. (Here and in the following, we will indicate constructions, that is form-meaning pairs that speakers of English will have stored in their long term-memory by SMALL CAPS.) Furthermore, it refers to something that happened in the past, as is made clear by the use of the PAST TENSE CONSTRUCTION. *In Belgium* and *on Thursday* represent constructions that take the form of a preposition and a noun and refer to place and time, and *to join demonstrations for action against climate change* is an infinitive construction expressing a purpose. The verb *skip* is used in a construction that describes the relationship between the children and school in a particular way, i.e., the MONOTRANSITIVE CONSTRUCTION (→

---

4. See also Matthews (2007: 9). Compare also Schönefeld (2006).

5. Code after authentic examples indicates the source, e.g., BNC = British National Corpus; COCA = Corpus of Contemporary American English, or NYT (New York Times).

Chapter 1. Introduction 5

5.4). Furthermore, *tens of thousands of N* can be seen as a QUANTIFYING CONSTRUCTION. Thus, a sentence such as (1) is made up of quite a large number of different constructions – and we have not even discussed all of them! – and they all contribute to the meaning of the sentence. A major goal of our CASA approach is to enable readers to provide a single analysis of such complex utterances that highlights all of the constructions that are combined to produce authentic utterances.

It is, however, by no means always straightforward to determine exactly what the constructions are that make up a particular construct, and, in fact, the definition of construction has changed considerably over the years. This ranges from seeing constructions as form-meaning pairings that are "not strictly predictable" from other constructions (definition 1) via a definition that includes predictable units "as long as they occur with sufficient frequency" (definition 2) to one that focuses on psychological and neurological criteria (definition 3):

1. C is a construction if and only if C is a form-meaning pair <Fi, Si> such that some aspect of Fi or some aspect of Si is not strictly predictable from C's component parts or from other previously established constructions.   (Goldberg 1995: 4)

2. Any linguistic pattern is recognized as a construction as long as some aspect of its form or function is not strictly predictable from its component parts or from other constructions recognized to exist. In addition, patterns are stored as constructions even if they are fully predictable as long as they occur with sufficient frequency. (Goldberg 2006: 5)

3. The present volume offers a still more inclusive understanding of what constructions are, motivated by a better appreciation of human memory, learning, and categorization. Here, as explained in the following chapters, constructions are understood to be emergent clusters of lossy memory traces that are aligned within our high- (hyper!) dimensional conceptual space on the basis of shared form, function, and contextual dimensions.   (Goldberg 2019: 7)

This latter definition underscores the fact that constructions are abstractions that speakers make over specific usage events – a view which is generally accepted within the usage-based framework (i.e., the kind of empirical research to which Construction Grammar belongs). The network of constructions that emerges in a speaker's brain, their **constructicon**, makes up the knowledge speakers have of a language (Diessel 2019; Goldberg 2019). Since different speakers quite obviously have different experiences of language, both quantitatively and qualitatively, there will also be inter-individual differences with respect to their constructicons. In fact, these differences between individuals can be rather remarkable: for instance, research has shown that there are adult native speakers of English who have trouble understanding passives (Street and Dąbrowska 2014). There is, consequently, no such thing as a single constructicon of English, but rather a vast amount of constructicons that all differ from one another, even if the differences may be relatively small or even minimal (after all, all speakers of English will have heard a great number of expressions such as *Good Morning!, Thank you!, What a lovely day!*, etc. quite often). It is perfectly obvious that the shape of a person's constructicon is highly dependent on social and regional factors as well, because they play an important part in determining that person's linguistic experience. Constructionist theory would not take a person's constructicon to be in any way stable from a certain age on, because, as Bybee (2010:19) puts it, "every token of experience has some effect on memory storage and organization for linguistic items".

1.3.2 Simple words as constructions

Although, as pointed out above, it is a little awkward to refer to single words as constructions, they undoubtedly constitute pairings of form and meaning and thus fall under any of the definitions of construction given in the previous section. Nevertheless, there is a problem because it is by no means clear what we mean by *word*. To take a very simple example, we can make out a case for saying that *tram, tram's* and *trams* in (2) are three different words just as we can say they are three forms of the same word.

(2) a. The city has a good idea of its own, though: take the tram.   NYT-27-Apr-2009

     b. On the east side of town at the tram's Linnaeusstraat stop, you can catch the Bredeweg Festival...   NYT-27-Apr-2009

     c. ... in France, slick modern trams run on electricity generated exclusively from water, wind, and the sun.   COCA-2014-NEWS

As we will explain in more detail in Chapter 13, we see the different word forms as part of larger constructions such as (a) the DEFINITE-SINGULAR-NP CXN (*the tram*), (b) the GENITIVE-SINGULAR-NP CXN (*the tram's*) or (c) the INDEFINITE-PLURAL-COUNT-NP CXN (*trams*). The **word-lemma construction** *tram* combines the form element that is common to all of these constructions with the meaning they contribute to all of these constructions (see 13.1.1).

1.3.3 Complex words as constructions

Word formation can be accounted for in terms of constructional schemata (Booij 2013; Hoffmann 2022b: 86–102). Words such as *lighthouse, climate change*, or *cleverness* are thus analyzed as instances of the corresponding word formation constructions (N-N COMPOUND CONSTRUCTION, and -NESS DERIVATION CONSTRUCTION). At the same time, they are also constructions in themselves because their meaning is not entirely compositional (which means speakers must store them in their long-term memory to use them correctly). A *lighthouse* is a building – however, not necessarily a building you'd refer to as a *house* as shown by German *Leuchtturm* ('light tower') and Dutch *vuurtoren* ('fire tower'). Furthermore, although *lighthouse* has to do with light, the precise relationship between the two elements is by no means clear from adding *light* to *house*. While a *beach house* is a house at the beach, a *lighthouse* is not a house at light. Similarly, a *brick house* is made out of brick, but a *lighthouse* is not made out of light. These first examples already illustrate that the meaning of such combined words is far from straightforward. On top of that, the term *lighthouse* stands for a very specific concept (a house that shines light to provide guidance for ships)[6] – which, in the present view, makes it necessary for speakers to store it in their long-term memory as a construction.

1.3.4 Idioms as constructions

After what we have said about the nature of constructions so far, it should be obvious that idioms, which by their sheer nature, are non-compositional in terms of meaning, must be regarded as constructions. What is interesting about idioms, however, is that they are not entirely fixed in their form, but display some variation, as the examples in (3) and (4) show:

(3) a. The early bird gets the worm, right? COCA-2014-NEWS
 b. This is the case where the early bird does not catch the worm. COCA-2013-SPOK
 c. The early bird gets the best cabin. COCA-2006-MAG
 d. The early bird may get the worm, but it's the second mouse that gets the cheese. COCA-2004-MAG
 e. The early surf photographer catches the best images. COCA-2010-ACAD

(4) a. Dad, you're driving me crazy. COCA-2016-SPOK
 b. … the windshield wipers are driving her bananas. COCA-2000-F
 c. Even a few drops of leaking salt water creating a spot of rust in a tank wall may emit enough of an electrical signal to "drive a shark nuts …" COCA-1994-ACAD

Bybee (2013: 61) suggests the following representation for the variation in (4):

> If each token of experience has an effect on representation, then each occurrence of the construction maps onto the exemplar cloud for the construction. The figure in (10) schematizes this exemplar cloud. …

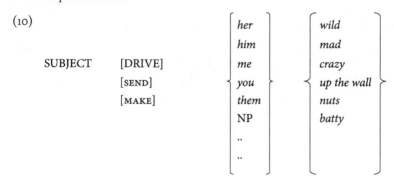

---

6. For concept-formation in word formation see Schmid (^{2}2011); for a more detailed account of word formation in a constructionist framework see Hoffmann (2022b: 86–102).

In (10) larger font is used to represent items that have a higher token frequency in the construction ...

We will come back to this kind of representation of exemplar clouds in later chapters.[7] What the variability illustrated by (3) and (4) shows very clearly is that although idioms are units of meaning of their own and may well be accessed holistically in the brain, they still seem to be analyzable with respect to formal structure (and, consequently, can display some variation with respect to, e.g., nouns that are used in them; cf. (3a) vs. (3e); see also 5.1.3.1). This dual interpretability is a very typical feature of many constructions, which we can compare to the phenomenon of ligature: a symbol such as the ligature ⟨æ⟩ stands for a sound value of its own, but can at the same time still be recognized as a combination of the graphemes ⟨a⟩ and ⟨e⟩ (see 12.1). In the same vein, many constructions can be perceived as individual units with their own idiosyncratic features (treating (3a) *The early bird gets the worm* as a holistic chunk), while it is nevertheless still possible to identify the units they were originally composed of (thus, e.g., allowing speakers to substitute parts of the idiom as in (3e)). This is not only true of multi-word constructions such as idioms, collocations (see 1.3.6) and the like, but also of compounds or other words that have been made up of different parts. Thus, although *lighthouse* has a very specific meaning that is not predictable from its component parts, these components parts are still clearly recognizable. Similarly, most speakers of English would probably not hesitate to analyze the noun *damages* as the plural form of the noun *damage*, although in a phrase such as *claim damages* it means 'compensation for damage caused'.

1.3.5 Schematicity of constructions

What Examples (3) and (4) illustrate very nicely is that some constructions contain schematic slots, which can be filled by different words or expressions. Take, for instance, the THE-TWO-OF-THEM CONSTRUCTION, which is a very common way in English of expressing how many members a group of people comprises. Depending on the level of abstraction we consider psychologically more plausible, we can represent the two slots of the construction either through category labels (such as cardinal number and personal pronoun, cf. Chapter 6.3.2 and 6.6.1) as in Figure 1.1A or as a list of the most frequent items occurring in the construction, which we refer to as a collo-profile, as in Figure 1.1B:

---

7. See also Herbst (2015).

Chapter 1. Introduction

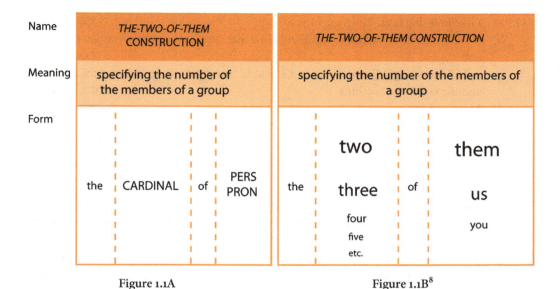

Figure 1.1A   Figure 1.1B[8]

(As mentioned above, we use SMALL CAPS for the names of specific constructions. Lexical items in the names of constructions will be printed in *ITALICS*; all components of the names of constructions will be hyphenated, as in the label THE-TWO-OF-THEM CONSTRUCTION.)

Furthermore, it would be difficult to decide whether the THE-TWO-OF-THEM CONSTRUCTION is a lexical or a grammatical phenomenon. Interestingly, we neither found it in the standard reference grammars (CGEL and CAMG) nor in the standard learners' dictionaries (OALD, LDOCE and MEDAL). And perhaps the answer is that you do not have to classify the construction as either lexical (Figure 1.1B) or grammatical (Figure 1.1A) – as pointed out in 1.2, Construction Grammarians reject the idea of a strict dividing line between syntax and lexis anyway. We are therefore not surprised by phenomena such as the THE-TWO-OF-THEM CONSTRUCTION, which to a certain degree can be analyzed as a lexical and a grammatical construction.

Another case in point is presented by the THE-X-ER-THE-Y-ER CONSTRUCTION, which was analyzed by Fillmore, Kay and O'Connor (1988) in a paper that turned out to be groundbreaking in the development of constructionist thinking, because it revealed the complexity of grammatical knowledge associated with a particular constellation of words, displayed in (5):

---

8. Note that font size can only give a very rough indication of the figures obtained from the corpus. A BNC search "the _CRD of (them|you|us)" produced 1221 hits (*them*: 708, *us*: 360, *you*: 156; *two*/2: 739, *three*/3: 344, *four*/4: 88, *five*/5: 19; see also Herbst 2016).

(5) a. I like fires. Big fires. The bigger the better. COCA-2014-F
b. It takes time and practice to instill polished manners, so the earlier you start the better. COCA-1997-M
c. ... Hubble thought that the fainter the nebulae the greater their distance from Earth – and the larger the redshifts... COCA-1999-MAG
d. Moreover, the longer you live, the longer you are likely to live. COCA-1991-MAG
e. You know, the more you do in life, the more successful you are, the more confident you get. COCA-2007-SPOK
f. The more data they have, the more accurate their models; the more accurate the models prove to be, the more data they'll continue to want. COCA-2014-MAG

As you can see, the *THE-X-ER-THE-Y-ER* construction (or, as we will call it, the COMPARATIVE-CORRELATIVE CONSTRUCTION, see Hoffmann 2019a) is fairly flexible, but it also has some idiosyncratic features. The *the* in this construction, e.g., is not a determiner (as outside of the COMPARATIVE-CORRELATIVE construction *the bigger* (5a), *the earlier* (5b) or *the more* (5e) would not be acceptable noun phrases; Fillmore, Kay & O'Connor 1988:508). A detailed analysis of this construction and its main features will be given in Chapter 11.5.3.

1.3.6 Collocations as constructions

The status of collocations as constructions is perhaps not quite so obvious, but, interestingly, the two prevailing concepts of collocation found in the literature find a parallel in the definition of the term construction outlined in 1.2. If we look at the co-occurrence of two words such as *guilty conscience* or *lay the table* from the point of view of a foreign language learner, there is an element of unpredictability that needs to be accounted for. This has given rise to the significance-oriented view of collocation propagated, for example, by Hausmann (1985) and in EFL-lexicography (Lea 2007; Klotz & Herbst 2016). The other main view, the statistical approach to collocation, highlights the fact that certain words have a strong tendency to co-occur such as *sandy* and *beach*, or *buy* and *shares* or *buy* and *house*. This approach is closely related to corpus linguistic research (Altenberg 1998; Sinclair 1991; Evert 2005).

Up to a point, a parallel can be established between the distinction between the significance-oriented and the statistically-oriented view of collocation (Herbst 1996, 2011a; Evert et al. 2017) and Goldberg's definitions of construction in 1995 and 2006. What this shows, at any rate, is that co-occurring words can be stored as constructions either because they are semantically salient or because they occur with high frequency.[9] There are various arguments in favor of such storage:

i. Native speakers show a high level of agreement as to "words that go together" (Dąbrowska 2014b), unsurprisingly more so than non-native speakers (Uhrig et al. 2022).

---

9. For a representation of collocation in the format introduced in the previous section see Herbst (2018b).

Chapter 1. Introduction

ii. We know that speakers have a strong tendency towards using familiar expressions, which presupposes that they are stored in the brain in some form or another (see Goldberg's 2019: 60–61 account in terms of accessibility and lossy memory traces).

1.3.7 Lexico-grammatical space

What we wanted to demonstrate in the previous sections is that the constructionist approach provides a suitable framework for the description of a wide range of linguistic units that traditionally have been dealt with under the headings of word formation, collocation and idioms, and in the chapters that follow we will show that this also applies to phenomena that in traditional models fall under the scope of grammar or syntax. It would be a mistake to see what may seem a rather inflationary use of the term construction as a kind of gimmick to set this approach apart from others. Rather, this use of the term construction signifies two basic convictions of constructionist theory:

– The linguistic knowledge speakers have at the different levels of description (words, collocations, idioms, syntactic structure) is essentially of the same type and can adequately be described in terms of symbols, i.e., form-meaning pairings.[10] Symbolic thinking (Deacon 1997) can, therefore, be considered the central property of human languages.
– There is no strict dividing line between lexis and syntax but rather we assume there to be a lexicogrammatical space without clear dividing lines.

This is not to say that it would not be possible to distinguish between, say, a collocation and a compound, or a collocation and an idiom, but such categories are best distinguished from one another by identifying their prototypical centers and allowing for elements to have an in–between or more-or-less status, as shown in Figure 1.2.

Taking such a spotlight view on the lexicogrammatical continuum makes perfect sense for certain purposes: if one wants to publish an idiom dictionary or a collocation dictionary, one needs to identify the items to be included. However, as far as the description of linguistic phenomena is concerned, it is totally irrelevant whether we describe THE-X-ER-THE-Y-ER or THE-TWO-OF-THEM as an idiom, a syntactic template or something else as long as we recognize its character as a complex form-meaning pairing, i.e., a construction with schematic slots.

Constructionist approaches offer a much more comprehensive framework than generative grammar, precisely because they do not separate lexis and phraseology from syntax and because they do not relegate all aspects of idiomaticity to the periphery of linguistic investigation as the generative approach does (Chomsky 1986: 147–151).[11] Both Langacker's Cognitive Grammar and Construction Grammar approaches emphasize the role of prefabricated items in language use:

---

10. For the advantages of a theory that draws upon one type of knowledge see Stefanowitsch (2011b).

11. See also Croft & Cruse (2004: 225) for the role of idiomaticity in the development of the approach.

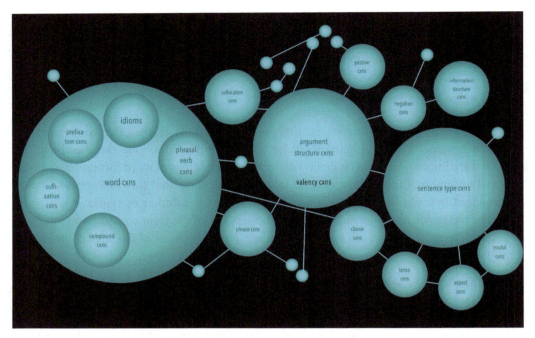

Figure 1.2 Constructional space. This two-dimensional representation can merely give an impression of several construction types of English and possible connections between them in a network in n-dimensional constructional space

> Becoming a fluent speaker involves learning an enormous inventory of expressions larger than words, representing usual ways of conveying certain notions. ... Without a substantial inventory of prefabricated expressions, fluent real-time speech would hardly be possible. Theorists have grossly exaggerated the novelty of "novel sentences". (Langacker 2008a: 19)

> ... all other things being equal, more familiar formulations are preferred over less familiar formulations and the more familiar, the better. (Goldberg 2019: 122)

> Competition between possible means of expressing a particular message leads to a preference for familiar formulations over novel formulations, whenever there exists a familiar formulation that is appropriate to express a particular message. (Goldberg 2019: 143)

These insights into the nature of language use are directly applicable to foreign language learning and teaching because they offer an explanation for the fact that (6b) is a much more native-like translation of (6a) than (6c) (Herbst 2011b):

(6)   a. Wir zwei waren ein halbes Jahr in England.
      b. The two of us spent six months in England.
      c. We two were in England for half a year.

1.4 How do we learn constructions

1.4.1 Segmentation and pattern finding

Constructions can be learnt. This has been shown in many experiments (e.g., Tomasello 2003; Dąbrowska & Szczerbinski 2006). Furthermore, Casenhiser & Goldberg (2005) showed that children were even able to learn constructions that at first glance seemed to violate the principles of their native language.

When children hear utterances, they will, as Tomasello (2003: 41) outlines, do two things at the same time:

> First, they extract from utterances and expressions such small things as words, morphemes and phrases by identifying the communicative job these elements are doing in the utterance or expression as a whole. Second, they see patterns across utterances, or parts of utterances, with "similar" structure and function, which enables them to create more or less abstract categories and constructions.

We can illustrate how this could happen by looking at a few utterances taken from a corpus of child language, the Thomas corpus, which contains exchanges between a young boy (from age 2;0 to 4;11) and his mother and other adults.

Without going into too much detail, you can see that these utterances are highly repetitive, which is a general feature of child-directed speech (Tomasello 2003): 12 out of 32 utterances are questions with *are you*, of the statements 5 are *you are* and 4 *Mummy is*. Only one third are statements, the rest being questions. These data make clear why usage-based language acquisition research puts such great emphasis on pattern recognition and the storage of chunks.

Let's look at another example: The verb form *let* occurs 4,276 times in the Thomas Corpus, 70% of these uses being *let's* or *let us* + *Verb* (3,100).[12] Since the Thomas corpus contains 379 hours of recording between age 2 (t2_00_12) and age 4 (t4_11_20), we can say that the child was exposed to *let's* or *let us* about 8.17 times per hour. If, like Dabrowska & Lieven (2005), we assume a child of that age to have around 8 hours of language input per day (which they say is a conservative estimate), then we can calculate that Thomas had heard (or used) *Let's verb* over 20,000 times in one year. It would be difficult to imagine how this type of exposure should not lead to a rather strong long-term memory representation of the construction. In usage-based terminology, this is dubbed **entrenchment**.

---

12. This also confirms the results of Stefanowitsch & Gries (2003: 233) about the use of imperative constructions as important devices to direct attention and discourse organization.

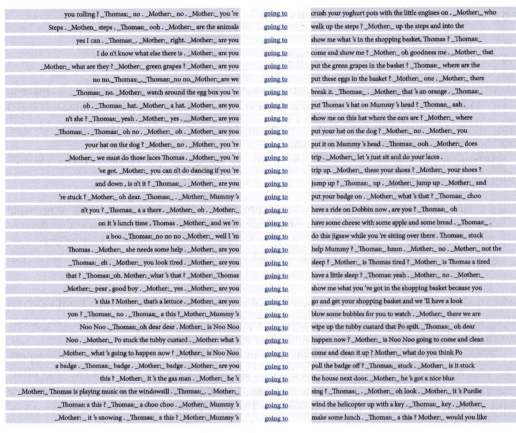

Figure 1.3 Childes Corpus. Thomas corpus. MacWhinney (2000). Two days of *going to* Thomas (t2_00_12 and t2_00_13)

1.4.2 Entrenchment and pre-emption

Entrenchment is one of the key factors determining language use (Schmid 2017, 2020). Speakers tend to be very conservative and make use of expressions that are firmly entrenched in their mental constructicons. No doubt, as has been noted by many scholars (Sinclair 1991: 110; Langacker as quoted above), we have an enormous inventory of stored expressions that we use in the appropriate situations. There are conventional ways of greeting people, answering the telephone, etc. However, it would be a gross misunderstanding of the constructionist approach to assume that it claims that speakers only retrieve constructions they have encountered and stored from memory in a parrot-like word-for-word fashion when they produce an utterance. Rather, they combine constructions in a productive and sometimes creative way.

Chapter 1. Introduction   **15**

(7) a. Pat sneezed the foam off the cappuccino.   (Goldberg 2006)
     b. Within 12 hours of the notice, he emailed us his observations. It became clear that
         this was no ordinary asteroid.   COCA-1996-ACAD

As Goldberg (2019: 73–94) points out, speakers will produce sentences such as (7) only if there is no established way of expressing the meaning in question (or to achieve a humorous or stylistic effect). The situation described in (7a) can rightly be said to be somewhat unusual (although since this example became so fashionable some linguists have started assessing cappuccinos according to degrees of sneezability), and (7b) is a relatively early use of the verb *e-mail* in the ditransitive construction – for the years 1990 to 1993, COCA only has noun uses of *e-mail*. Speakers will come up with such novel expressions if there is a need for them.

Thus, native speakers of English are not likely to produce utterances like the ones under (8):

(8) a. Explain me this.   (Goldberg 2019)
     b. What did you say her?

The reason for this is quite simply that there are already conventional ways of expressing these meanings in English:

(9) a. Explain this to me.   COCA-2015-SPOK
     b. What did you say to her?   COCA-2019-F

In the usage-based account, the term **pre-emption** (Tomasello 2003; Goldberg 2006) is used to describe the phenomenon that the existence of one way of expressing a certain meaning may block another.[13]

1.5 How do constructions combine

As we said in Section 1.3.1, a specific token of use that a speaker produces is called a construct. Take a look at (10):

(10) Would you like tea or coffee?   COCA-1997-TV

This short and simple utterance is a construct that involves the following constructions:

---

13. In morphology, this is often called "blocking". Burgschmidt (1977: 43) speaks of a "Regel der besetzten Stelle" with respect to word formation, see also Bauer (1983: 87) and Clark & Clark's "principle of pre-emption by synonymy" (1979: 798). As far as restrictions on the use of argument structure constructions (see Chapter 6) are concerned, see the valency realization principle suggested by Herbst (2011a, 2014a, b), which states that creative uses such as the ones under (8) can only occur if there is no corresponding valency construction expressing the same meaning.

a. *YES/NO*-QUESTION CONSTRUCTION (see Chapter 3)
b. *DO*-SUPPORT CONSTRUCTION (see 4.8)
c. MONOTRANSITIVE CONSTRUCTION (see 5.4)
d. *OR*-COORDINATION CONSTRUCTION (see Chapter 10)
e. *you, want, tea, coffee* WORD constructions

Remember that constructions are form-meaning pairings that are stored in the long-term memory. In contrast to this, concrete utterances that are produced in the working memory (Cowan 2008; Diamond 2013) are called constructs. Even though speakers heavily rely on entrenched, pre-fabricated expressions, they only rarely draw on only a single construction to create a construct (e.g., when greeting someone with *Good evening!*, or using a saying such as *Don't judge a book by its cover.* – or if you are a flight attendant and have uttered (10) hundreds of times, so that it became entrenched in your mind as a single pre-fab). More frequently, however, a construct will be 'constructed' in the working memory by activating several constructions from the long-term memory (Hoffmann 2018, 2020). Whether a particular expression has been constructed by a speaker on the fly through a process of blending or whether this speaker draws upon it as a unit, is often impossible to say.[14]

What is the process by which constructions are combined in the working memory? Previously, we have argued that conceptual blending is the domain-general process that can best explain the combination of constructions (Herbst & Hoffmann 2018; Hoffmann 2023).[15] Conceptual Blending has already been used to explain how humans can combine existing sources of knowledge to create novel ideas in diverse fields such as art, music, mathematics or social cognition (http://blending.stanford.edu). It assumes that humans can take two or more input spaces to create a novel thought or idea with emergent meaning properties – exactly the kind of process that characterize constructs. (11) is a classic example that illustrates how Conceptual Blending works:

(11) Vanity is the quicksand of reason.   (Turner & Fauconnier 1999: 413)

If you were asked to paraphrase (11), you probably would have no problem saying that it means something like 'vanity can stand in the way of reason' or 'your ability to think logically can be affected if you're too vain'. But how did you arrive at that meaning and what does quicksand have to do with this? As Turner and Fauconnier (1999) explain, (11) involves at least two input spaces, one for mental processes (*vanity* and *reason*) and another for a physical phenomenon (*quicksand*). What Conceptual Blending enables you to do is to com-

---

14. Compare the cautious wording by Langacker (2009/2003: 11): "It is not being claimed that, in terms of actual processing, the component structures exist first, and the composite structure only subsequently. Nor is the composite structure seen as being constructed out of the component structures, which supply all its content. The composite structure is viewed as an entity in its own right, which may have properties not derived from either component." We will take up this issue in Chapter 12.1.

15. For conceptual blending see, e.g., Fauconnier & Turner (2002); Ungerer & Schmid (2006: 275–227); Turner (2018); Hoffmann (2019b) or Herbst (2020a).

bine these two into a new blended space that expresses a new idea: vanity is to reason what quicksand is to – well what exactly? Even though it is not overtly mentioned, you can access your frame-based knowledge about quicksand. As we know, it is treacherous ground that is very dangerous because you can drown in it and die. Mapping quicksand and vanity in your mind, you can then project this meaning of 'dangerous' from quicksand to vanity, which allows you to process the intended meaning of (11) – vanity is a danger to reason!

The concept of conceptual blending is widely used in Cognitive Linguistics for creative and exceptional uses of language (see, e.g., Ungerer and Schmid 2006: 277) on how it can offer an analysis for L2 errors such as *Susan remembered Tom of Grandma's birthday, for the L1 target structure Susan reminded Tom of Grandma's birthday.). Recently, however, several linguists raised the question whether conceptual blending might not also be the best metaphor to describe all types of combination of constructions (Fauconnier & Turner 2002; Hampe & Schönefeld 2003; Herbst 2018a; Hoffmann 2022b). If you can use it to account for creative constructs such as (11), which involves mapping two input domains (mental processes and physical phenomena) that appear incompatible at first glance, why should speakers not also draw on it to create constructs such as (10) *Would you like tea or coffee* discussed above?

Following this line of thinking, whenever we speak of the combination of two or more constructions in this book, we mean that these input constructions are blended into a construct in a speaker's or writer's working memory.

A phrase such as *tea or coffee* in (10) can thus be seen as a blend of the two words *tea* and *coffee* with the OR-COORDINATION CONSTRUCTION, as shown in Figure 1.4:

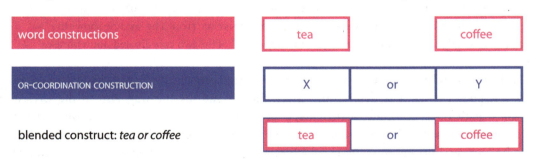

Figure 1.4 Blending the word constructions *tea* and *coffee* with the OR-COORDINATION CONSTRUCTION. Figure 1.4 uses coloured boxes to show how the two word constructions (the red boxes) blend with the two slots of the OR-COORDINATION CONSTRUCTION (which is surrounded by a blue box)

The OR-COORDINATION CONSTRUCTION consists of one fixed lexical item, *or*, and two schematic slots that can be filled by numerous word and phrase constructions (e.g., *wine or beer, boy or girl, now or never, to be or not to be*, etc.).

Actual sentences (or constructs) are combinations of a large number of constructions, and it is the main aim of the present book to develop a framework for a full constructional analysis of any authentic construct one may encounter. Figure 1.5 illustrates what such an analysis will look like for a construct such as (10):

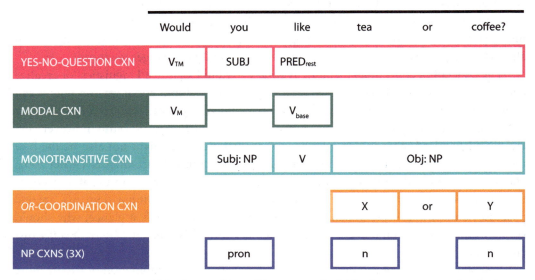

Figure 1.5 Construction grid for (13 *Would you like tea or coffee?*) The boxes represent slots in the respective constructions; the horizontal line connecting the two boxes of the MODAL CONSTRUCTION is meant to signify that the MODAL CONSTRUCTION has two slots, V_M (modal) and V, but that we do not consider the subject to be part of this construction. The MONOTRANSITIVE CONSTRUCTION in the next line consists of a verb, a subject argument and an object argument. The object argument *tea or coffee* is a noun phrase that involves a COORDINATION CONSTRUCTION. The last line shows the realization of the argument functioning as the subject and of the two coordinated noun phrases

Each horizontal row represents one of the constructions that will be identified in detail in Chapters 3 to 12. The descriptions given there – and, by the way, also in the CASA-ConstruCtiCon (www.constructicon.de) – provide information about the form and the meaning aspect of each construction. Construction grids such as Figure 1.4. and 1.5 are thus to be seen as short-hand notations which can serve as the basis of an exhaustive cognitive analysis of the formal and semantic interaction of all the constructions making up a particular construct. One reason for choosing this grid format is that it enables us to indicate the points of overlap, i.e., the locations where the various constructions are blended.

1.6   Form and meaning in Construction Grammar

Since constructions are generally defined as form-meaning pairings, we need to clarify what exactly we mean by *form* and by *meaning*. Linguistic **form** can be identified at different levels:

i.   the level of speaking in terms of phones or combinations of phones,
ii. the level of writing in terms of letters or combinations of letters.

In this book, we will normally characterize the form-component of constructions in terms of the written language and refer to the spoken language only in cases in which particular phonetic properties – such as rising or falling intonation – are an integral part of the description of a construction. This does not mean in any way, however, that the analysis of the written language should be given priority over that of the spoken language. Quite the contrary, the constructionist framework has successfully been applied to the analysis of spoken language with respect to human interaction (e.g., Imo 2005) and with respect to gestures (Hoffmann 2017, 2021a; Uhrig 2021). Furthermore, it is the analysis of spoken language and especially of phonetic reduction that provided important cues for the identification of chunks and thus also for constructions (Bybee & Scheibman 1999; Bybee 2010).

In addition to phonetic or orthographic features, form in our analysis will also include information on syntactic form (e.g. that *the children* is a noun phrase; for details see Chapter 6) and function (e.g. that the noun phrase *the children* functions as a subject in (12a) and as an object in (12b) (for details see Chapter 5).[16]

(12) a.   Do the children like school?   BNC-AND-468
      b.   I'll tell the children.   TV-1965-Addams

In line with mainstream cognitive linguistics, we hold the view that constructional **meaning** can include semantic as well as pragmatic information (cf., e.g., Leclercq 2020). This is most adequately described in terms of frame semantics which is based on the idea that words, for example, evoke a wide range of knowledge that a speaker has acquired over many instances of language use (see, e.g. Goldberg 2019: 13). Another aspect of meaning is concerned with semantic roles, describing, e.g., the element of meaning that *the children* and *I* in (12) have in common on the basis of being used in the subject-slot of the MONOTRANSITIVE CONSTRUCTION (see 5.4).

In contrast to this, pragmatic meaning is context-specific and includes a range of contextual pieces of information (see Hoffmann 2022b: 40–43). The two phrases *Good morning!* and *Good evening!* are both greetings, but in order to use them correctly you will need to take into account the specific time of the day that you meet someone. Pragmatic conditions are thus an integral part of using constructions adequately in a particular situation. In the present book, we will provide pragmatic information when it is an integral part of the description of a construction.

---

16. In the case of the examples in (12), the position of the noun phrase can be taken as a formal criterion to distinguish between the subject and the object. As soon as semantic criteria are drawn upon in the definitions of these categories, as is often the case, they are not strictly formal categories anymore, which can be problematic in some cases.

Note that there is no clear dividing line between semantic and pragmatic meaning, as Langacker (2008a: 39–40) points out in a very amusing way. It is perfectly clear that pragmatic meaning arising from so-called bridging assumptions (Brown & Yule 1983: 256–257) cannot be seen as a property of particular constructions.

(13) We're so hungry. I can't get the burrito place on Coda Street out of my mind. They're
      open late.   TV-2008-Psych

The first two sentences in (13) crucially depend on such a bridging assumption: the link between being hungry and the fact that the speaker cannot get the burrito place out of their mind is obviously that we know that the burrito place is a kind of restaurant and that restaurants are places where you can satisfy your hunger.

However, the fact that constructs such as (14) are more likely to be interpreted as requests rather than ability questions can be taken as evidence in favour of postulating a separate construction (cf. Leech 1983: 193–195):

(14) a. Shawn, can you just not talk for a few seconds?   TV-2008-Psych
      b. Speaking of help, can you carry these two plates in for me?   TV-1970-Bewitched

1.7   Construction Grammar as a model of linguistic description

It is certainly too early to come to any final conclusions about the place of Construction Grammar in the development of linguistics, and in particular whether in the long run it will replace generative theory and its claims concerning Universal Grammar, or whether at the end of the day a new theory will be developed that combines elements of both approaches. It is not totally unrealistic to assume that neurolinguistics research will eventually lead to a greater understanding of the nature of language, but it would be naïve to expect this to happen in the very near future.

At the present moment, however, there is a whole plethora of reasons to pursue the constructionist route further:

–   Construction Grammar provides a theoretical framework that is equally suitable to accommodate insights of corpus linguistics (such as Sinclair's idiom principle),[17] of foreign language linguistics (e.g., concerning the central role of item-specific knowledge as in the areas of collocation and valency; see Section 5.1.3.1) and of the philosophy of Cognitive Grammar.
–   The model of first language learning developed in the usage-based paradigm is not only extremely plausible, it is also based on an enormous number of empirical studies that support this line of research.

---

17. See Sinclair (1991, 2004) and Chapter 11.

Chapter 1. Introduction

- The mechanisms relevant to L1 learning have been shown to be equally valid when it comes to second and foreign language acquisition (Ellis 2003; Gries & Wulff 2005; Boas 2022).
- Unlike some other theories of language, the constructionist approach is compatible with applied disciplines such as lexicography and grammar-writing; in fact, there is already an emerging new discipline of constructicography (Herbst 2016b, 2019; Boas, Lyngfelt & Torrent 2019; Patten & Perek 2019; Lyngfelt et al. 2018; Ziem & Feldmüller 2023; Patel et al. 2023); see also the CASA-ConstruCtiCon at https://constructicon.de).[18]
- Constructionist theory lends itself to be applied to foreign language teaching methodology and foreign language teaching materials (Ellis & Wulff 2015; de Knop & Gilquin 2016; Gilquin 2022, 2023; Herbst 2016a; Siepmann 2007; Tyler 2012; Tyler et al., 2018; Boas 2022; see also Langacker 2008b).

For the reasons outlined above, we are convinced that the constructionist approach is a very promising one when it comes to describing languages and to understanding the nature of language and language learning. We consider it essential for the overall success of this line of thinking that it should be made part of situations in which people (as opposed to linguists) talk about language, most importantly of course in practical language teaching. The CASA project is a proposal how this could be done.

> **Note on alternative approaches:** There are different ways of looking at the question of how constructions are combined into constructs and how this should be modelled in Construction Grammar. Some approaches merely claim, e.g., that "constructions [...] combine freely as long as there are no conflicts" (Goldberg 2006: 22), without specifying in detail how this is supposed to work. In contrast to this, formal approaches (such as Fluid Construction Grammar or Sign-based Construction Grammar), draw on a technical operation called "constraint-satisfaction" to model construction combination. Simplifying somewhat, in these approaches a construction is seen as a constraint on possible structures. If there is no constraint ruling out a particular combination of constructions, constructions can combine freely (for details see Müller 2023: 511–515). Constraint-based approaches have successfully been implemented in computational programs that are able to parse large amounts of natural language data. However, as cognitive linguists we must always raise the question whether an operation such as constraint-satisfaction is also a plausible cognitive process. Would we like to argue that constructions are combined in the working memory by the process of constraint-satisfaction? Moreover, should constraint-satisfaction be interpreted as a language-specific or domain-general process?

---

18. For the FrameNet constructicon see also Fillmore, Lee-Goldman, & Rhomieux (2012).

CHAPTER 2

Conventional wisdom
A chapter some readers might want to skip

2.1 The purpose of this chapter: Reminding you of things you already know

Like all sciences, linguistics has its own terminology. Regrettably, however, there is not one single terminology that all linguists can agree on. Rather, each linguistic theory tends to come with its own theoretical framework. This is a little annoying at times, but can hardly be avoided since every linguistic theory will develop concepts that are not necessarily identical with those employed in other approaches.

At the same time there is a common core of linguistic terms that most people are happy to use – many of these terms have been used for centuries in so-called "traditional" grammar and language teaching. Most linguistic models make use of terms such as object, noun, verb, case, tense, etc. Unfortunately, this does not mean that everybody uses these terms in the same way.

While the remainder of this book is concerned with developing Construction Grammar and explaining the terminology of this particular model of language, the present chapter will provide a list of commonly used terms that are not specific to Construction Grammar with brief explanations of how we are going to use them in this book. Readers who feel confident that they are sufficiently familiar with these terms are invited to skip Section 2.2. The short characterizations of the terms provided below are intended to remind readers of terms they already know and are **not to be interpreted as comprehensive definitions** in any way. Our own view of word classes will become clear from the discussion of the constructions in which they are typically used and be summarized in Chapter 13.

2.2 Word classes

In this section, we will provide a list of terms that are used in many accounts of language to indicate particular word classes (also known as parts of speech). The traditional labels will be given first together with their standard abbreviation, followed by the domain that the term is normally used in, and examples.

Label (Abbreviation) – domain of use – *examples*
Adjective (Adj) – traditional word class – *apparent, nice, necessary, probable, parallel, etc.*

There are two positions in which adjectives typically occur:[19]

---

19. Some adjectives also occur in postpositive position: *heir apparent, something new* (CAMG 2002: 528–529).

Chapter 2. Conventional wisdom 23

- **attributive position**, i.e., before a noun: *a nice person, an apparent mistake*
- **predicative position**, i.e., after a verb: *They are nice. The mistake was apparent.*

Adverb (Adv) – traditional word class – *nicely, necessarily, probably, well, here*, etc.

Adverb is a very problematic word class in that it tends to be a sort of dustbin category for words that do not clearly fall into any other word class. For example, traditionally all of the following are classified as adverbs although they have very little in common: *very nice, sing beautifully, come in, here* and *they both came.* We will not use the term adverb in this wide sense (see Chapter 13).

Article (Art) – traditional word class – *a, an, the*

- definite article: *the*
- indefinite article: *a/an*

Articles are often subsumed under the category of determiners or determinatives.

Conjunction (Conj) – traditional word class – *and, if, since*, etc.

- coordinating conjunctions: *and, or*
- subordinating conjunctions: *because, while, etc.*

See Preposition (P or Prep) below.

Determiner (Det) – word class – a/*an, the, no, each, every, some, these, etc.*

The term determiner (or also determinative) is often used to subsume elements of traditional word classes such as the articles, demonstrative pronouns, indefinite pronouns and others on the basis of the common function they have within the noun phrase. See 6.9.

Interjection (Interj) – traditional word class – *hello, oh, etc.*

Interjections cover expressions that are not integrated into their syntactic environments, but only considered emotional add-ons: *Oh, what a beautiful day!*

Noun (N) – traditional word class – *canal, ocean, language, Langacker*, etc.

- **count nouns:** *bicycle, ocean*, etc.
- **mass nouns/uncount nouns/non-count nouns:** *traffic, ice*, etc.
- **proper noun/name:** *Amsterdam, Geoffrey*, etc.

Many nouns in present-day English show contrast between

- **number: singular:** *bicycle, ocean* – **plural:** *bicycles – oceans* (count nouns only)
- **case. common case:** *bicycle* – **genitive:** *bicycle's, children's, linguists'*

Number and case are often called 'inflectional categories'. Many languages have more case forms than English (such as nominative, accusative or dative).

A Construction Grammar of the English Language

Numeral (Num) – traditional word class – *one, three thousand, first, last, etc.*

–   **cardinal numbers**: *one, two, 407, three thousand,* etc.
–   **ordinal numbers**: *first, second, seventeenth,* etc.

Preposition (P or Prep) – traditional word class – *about, into, over, etc.*

There is a certain overlap between the uses of the terms preposition and conjunction in traditional grammars. Traditionally, conjunctions are defined as coordinating two phrases (1ab) or clauses (1c) or introducing a subordinate clause (which forms a constituent of a main clause (1d), while prepositions are regarded as elements that introduce prepositional phrases (2).

(1) a. They went to Amsterdam and Hoorn.
         [noun phrase – conjunction – noun phrase]
     b. They went to Amsterdam and to Hoorn.
         [prepositional phrase – conjunction – prepositional phrase]
     c. She taught at Rummidge and he worked on his PhD in Cambridge.
         [main clause – conjunction – main clause]
     d. She taught at Rummidge while he worked on his PhD in Cambridge.
         [main clause – conjunction – subordinate clause]

(2) a. They went to Amsterdam.
         [preposition + noun phrase = prepositional phrase]
     b. In Amsterdam's Stedelijk Museum you can see original paintings by Mondrian.
         [preposition + noun phrase = prepositional phrase]

The traditional distinction between conjunctions and prepositions has often been criticized in its application to English grammar. We will discuss this in Chapter 13.2.4.

Pronoun (Pron) – traditional word class – *she, they, himself, someone, this, etc.*

Pronouns are sometimes described as "substituting" or "standing for" a noun, which is an informal and not very precise way of saying that they on their own can appear in positions in which full noun phrases occur.

(3) The Stedelijk Museum / This / It /, etc. [NP] is a nice place to visit.

Traditional grammars distinguish a relatively large number of different types of pronouns such as personal pronouns, demonstrative pronouns, indefinite pronouns, etc. We discuss these differences in detail in Chapters 6.2–6.4.

Verb (V) – traditional word class – *eat, love, pray, etc.*

There exist a number of terms to describe certain properties or functions of particular types of verbs. Depending on the function they can have in the clause, one can distinguish between **main verbs or lexical verbs** that express the event type (the kind of 'action', 'activity', 'process' or 'state' described) and **auxiliary verbs**, which mainly have a grammatical function in a clause.

(4) a. They may [auxiliary] visit [main verb] the Museum of Modern Art in New York.
b. They had [auxiliary] been [auxiliary] invited [main verb] to the meal.

A different level of categorization is captured by the following distinction:

- **full verb**: a verb that can be marked for tense (*She laughs – She laughed*), person (*I know – He knows*) and/or number (*She knows – They know*). Furthermore, the following terms are used for different forms of full verbs:[20]
  - **base form** (*go*), a form without any inflectional suffixes
  - **infinitive**: bare infinitive (*go*), *to*-infinitive (*to go*)
  - **participle**: present participle V-*ing* (*laughing*), past participle V-*en* (*laughed, taken*)

- **modal verb**: a verb that expresses some kind of modality (broadly speaking, necessity or obligation, etc.),[21] has no infinitive form, no participles and does not take {-S} in the 3rd person singular: *can, could, may, might, must, shall, should, will, would*.

(5) a. This could lead to war.   (possibility)
b. You may have one ice-cream per day.   (permission)

Sometimes the verbs *be, do* and *have*, which can occur both as auxiliaries and main verbs are referred to as *primary verbs*.

Verbs will be discussed in detail in Chapters 4 and 13.

2.3 Phrases, clauses and sentences

The following terms are used to describe larger units:

Phrase – constituent label introduced first in structuralist linguistics – AdjP, AdvP, NP, PP, etc.

Phrases are constituents of clauses or of other phrases that are characterized by the presence of a member of a particular word class. In the case of **adjective phrases** (AdjPs) and **adverb phrases** (AdvPs), for example, adjectives and adverbs, respectively, are seen as the **head** of the phrase. Other, optional, elements in these phrases are called **pre-** and **postmodifiers**.

(6) a. very [premodifier] interesting [head] – adjective phrase
b. open [head] to the public [postmodifier] – adjective phrase
c. almost [premodifier] always [head] – adverb phrase

---

20. Note that to a certain extent these terms reflect a certain perspective. Thus, the base form of an English full verb can be used to express present tense (except for the 3rd person singular) as well as in infinitive and imperative constructions.

21. See 4.2.2.

Prepositional phrases (PPs) consist of a preposition (seen as a head in some, but not all models), and a prepositional complement (traditionally also called prepositional object):

(7) They were worried about [preposition] climate change [complement/object of prep.]

Noun phrases (NPs) have heads (nouns, pronouns or numerals) and can have pre- and/or postmodifiers as well as elements that function as determinatives or determiners:

(8) a. an [determinative/determiner] interesting [premodifier] question [head] of great importance [postmodifier]
     b. They [head] had a [determinative/determiner] very nice [premodifier] meal [head] that [determinative/determiner] evening [head]

The term **verb phrase** (VP) is used in different ways. In structuralist and generative models, clauses are generally analyzed into two immediate constituents – a noun phrase and a verb phrase, which largely correspond to the division into subject (topic) and predicate (comment) in other approaches.[22] The verb phrase then comprises all verbs, but also objects and adverbials.

(9) She sneezed the foam off the cappuccino [verb phrase]

Differing from this established terminology, Quirk et al. (CGEL 1985) use the term verb phrase to refer only to the verbal elements (auxiliaries and the main verb of a clause; Herbst and Schüller 2008 call this constituent 'verbal head complex'):

(10) They should have enjoyed [verb phrase] the conference.

Other models see clauses as verb phrases.[23]

Clause – traditional term

Conventionally, the difference between a phrase and a clause is (a) that a clause usually contains a verb as a central element and (b) that a clause can be analyzed in terms of the clause constituents (or elements of clause structure) outlined in 2.4 below.

– Subordinate clauses are constituents of other clauses (called superordinate or main clauses):

(11) a. Seeing original Rothkos and Mondrians in the Museum of Modern Art in New York [subordinate clause as subject of superordinate clause] is great [*Seeing ... great*: superordinate clause].
      b. When you are in Amsterdam [subordinate clause as adverbial of superordinate clause], you must go and see Rembrandt's Night Watch in the Rijksmuseum [*When ... Rijksmuseum*: superordinate clause].

---

22. The difference is, however, that the distinction between NP + VP refers to formal units, whereas subject and predicate are functional units.

23. See Fillmore (1988: 43) and Herbst & Schüller (2008: 23–26). See also CAMG (2002: 24).

Chapter 2. Conventional wisdom   **27**

At a different level of analysis, a distinction can be made between **finite clauses**, which contain a modal verb or one that is marked for tense and/or number (*goes, are, was*), and **non-finite** clauses, in which the verb is neither a modal nor marked for tense and/or number. English has two types of non-finite clauses:

- **infinitive clauses:** She had always wanted to be a linguist.
- **participle clauses:**[24] Visiting Amsterdam was great.

Sentence – traditional term

A sentence can either consist of

- a single clause that is not a constituent of another clause (12a) or
- several such clauses in coordination (12b).

(12) a. They went to Montauk.
      b. I went to Austin and my son stayed in New York.

2.4   Clause constituents

Clauses can be divided into several constituents. One very fundamental distinction is that between subject and predicate:

Subject – traditional term

Various criteria can be used to define the subject of a clause. A "typical" subject

- shows concord with the finite verb of the predicate, i.e., agrees with it in terms of person and number: *He is ill.* vs *They are ill.*,
- frequently can be seen as the most AGENT-like constituent of the clause,
- very often is that element of a clause about which information is provided (topic).

(13) Charles Fillmore [subject] was a very nice person.

Predicate – traditional term

Loosely speaking, the predicate can be seen as that part of the clause that is not the subject; in the analysis of English, the term is often used to refer to that part of a clause that follows the subject (and thus overlaps with what some analyses would identify as a VP; see above).

(14) You can leave the books on the table.

---

24. Note that some teaching grammars use the term *gerund* in the description of English. Most linguists agree with the point of view taken in CGEL (1985: 1292), CAMG (2002: 1220–1222) that there is no justification for distinguishing between a gerund and a participle in English (which is why CAMG uses the label gerund-participle). See also Aarts (2011); Esser (1992), or Herbst (2005, 2013).

In a narrow view, the term predicate comprises the verb and its objects; in a wider sense, the verb, objects and adverbials.

Generally, a distinction is made between objects, complements/attributes and adverbials for the elements in the predicate that depend on the verb:

Object – traditional term

Usually, the term object is used only for non-subject noun phrases, but sometimes also for elements such as infinitive- or V-*ing* clauses that occur in the same slot as a noun phrase:

(15) a. Would you like another glass of wine [noun phrase as object]?
    b. Would you like to have another glass of wine [infinitive clause as object]?

Traditionally, a distinction is made between

– **direct objects**, which refer to a person or 'thing' that is affected by the action expressed by the verb, and
– **indirect objects**, which usually refer to people benefitting from the action.

(16) She sent him [indirect object] a copy of her new book [direct object]

Subject Complement / Object Complement / Subject Attribute and Object Attribute – traditional terms

The terms subject and object complement (sometimes also called predicative or subject and object attribute) are used predominantly for noun phrases or adjective phrases that describe or identify the subject or the object respectively.

(17) a. Fillmore was a great linguist.   [subject complement]
    b. Many linguists consider Langacker's ideas ground-breaking.   [object complement]

Adverbial – traditional term

Like adverb at the level of word classes, adverbial is a rather vague category that is best described as a constituent that is neither an object nor a complement. Adverbials often express the circumstances or the setting against which an 'action' or a 'state' can be seen, e.g., time, place, manner, cause, etc.

(18) In Amsterdam, one should not miss the Stedelijk Museum, if one takes an interest in modern art and design.

2.5 Semantic roles

Since the 1960s, it has become common practice to describe the semantic functions of clause constituents in terms of **semantic roles** (Halliday 1967–8, 1970; Fillmore 1968: 196). Different approaches have various names for these semantic functions and have called them **partic-**

ipant roles, argument roles, theta roles or **semantic roles.** Thus, roles such as AGENT and PATIENT have been used to distinguish between the entity carrying out the action described by the verb and the entity affected by the action.

(19) a.   The cat [AGENT] is chasing the mouse [PATIENT].
 b.   The mouse [AGENT] is chasing the cat [PATIENT].
 c.   The mouse [PATIENT] is being chased by the mouse [AGENT].

We will address the issue of semantic roles from a cognitive perspective in Chapter 5.2.4.

This concludes our overview of traditional syntactic labels – the next chapters will now illustrate how the above notions have to be (re-)interpreted from a cognitive, CASA approach.

CHAPTER 3

Sentence type constructions

3.1   Starting with children

A very important tenet of usage-based approaches in general, and of Construction Grammar in particular, is the conviction that the form-meaning pairings that form speakers' constructicons are learnt. Taking this observation as our starting point, we adopt what might seem a rather unconventional way of introducing our readers to some of the basic categories of the constructionist description we are going to develop in this book. This includes pointing out the way in which we use some of the categories briefly discussed in the previous chapter – categories such as verb, noun phrase, subject and predicate. These terms have been used for centuries and been given slightly different interpretations by traditional grammarians and structuralist linguists. What we are attempting to do in this chapter is to illustrate what kind of unconscious categories young first language learners *could* arrive at given the actual input they are receiving.

In order to do this, we will make use of example sentences taken from a corpus of child language, the so-called Thomas-corpus, which is part of the CHILDES-database (MacWhinney 2000) and which we already referred to in 1.4.1.2. The child named Thomas was recorded, in varying degrees of intensity, for a period of two years, but here we will only draw upon the 5 hours of recording carried out during the first complete week of the observation (t2_00_16 to t2_00_20), i.e., a time when the child had just turned two. It is important to be aware of the fact that these data do not only contain the child's utterances, but also those of his mother (and later of other caretakers), which are by far in the majority. The data presented below are thus typical of so-called child-directed language, i.e., the way that parents and other people tend to talk to young children.[25]

3.2   From illocution to the semantic properties of different sentence types

A two-year old will hear such sentences as:

(1)   a.   Alright, Thomas, let's put your shoes and socks on.   t2_00_16m
      b.   Let Mummy put your shoes on.   t2_00_20m

(2)   a.   I think the postman is going to drive off in a few minutes in his red van.   t2_00_16m
      b.   ... he's knocking on somebody else's door.   t2_00_16m
      c.   Mummy's going to the kitchen to make a cup of tea.   t2_00_17m

---

25. Orthography and punctuation of examples taken from the Thomas corpus have been changed slightly to increase readability. The code indicates the age of the child (y-m-d), m/t identify the speaker (mother/ Thomas), so 't2_00_16m' stands for an utterance the m(other) made when Thomas was two years and 16 days old.

| (3) | a. | oops | t2_00_17m |
| | b. | oh, oops, oh dear | t2_00_17t |

| (4) | a. | Is she hiding? | t2_00_17m |
| | b. | Is he clearing away the mess? | t2_00_19m |

One of the most important things language learners have to do is work out the meanings of the utterances directed at them. This does not only mean that they have to learn to understand the meanings of individual words, but it also entails recognizing syntactic patterns and their overall semantic functions. We cannot go into the details of these learning processes here, in which facial expressions and gestures play a major role (see Tomasello 2003; Hoffmann 2020: 17–37), but one factor that facilitates pattern recognition and analysis is the frequency with which these patterns occur: Let us assume that those five hours in the corpus are more or less typical of the speech that the boy encountered. If we further assume that children of this age will have 8 hours of linguistic input of this kind, we can estimate how often they experience particular types of expression in a single week:[26]

Table 3.1

		5 hours	1 week (estimate)
(1)	let's	39	> 400
(2)	(he|she|it) is/'s *ing	60	> 650
	is/'s *ing (without *wh*)	131	> 1400
	oops	39	> 400
(3)	oh (without *oh dear*)	411	> 4,500
	oh dear	141	> 1,500
(4)	is (she|he|it) *ing	15	> 150
	is + *ing (without *wh*)	27	> 300

One of the most important tasks for children is to find out what utterances mean and how they should respond in a particular situation. Children must learn that the utterances in (1) mean that a certain type of action or behavior is expected of them, whereas those in (2) provide information by describing events. Those in (3) express some kind of emotion on the part of the speaker, while utterances such as the ones in (4) require them to provide some kind of (verbal) response. Initially, these utterances will, therefore, have a strongly context-dependent meaning for children. At the same time, the linguistic structures that are associated with these pragmatic functions have conventional, prototypical forms. In tra-

---

26. To arrive at an estimate for input per week, we thus first project the observed data from 5 days (one hour each) to 8 hours a day ($39/5*8 = 62.4$) and then multiply this result by seven days ($62.4*7 = 436.8$). Compare the slightly different calculation in 1.4.1.

ditional approaches, these conventional structures are often captured by semantic/pragmatic labels such as *command, statement, exclamation,* or *question,* respectively (CGEL 1985: Chapter 11.1–11.2).

Adopting a usage-based Construction Grammar approach, let us explore now what the sentence-level constructions look like that children can be expected to learn from their input. Note that children (as well as most adults) will only acquire this knowledge subconsciously. They learn to use their language, without necessarily being able to explain what it is they have learnt. So, what we present in the following is a constructionist analysis that outlines the subconscious knowledge that speakers of English seem to acquire and that helps us to analyze authentic utterances they produce. (Note, however, that we do not claim that all these constructions are also 'psychologically real' – much more psycholinguistic and neurolinguistic research is needed to test this claim. Instead, our analyses should be seen as representational descriptions that can reasonably be postulated given the authentic input that children receive and that we believe are helpful tools for foreign language teaching and learning.)

3.3 Basic sentence type constructions

3.3.1 Subject and predicate

Syntactic theories have postulated a great number of categories for which there is surprisingly little cognitive evidence (e.g., the number and types of semantic roles and the syntactic functions they establish; cf. Chapter 5). Throughout this book, we will, therefore, only adopt terms for concepts that speakers can realistically be expected to have entrenched. One such traditional term that turns out to have cognitive relevance is the notion of 'subject':

In his model of Cognitive Grammar, Langacker (2008a:365) defines the subject as a "a nominal [i.e., a noun phrase] that codes the trajectory of a profiled relationship" – the trajectory being "the primary focus, as the entity being located, evaluated, or otherwise described". Up to a point, such a semantic approach towards the definition of subjects seems very plausible with respect to the language learning situation sketched out above. Although children seem to reach a full understanding of the notion of subject rather late in acquisition, young children rely on three factors in identifying subjects, which are covered by Langacker's definition, namely animacy, first-mentioned participant, and agent (Tomasello 2003:169).

What makes subjects so important is that, in English, the position of the subject can be crucial for interpreting a sentence as either a statement or as a question:

(5) a. Climate change is affecting the national parks' most ancient and critical cycles.

COCA-2011-MAG

b. Is climate change affecting the insect populations?

COCA-2019-SPOK

Most theories of linguistic description make a distinction between **subject** and **predicate**: we will classify the first noun phrase in (5a), i.e., *climate change*, as the subject and the remaining part of the sentence as its predicate. Cases such as (5b), in which a verb precedes the subject, we will refer to as **split predicates**. From a cognitive perspective, subjects often function as topics (the vantage point from which a scene is described; van Trijp 2014), while predicates encode a comment on the topic (the *Let me tell you about* [TOPIC] construction is a way of highlighting the topic of a sentence, take, e.g., the paraphrase of (5a): *Let me tell you about climate change, it is affecting the national parks' most ancient and critical cycles.*; see also Hoffmann 2022b: 151–153, 203–205).

3.3.2 Declarative and interrogative constructions

In English, there is generally **concord** between the subject and the predicate, which means that a noun phrase subject and the first verb of the predicate must agree in number and person (see 4.3.1):

(6) I don't think she's going to listen to a word you say.   TV-2007-Psych

This means that the predicate will have to contain a verb form that has the potential of being interpreted in terms of a contrast with respect to number and person (7) (showing concord) as well as tense (8) or modality (9). We will indicate this by the following specification: $V_{TM} \in$ PRED:

(7) a. She is a linguist.   [number: singular]
     b. We are linguists.   [number: plural]

(8) a. She blushes.   COCA-2011-FIC [present tense; person: 3]
     b. He blushed.   COCA-2019-FIC [past tense]

(9) a. We made a mistake.   TV-2010-Psych [presented as a fact]
     b. I might have made a mistake.   TV-2010-Psych [presented as a possibility]

Constructions of this kind are referred to as **finite constructions**.[27] For English, we can identify the following five types of finite sentence type constructions (see Herbst & Schüller 2008: 146–153, see also Hoffmann 2022b: 211–221):

---

27. The traditional distinction between finite and non-finite is difficult to apply to isolated verb forms in English since there is no way of telling whether a decontextualized form such as *take* is the one or the other. We thus apply the terms finite and non-finite only to constructions and say that a base form such as *take* can be used in, e.g., a finite DECLARATIVE-STATEMENT CONSTRUCTION (*I take our job seriously.*(TV-2007-Psych)) or a non-finite IMPERATIVE CONSTRUCTION (*Take a look at this article, Shawn.* (TV-2007-Psych)), but we will not classify the verb form *take* as finite in the first sentence and as non-finite in the second, and simply refer to it as the base form in both cases.

1. The DECLARATIVE-STATEMENT CONSTRUCTION is characterized by the fact that the subject precedes the predicate, that it is realized with a falling intonation and that it expresses a statement.

Name of cxn	DECLARATIVE-STATEMENT CONSTRUCTION (DECS)	
Meaning	Making a statement	
Form	SUBJ	$V_{TM} \in$ PRED
	falling intonation	
Example	*The Paris climate agreement is the first to unite all of the world's nations in a single accord to fight climate change.* COCA-2018-MAG	

   Figure 3.1 The English DECLARATIVE-STATEMENT CONSTRUCTION

2. If a sentence with the same word order is pronounced with a rising intonation, it is interpreted as a question; we refer to this construction as DECLARATIVE-QUESTION CONSTRUCTION because it combines declarative word order with the meaning of a question:

DECLARATIVE-QUESTION CONSTRUCTION (DECQ)	
Asking a question, often as an echo question or signaling surprise	
SUBJ	$V_{TM} \in$ PRED
rising intonation	
You found it? COCA-1996-F	

   Figure 3.2 The English DECLARATIVE-QUESTION CONSTRUCTION

3. More prototypically, questions are distinguished from the DECLARATIVE-STATEMENT CONSTRUCTION with respect to word order. In the case of the YES/NO-QUESTION CONSTRUCTION the first element is an operator verb which precedes the subject as a part of a split predicate):[28]

---

28. If a YES/NO-QUESTION CONSTRUCTION is combined with an *OR*-COORDINATION CONSTRUCTION, the result is an alternative question. Depending on the intonation, a sentence such as *Would you like tea or coffee?* (COCA-1997-TV) can either be interpreted as a question of whether the addressee wants a drink of some kind or whether it is *tea* or *coffee* they would like to have.

YES/NO-QUESTION CONSTRUCTION (YNQU)		
Asking a question that can be answered by yes or no		
$V_{TM} \in$ PRED	SUBJ	PRED$_{rest}$
rising intonation		
Is CNN fake news? COCA-2017-SPOK		

Figure 3.3 The English YES/NO-QUESTION CONSTRUCTION

The function of an **operator verb** (V_{TM} in Figure 3.3) is usually fulfilled by the first auxiliary verb of a corresponding declarative sentence, i.e., a verb that is part of one of the modal, aspect or voice constructions that will be introduced in Chapter 4 (in other words a form of *be, do,* or *have* or a modal). It is this operator verb that shows concord with the subject:

(10) a. This **is** Juliet's investigation.   TV-2008-Psych [DECS]
     b. **Is this** Shawn Spencer?   TV-2010-Psych
     c. **Are you** going out to the pottery today?   BNC-GWB-2682

If there is no operator provided by a modal, aspect or voice construction, a *DO*-OPERATOR CONSTRUCTION is used (see 4.8):

(11) **Does she** answer the phone?   TV-2006-Psych

4. The same situation applies to the *WH*-NONSUBJECT-QUESTION CONSTRUCTION, in which the operator verb is preceded by a phrase containing a *wh*-element as in the following examples:

(12) a. 'Where were you this morning between, say, nine and midday?'   BNC-GWB-1677
     b. What exactly does the president hope to achieve?   TV-HouseofCards2015

We can describe this construction as follows:

WH-NONSUBJECT-QUESTION CONSTRUCTION (WHQU)				
Asking for an element expressed in the predicate				
wh		$V_{TM} \in$ PRED	SUBJ	PRED$_{rest}$
falling intonation				
Where did you go in York? TV-2014-Downton				

Figure 3.4 *WH*-NONSUBJECT-QUESTION CONSTRUCTION

5. There is one subtype of *WH*-QUESTION CONSTRUCTION in which no operator verb is required, exemplified by (13):

   (13) Who knows what the future may hold?   TV-2014-Downton

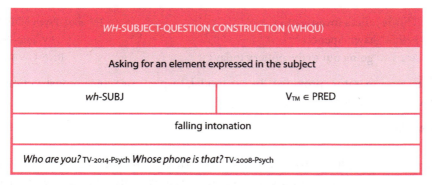

Figure 3.5 The English *WH*-SUBJECT-QUESTION CONSTRUCTION

3.3.3 Imperative constructions

The following type of construction expresses a command, or, very often an invitation to another person to take a certain course of action (Stefanowitsch & Gries 2003). The predicate contains a verb that is not marked for mood or tense. Only in rare cases (such as 14b) does the construction occur with a reinforcing subject *you*:

(14) a. Let's start with Greta Thunberg because this is a 16-year-old girl who managed to convince some massive school districts – including New York City – to let kids walk out for a day.   COCA-2019-SPOK
   b. You be careful, now.   TV-2018-HawaiiFive0

Since there is a difference in form, and to a certain extent also in the semantic function, between the cases with (14a) and without *you* (14b), we will identify two different constructions (which, however, are strongly related in the network of constructions that we believe language to be):

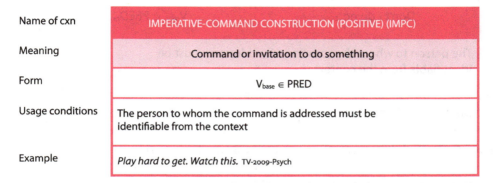

Figure 3.6 The English POSITIVE-IMPERATIVE-COMMAND CONSTRUCTION

Name of cxn	YOU-IMPERATIVE-COMMAND CONSTRUCTION (POSITIVE)	
Meaning	Command or invitation to do something (used to single out one or more individuals from a group)	
Form	SUBJ: you	$V_{base} \in$ PRED
Usage conditions	The person to whom the command is addressed must be identifiable from the context	
Example	*Here, come here. You watch this video. You watch this.* TV-2013–Chosen	

Figure 3.7 The English POSITIVE-*YOU*-IMPERATIVE-COMMAND CONSTRUCTION

As you can see, our description of these constructions contains a type of information that we have not introduced so far: Usage conditions. We will add this level whenever we have a construction that has specific pragmatic co- or contextual usage constraints, to cover the property of "contextual dimensions" of Goldberg's (2019: 7) definition of constructions.

Negative imperatives require a separate constructional template (see also Hoffmann 2022b: 216–218). Although the DO-SUPPORT CONSTRUCTION is generally used with lexical verbs in negation, in this case it is also used with *be*, which is not the case in negated declaratives and interrogatives (Croft and Cruse 2004: 320–321):

(15) a. Don't worry, be happy!
 b. Don't be cruel!

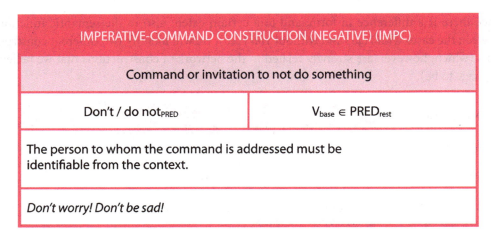

Figure 3.8 The English NEGATIVE-IMPERATIVE-COMMAND CONSTRUCTION

Again, there is a related construction with *you*:

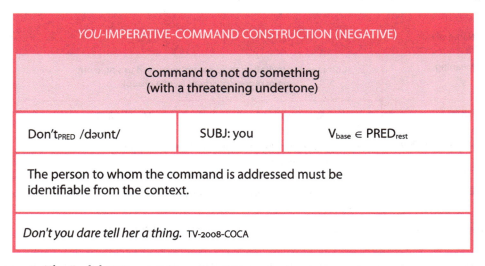

Figure 3.9 The English *YOU*-NEGATIVE-IMPERATIVE-COMMAND CONSTRUCTION

Note that proper names that occur together with imperative constructions are better treated as constructions in their own right, namely as VOCATIVE ADJUNCTS (see 8.8.6).[29]

(16) a. Take a look at this article, Shawn. TV-2007-Psych
 b. Don't you dare lecture me, Shawn. TV-2009-Psych

---

29. For a more detailed description of imperative constructions in English see Stefanowitsch (2003).

3.3.4 Exclamative constructions

There is a construction that exhibits formal similarities with the two types of *WH*-QUESTION CONSTRUCTIONS in that it is introduced by *what* and *how*. However, this construction does not express a question, but rather an 'evaluation' or 'surprise' as in (17):

(17) a. What a torrent of inventions and scientific discoveries the past 120 years have seen!

COCA-1992-MAG

    b. How strange this place is!

COCA-2004-FIC

We can thus identify an exclamative construction of the following type (see www.construct icon.de and Hoffmann 2022b: 219), in which the initial slot is a valency complement of the verb, i.e., part of the corresponding argument structure construction and thus part of the predicate:[30]

EXCLAMATIVE CONSTRUCTION (EXCL)		
Exclamation expressing surprise or evaluation		
WH ∈ PRED	SUBJ	V_{TM} ∈ PRED$_{rest}$
What mistakes he made! How old he is!		

Figure 3.10 The English EXCLAMATIVE CONSTRUCTION[31]

3.4 Sentence type fragments

The sentence-type constructions identified in this chapter can be seen as forming the basis for the great majority of sentences – at least as far as written language is concerned. In spoken language, however, we often also find passages that do not conform fully to these patterns. Look at the following passage of running text taken from a crime novel by W. J. Burley, i.e., from a written text containing dialogue.

(18) [a] 'I don't suppose it's important, but I thought I ought to tell you that I saw Mr Riddle on Friday evening.' She had innocent, dark-blue eyes and a cupid's-bow mouth which would certainly get her into trouble one day. [b] 'I was out with my boyfriend and we

---

30. Strictly speaking, one can distinguish between a *WH*-NONSUBJECT-EXCLAMATIVE CONSTRUCTION, in which the wh-phrase can realize a number of syntactic and semantic functions but not that of a subject, and a *WH*-SUBJECT-EXCLAMATIVE CONSTRUCTION which, however is rare (cf: *What an enormous crowd came!*; CGEL: 833).

31. The form (exclamative) and the function (expressives) of this construction coincide so frequently that, in contrast to the other constructional labels, we only use a single label 'exclamative' here.

passed him in Albert Terrace.' [c] 'Where is that?' [d] 'Not far from where he lives.' [e] 'Was he going towards his house or away from it?' [f] 'Away from it. I suppose he was going down the hill to Moorgate Road, there's nowhere else to go from Albert Terrace.'

BNC-GW3-661-667

Quite clearly, the green utterances in [d] and [f] are not what traditional grammarians would call complete sentences: rather, both take up an element of the previous sentence, an attribute (as defined in 5.2.2), and only express what is relevant in the context. This is also typical of authentic spoken language as in (19):

(19)   a.   When did you first start surfing? – When I was about seven years old, here.

COCA-2013-SPOK

   b.   Why does that matter? Because you look at Hillary Clinton if she wants to run in 2016.

COCA-2014-SPOK

A similar phenomenon can be observed in situations in which a person talks about a series of actions they have carried out without expressing the Subj-argument as in (20a), a style also typical of diaries as in (20b):

(20)   a.   Well, we just did a cruise last year in – in the Baltics. Went to eight different countries. – : I see. – Oh, it's great. – I like that. – Norway, Sweden. Went to Russia. Went to Finland.

COCA-2019-SPOK

   b.   Peeled potatoes, chopped up cabbage, cut finger, rinsed blood off cabbage. Put chops under grill, looked in cookery book for a recipe for gravy. Made gravy. Strained lumps out with a colander. Set table, served dinner, washed up. Put burnt saucepans in to soak.

Sue Townsend-*TheSecretDiaryofAdrianMole*-Monday March 9th

In (21), we can observe uses of impersonal constructions without the *it*-subject, which, it could be argued, could be regarded as a special type of phraseological construction (Bauer & Hoffmann 2020):[32]

(21)   a.   Seems like this holding escalated quickly.   COCA-2015-SPOK
   b.   Turns out it was an explosion at a power plant.   COCA-2018-SPOK

In a similar way, the NICE-OF-YOU CONSTRUCTION has uses of the following kind (Goldberg & Herbst 2021):

(22)   a.   Good of you to join us today.   COCA-2005-SPOK

---

32. As Bauer & Hoffmann (2020) show, these constructions appear even more frequently in spoken language than the 'non-reduced' forms with a subject (such as *It seems ...* or *It turns out ...*). On top of that, they exhibit a different complementation preference and express different emotional content. Consequently, Bauer & Hoffmann argue that 'reduced' and 'non-reduced' are two separate, albeit related constructions without one being derived from the other.

> b. How strange it is, strange and sad, to see all these tropical faces amid the slush and dirty snow, the grey gritty hopelessness of an English industrial city in the middle of winter. BNC-ANY-1594
>
> c. How nice of you. TV-2013-Downton

All of these examples present perfectly normal patterns of usage, although they do not lend themselves to an analysis in terms of categories such as subject and predicate in a *what-you-see-is-what-you-get* approach. Obviously, all the elements needed for a meaningful interpretation of these utterances can be retrieved from the context, but in a constructionist model one would not make any assumptions about any kind of "underlying" form. Since the four cases above follow clearly distinguishable patterns, we can postulate the following four fragment constructions, which, when spoken with falling intonation, all fall under the label of declarative-statement (DECS):

- DECS-FRAGMENT CONSTRUCTION WITH PARTIAL REALIZATION OF PREDICATE (18d/f),
- DECS-FRAGMENT CONSTRUCTION WITHOUT EXPRESSED SUBJECT REFERRING TO SPEAKER (20),
- IMPERSONAL DECS-FRAGMENT CONSTRUCTION WITHOUT *IT* (with verbs such as *seems, appears, looks, turns out,* (21)) and
- EVALUATIVE-DECS-FRAGMENT CONSTRUCTION WITHOUT *IT* AND *BE* (22).

Spoken with rising intonation, these patterns form the corresponding DECLARATIVE-QUESTION-FRAGMENT CONSTRUCTIONS. More importantly though, we must mention one other type of short question constructions, which act as turning-taking signals in spoken discourse:

> (23) **Ted:** First movie you ever saw. -
>
> **Stella:** Benji, 1981. I watched it recently with Lucy and I just thought, "Oh, that dog is so dead right now." What about you?
>
> **Ted:** My dad took me to an old drive-in to see the original Star Wars. TV-2008-HowImet

In (23), the conventionalized turn-taking question *What about you?* does not lend itself to an analysis in terms of subject and predicate, and, consequently, relies heavily on the context for its interpretation. It can roughly be paraphrased as 'How does the event just outlined relate to you?' and has the pragmatic force of directing the addressee to respond by giving a relevant answer.

As you can see, any exhaustive description of these types of constructions must comprise a specification of their usage conditions concerning the required preceding context or genre, for instance. By usage conditions we refer to all the factors determining the use of a construction in the sense of the "shared contextual dimensions" of Goldberg's (2019:7) definition of constructions.

You may have noticed that we are using the term **fragment** here for what in other approaches is called **ellipsis**. There are two reasons for this:

i. Ellipsis is sometimes defined in terms of "recoverability" (e.g., CGEL 1985: 861–862), which somehow suggests that something got lost in the process of formulating the utterance. In a surface-based approach to syntax it is difficult to see how you can recover something that was never there.

ii. Cognitively, we would assume that some of these fragments – especially those exemplified by (18) and (19) – can only be used because the corresponding structure is still activated in the speaker's mind (in a way similar to a priming effect). Other fragment constructions – like those in (20) and (21), for instance – carry a special kind of stylistic and affective meaning (Leech 1981: 14–16) and due to these unique usage conditions – have to be considered constructions in their own right.

3.5 The role of sentence type constructions in CASA

In the CASA-model, sentence type constructions constitute the first step of syntactic analysis. This means that these constructions provide a first template, which serve as the basis for a construction grid. For sentences (5a) and (5b), at this level of specification, we would thus set up the following construction grids:

	Climate change	is affecting the national parks' most ancient and critical cycles.
DECS	SUBJ	$V_{TM} \in$ PRED

Figure 3.11 Construction grid representation of the DECLARATIVE-STATEMENT CONSTRUCTION (DECS) in construct (5a). The construction has two slots – one for the subject, and one for the predicate which must contain a verb

	Is	climate change	affecting the insect populations?
YNQU	$V_{TM} \in$ PRED	SUBJ	PRED$_{rest}$

Figure 3.12 Construction grid representation of the YES-NO-QUESTION CONSTRUCTION (YNQU) in construct (5b). The construction has three slots – one for the operator verb ($V_{TM} \in$ PRED), which is part of the predicate, one for the subject, and one for the rest of the predicate

In the next chapter, we will now look at the next level of a CASA analysis: the constructions that express the tense, aspect and modality of events.

CHAPTER 4

The roles of verbs

4.1 Introduction

4.1.1 Language acquisition and adult language use

There can be no doubt that the words that linguists call verbs play an immensely important role in the construction of sentences in English. This has to do with their overall function in language, which Langacker (2008a: 108) describes as follows:

> The schema for verbs presupposes two fundamental cognitive abilities: the capacity for apprehending relationships and for tracking relationships through time.

Basically, what this means is that many verbs can be used to refer to processes (cf. Langacker 2008a: 100), but some verbs (e.g., *be* or *resemble*) can also refer to stative relations.[33] In any case, comprehending the relation underlying the use of *chase* in *The cat chased the mouse* is bound to require greater intellectual effort than learning that the word *cat* refers to a particular kind of animal.[34] Let us look at a few examples from the Thomas corpus, which are all taken from the first hour of recording, in which the boy is two years and twelve days old (age: 02_00_12).

(1) a. Mother: that's the giraffe. Mother: and that's the lion. Child: grrr. Mother: what does the lion say? Mother: grrr.   t2_00_12
    b. Mother: is it a bear? Child: no. Mother: oh I think it's the bear.   t2_00_12
    c. Mother: what is it? Child: bus. Mother: no it's not a bus.   t2_00_12
    d. Child: where the bus. Mother: the bus is over there. Mother: there's the bus. Thomas: bus.   t2_00_12
    e. Mother: and which one's the blue engine?   t2_00_12

In this recording, we find a rather high number of uses of *is* in the mother's speech as well as that of a few other verbs, but none really of the child.

Six months later, there are a few uses of participles (*gone* (2a), *chasing* (2b)), which are then echoed by the Mother:[35]

---

33. For a discussion of *be* see Langacker (2008a: 396–398). For a more complex definition of verbs that also draws upon formal criteria see 13.3.3.1. Compare, e.g., CGEL (1985: 96–97) or Herbst & Schüller (2008: 37–38). See also Taylor's (1989: 190–196) discussion of verbs and nouns in terms of prototypes, who refers to Givón's (1979: 250) analysis of prototype nouns and verbs in terms of time-stability and temporal instability.

34. For the role of nouns and verbs in L1-acquisition see Behrens (1999) and Tomasello (2003: 43–93).

35. The transcript contains a number of unclear passages that have been marked by symbols such as 0, ? and =; see https://childes.talkbank.org/access/Eng-UK/Thomas.html.

44   A Construction Grammar of the English Language

(2) a. CHI: where ohave [*] hands gone now ? MOT: where've your hands gone now?

t2_06_12 [ohave * = very unclear in recording]

   b. CHI: chasing afte(r). MOT: chasing after. CHI: chasing after now. MOT: who was chasing after who?

t2_06_12

Another four months later, the child produces utterances like the following:

(3) a. CHI: where (h)as he gone? MOT: it (h)as gone away now, darling. CHI: where (h)as it gone?

t3_00_14

   b. CHI: Mummy, what are you doing? MOT: Mummy, what are you doing? MOT: I'm folding this up, darling.

t3_00_14

Obviously, it cannot be our intention to provide a systematic study of the development of the verbal system by Thomas, let alone by children in general, but it is perfectly clear that the development from (1) to (3) does take a considerable amount of time – and is still a far cry from the complexity of adult sentences as the ones in (4):

(4) a. Can you suggest where he might have been going?'   BNC-GW3-1774

   b. Who did you say you bought this land from?   TV-2017-MurdochMysteries

Note, however, that combinations such as (4a) or (4b) are obviously also rare in adult speech, as shown by the figures in Table 4.1:

Table 4.1 Combinations of verbs in BNC

Pattern (with example)	Search string	Frequency	Frequency per million	Percentage of total
HAVE + en-participle (*have seen*)	(have | has | had) (_VBN | _VDN | _VHN | _VVN)	585,302	5953.43	31.11%
modal + verb (*will be*)	_VMo (_VBI | _VDI | _VHI | _VVI)	466,412	4744.13	24.79%
BE + en-participle (*was made*)	(am | are | is | was | were) (_VBN | _VDN | _VHN | _VVN)	456,672	4645.06	24.27%
BE + ing-participle (*was going*)	(am | are | is | was | were) (_VBG | _VDG | _VHG | _VVG)	188,011	1912.36	9.99%
modal + have + en-participle (*would have been*)	_VMo have (_VBN | _VDN | _VHN | _VVN)	58,666	596.72	3.12%
modal + be + ing-participle (*will be working*)	_VMo be (_VBGI | _VDG | _VHG | _VVG)	14,277	145.22	0.76%
BE + being + en-participle (*is being used*)	(am | are | is | was | were) being (_VBN | _VDN | _VHN | _VVN)	15,296	155.58	0.81%

Chapter 4. The roles of verbs 45

Table 4.1 *(continued)*

Pattern (with example)	Search string	Frequency	Frequency per million	Percentage of total
HAVE + been + en-participle (*have been made*)	(have | has | had) been (_VBN | _VDN | _VHN | _VVN)	96,017	976.64	5.10%
modal + have + been + ing-participle (*must have been doing*)	_VMo have been (_VBG | _VDG | _VHG | _VVG)"	913	9.29	0.05%
Total		1,881,566		100.00%

Some of the combinations of two or three words (such as *would be*, which occurs 555 times per 1 million words in the BNC) may well occur frequently enough to be stored as constructional chunks by at least some speakers, as we will show in more detail in Chapter 12. However, for most constructs of this type, especially long ones such as (5), this is probably not the case:

(5) Well, surely you must have been doing something illegal. TV-2014-BlueBloods

Rather, such sequences of verbs will be interpreted as combinations of constructions. What seems to be instrumental in this respect is the knowledge that speakers have of transitional probabilities, i.e., knowledge what word(s) can be expected to follow (or precede) a particular word (see Chapter 14 for details). Jurafsky (2003:9) defines transitional probability as the number of occurrences of a combination of a word n-1 and a word n as the number of occurrences of the sequence $[w_{n-1} + w_n]$ divided by the number of overall occurrences of w_{n-1} in a corpus.[36] So, for instance, if you take a modal verb such as *can*, in 66% of all cases in the BNC, it will be followed by the infinitive or base form of a verb, 70% of occurrences of *is/am/are/was/were* are followed by *V-ing* and 17% by *V-en*. We can thus argue that transitional probabilities play an important part in the production and comprehension of such sequences (and their potential subsequent entrenchment as single constructional chunks).

4.1.2   A methodological question

One way of analyzing the sequences of verbs listed in Table 4.1 is to see them as combinations of one or more of the following constructions:

i.   **modal constructions** that present the process described as not being 'factual' but as being subject to some kind of modification with respect to factors indicating the feasibility or necessity of it happening, volition, etc.

---

36. Cf. Jurafsky (2003:9): $P(w_i|w_{i-1}) = C(w_{i-1}w_i): C(w_{i-1\pm})$.

(6)   Climate change *may shift* timing of summer thunderstorms   COCA-2019-MAG

ii.   **tense constructions** – i.e., in English, PRESENT-TENSE CONSTRUCTIONS and the PAST-TENSE CONSTRUCTIONS,

(7)   a.   Is St. Ives in Cornwall?   COCA-2011-TV
      b.   Universities everywhere *were* in disarray ...   BNC-ANY-696

iii. the PROGRESSIVE CONSTRUCTION [BE+V-ING], which presents the action described as being in progress,

(8)   Climate change *is causing* the Antarctic to melt, but glaciologists are still mapping how, where and why.   COCA-2019-MAG

iv.   the PERFECTIVE CONSTRUCTION [HAVE+V-EN],[37] which expresses some relevance of the action described in relation to the time of the utterance,

(9)   I've *been* to the MOMA, like, a hundred times.   COCA-2008-MOV

v.   **voice constructions**, i.e., the ACTIVE CONSTRUCTION and the PASSIVE CONSTRUCTION [BE+V-EN] in English.

(10) a.   ... the current climate change *causes* westerly winds to increase ...
                                                                        COCA-2016-MAG
      b.   Rising sea levels ... *are caused* by the melting of ice sheets, as well as the thermal expansions of the ocean.   COCA-2019-NEWS

However, for two reasons, this list makes things look simpler than they are. There are two issues that deserve some discussion from a theoretical point of view.

a.   Firstly, we analyze modals such as *may* and *might* as two different modal verbs because they clearly express different degrees of possibility:

(11) a.   Climate change *may* disrupt production processes and service delivery ...
                                                                        COCA-2013-MAG
      b.   Climate change *might* hasten these invasions or might mediate their effects on forest structure.   COCA-2012-ACAD

At the same time, one can also argue that forms such as *could, should, would* and *might* can be considered past tense forms: firstly, they occur in past tense contexts as in (12), and, secondly, they are often used in indirect speech introduced by a past tense verb in places where past tense is normal with other verbs (and, thirdly, historically, *could,*

---

37. V-EN stands for past participles such as *looked, known, added* or *given*. To avoid confusion with past tense forms [V-ED], [V-EN] is used for participles ending in *-ed*, too.

should, would and *might* do indeed go back to the past tense forms of *can, shall, will* and *may*). Compare:

(12)   It was not raining, but droplets of moisture condensed on every cold surface and
       Wycliffe could taste the salt on his lips.   BNC-GW3-466

(13)   a.   She says we may not be where we think we are.   TV-2009-Psych
       b.   I said they might be.   TV-2998-Psych

Nevertheless, there is no way of knowing whether *might* in (13b) corresponds to *may* or *might* in a hypothetical direct speech equivalent. Furthermore, a past tense introductory verb does not necessarily rule out the use of *may* or *will*:

(14)   a.   But you said there may not be time to find another donor.   TV-1987-Dynasty
       b.   The clerk said it 'll take a few more minutes to process our check.   TV-2009-Psych

For these reasons, we prefer not to analyze forms such as *might* or *would, etc.* as past tense forms of *may* or *will*.

b.   The second problem is even more intricate. The way we have presented the constructions, there is one case in which speakers have to make a choice between two constructions, namely that between the PRESENT-TENSE CONSTRUCTION and the PAST-TENSE CONSTRUCTION.[38] In the case of the MODAL CONSTRUCTION, the PERFECTIVE CONSTRUCTION, and the PASSIVE CONSTRUCTION, the choice speakers have is one of "adding" a particular dimension of meaning or not. In a structuralist way of thinking, this problem can be solved by saying that (15), which contrasts with (8), is 'non-progressive' (or 'simple'), (16), which contrasts with (9) 'non-perfective', and (17), which contrasts with (15), as 'non-passive', i.e., active:

(15)   [There is evidence to suggest that] the current climate change causes westerly winds
       to increase ...   COCA-2016-MAG

(16)   I have the experience.   COCA-2019-SPOK

(17)   Climate change is caused by pollution.   COCA-2012-MAG

On the other hand, we do not call constructs such as (7) or (15–17) 'non-modal' – nor do we have a category 'non-cat' for all nouns that cannot be used to refer to cats. In this line of thinking, one could argue that in (8), for example, the use of the PROGRESSIVE CONSTRUCTION adds an additional element of meaning in comparison to (14). The counter-argument is, of course, that certain meanings of PRESENT-TENSE CONSTRUCTIONS do not combine with the meaning of the PROGRESSIVE CONSTRUCTION, e.g., meanings that can be described as 'general truths' or 'habitual action':

---

38. In fact, in present-day English, one could also argue that the case for a PRESENT-TENSE CONSTRUCTION is relatively weak since for almost all verbs it is only the third person form that is not identical with the base form of the verb. It is only the verb *be* where 1st and 2nd person tense forms differ from the base form.

(18) a. The satellites orbit the globe every ninety minutes while the Earth rotates
beneath them ...   COCA-2019-SPOK

b. Why do you smoke?   COCA-2004-MAG

However, we cannot make out a case for a simple-form construction on that basis either, because such meanings do not normally combine with the PROGRESSIVE CONSTRUCTION.

In the construction grids that we will use to show the constructions that make up a construct, we will thus restrict ourselves to the constructions listed under (i)–(v). Constructs that do not involve a passive construction can be classified as active, constructs that do not involve a progressive construction can be classified as simple, but this does not necessarily commit us to postulate an active or a simple-form construction.

4.2 Expressing different degrees of certainty

4.2.1 Yes, no, possibly or perhaps

Put yourself in the position of a two-year-old hearing sentences such as the ones under (19) and (20).

(19) a. ... there is another car there.   t2_00_19m

b. ... but there isn't any chocolate.   t2_01_06m

(20) a. There may be a little drop of water left in there.   t2_01_26

b. Well, when Nana comes she may very well have some chocolate hidden in her bag.

t2_02_13

The first thing children will have to learn is that all of these constructs relate to the existence or, from the children's perspective, the availability of a 'thing' in the context of the situation they are in. Furthermore, they will have to understand that the sentences in (19) express a definite statement as to whether or not something is the case, whereas those in (20) contain an element of uncertainty, and that this has to do with the word *may*, or, to be more precise, the MAY-CONSTRUCTION, which also involves the use of *be* or *have* rather than *is*. Once they have grasped the nature of *may* + infinitive as a construction, they will have to work out that the 'uncertainty' associated with *may* can be of different kinds since the uses in (21) are not quite the same as those in (20):

(21) a. Please, may Mummy wear your badge?   t2_00_13

b. Please, may Mummy come and sit next to you?   t2_01_15

c. Please, may I have the truck?   t2_01_18

Chapter 4. The roles of verbs   49

4.2.2   The English modals

Verbs like *may* are called modal verbs and the distinction exemplified by the examples
in (20) and (21) reflect a very basic distinction between two uses of modals, namely that
between

- **intrinsic** (or **root**) **modality**, expressing human control over something happening
  ('obligation', 'permission', 'intention', 'ability'; Langacker 2008a: 305), and
- **extrinsic** (or **epistemic**) **modality**, providing the speaker's evaluation of the likelihood
  of something happening or being the case.[39]

What children also have to work out is that *may* is very much like some other words such
as *can* or *will*, not only with respect to the type of meaning they can be used to express, but
also with respect to some formal properties.[40] Modal verbs

i.   can be followed by an infinitive, i.e., the base form of the verb,
ii. can function as auxiliaries in negation and question constructions (like *be, do* and *have*),
iii. unlike all other English verbs do not have a separate form for the 3rd person present
     tense,
iv. do not occur in non-finite clauses.

English has the following set of core modal verbs to which these criteria apply: *can, could,
may, might, must, shall, should, will, would*.[41]

4.2.3   Form and meaning of modal constructions

At the level of form, a **modal construction** consists of a modal verb (V_M) and a schematic
V slot and semantically it expresses some kind of reservation on the factual character of the
'process' described by the subject and the infinitive clause. Like certain types of adverbs (e.g.
perhaps, possibly), the semantic scope of modal constructions extends to the content of the
whole clause.

While such a general construction captures the semantic properties shared by all modal
constructions, for many purposes it is the less abstract and more specific level of the type

---

39. Compare CGEL (1985: 219), who point at the gradient character of the distinction, or Langacker
(2008a: 305–309). For a distinction between epistemic, deontic and dynamic modality see CAMG
(2002: 178–179) and Aarts (2011: 276–277). See also Radden and Dirven (2007: 262–263).

40. Searching the first full week of the Thomas corpus (5 hours: t2_00_16 to t2_00_20) produced 353
instances of "may|can|will|shall|'ll|would|could|might|must|should". We can thus estimate that Thomas
experienced almost 4,000 instances of modals in that week (8 hours per day, 7 days).

41. *Dare* and *need* can be used like modals or like other verbs with respect to criteria (i)–(iii), *ought* is like a
modal with respect to (i), (ii), and (iv), but can only be followed by a *to*-infinitive. CGEL (1985, Ch. 3.41–43)
includes these verbs under *marginal modals*. See 13.3.3.2.

50 A Construction Grammar of the English Language

Name	MODAL CONSTRUCTIONS		
Meaning	Epistemic or root modification of the proposition expressed by the verb and its participants		
Form	V_M		
	can may will must shall could might should would dare need		V_{base}
	ought	to	

Figure 4.1 The English MODAL CONSTRUCTIONS

MAY-MODAL CONSTRUCTION, WILL-MODAL CONSTRUCTION – or, simply, MAY-CONSTRUCTION, WILL-CONSTRUCTION, ETC. – that are of greater relevance for the description of English.[42]

4.2.4 Combining modal and other constructions

Modal constructions can be combined with sentence-type constructions in very much the same way as tense constructions (see 4.3), e.g., with the DECLARATIVE-STATEMENT CON-STRUCTION or the YES-NO-QUESTION CONSTRUCTION:

In a sentence such as

(22) She might have seen something. TV-2006-Psych

might is the verb required in the predicate of a DECLARATIVE-STATEMENT CONSTRUCTION (see 3.3.2). It also fills the modal slot of the MODAL CONSTRUCTION, whose second slot is filled by the base (or infinitive) form *have*. The modal *might* thus functions as a nexus of two

---

42. See Hilpert (2020: 116–117), who supports this view on the grounds of the different collocational behavior of these verbs.

blended constructions, as shown in Figure 4.2 (which is just a part of the construction grid for the whole sentence, of course):

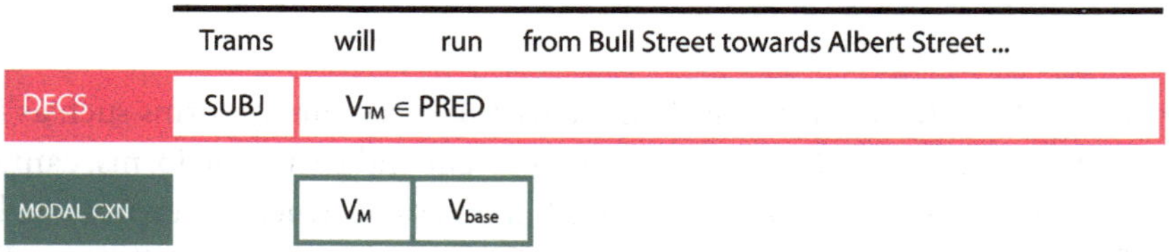

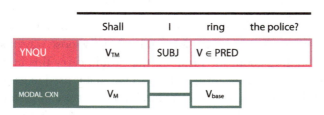

Figure 4.2 Construction grid representation of the DECLARATIVE-STATEMENT CONSTRUCTION and the MIGHT-MODAL CONSTRUCTION in the construct *Trams will run from Bull Street towards Albert Street* … NOW-22-07-17-GB

If combined with the INTERROGATIVE-YES/NO-QUESTION CONSTRUCTION, which demands that an operator verb appears before the subject, the modal verb functions as the operator:

Figure 4.3 Construction grid representation of the YES/NO-QUESTION (YNQU) and the MODAL CONSTRUCTION in the construct *Shall I ring the police?* TV-2011-Psych

In the construction grid representation, every construction will be surrounded by a box surrounding the area ranging from the first to the last slot of the construction. Should not all slots of a construction be immediately adjacent to each other, this is shown by a connecting line as in Figure 4.3 (where the line connects the non-adjacent modal and V_{base} slots).

4.3 Using verbs to refer to time

4.3.1 Problems of the morphological analysis of English verb forms

As outlined above, we will identify two groups of tense constructions for English – PRESENT-TENSE CONSTRUCTIONS and PAST-TENSE CONSTRUCTIONS (though there are, of course, more constructions that allow us to express temporal information, see, e.g., Section 4.3.3). Formally, some of these constructions can be characterized in terms of suffixes that combine with the base form of a verb (see Hoffmann 2022b: 57–63):

52 A Construction Grammar of the English Language

- V-{S}, i.e., V_{base} + /s/, /z/ and /ɪz/ (*hates, coincides, finishes*) THIRD-PERSON-PRESENT-TENSE-CONSTRUCTIONS and
- V-{D}, i.e., V_{base} + /t/, /d/ and /ɪd/ (*finished, surprised, hated*) PAST-TENSE CONSTRUCTION

However, these schematic descriptions do not cover all cases. Firstly, forms such as *is, am* or *was, sang, came* and *took*, which quite clearly are present and past tense forms, cannot really be separated into two bits, but have to be looked upon as constructions expressing both the meaning of the verb and the respective tense (Hoffmann 2022b: 65–69).[43] Secondly, some verbs such as *put* or *cut* have distinct present tense forms only in the 3rd person singular.[44] In these cases, the distinction between present and past tense is neutralized in the sense that the same form receives a present tense or past tense interpretation which is entirely dependent upon the context.

(23) a. You know, they often put apples and oranges together. COCA-1998-SPOK
      b. Here's one of the tweets that the President put out today. COCA-2018-SPOK

When you think about it carefully, it is thus pretty obvious that calling *put* a present tense *form* in (23a) and a past tense *form* in (23b) is at best a very loose way of speaking because there is absolutely nothing about the form *put* that would carry this information. It is far more precise to say that ⟨put⟩ is the form of the verb *put* that is used in PRESENT-TENSE CONSTRUCTIONS (1st/2nd person and 3rd person plural) and the PAST-TENSE CONSTRUCTION.

A similar point can be made with respect to the distinction between finite and non-finite forms because, again, in English there is no difference in morphological form in the verb between uses in constructions traditionally classified as finite (such as a PRESENT-TENSE CONSTRUCTION as in (24a) and non-finite (such as the infinitives in (24bc) (see 2.3):

(24) a. With all the work I have as Dean?' BNC-ANY-1412
      b. We'll have wine with dinner. COCA-1994-FIC
      c. She wanted to have wine with lunch. COCA-2003-FIC

The only way of arriving at a present tense interpretation of *have* in (24a) is thus that it occurs together with a subject. While we will not go so far as to make the subject an integral part of PRESENT-TENSE CONSTRUCTIONS, we will treat the fact that such constructions can only be used if a subject is realized in the clause (or, in rare cases, can be identified from the context) as a usage-condition of such constructions. In fact, if we take the usage conditions of the various tense constructions to comprise information about the types of subject with which they can occur, this provides a straightforward and convenient way of accounting for the agreement between subject and the finite verb of the predicate. As far as agreement is

---

43. In structuralist linguistics, such forms are called portmanteau morphemes.

44. Some analyses posit a zero-morph or zero-morpheme to be able to analyze such cases as being compositional.

concerned, there is also the option of specifying accordingly those sentence type constructions that contain a SUBJ and a PRED or saying that subject-verb agreement is a by-product
of the fact that both the verb and the subject-NP refer to one (singular) or more (plural)
things (Kibrik 2010; Hoffmann & Herbst, forthc.). Agreement actually seems to present a
strong argument for considering subjects as integral parts of present-tense constructions. To
be perfectly honest, in the course of writing this book we changed our minds more than
once with respect to the question of whether we should include the subject as a slot in tense
constructions or whether we should see the fact that the various tense constructions as usage
conditions – in terms of Goldberg's (2019:7) "contextual dimensions". In terms of the psychological processes underlying the use of tense constructions, this probably does not make
any difference, let alone a difference that could be proved by psychological or neurolinguistic evidence. In the end, we considered the solution in terms of usage conditions preferable –
mostly, because the difference in meaning between present-tense constructions and past-
tense constructions.

Note, moreover, there are fragment constructions that do not contain SUBJs (as in
diaries or informal spoken language, see (25)). In these cases, the element that could have
been realized in the subject slot must be identifiable from the context. We will call this a
contextual anchor. Compare:

(25) a.   Said everything came down to sex, didn't he?   BNC-ANY-2578
      b.   It's still me. Still love you. I need some air.   COCA-2013-TV

(26) Alright. Can do or I'll ring him later on.   BNC-KCI-1962-3

The subject of a tense construction – like that of a modal construction – must thus be
regarded as an element that will only be realized if the corresponding sentence type construction provides for a SUBJ slot.

4.3.2   Tense and person constructions

4.3.2.1   *Present and past-tense constructions*

In light of the above considerations, we consider it appropriate to propose a somewhat
unorthodox classification of tense in English, which is driven by cognitive considerations
based on the characteristics of the English language and independent of classifications
which have proved to be a suitable framework for other languages, but may not be ideal for
English.

With the exception of modals, all English verbs have distinct forms for the third person
singular in the present tense, and most have different forms in present and past tense constructions. Notably, *be*, which is by far the most frequent verb of the English language, is also
the only one that has a separate 1st person singular form in the present tense and that distinguishes between singular and plural in the past tense.

This leads us to postulate the following five tense constructions:

A Construction Grammar of the English Language

1. FIRST-PERSON-PRESENT-TENSE CONSTRUCTION
2. THIRD-PERSON-PRESENT-TENSE CONSTRUCTION
3. GENERAL-PRESENT-TENSE CONSTRUCTION (2nd person sg and all plurals)
4. FIRST-AND-THIRD-PERSON-SINGULAR-PAST-TENSE CONSTRUCTION
5. GENERAL-PAST-TENSE-CONSTRUCTION (2nd person sg and all plurals)

We will employ the following format for the description of these constructions, using the abbreviations V_T for forms that allow an interpretation in terms of present or past tense, V_{Tpres} and V_{Tpast}, indications of person (1=speaker, 2=addressee, 3=other) and number (SG, singular=one, PL plural=more than one).[45]

Name of cxn	FIRST-PERSON-SINGULAR-PRESENT-TENSE CONSTRUCTION	
Meaning	Relating a 'process' with the speaker as participant to the time of the utterance or giving it a neutral "timeless" interpretation.	
Form	$V_{TPres1SG}$	
	am	
	V_{base}	← *have/'ve do think know mean want love guess need feel see get believe like hope get etc.*
Usage condition	The construction can only be used in combination with a sentence-type construction in which the subject is I or in contexts in which the subject can be identified from the context.	

Figure 4.4 The English FIRST-PERSON-PRESENT-TENSE CONSTRUCTION

This way of representing constructions indicates the semantic function of the construction as well as the formal realization: What we attempt to visualize in this format is the view propagated by Bybee (1995, 2010), who argues that speakers do not only store irregular forms (such as *am* in Figure 4.4), but also a large number of frequent forms (which serve as a basis for the generalization of a schema). We refer to such items as 'itecxes' – itecx stands for 'item as an element of a construction': it∈cx (Herbst 2018b). We show itecxes by listing a few of the most frequent ones in the constructional description to symbolize forms that could provide a basis for the emergence of the abstract category shown to the left of the arrow.[46]

---

45. In construction grids we will not usually make specifications beyond V_T.

46. In this chapter, itecxes are given in the order of their frequency on the basis of simple COCA searches of the type "I _v*" (based on the first 100 hits; without taking into account of whether forms of *be, do* or *have* are part of, e.g., a passive construction.)

In very much the same way, we can capture the lexical basis for the emergence of a schematic representation of what in structuralist linguistics is described in terms of different allomorphs of one morpheme (see also Hoffmann 2022b: 59–61):

THIRD-PERSON-SINGULAR-PRESENT-TENSE CONSTRUCTION		
Relating a 'process' with a third-party participant to the time of the utterance or giving it a neutral "timeless" interpretation.		
$V_{Tpres3SG}$		
is has does says		
V_{base}	/z/	← *comes seems goes means knows needs happens shows gives appears turns includes sounds becomes feels etc.*
	/s/	← *makes looks wants gets takes works thinks starts suggests etc.*
	/ɪz/	← *increases raises etc.*
The construction can only be used in combination with a sentence-type construction in which the subject is $NP_{count-sg}$ NP_{mass} *he/she/it* clause or in contexts in which the subject can be identified from the context.		

Figure 4.5 The English THIRD-PERSON-SINGULAR-PRESENT-TENSE CONSTRUCTION[47]

GENERAL-PRESENT-TENSE CONSTRUCTION (second person singular and all plurals)	
Relating a 'process' in which the subject is a participant to the time of the utterance or giving it a neutral "timeless" interpretation.	
are	
V_{base}	← *know want think get need see go like etc.*
The construction can only be used in combination with a sentence-type construction in which the subject is *you*, a plural NP or in contexts in which the subject can be identified from the context.	

Figure 4.6 The English GENERAL-PRESENT-TENSE CONSTRUCTION

---

47. Based on COCA ("_v?z*").

56 A Construction Grammar of the English Language

Figure 4.7 and 4.8 show our representation of the English PAST-TENSE CONSTRUCTIONS:

FIRST & THIRD-PERSON-SINGULAR-PAST-TENSE CONSTRUCTION		
Relating a 'process' in which the subject is a participant to the time of the utterance or removing it from the reality of present time.		
$V_{Tpast3SG}$		
was said had did told knew went thought took saw came felt found gave left wrote put began		
V	/t/	← *looked asked walked worked liked stopped etc.*
	/d/	← *turned called tried died loved seemed used pulled moved etc.*
	/ɪd/	← *wanted started needed added decided etc.*
The construction can only be used in combination with a sentence-type construction in which the subject is *I* *he/she/it* $NP_{count-sg}$ NP_{mass} clause or contexts in which the subject can be identified from the context.		

Figure 4.7 The English FIRST & THIRD-PERSON-SINGULAR-PAST-TENSE CONSTRUCTION

GENERAL-PAST-TENSE CONSTRUCTION (2nd person singular and all plurals)		
Relating a 'process' in which the subject is a participant to the time of the utterance or removing it from the reality of present time.		
$V_{Tpast2SG123PL}$		
were did had got said found went saw thought, etc.		
V_{base}	/t/	← *talked asked looked* etc.
	/d/	← *called mentioned tried* etc.
	/ɪd/	← *wanted started needed* etc.
The construction can only be used in combination with a sentence-type construction in which the subject is *I* *you* NP_{pl} NP and NP or in contexts in which the subject can be identified from the context.		

Figure 4.8 The English GENERAL-PAST-TENSE CONSTRUCTION

It must be understood that this is not the only conceivable way of representing these constructions. From a cognitive point of view, we could imagine making finer distinctions and seeing, e.g., the various allomorphs (such as /t/, /d/ or /ɪd/) as specific constructional instances of the abstract GENERAL-PAST-TENSE CONSTRUCTION or also distinguishing between 1st and 3rd person singular constructions in the past tense (see Hoffmann 2022b: 57–67).[48]

4.3.2.2 *Combining tense constructions with other constructions*

Note that we consider tense constructions as not being marked for word order. In actual sentences, tense constructions always blend with either the DECLARATIVE-STATEMENT CON-STRUCTION or some other sentence-type construction identified in Chapter 3. In fact, these constructions are characterized by the fact that their predicate must contain a modal verb

---

48. We would like to point out an alternative to the present account could be to include the respective subjects in the description of the various tense constructions identified instead of capturing the relation between subjects and verb forms in terms of usage conditions. In fact, it is likely that children learn tense constructions in combination with the respective types of subjects. On the other hand, one can also find "errors" of the following type in early child language: ... *and then Mummy just ring the bell;* ... *and then Mummy go rat a tat tat*$_{Thomas}$ (t3_03–06). Ambridge & Lieven (2011: 144–157) provide a detailed survey of generativist and constructionist accounts of childrens' failure to mark tense and agreement. See also Tomasello (2003: 230–232). In this context, it is important to note that "grammatical function words and bound inflections tend to be short and low in stress ... with the result that these cues are difficult to perceive" (Ellis 2006: 170–171).

or a verb form that can be interpreted as an indication of present tense (V_{TPres}) or past tense (V-ed) (either through the form as such as with *laughed* or by relying on the context as with *put*). There is thus a large amount of overlap between these constructions. Tense constructions of the form identified above can be imagined to fuse with the various sentence type constructions: the tense construction provides a verb form of the type required by the sentence type construction. We indicate this identity of elements by putting them underneath each other in the grid:

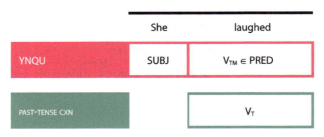

Figure 4.9 Construction grid for *She laughed*. COCA-2019-TV

In the final construct, we thus assume that the two V boxes of Figure 4.9 blend / overlap with each other. In cases where two constructions contain the same identical slot (as with the V slot here), this is straightforward. When constructions have similar slots with slightly different information, the result is a blended unit of all pieces of information (in this case: V-ed ∈ PRED).

4.3.3   Referring to the future

4.3.3.1   *Referring to future time with the* WILL CONSTRUCTION

Time – an extralinguistic category – is construed in many languages as a relational system that depends on the present as a primary reference point, which divides the time continuum up into

- the 'past', i.e., the stretch of time before the present,
- the 'present', i.e., strictly speaking, the present moment, or, for most intents and purposes, a small time segment around the present moment,
- the 'future', i.e., the stretch of time following the present.

We have already seen that 'past time reference' is often established by the PAST-TENSE CONSTRUCTION (although it has other uses, too; see I.4.4). PRESENT-TENSE CONSTRUCTIONS typically refer to 'processes' related to 'present time' (as in 27a) and, as pointed out above, to 'processes' that we tend not to relate to the past, the present or the future, as in (27b). It can also be used, however, to refer to 'past processes' as in newspaper headlines as in (28), or to 'processes' located in 'future time' as in (29):

Chapter 4. The roles of verbs   **59**

(27) a.   Why is Harris the 49th Vice President when Biden is the 46th President?

NOW 21-01-22 US

    b.   The return train leaves Llandovery at 14:40 and arrives in Knighton at 16:38, Craven Arms at 17:03 and Shrewsbury at 17:30.   BNC-HHU-216

(28) Biden arrives in Europe for first foreign trip as president # President Biden arrived in Europe on Wednesday ...   NOW-21-06-09-US

(29) As the G7 meets this week, Governments must go further to incentivize ambitious science-based target setting.   NOW 21-06-09-US [before summit began]

Quite obviously, there is no direct 1:1-correspondence between the segments into which we tend to divide 'time' and linguistic structure, but the classification of the linguistic means that can be used in English to refer to the 'future' is particularly tricky.[49] One of the most common ones is exemplified by (30):

(30) a.   The G7 Summit will take place at Carbis Bay, Cornwall, U.K. from Friday 11 through Sunday 13.   NOW 21-06-09 US

    b.   On Saturday and Sunday, the president will attend the G7 Summit in Cornwall.

NOW 21-06-09 US

    c.   Will you do me a favor? In your funny accent, will you say, "magically delicious"?

TV-2007-Psych

The *WILL*-CONSTRUCTION, which we already mentioned in 4.2.2.2 is a modal construction whose meaning spectrum ranges from clear cases of referring to 'future time' (27a) to the expression of 'willingness' (30b) or 'intention' (30c).[50]

4.3.3.2   *The BE-GOING-TO-V CONSTRUCTION*

Another very common means of referring to 'future time' events is the use of the *BE-GOING-TO*-V CONSTRUCTION, as in (31):

(31) a.   I think you were going to say something beginning with But.   BNC-ANY-957

    b.   'I'm going to be very late.'   BNC-ANY-1673

    c.   Looks like it's going to rain. You think? Nah, it's going to pass.   COCA-2016-MOV

---

49. Cf. the discussion of the issue of whether it makes sense to identify a future tense in English by Hilpert (2008: 17–22), who concludes: "The view that a given form must be either a tense marker or a modality marker is thus rejected in the present study in favour of a constructional view that embraces the multifunctionality of future constructions."

50. It should be noted that we follow the big reference grammars like CGEL (4.3, 4.41–42) and CAMG (2002: 208–210) here by not making a distinction between a modal *will* and a future tense *will*. Some linguists refer to this construction as the future tense all the same, but – if you define tense as an inflectional category – then there is no justification for this in English (see also Herbst 2010).

This construction is often associated with an element of meaning in terms of 'predictability' in the sense of there being causes in the 'present' that lead your expectations about some future development.

Let us digress for a moment, because the historical development of this construction is a wonderful example of what can happen in language (see Hoffmann 2022b: 250–252). As Traugott (2015) has shown, this construction originated from a combination of an explicit motion event and the naming of its purpose as in (32a), went through a stage where the goal of the motion did not have to be mentioned any more as in (32b), until it was used with impersonal subjects and lost its purpose meaning as in (32c) or the examples in (31) above:

(32) a. "and now I *am going* to the court to prefer my petition"
          (1594 Anon., *A Knacck to Know a Knave* [CED DICKNAVE]"   (Traugott 2015: 66)
      b. "... and as he *was going to* make a nooze, I watch'd my time and ranne away."
          (1611 Tourneur, *The Atheist's Tragedie* [LION: Early English Books Online; Garrett 2012: 69)"   (Traugott 2015: 67)
      c. "You hear that there is money yet left, and it *is going to be* layd out in Rattels ..."
          (1647 Field and Fletcher, *The Honest Man's Fortune* [LION; Garrett 2012: 70])
                                                              (Traugott 2015: 68)

The BE-GOING-TO-V CONSTRUCTION, which interestingly has parallels in quite a few other languages such as Spanish, Portuguese or French (Bybee 2015: 123 & 137), is the result of a historical process called **grammaticalization**, in which a new "grammatical" construction emerges out of the repeated use of a sequence of lexical items.

It should be noted that the BE-GOING-TO-V CONSTRUCTION, while relating to 'future time', does not necessarily do so from a 'present-point-in-time'-perspective (but rather with respect to a contextually-given reference time):

(33) a. On the other hand, she wasn't going to show excessive respect by wearing her olive-green tailored interview suit.   BNC-ANY-1543
      b. Tony did some sketches last year and he was going to work them up into a picture – why haven't you, Tony?   BNC-GW3-86

4.3.4 Other multi-word constructions used to express 'time'

The BE-GOING-TO-V CONSTRUCTION is by no means the only construction of its kind, although a particularly frequent one. In fact, there are numerous such item-based constructions with some reference to 'time' such as

– the BE-ABOUT-TO-V CONSTRUCTION:

   (34) Robyn was about to say, 'The Government,' when she saw the trap ...   BNC-ANY-1937

– the USED-TO-V CONSTRUCTION (pronounced /juːst tə/):

   (35) They used to camp out there in the summer holidays.   BNC-GWB-2266

4.4 The PROGRESSIVE CONSTRUCTION

At the level of form, the PROGRESSIVE CONSTRUCTION consists of a form of BE and a present participle form of the verb (Hoffmann 2022b: 211):

(36) a. Robyn Penrose is making her way to Lecture Room A... BNC-ANY-1081
b. Then, in 1984, just when Robyn was beginning to despair, the job at Rummidge came up. BNC-ANY-706
c. Then I was interviewing all last week. BNC-ANY-981
d. As the coronavirus rages out of control across much of the United States, Americans are acting curiously helpless. NYT-1-July-2020

The range of meanings expressed by the PROGRESSIVE CONSTRUCTION centers around the idea of putting emphasis on the fact that an action is "in progress" (36a), often as a background to another action (36b), but also to express duration or to give special emphasis to the action as such (36cd).

PROGRESSIVE CONSTRUCTION		
Putting emphasis on an action being in progress in a certain time span.		
BE	V-ing	← *going doing being trying looking getting talking coming saying working making happening taking thinking having sitting wearing running standing using etc.*

Figure 4.10 The English PROGRESSIVE CONSTRUCTION

The PROGRESSIVE CONSTRUCTION is a nice example of how the meaning of a construction and its verbal slot fillers interact (Leech 1971: 14–30; Hoffmann 2022b: 142–148). This is particularly noticeable with 'transitional event verbs', which express processes leading to an endpoint. Their use in the PROGRESSIVE CONSTRUCTION can result in a construal of opening up a time span and putting the focus on the approach to the endpoint (of arriving and drowning, respectively, in (37)).

(37) a. Attention passengers, the taxi is arriving at Gate 1. COCA-2014-MOV
b. I was drowning, and Louis threw me a lifeline. COCA-2014-TV

On the other hand, verbs that can be used to refer to actions consisting of a single moment, tend to be interpreted in the sense of repeated actions:

(38) a. The horse jumped over the fence and galloped down the hill... COCA-2004-FIC
b. Kids were jumping around playing hopscotch ... COCA-2017-FIC

Note that verbs expressing states do not normally occur in the PROGRESSIVE CONSTRUCTION, but when they do, they tend to receive an activity interpretation:

(39) a. The wine tasted very nice.
     b. They were tasting the wine.

Despite this focus on the process, one can draw a parallel to the ATTRIBUTIVE CONSTRUCTION with adjectives (as in 40b) or a prepositional phrase containing a noun indicating 'process' (as in 41b and 42b) and interpret the present participle as a state a person is currently in.

(40) a. The squirrel was sleeping when she entered … BNC-JYE-902
     b. He was fast asleep when the telephone rang beside his bed. BNC-GV8-3028

(41) a. … they are interviewing candidates right now. COCA-2012-BLOG
     b. We're in the process of interviewing right now. COCA-2017-SPOK

(42) a. … researchers at NOAA's National Severe Storms Laboratory are developing a system called Warn-on-Forecast. COCA-2015-MAG
     b. They're in the process of developing a computer database to identify high-risk households. COCA-1994-SPOK

The PROGRESSIVE CONSTRUCTION can combine with the PRESENT- and PAST-TENSE CONSTRUCTIONS. In that case, BE fills the verbal slot of these constructions.

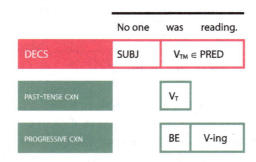

Figure 4.11 Construction grid for *No one was reading*. COCA-2006-FIC

4.5 The PERFECTIVE CONSTRUCTION

4.5.1 Form and meaning of the PERFECTIVE CONSTRUCTION

Another way of taking a certain perspective on an event or action is to relate it either to the time of speaking or to the time referred to in the text. In English, such a relation can be established by making use of the PERFECTIVE CONSTRUCTION (see also Hoffmann 2022b: 209–211).

At the level of form, the PERFECTIVE CONSTRUCTION consists of a form of the verb *have* and the past participle of a verb. Semantically, it can be characterized in terms of relevance with respect to the time referred to.

PERFECTIVE CONSTRUCTION			
Construing a fact, event, process or event that occurred previously as relevant to the time of speaking or the time frame of the text			
HAVE	V	-en	
		been got done seen made come become taken gone found heard given lost gotten known shown spent written brought grown begun won fallen met led chosen kept sent built	
	V	/t/	← *worked helped passed developed reached talked*
		/d/	← *changed happened learned tried turned received lived moved died killed played failed, etc.*
		/ɪd/	← *created decided*

Figure 4.12 The English PERFECTIVE CONSTRUCTION[51]

As you will know, the meaning of the PERFECTIVE CONSTRUCTION is often contrasted with that of the PAST-TENSE CONSTRUCTION. For instance, the PAST-TENSE CONSTRUCTION in (43a) refers to a 'process' as having happened at some concrete time in the past, whereas (43b) relates it to the time of speaking by combining a PRESENT-TENSE CONSTRUCTION with the PERFECTIVE CONSTRUCTION:

(43) a. Did you go to the Construction Grammar conference in Austin?
      b. Have you ever been to a Construction Grammar conference?

In a very loose way, we can see a relation between the core meaning of *have* as expressing 'possession' and its use in the PERFECTIVE CONSTRUCTION if we are happy to analyze (43b) in a sense of 'possess the experience of having attended a Construction Grammar conference', for instance.

---

51. Top 50 verb forms from COCA search "HAVE _v?n*".

4.5.2 Relating the PERFECTIVE CONSTRUCTION to other constructions

The PERFECTIVE CONSTRUCTION can combine with the tense constructions as in Figure 4.13, but also with modal constructions as in Figure 4.14:

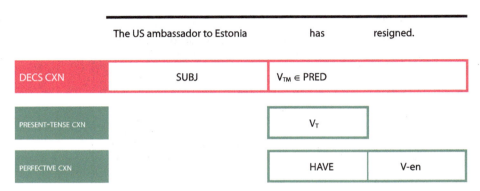

Figure 4.13 Construction grid for *The US ambassador to Estonia has resigned ...* COCA-2018-NEWS

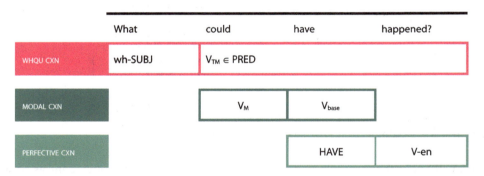

Figure 4.14 Construction grid for *What could have happened?* COCA-2015-FIC

4.6 The PASSIVE CONSTRUCTION

4.6.1 Active and passive

The option of choosing to present a message either in the form of an active clause or in the form of a passive clause is another way in which speakers can take a certain perspective on the situation described. The passive does not force the speaker to say who performed an 'action' (i.e., who is the ÆFFECTOR). Instead, it takes as a starting point of the message the participant that is the subject of the passive clause, usually the 'thing' at which the action is directed (i.e., the participant for which labels such as PATIENT, ÆFFECTED or THEME are being used in the literature), or the person that benefits from the action (i.e., a BENEFICIARY or a RECIPIENT).

(44) a. Oswald shot Kennedy from a warehouse and hid in a theatre and Booth shot Lincoln in a theatre and hid in a warehouse. COCA-2000-FIC

b. President Lincoln was assassinated because he signed the Emancipation Proclamation and freed those who were chained by slavery. COCA-2019-NEWS

Since the use of the passive is closely connected to the question of argument structure constructions, we will discuss such aspects in Chapter 5. At this stage, let us simply say that the PASSIVE CONSTRUCTION can be characterized as follows:

PASSIVE CONSTRUCTION			
Presenting an action that involves an ÆFFECTOR with an ÆFFECTED or other element that is not the ÆFFECTOR as a starting point.			
BE	V	-en	
	V_base		*been made done found got taken gone given born seen told known left held set built written lost shown brought shot*
		/d/	← *called considered killed allowed required paid prepared determined published raised filled*
		/t/	← *based forced needed released arrested*
		/ɪd/	← *expected treated created reported presented associated*

Figure 4.15 The English PASSIVE CONSTRUCTION[52]

As in the case of the PROGRESSIVE CONSTRUCTION, we can make out a parallel between the PASSIVE CONSTRUCTION and constructions with an attributive complement; compare, e.g.: *She was killed.* and *She was dead.* Historically, this parallel has given rise to many *-ed*-adjectives derived from verbs in English (*interested, convinced,* etc.). Compare also:

(45) a. Margaret Thatcher was elected Prime Minister of Britain ... NOW-19-12-08-US
b. Thatcher became prime minister ... NOW-22-02-14-CA
c. Thatcher was Prime Minister ... NOW-23-02-15-GB

What these examples show is the complex interaction between grammatical and lexical constructions.

---

52. Top 50 collocates for COCA query "BE _v?n*" (excluding used); ? means doubtful.

4.6.2 Combining the passive construction with other constructions

The combination of the PASSIVE CONSTRUCTION with, e.g., the PAST-TENSE CONSTRUCTION, is illustrated in Figure 4.16:

	My flight	was	cancelled.
DECS CXN	SUBJ	$V_{TM} \in$ PRED	
PAST-TENSE CXN		V_T	
PASSIVE CXN		BE	V-en

Figure 4.16 Construction grid for *My flight was cancelled.* COCA-2014-MOV

4.7 More complex combinations

The sequences discussed in 4.1 can now been interpreted as sequences of the constructions identified above:

(46) a. The furniture is looking a bit shabby, though.   BNC-ANY-429
PRESENT-TENSE CXN + PROGRESSIVE CXN
b. Somebody will be asking you questions more formally …   BNC-GWB-31
MODAL CXN + PROGRESSIVE CXN
c. Can you suggest where he might have been going?   BNC-GW3-1774
MODAL CXN + PERFECTIVE CXN + PROGRESSIVE CXN
d. I mean the train could have been cancelled … or something.   BNC-HWM-2782
MODAL CXN + PERFECTIVE CXN + PASSIVE CXN

When this is done, the constructions occur in the following order (Hoffmann 2022b: 148–151):

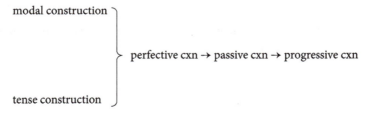

Figure 4.17 Order in which tense, modal and aspect constructions can be combined

Chapter 4. The roles of verbs **67**

In our view, the approach taken here has several advantages:

i.   In contrast to a comparable generativist account such as the one presented by Lohndahl & Haegeman (2020), for example – it does not consist of a sheer endless tree with nodes and branches for syntactic elements which to a large part represent theory-internal categories bearing no relation to meaning. Quite the contrary, the grid representations of the CASA-model, although displaying a considerable degree of complexity as well, outline a way in which the constructions making up a construct can be imagined to interact or combine, showing at every single point what the contribution of each of these constructions is with respect to form and meaning.

ii. Although our model allows an analysis in terms of the constructions illustrated in Figures 4.17, the conception of constructions explicitly also provides for the emergence of new constructions on the basis of frequency, even if they can be analyzed as being compositional. This means that the model is perfectly open to the idea that some – or perhaps even all – speakers entrench item-based constructions such as *may have been* or store something such as an abstract PRESENT-PROGRESSIVE CONSTRUCTION. In other words, our model allows for individual differences between speakers to be incorporated into the analyses.

4.8 Subjunctive mood constructions

The outline given in Figure 4.17 is not entirely complete in that we have not yet mentioned a number of English verb forms that are generally dealt with under the heading of mood. Many languages have different verb forms for an indicative mood that usually expresses an idea of 'reality' or 'factualness' and a subjunctive mood that is associated with 'non-factualness'. In Old English, there was a so-called optative mood indicating something like 'desirability'. As with the tense forms, where, as we pointed out in 4.3.1, it is difficult to establish a consistent distinction between indicative and subjunctive forms in present-day English. Although subjunctives tend to be marked as 'formal' or even 'slightly stilted', at least in British English, we can identify a PRESENT-TENSE-SUBJUNCTIVE CONSTRUCTION, which only shows in the third person singular because it combines a singular subject with the base form of the verb, as in (47a), (b). In the plural a subjunctive can only be made out in the case of the form *be*, as in (47c):[53]

(47) a.   Cat was the firstborn daughter after all. It was important that she remain desirable so Father could arrange a good match for her …   TV-2014-GameofThrones
      b.   Well, I only intended that she be ticked off, not beheaded.   TV-2015-Downton
      c.   I pronounce that they be man and wife together.   TV-2015-Downton

---

53. For a distinction between mandative and formulaic subjunctive see CGEL (1985: 3.59–3.61).

The other construction that must be mentioned here is the so-called *were*-subjunctive, which tends to be used in conditional constructions with unrealistic conditions (see 9.4.4.):

(48) a. I'd be embarrassed if I were you.   TV-2007-Psych
     b. I'd do the same thing if I were in your shoes.   TV-2013-Psych

4.9 Negation and the DO-SUPPORT CONSTRUCTION

If a sentence is negated, the speaker presents the information expressed as being not true. Negation can be achieved by the particle *not*, which is usually positioned after the operator verb, i.e., a form of *be, do,* or *have* or a modal, as in (49):[54]

(49) a. She hasn't called in a month.   TV-2007-Psych
     b. Why hasn't she told me?   TV-2013-Psych

If no such operator verb is provided by any of the constructions identified above, the DO-SUPPORT CONSTRUCTION is used:

(50) a. It doesn't look new.   BNC-ANY-2428
     b. No, I didn't say that, sir.   BNC-GW3-97

Since sequences such as *does not, do not, is not, etc.* occur very frequently, they are often pronounced as one unit with elision of the vowel in *not*, something that is often indicated by the apostrophe in the spelling of the examples above (*n't*).

A number of rather idiosyncratic facts have to be noted in this context:

–   The combination of the modal verb *must* and *not* expresses 'prohibition', i.e., the negation of the 'permission'-use of *may*, whereas the negation of 'obligation' is expressed by means of the multi-word construction *have* + to-infinitive:

(51) a. You must not travel before the baby's born.   TV-2012-Downton
      [prohibition ≈ obligation not to do something]
     b. His GPS must not be working.   TV-2007-Psych
      [conclusion, assumption]
     c. Obviously you do not have to answer at this stage if you would prefer not to ...
      [negated obligation]   BNC-GW3-1095

–   *Have* is sometimes negated without *do*-support even if it does not function as an operator verb:

(52) a. ... her budget hasn't the slightest chance of passing the House with a trillion dollar tax increase.   COCA-2013-SPOK

---

54. For a more detailed account see Hoffmann (2022b: 149–151).

Chapter 4. The roles of verbs   **69**

    b.   He has not a clue as to how to solve his underlying economic problems ...

COCA-2009-MAG

–   *Have got* is always negated without *do*-support:

    (53)   I haven't got one, sir. (BNC-GW3-3147)

–   *Be* does not take *do*-support in declarative and interrogative constructions, but it does not occur without *do* in the IMPERATIVE CONSTRUCTION (see 3.3.3):

    (54)   a.   I am not silly. In fact, I'm quite the opposite.   TV-2012-Psych
            b.   Don't be silly!   BNC-HWM-316

Finally, it ought to be mentioned that the DO-SUPPORT CONSTRUCTION can also be used in assertive (i.e., non-negated) sentences to put special emphasis on the action described:

(55)   He does love acronyms, doesn't he.   BNC-ANY-1356

CHAPTER 5

Who does what to whom?
Argument structure constructions

5.1 General introduction

5.1.1 Ways of looking at argument structure

The structure of a sentence is not only determined by the sentence type constructions described in Chapter 3 and the constructions illustrated in the previous chapter, but to a large extent also by the argument structure construction containing the last verb in the predicate (cf. Herbst & Schüller 2008: 10).

Argument structure constructions are one of the best-researched areas within the constructionist framework. This is partly because Adele Goldberg's 1995 and 2006 books have played a key role in propagating constructionist theory and have instigated a lot of research in this area. In addition to this, what she describes in terms of argument structure constructions has always formed an important part of linguistic description, albeit without the cognitive dimension of Goldberg's and other constructionist models.

Reference grammars such as CGEL (1985: Chapter 16), for instance, deal with the same phenomena under the label of 'complementation', generative theory addresses them through concepts such as subcategorization or theta-theory, and a considerable amount of research in this direction has been done in various theoretical models under the name of valence or valency, especially in Germany.[55]

For the relation between the account of argument structure constructions presented here and Fillmore's (1968) Case Grammar, Valency Theory and FrameNet see the blue box at the end of this Chapter.

5.1.2 The emergence of argument structure constructions

While children are learning their mother tongue (L1), they are learning lots of other things as well, they have to learn to walk, to hold a cup without spilling its contents, or how to pour something into a cup or a glass. Furthermore, and more importantly in our context, they will have to get an understanding of basic relations and processes, i.e., the relation of identity ($X \equiv Y$, e.g., that a particular person X is the postman Y), the relation between an attribute and the object described by it (e.g., that a ball can be red or blue, that some toys are new, and others are broken), or the relation of causation (X causes Y, e.g., *Mummy turns on the lights*, etc.).

---

55. For a constructionist account of verb-headed constructions in English see Bierwiaczonek (2016: 95–125).

The development of children's cognitive abilities and their linguistic development must not be imagined as independent processes. In fact, a look at the data from the first full week of recordings of the Thomas corpus – Thomas is two years old at this stage – provide ample evidence for the verbalization of such basic processes:

(1) Identity:
This is cooking chocolate.
Is that Pooh Bear?

t2_oo_16m
t2_oo_17m

(2) Attribution:
Your face is all dirty.

t2_oo_16m

(3) Change of position:
Are you going to put them into the washing machine?

t2_oo_16m

(4) Change of possession:
I'm going to give my teddy a piece of apple.

t2_oo_12m

The learning of the meanings of verbs and of the constructions in which they occur (and vice versa) can be seen as instrumental in this process. Very often, they go hand in hand. For instance, looking at sentences involving more than two arguments in the first full week of the Thomas corpus (t2_oo_16–t2_oo_20), two verbs occur particularly frequently – *give* and *put*:

(5) You're giving Mummy a lovely cuddle but you've got jam all over your fingers. t2_oo_18

(6) You put them into the right holes. t2_oo_16

Interestingly, more than 95% of all uses of *give* and more than 90% of all uses of *put* in these five hours of recording are in these two constructions expressing transfer and caused motion, respectively. This consistent pairing of form and meaning explains how children can associate the meanings of the verbs with those of the corresponding patterns, [X Verb Y Z] and [X Verb Z W] (which will be described in a more sophisticated fashion below) (Goldberg 2006). At the same time, they will be able to make generalizations about the roles of the various arguments: X as the one doing something, Y as a person who gets something, Z as the argument to which something happens, and W as a kind of place. Construction grammarians believe that children build up an inventory of so-called argument structure constructions in this way when they are learning their L1.

Argument structure constructions are schematic form-meaning pairings that express basic human scenes that are particularly salient to children: "someone transferring something to someone, something causing something to move or to change state, someone experiencing something, something undergoing a change of state or location, and so on" (Goldberg 1995:224–225). Sentences (5) and (6), e.g., represent two different argument structure constructions, as shown in Figures 5.1 and 5.2 (simplified from Goldberg 1995):

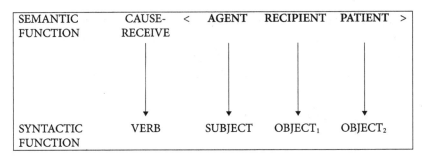

Figure 5.1 The DITRANSITIVE CONSTRUCTION (adapted from Goldberg 1995: 77)
Meaning of the construction: CAUSE-RECEIVE
AGENT, RECIPIENT and PATIENT are argument roles
VERB, SUBJECT, OBJECT1 and OBJECT2 are syntactic roles

(5')   You (AGENT) are giving Mummy (RECIPIENT) a lovely cuddle (PATIENT)

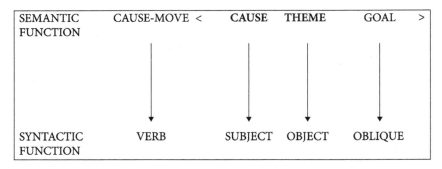

Figure 5.2 The CAUSED-MOTION CONSTRUCTION (adapted from Goldberg 1995: 78)
Meaning of the construction: CAUSE-MOVE
CAUSE, THEME and GOAL are argument roles
VERB, SUBJECT, OBJECT and OBLIQUE(i.e., adverb phrase or prepositional phrase) are syntactic roles

(6')   You (CAUSE) put them (THEME) into the right holes (GOAL).

There are a number of reasons for giving such patterns constructional status:

i. There is plenty of evidence that argument structure constructions can be learnt (Goldberg 2006; see also Chapter 1).
ii. Speakers of a language are able to associate a particular meaning with a construction, as can be shown in experiments with Jabberwocky sentences containing non-existent verbs, where *She mooped him something* is interpreted in a 'transfer'-sense, and priming experiments of a similar nature (Goldberg 2019: 29 & 33).
iii. Furthermore, Goldberg's (2006) model can explain why utterances such as (7), in which the meaning of a verb is combined with that of an argument structure construction in

Chapter 5. Who does what to whom?

which the verb is not normally used, are perfectly possible (not only in English, but also in other languages):

(7) a. She sneezed the foam off the cappuccino.   (Goldberg 2006:94)
     b. Schmeck dich spritzig.   Em-Eukal advert ('Taste yourself sparkly')

The point here is that verbs such as *sneeze* in English or *schmecken* in German by themselves neither express a resultative meaning nor do they usually occur in these syntactic patterns. The resultative meaning of (7) is thus provided by the abstract constructional argument structure template in Figure 5.2. This provides an important argument in favor of a constructionist analysis of sentences.

There are thus very good reasons to assume that speakers make generalizations of the sort described above. This is not to say, however, that all uses of verbs could be subsumed under a very small number of argument structure constructions. Nor does it mean that very abstract argument structure constructions play a role in language learning from the beginning – quite the contrary, because we imagine such argument structure constructions to emerge as generalizations over experienced input. When we look at language acquisition, it certainly seems reasonable to assume that children do not learn words in isolation, but in and together with the constructions in which they occur (Behrens 2011:382).[56] There must thus also be a place for argument structure constructions at a very low level of abstraction, which are strongly associated with particular verbs (verb-specific argument structure constructions; see Croft 2012:374–392; Herbst 2014a). Thus, being exposed to utterances such as the ones in (8a)–(d) may well lead to a mental representation of the type shown in (8e):

(8) a. ... and then we can give the teddy something to eat, can't we?   t2_oo_20
     b. ... and would you like to give the teddy bears a drink.   t2_oo_20
     c. ... are you going to give Mummy's teddy a drink?   t2_oo_20
     d. ... I'm going to give my teddy a piece of apple.   t2_oo_20
     e. NP^{GIVER} – GIVE – NP^{GIVEE} – NP$^{\text{THING GIVEN}}$

There is also some evidence pointing in the direction of a strong link between particular verbs and particular constructions with children. Tomasello (2003) observes that children tend to use verbs in only one of several argument structure constructions for several months, although they (i) have experienced the verb in other constructions, and (ii) use these other constructions with other verbs. This so-called **verb-island construction hypothesis** is very much in line with the idea of chunk learning and the gradual development of schematic slots

---

56. Behrens (2011:382) outlines a holistic view of language acquisition as follows: "Kinder erwerben nicht die Wörter mit ihren Subkategorisierungseigenschaften, die dann bestimmen, an welchen syntaktischen Strukturen ein Wort partizipieren kann, sondern sie erwerben das Lexikon durch und in den Konstruktionen, in denen sie auftauchen." 'Children do not acquire the verbs with their subcategorization features, which then determine in which syntactic structures a word can participate, but they acquire the lexicon through and in the constructions in which they appear.'

A Construction Grammar of the English Language

on that basis.[57] (Whether this is a general strategy that children employ or only occurs sporadically remains to be seen.)

Within a usage-based account of language acquisition, it thus seems perfectly feasible to imagine a scenario of the following kind: (i) Children use the input they receive to generalize over various usage events; (ii) in the early stages, these generalizations tend to take the form of item-based constructions with verb-specific roles such as GIVER and GIVEE; (iii) once they have acquired a number of similar item-based argument structure constructions for different verbs (NP^{SHOWER} – SHOW – NP^{SHOWEE} – NP$^{THING\ SHOWN}$), they can generalize across these, which eventually will result in the emergence of more abstract argument structure constructions.

5.1.3 Argument structure constructions at different levels of abstraction

5.1.3.1 *Valency constructions and pre-emption*

In a cognitive model of language, the emergence of a generalization does not mean that the lower-level representations on which they are based are lost. In fact, it is quite useful to acknowledge that speakers' constructicons comprise low-level constructions alongside more general argument structure constructions. We will refer to these low-level constructions of the type sketched out in (8e) above as **valency constructions**, because they cover the same facts of usage as traditional valency descriptions. (Croft 2012, speaks of 'verb-specific constructions', and Boas 2003, 2011, of 'mini-constructions' in this context.)

However, it is also important to note that although constructions such as the DITRANSITIVE CONSTRUCTION or the CAUSED-MOTION CONSTRUCTION are generalizations across many verbs, it does not mean that any verb can occur in a particular construction. For instance, while verbs such as *give, tell* and *send* occur both in the DITRANSITIVE and the CAUSED-MOTION CONSTRUCTIONS, for no obvious reason, verbs such as *explain* or *say* do not:[58] (Note that in the case of *tell*, etc. the term caused-motion has to be seen metaphorically in the sense of 'cause a message to move to a RECIPIENT').[59]

(9) a. I shall certainly send her a present. [DITRANSITIVE CXN]   COCA-2000-FIC
    b. Never send a present to someone who won't send one back. [CAUSED-MOTION CXN]
                                                      COCA-1990-TV

(10) a. I told you that. [DITRANSITIVE CXN]   TV-2007-Psych
     b. I never told that to anyone before. [CAUSED-MOTION CXN]   TV-2006-Psych

---

57. See Tomasello (1992), Diessel (2013: 353), for a critical view Ambridge & Lieven (2011: 217).

58. See, e.g., Gries & Stefanowitsch (2004) or Colleman (2011).

59. In other cases, it is obvious from the meaning of the constructions why a particular verb should occur in one of the two constructions but not the other. Cf. *He might have addressed the letter to me ...*
                                                  COCA-2018-TV

Chapter 5. Who does what to whom? 75

(11) a. ??Explain me this [DITRANSITIVE CXN]   (Goldberg 2019)
      b. Explain this to me again. [CAUSED-MOTION CXN]   COCA-MOV-2018

(12) a. ??What did you just say me? [DITRANSITIVE CXN]
      b. What did you just say to me? [CAUSED-MOTION CXN]   TV-2013-Psych

We can explain such unpredictability by saying that speakers' constructicons comprise verb-related valency constructions such as a *TELL*-DITRANSITIVE CONSTRUCTION, a *TELL*-CAUSED-MOTION CONSTRUCTION and a *SAY*-CAUSED-MOTION-CONSTRUCTION, but since they will never have experienced a use of the verb *say* in the DITRANSITIVE CONSTRUCTION, they will not have a corresponding valency construction. In other words, the level of valency constructions is necessary, but also sufficient to account for constraints of the *say me* or *explain me this*-type (see also Herbst 2014a, b; Hoffmann 2022b: 189–199). This phenomenon is called **pre-emption** and described in the following way by Goldberg (2019: 74):[60]

> ... productivity is curtailed by the existence of an alternative formulation that conveys the intended message-in-context and is more accessible at the moment of speaking.

In other words: If speakers have a familiar (often conventionalized) way to express a particular meaning, they will make use of that rather than thinking of a novel way of expressing the same meaning in a new construction (by, e.g., creatively combining a verb with an argument structure construction as in the case of *She sneezed the foam off the cappuccino* in (7a) above).

Speakers thus need to have

i.   knowledge related to particular items, i.e., low-level valency constructions because otherwise they would overgeneralize and produce constructs such as (11a) or (12a), and
ii. knowledge of more abstract argument constructions such as the CAUSED-MOTION CONSTRUCTION because otherwise they could not produce constructs such as (7a).

5.1.3.2 *Participant roles and argument roles*

Ever since their introduction into linguistic theory in the late 1960s (Halliday 1967; Fillmore 1968), semantic roles have been used in various frameworks to characterize the semantic function of clause constituents. The distinction between valency constructions and fully schematic argument structure constructions can be fruitfully drawn upon to capture the complexity of a construct's meaning.[61]

---

60. The observation that an existing expression can block the creation of new ones is not new. See note 9 in Chapter 1.4.

61. Herbst & Schüller (2008: 155–160) introduce semantic roles, so-called clausal roles, too: thus, e.g., subjects of active clauses can be characterized by a role *AGENTIVITY*. This provides an opportunity to capture the difference between sentences oft he following type: (a) *Could you [ÆFFECTOR+AGENTIVITY] close the shop and drive me to Dublin?* (BNC-CCM-2521), (b) *The shops [ÆFFECTED+AGENTIVITY] don't*

76 A Construction Grammar of the English Language

The **participant roles** of valency constructions are based on generalizations over the uses of a syntactic pattern with one particular verb and thus reach a relatively low level of abstraction. Describing the participants of the verb *send* in (11) as SENDER, SENDEE and THING SENT does not require any great effort of abstraction:

(13)   Lassie, you [SENDER] can send me [SENDEE] a thank you note [THING SENT] later.

TV-2010-Psych

These labels come in quite useful, however, when we want to refer to these participants and their use in other constructions. Thus, we can say that the SENDEE can have two different formal realizations, as an NP in the DITRANSITIVE CONSTRUCTION as in (14a) and a PP_{to} in the CAUSED-MOTION CONSTRUCTION as in (14b):

(14)   a.   My folks sent me some money   TV-2007-LasVegas
       b.   Crosby sent the list to me.   TV-2012-Scandel

Since more general argument structure constructions represent generalizations across a number of verbs, their so-called **argument roles** tend to capture meaning elements that are primarily determined by the meaning of the construction rather than that of a particular verb. This works similarly for the verb *give*:

(15)   a.   The Chief just gave me some really weird advice.   TV2008-Psych
       b.   You want to give any advice to our viewers out there?   COCA-2010-SPOK

Thus, in the analysis by Goldberg (2006), the GIVEE participant of *give* can be expressed in terms of two different argument roles – RECIPIENT in (15a) and GOAL for (15b). These different role labels are to indicate that – prototypically! – the DITRANSITIVE CONSTRUCTION expresses a successful transfer event, whereas the CAUSED-MOTION CONSTRUCTION does not entail that the intended GOAL was actually reached. Although this analysis may be more convincing in some cases than in others, it provides one way of explaining why you can *send something to another person, to your office, to a place or a particular address*, but why you would not normally say *send a place* or *an address something*.

Goldberg (2006: 40) exploits this difference between item-related participant roles and general argument roles in terms of construal:

> The Semantic Coherence Principle ensures that the participant role of the verb and the argument role of the construction must be semantically compatible. In particular, the more specific participant role must be construable as an instance of the more general argument role.

Construal, i.e., the particular conceptualization of an event you choose to pursue – seeing or describing a glass as half-full or half-empty, for example – may thus be one of the factors affecting the choice of a particular construction over another.

---

close until about midnight ... (BNC-AM0-1427), and (c) ... *in 1824 the shop* [ÆFFECTED] *was closed* ... (BNC-GT0-1107). See 5.8.4 for the MEDIOPASSIVE CONSTRUCTION.

Chapter 5. Who does what to whom? 77

5.1.3.3 *Levels of knowledge associated with argument structure constructions*

Obviously, it is very difficult to say anything definitive about the way argument structure constructions are represented in the mind. From a linguistic (as opposed to a psychological or neurological) point of view, we would argue that speakers' knowledge of an argument structure construction is likely to comprise information about

i.   the semantic function of the construction as a whole,
ii. the semantic roles of the slots of the construction – either in the form of item-related participant roles and/or in the form of generalized argument roles,
iii. the formal realization of argument slots, including information about which argument has subject status (in the sense that it can be the subject of a finite clause and need not be realized in some types of non-finite clause).

However, our knowledge may extend far beyond these three pieces of information and reflect the usage events. Even low-level abstractions such as participant roles cannot capture relatively idiosyncratic preferences of particular nouns for the one or the other construction illustrated by the following examples:[62]

(16) a. And he gave her a hug.   COCA-2019-FIC
          [1,625 similar examples in COCA]
      b. ... Kathleen gave a hug to the ever-cheerful Kyle...   COCA-1994-FIC
          [10 similar examples]

(17) a. Let me give her a call.   COCA-2019-TV
          [3,921 similar examples in COCA]
      b. I'll check missing persons, also give a call to the state guys... COCA-2015-FIC
          [10 examples]

Similarly, we can take the verb *offer* and look at the lexical items representing the THING (that is) OFFERED. As Table 5.1 shows for data from COCA, this participant role is realized by markedly different nouns and pronouns in the RECIPIENT slot of the DITRANSITIVE CONSTRUCTION and the GOAL slot of the CAUSED-MOTION CONSTRUCTION:

---

62. Figures based on queries "GIVE * a hug/call" and "GIVE a hug|call to", excluding examples like *call to action*.

Table 5.1 Colloprofiles for THING OFFERED in the DITRANSITIVE construction and the CAUSED-MOTION CONSTRUCTION with *offer* (only with pronominal indirect objects and pronominal PPs respectively) based on COCA[a]

Frequency range within respective construction	Hits in the *OFFER*-DITRANSITIVE CXN (total: 3,198)		Hits in the *OFFER*-CAUSED-MOTION CXN (total: 717 hits)	
> 50%			*it*	361
20–30%	*job*	726		
10–20%	*something*	335		
5–10%	*chance*	218	*them*	41
	opportunity	210		
< 5%	*money ride anything drink one deal position scholarship nothing coffee contract tea place protection advice hand food* etc.		*myself herself yourselves itself hand one advice condolences help something himself reward services support $ 5,000 food money protection resistance themselves* etc.	

a. Based on the following searches in COCA (1 billion words, 2020): "OFFER _p* _nn*", "OFFER _p* * _nn*", "OFFER _p* _p*" vs. "OFFER _p* to _p*", "OFFER _nn* to _p*" and "OFFER * _nn* to _p*".

It is worth noting that such differences in collo-profiles provide a strong argument in favor of the autonomy of different constructions. They also constitute empirical evidence against approaches that would argue that one of these constructions is the more basic one and the other 'only' derived from the former.[63]

Within an approach that draws heavily on exemplar theory, as outlined in Chapter 1.3.4, it makes sense to assume that collo-profiles form a part of the lossy memory representations of argument structure constructions (Goldberg 2019: 6–7). Up to a point, one can even argue that the collo-items of a constructional slot form a basis for the abstract participant roles of verb-specific argument structure constructions. Integrating the collo-profiles of the verb slot into the representation of the more general argument structure constructions, has the enormous descriptive advantage of linking generalizations to the items with which they occur. **Item-relatedness** of several competing constructions is a very common phenomenon in language (Herbst 2020a): think, for instance, of general correspondences between the phoneme /i:/ in English and spellings such as ⟨ea⟩ and ⟨ee⟩, where speakers have to know (or learn) which grapheme applies to which item (*sea* 'ocean', *see* 'bishopric' and 'perceive visually', cf. also *lead, feed*, etc.) or of word formation, where the suffixes {-ness}, {-ity} and {-ery} can all be used to form abstract nouns from adjectives, but not each of the suffixes can combine

---

63. For further arguments against derivational accounts see Goldberg (2006: 28–34). See also Hoffmann & Herbst (forthc.).

with any noun (*kindness, brevity, bravery, etc.*) and the existence of a noun often blocks (or pre-empts) the creation of a new one. We can cover this item-relatedness by choosing the following format outlined in Figure 5.3 for representing the general argument structure constructions (Herbst 2020a):

The English DITRANSITIVE CONSTRUCTION				
ÆFFECTOR makes recipient receive effected ÆFFECTED.				
ÆFFECTOR			RECIPIENT	ÆFFECTED
Subj	V		Obj: NP	Obj: NP
>	**GIVE** TELL BRING COST OFFER SEND SHOW ALLOW ASK BUY CAUSE COST DO FIND GET GRANT HAND OWE LEND MAKE PAY SAVE TAKE WISH AFFORD AWARD BID BUILD DENY EARN FEED FINE GAIN GUARANTEE LEAD LEAVE LOSE PASS POUR PROMISE REFUSE SELL SERVE SET SHOOT SPARE THROW WRITE etc.			
I can give you a hint. COCA-2017-SPOK - *Can I give you a hug?* COCA-2017-SPOK *She told me a lot about their relationship...* COCA-2017-SPOK *On Air Force One, the president told us a story he has never told before on television ...* COCA-2002-SPOK *... spare me the details if that's possible.* COCA-2014-F				

Figure 5.3 The DITRANSITIVE CONSTRUCTION with collo-profile (Herbst 2020b):[64] Rough BNC-frequency ranges indicated by typeface: *give* > 50%, *tell* > 5%, *bring ... show* > 2%, *allow ... wish* > 0.5%

This format of representation does not only contain a list of the most frequent items occurring in the verb slot (which, as explained in 1.3.5, we will refer to as a **collo-profile**), but also a more explicit characterization of the argument slots in terms of formal categories (NPs) than just indicating syntactic functions such as subject or object.

---

64. The semantic roles will be discussed in sections 5.4–5.5, see 5.4.2 for a slightly modified version of the DITRANSITIVE CONSTRUCTION within the CASA framework.

5.1.3.4 *Summary*

In any case, when it comes to the issue of the mental representation of low level versus more general argument structure constructions, we would like to emphasize that for a number of reasons these should not be seen as mutually exclusive alternatives:

i.   If people form a generalization, this does not mean that they necessarily lose the essence of the more specific knowledge on which it is based (Behrens 2007; Goldberg 2019).[65]

ii. We cannot say for certain whether all low-level argument structure constructions can be abstracted into more general constructions of the type DITRANSITIVE CONSTRUCTION or CAUSED-MOTION CONSTRUCTION or whether the latter are the exception rather than the rule (although they have received the most attention by cognitive linguists).

iii. We will certainly have to allow for individual differences between speakers. Currently, there is no way of knowing whether they (all) form classes of this kind or store the patterns as more or less item-specific properties of the verbs in question, i.e., at a level that we refer to as valency constructions.

5.2 The CASA framework of argument structure constructions

5.2.1 Specification of argument structure constructions in CASA

As pointed out in Chapter 1, the main goal of this book is to provide a cognitively plausible syntactic analysis of English sentences that is nevertheless fairly straightforward and relatively easy to do. In our account of argument structure constructions we will thus make a few slight terminological simplifications, which will, we hope, make it easier for users whose thinking is strongly determined by traditional reference grammars such as CGEL (1985), CAMG (2002), Aarts & Aarts (1982/1988) or valency models (Herbst & Schüller 2008). We will, however, use these terms in clearly defined ways which make their use appropriate to the constructionist framework we are aiming to develop.

In CASA, we will use the term **argument structure construction (ASC)** for constructions that have a verb (adjective 5.10 or noun 5.11) slot and one or more argument slots that can be characterized in terms of argument roles such as AGENT, CAUSER, etc. Goldberg (2019: 28) points out that argument structure constructions "constrain the interpretation of 'who did what to whom.'" One could also say that argument structure constructions underlie that part of an expression that represents a **proposition**, i.e., the type of relation between the arguments, abstracting from factors such as 'time', 'likelihood', etc. Thus, the following sentences all express the same proposition (i.e., a relation between a verb and two arguments – 'have (she, another glass of wine)' – which is independent of any situation in time or modality):

---

65. Cf. Goldberg's (2019) concept of lossy memory traces.

Chapter 5. Who does what to whom? 81

(18) a. Then she had another glass of wine ... COCA-1990-FIC
b. Can she have another glass of wine ...? COCA-2013-TV
c. Maybe she'd have another glass of wine. COCA-2003-FIC

In the same way, the order in which the elements of an argument structure construction occur in a sentence is not determined by the argument structure construction alone.[66] The examples under (19) illustrate how a RELATIVE-CLAUSE CONSTRUCTION or factors of processing complexity can influence word order:

(19) a. ... I dialed the number that he had **given** me. COCA-2014-SPOK
b. We must never **regard** as normal the regular and casual undermining of our democratic norms and ideals. COCA-2017-SPOK

Argument structure constructions are combined with other constructions such as the various sentence type constructions, tense constructions, etc., and, of course, the constructions that fill the respective argument slots. (How we envisage this to happen in a speaker's working memory will be explored in Chapter 13).

5.2.2 Specification of argument slots: Subj-, Obj- and Attr-arguments

In order to achieve maximal compatibility with established terminology, we will use the following labels to characterize the syntactic argument slots on the expression side of argument structure constructions, i.e., their morphological form or syntactic function. Since these terms receive slightly different interpretations in the various models that use them, we will provide the following short definitions:[67]

Subj **SUBJECT** an argument that can function as a subject in a sentence type construction.[68]
Close to 100 percent of earth and climate scientists agree: Climate change is advancing, and we have little time left to change course to avoid a catastrophic earth. COCA-2012-NEWS
Oxford is a city for walkers or cyclists, not drivers. COCA-2002-NEWS

Attr **ATTRIBUTE** an argument with the semantic role ATTRIBUTE that refers to Subj or Obj and characterizes it with respect to a certain feature or place.
Amsterdam is a city for walkers and bikers. COCA-1999-MAG
Call this a pleasant surprise. COCA-209-NEWS

---

66. "ASCs do not necessarily specify word order, as word order can instead be captured by independent constructions – such as the subject-predicate construction and the verb phrase construction – that combine with ASCs (...)" (Goldberg 2019: 39). See also Hoffmann and Herbst (forthc.) and Chapter 14.

67. Note that our definition of object does not refer to passivization as a criterion. Objects and attributes correspond to the complements in the predicate in Aarts & Aarts (1982: 136–143); the subjects, objects and attributes of CASA correspond to the complements in valency theory.

68. See 3.3.1. for the definition of subject in sentence-type constructions.

Obj	**OBJECT** an argument in the predicate that is not an ATTRIBUTE. This category can be subdivided into:

Obj_{NP} **NOUN PHRASE OBJECT**: an argument expressed by a noun phrase with argument roles such as ÆFFECTED or RECIPIENT.

Would you like some wine?.	COCA-2015-TV
Can I buy you a drink or something?	COCA-2017-SPOK

Obj_{PP} **PREPOSITIONAL OBJECT**: an argument that is realized by a prepositional phrase; its semantic role is dependent on the preposition and the construction in which it occurs.

... we'll talk about climate deniers in the Trump administration ...	COCA-2017-SPOK

Obj_{CL} **CLAUSAL OBJECT**: an argument that is realized by a clause; the semantic role depends on the type of clause and the construction in which it occurs.

They enjoy living in New York.	COCA-2010-M

Subj, Obj and Attr only provide a first step in the description of arguments, which will have to be complemented by much more detailed specifications of the semantic role of the arguments and possible forms of realization. So, for instance, the prepositional argument in

(20)	... we'll talk **about climate deniers in the Trump administration** ...	COCA-2017-SPOK

can be specified as $Obj_{PP:about}{}^{TOPIC\text{-}AREA}$ (prepositional object with the preposition *about* expressing the argument role of TOPIC-AREA; 5.7.2).[69]

5.2.3 Why Subj does not automatically mean SUBJ

Note furthermore that we are using the labels Subj, Obj and Attr to characterize the arguments of argument structure constructions that have the potential to occur, e.g., in the SUBJ-slot of a sentence type construction. Whereas capitalized SUBJ indicates a slot in a sentence type construction that **must** be filled, Subj indicates that this is the argument that has the **potential** to occur in such a slot as in (21a). At the same time, the Subj-arguments of argument structure constructions need not have a formal expression at all in other types of sentence or clause constructions: thus, in (21b) the Subj-argument of the verb *live* can be interpreted as having the same referent as the Subj-argument of *put*, although formally this noun phrase is not the subject of *live*. If there is no such referent to be found in the linguistic or extralinguistic context as in the case of (21c) or (21d), the Subj-argument receives an indefinite interpretation:

---

69. Note that we follow established usage by speaking of *prepositional objects, prepositional arguments* and *prepositional phrases*, although we do not identify a word class *preposition*. For the reasons explained in 13.2 we see traditional prepositions and conjunctions as forming a word class *particle*. Expressions such as prepositional phrase and particle phrase can thus be seen as equivalent. We use the term preposition like the term determiner to refer to the function these words have within such constructions (see 13.2).

Chapter 5. Who does what to whom? **83**

(21) a. The president **lives** in the White House. COCA-1997-NEWS
   b. **Living** in New York City, nursing and teaching, she put on a lot of weight ...
      COCA-1992-MAG
   c. **Living** in New York City creates enormous opportunities for wealth ...
      COCA-2017-SPOK
   d. The rising cost of **living** in Austin, though perhaps an inevitable twin to the city's
      success, undercuts some of the notions ingrained in the city's ethos ...
      COCA-2014-NEWS

In the terminology of FrameNet (Fillmore 2007), cases such as (21b) are referred to as **definite null instantiation** and contrasted with the **indefinite null instantiation** in (21c) and (21d).

In very much the same way, Obj-arguments need not be expressed under certain conditions:

(22) a. George, do you wear your glasses out on the battlefield? Oh, I want to, but Lassiter
      won't **let** me. TV-2006-Psych
      [DITRANSITIVE CONSTRUCTION in which the argument is retrievable from previous
      sentence]
   b. Lassie spoke to us all about a week ago about wearing sunglasses to all autopsies
      moving forward to show respect for the dead. I simply **forgot**, and Gus **refused**, ...
      TV-2011-Psych
      [MONOTRANSITIVE-CONSTRUCTIONS in which the slots for the 'thing forgotten/
      refused' do not have to be expressed because they can be retrieved from the context]

It has to be pointed out, however, that definite and indefinite null instantiation can be seen as properties of Subj-arguments in general (Herbst et al. 2004: xxx–xxxi; Herbst & Schüller 2008: 107–108), with Obj-arguments definite null instantiation – called contextual optionality in Valency Theory – being a property of the valency constructions of particular verbs. Since this degree of lexical specificity falls within the realm of lexicographical reference works like the *Valency Dictionary of English* and is less relevant to the purposes of the present approach, we will refrain from distinguishing in the descriptions provided here between Obj-slots whose formal expression is obligatory and Obj-slots that are contextually optional by typographic means. Instead, we will treat cases that could be analyzed as indefinite null instantiations of Obj-slots as separate argument structure constructions. Thus (23a) will be interpreted as an instance of the INTRANSITIVE CONSTRUCTION although it is obvious that whenever someone is cooking, they are cooking something, as made explicit in the MONOTRANSITIVE CONSTRUCTION in (23b):

(23) a. He was cooking; murder was, for the moment at any rate, not in his thoughts ...
      BNC-H8A-3499
   b. I understand your Mrs Chalk is cooking pheasant in red wine tonight.
      BNC-JY3-2293 TV-2012-Downton

A Construction Grammar of the English Language

Cases involving definite null-instantiation of objects, i.e., cases in which an object is not expressed but its referent can be identified from the context, will be analysed in terms of the "larger" argument structure construction. Thus, in contrast to (23a), we analyse the constructs in (24) as examples of the MONOTRANSITIVE CONSTRUCTION, although the object is not explicitly expressed:

(24) a. I had no idea it was your birthday. I forgot.   TV-2008-BigBang
      b. I'm a psychic detective, remember?   TV-2010-Psych

In very much the same way, Attr-slots of *be* need not be expressed under special circumstances in which the Attr-argument is retrievable from the context as in ellipsis, for example:

(25) a. 'She's all in favour.' 'Yes, I bet she is.'   BNC-ANY-2639-2640
      b. 'I've seen Gifford Tate's portrait of Garland's wife; she must have been a very lovely
          girl.' 'Oh, she was.'   BNC-HWP-2150-2151

5.2.4 Argument roles

As far as the semantic roles of argument structure constructions are concerned, we will try to make use of established labels – as far as this is possible. Definitions of the general argument roles employed will be provided with the respective constructions; a complete list can be found in Appendix I.

As pointed out in the previous chapter, most constructionist research on argument structure focuses on a rather small number of rather general constructions such as the CAUSED-MOTION and DITRANSITIVE CONSTRUCTIONS. For the vast array of argument structure constructions involving prepositional and clausal realizations (Obj_{PP} and Obj_{CL}), however, it seems perfectly justified to make use of verb-related labels at a lower level of abstraction if none of the established roles seems appropriate.

5.2.5 Names of constructions

Argument structure constructions can be classified according to the number of arguments they contain:

-   constructions with one argument: the INTRANSITIVE CONSTRUCTION;
-   constructions with two arguments: MONOTRANSITIVE CONSTRUCTIONS, the SELF-MOTION CONSTRUCTION and the ATTRIBUTE CONSTRUCTIONS;
-   constructions with three arguments: e.g., the DITRANSITIVE CONSTRUCTIONS and the CAUSED-MOTION CONSTRUCTION.

Note that these labels are based on the number of arguments that are integral parts of the construction, even if one or two of these arguments do not have a formal expression in a particular construct, as in the Examples (21) and (24) discussed above or in the imperative

Chapter 5. Who does what to whom?

construction, in which the Subj-argument is not explicitly given but instead interpreted as the addressee of the utterance:

(26) **Have** another glass of wine.   COCA-1997-TV
[MONOTRANSITIVE CONSTRUCTION in combination with IMPERATIVE-COMMAND CONSTRUCTION so that AGENT does not have to be realized because identifiable from context]

5.2.6   Subj-arguments

Subj-arguments are special in a number of respects:

First of all, Subj-arguments can only be expressed when the argument structure construction is combined with a sentence- or clause-type construction that provides for a subject. Looking at it from a different perspective, we can say that Subj-arguments are not explicitly expressed in IMPERATIVE-CONSTRUCTIONS like (26) and certain types of subordinate clauses as in (27):

(27) a.   I want to **know** how, I want to **know** who, I want to **know** why.   TV-2006-Psych
      b.   They enjoyed **having** a meal together.

The referents of the Subj-arguments of *know* and *having* are perfectly identifiable from the linguistic context in (27) in that they are clearly identical with the referent of the Subj of *want* and *enjoy*. In other cases, non-expressed Subj-arguments receive an indefinite interpretation:

(28) a.   Living on the ISS is no picnic...   COCA-2019-MAG
      b.   Visiting relatives can be a nuisance.   (Palmer 1971: 133)

While the great majority of subjects takes the form of noun phrases, there are also a number of clausal realizations as in (28) and (29):

(29) a.   To suggest otherwise is intellectually felonious.   COCA-2018-NEWS
      b.   Whether this objective was met is currently the subject of some debate.
                                                                          COCA-2001-ACAD

Since the use of clausal subjects is dependent on a great variety of factors, we will refrain from providing Subj slots with formal (phrasal) specifications (see Uhrig 2018).[70]

---

70. For a specification of subject slots see, however, the *Valency Dictionary of English*.

5.3 A one-argument construction: The English INTRANSITIVE CONSTRUCTION

The INTRANSITIVE CONSTRUCTION consists of a verb and one argument whose semantic role is rather difficult to capture because its interpretation depends strongly on the meaning of the individual verb. We'll use the rather neutral term **UNDERGOER**[71] to cover this.

(30) a. Where did you **sleep** last night?   BNC-HWP-1550
      b. There's no doubt our climate is **changing**...   COCA-2019-NEWS
      c. The first fireworks **exploded** ...   BNC-GW3-59
      d. Climate change **exists**.   COCA-2016-SPOK

INTRANSITIVE CONSTRUCTION	
An UNDERGOER does or experiences something.	
UNDERGOER	
Subj	V

Figure 5.4 The English INTRANSITIVE CONSTRUCTION

5.4 ÆFFECTOR and ÆFFECTED: Monotransitive constructions

5.4.1 Monotransitive constructions

5.4.1.1 *The MONOTRANSITIVE CONSTRUCTION with Obj*NP

The MONOTRANSITIVE CONSTRUCTION covers a rather wide range of meanings. There are cases in which someone performs an action that acts on a 'thing' that exists prior to the action, as in (31).

(31) a. We always destroy the evidence.   COCA-2002-FIC
      b. I've read the book.   COCA-2010-SPOK
      c. You should interpret the data.   COCA-1990-ACAD

A role label such as AFFECTED can be assigned to the objects in cases such as (31). In other cases, however, the 'thing' does not exist prior to the action, but is the outcome of the action as in (32):

---

71. The term UNDERGOER can be seen as a very general cover term which comprises argument roles such as ÆFFECTOR and ATTRIBUTE, which we will introduce in 5.4.1 and 5.4.2.

(32) a. Kasimir Malevich, Wassili Kandinsky and Piet Mondrian were painting abstract
         arrangements...   COCA-1998-NEWS
      b. Barbara Hepworth created some of her wide-eyed, huge hearted sculptures here.
                                                                                  COCA-1999-FIC

In the sense that the thing is the effect of the action, such roles can be characterized by the label EFFECTED (taking up the traditional distinction between affected and effected objects). Since the two are not always easy to distinguish, we subsume them under ÆFFECTED, which corresponds to the labels PATIENT and THEME commonly used in American work.[72]

However, one would have to stretch one's imagination quite a bit in order to say that it fits cases such as the ones in (33):

(33) a. A fraction of a second later, he heard the roar of the jet's engine.   COCA-2010-FIC
      b. President Obama enjoyed much broader and more unified congressional support
         than President Clinton did...   COCA-2011-MAG

It seems more appropriate to analyze these subjects as EXPERIENCERs and the objects as STIMULI in (33). We will interpret the AGENT-ÆFFECTED or EXPERIENCER-STIMULUS constellations as two prototypical centers of the meaning of the construction because the interpretation of the construction is largely dependent on the verb, but not always clear-cut:

(34) Enjoy your meal.

Alternatively, Croft (2012:198–219) suggests a more abstract semantic representation of the two roles of the MONOTRANSITIVE CONSTRUCTION as INITIATOR and ENDPOINT, respectively. Under this view, the prototypical meaning of this construction is a force-dynamic one in which the INITIATOR exerts physical or abstract force onto the ENDPOINT. In the spirit of Croft's analysis, we will follow this force-dynamic idea, but use the slightly more general terms ÆFFECTOR and ÆFFECTED to describe the respective argument roles.

– ÆFFECTOR is the argument role that applies to a 'thing' that performs an action (marked in this chapter by the colour teal).[73]
– ÆFFECTED is the argument role of a 'thing' that is either the outcome of an action or that is primarily affected by the action carried out by the ÆFFECTOR (printed in blue in this chapter).

We can then describe the English MONOTRANSITIVE CONSTRUCTION as in Figure 5.5:

---

72. PATIENT is a label used to refer to a participant that is passively affected by some external force and, as a result, changes its internal state, THEME refers to a participant that is passively involved in an event without changing its internal state. Note that in European linguistics, the term theme is commonly used in contrast to rheme in the analysis of the information structure of sentences. See Chapter 10.1.

73. The term ÆFFECTOR is meant to cover both animate AGENTs and inanimate FORCES.

MONOTRANSITIVE CONSTRUCTION		
An ÆFFECTOR does something to an ÆFFECTED		
ÆFFECTOR		ÆFFECTED
Subj	V	Obj: NP
She *kissed him*. COCA-2010-FIC *He* **opened** *the window*. COCA-2012-FIC		

Figure 5.5 The English MONOTRANSITIVE CONSTRUCTION

5.4.1.2 *Monotransitive constructions with clausal objects*

In a way, Figure 5.5 represents the prototype of the English MONOTRANSITIVE CONSTRUC-TION, in which the Obj-slot is expressed by a noun phrase. However, there are a number of constructions that express the same meaning relations between two arguments as those in the previous section, but are different in form because the second argument is realized by a clause. We subsume these constructions under the label of CLAUSE-MONOTRANSITIVE CONSTRUCTIONS, or, if we want to be more specific, we will refer to them by labels such as the *THAT*-CLAUSE-MONOTRANSITIVE CONSTRUCTION, or the MONOTRANSITIVE-V-ING-CONSTRUCTION, etc. (Note that when we use "MONOTRANSITIVE CONSTRUCTION" without a label specifiying a type of clause, it refers to the construction with a noun phrase object.)

If the clausal object is expressed by a V-*ing* or a *to*-INF-clause, the Subj-argument of the respective argument structure constructions is not expressed formally (null-instantiation) (see 5.2.3). Such Subj-arguments have the same referent as the Subj-argument of the MONO-TRANSITIVE CONSTRUCTION. Thus, in *Nancy Pelosi (D-CA) wants to have a climate bill on the House floor by July 4* we consider *Nancy Pelosi* to be the Subj of the *WANT*-MONOTRANSITIVE CXN, but not as the grammatical subject of the infinitive clause with *have*, although seman-tically *Nancy Pelosi* is interpreted as the ÆFFECTOR of *have*.

Note that in the analysis proposed **NP Ving, NP to-INF-CL, NP to-INF-CL and NP V-en-CL** are seen as fillers of one argument slot because they fall under the role of ÆFFECTED. Seeing them as a single constituent is further justified by the fact that they can be replaced by one pro-form such as *it* or *what* ('*What do you want, Elizabeth? Do you want me to be struck off?*' (BNC-GoX1549-1550) – *Is that what you want ? Her to be like you?* (TV-2012-Vampire Diaries).)

5.4.2 Introducing a RECIPIENT: Ditransitive constructions

5.4.2.1 *The DITRANSITIVE CONSTRUCTION with Obj_{NP}*

The English DITRANSITIVE CONSTRUCTION (sometimes referred to as DOUBLE-OBJECT CON-STRUCTION) is probably one of the best-studied constructions of English (Goldberg 2006, 2019; Herbst 2020a). What is special about the DITRANSITIVE CONSTRUCTION is that it is the only construction in English that has slots for two objects that can be realized by noun

Chapter 5. Who does what to whom? **89**

MONOTRANSITIVE CONSTRUCTIONS (CLAUSAL OBJECTS)				
An ÆFFECTOR does something to an ÆFFECTOR.				
ÆFFECTOR			ÆFFECTED	
Subj	V	Obj	V-ing-CL	*They **enjoy** seeing each other and talking and so on.* COCA-1999-M
			to_INF-CL	*... Nancy Pelosi (D-CA) **wants** to have a climate bill on the House floor by July 4 ...* COCA-2007-MAG
			that_CL	*Scientists **argue** that human activity has placed the planet in uncertain but potentially calamitous peril.* COCA-2012-NEWS
			wh-CL	*I **don't see** how the president benefits by belittling and criticizing the Republican leadership on the Hill.* COCA-2017-SPOK
			wh_to_inf-cl	*Donald Trump **knows** how to put on a good show.* COCA-2016-SPOK
			NP V-ing	*She **heard** the wind skittering dried leaves around the balcony ...* COCA-2010-F
			NP to_inf-cl	*They **want** Obama to run for president.* COCA-2014-SPOK
			NP inf-cl	*She **heard** the door close.* COCA-2012-F
			NP V-en-cl	*At this point, who **doesn't want** Trump impeached?* COCA-2017-M
			NP PP	*... most Republican voters **want** Trump at the top of the ticket.* COCA-2016-SPOK

Figure 5.6 Active clausal monotransitive constructions

phrases. At the level of form, we will distinguish between these two objects by the subscripts 1 and 2 indicating the order in which they prototypically appear in clauses. Semantically, both objects can be seen as being affected by the action expressed by the verb, but since – in the order in which they are presented in the DITRANSITIVE CONSTRUCTION – the second object has more of an endpoint character than the first one, it seems appropriate to restrict the label ÆFFECTED to Obj_{NP_2}. This is all the more so since it is perfectly possible to characterize Obj_{NP_1} in terms of the rather specific argument role of RECIPIENT:

DITRANSITIVE CONSTRUCTION (NP-OBJ)			
ÆFFECTOR **makes** RECIPIENT **receive** ÆFFECTED.			
ÆFFECTOR	V	RECIPIENT	ÆFFECTED
Subj	V	Obj$_{NP1}$	Obj$_{NP2}$
*She **gave** him a quick hug.* COCA-2017-FIC – *And he **told** me the very same thing.* COCA-2017-SPOK – *...could you **read**? me a story?* COCA-2012-FIC			

Figure 5.7 The English DITRANSITIVE CONSTRUCTION

As Goldberg (1995: 38) points out, the DITRANSITIVE CONSTRUCTION has a prototypical meaning of "agent successfully causes recipient to receive patient" (translated into our terminology: ÆFFECTOR causes RECIPIENT to receive ÆFFECTED) in which it occurs with verbs such as *give, pass, kick, bring,* but in combination with other verbs may receive a slightly different interpretation.

(35) a.   He never actually refused us an interview, but he simply was unavailable.

COCA-1996-SPOK

['AGENT causes recipient not to receive patient']

 b.   ... and until 20 years ago, they did not even allow women the chance to compete for these jobs.   COCA-2009-SPOK

['AGENT enables recipient to receive patient']

 c.   ... we and our allies have a chance to leave our children a Europe that is free, peaceful and stable.   COCA-1999-SPOK

['AGENT acts to cause recipient to receive patient at some future point in time'][74]

> In classic terminology, Obj$_{NP1}$ corresponds to what is called an **indirect object**, whereas the term **direct object** corresponds to our Obj$_{NP2}$.

5.4.2.2   *Ditransitive constructions with clausal objects*

As with the MONOTRANSITIVE CONSTRUCTION, there are a number of DITRANSITIVE CONSTRUCTIONS with clausal objects. There is a clear parallel between (36a) and (36b), which provides a justification for subsuming (36b) under the label DITRANSITIVE:

(36) a.   ...we have to tell you the news of the day.   COCA-2011-SPOK
 b.   Did anyone tell you that your hair smells like strawberries?   TV-2008-Psych

This is not quite so obvious in the following examples:

(37) a.   I specifically told you guys to stay at my dad's.   TV-2009-Psych
 b.   O'Hara, I forbid you to buy into this load of crap.   TV-2013-Psych

---

74. All descriptions taken from Goldberg (1995: 38); bold in original.

c. Allow me to say that I'm not impressed. TV-2008-Psych

What distinguishes the examples in (37) from those in (36) is that the RECIPIENT-argument can also be interpreted as a (potential) ÆFFECTOR with respect to the infinitive clause. We could thus analyze (37a)–(c) as monotransitive in which the ÆFFECTED argument is realized by a non-finite clause of the form NP to-INF (*you guys to stay at my dad's* in (37a)). Alternatively, (37a)–(c) can be seen as creating (or prohibiting) a possible course of action, which one might take as an argument for establishing a special AUTHORIZATION CONSTRUCTION. However, at a higher level of abstraction, it seems legitimate to subsume these under the DITRANSITIVE CONSTRUCTION by analyzing them in terms of a transfer of a permission to the RECIPIENT to carry out the action expressed by the infinitive clause. We can therefore subsume a number of constructions under the label DITRANSITIVE, which is not to obscure the fact that each of these constructions can be provided with a much more specific description at lower levels of abstraction:

DITRANSITIVE CONSTRUCTIONS (CLAUSAL OBJ)					
ÆFFECTOR **makes** RECIPIENT **receive** ÆFFECTED.					
ÆFFECTOR		RECIPIENT	ÆFFECTED		
Subj	V	Obj: NP	Obj:	to-INF	*I've persuaded him to change his mind.* TV-1971-DoctorWho
				INF	*Just let me do the talking.* TV-2006-Psych
				CL$_{fin}$	*Trump told us he will pay for his campaign all the way through the nomination.* COCA-2015-SPOK
				that_CL$_{fin}$	*Obama told me that he did not find the Senate boring.* COCA-2007-M
				wh_CL$_{fin}$	*... many locals asked reporters when the aid was coming.* COCA-2003-NEWS
				wh_to_INF	*... she could have asked somebody how to dress when you go to the Masters.* COCA-2005-F

Figure 5.8 English DITRANSITIVE CONSTRUCTIONS with clausal objects

> Note that there is no difference in form between sentences such as ... *she allowed him to give her his number* ... (COCA-2015-FIC) and sentences such as *Why had she allowed this to happen?* (COCA-2013-FIC), where, for obvious semantic reasons, an analysis in terms of a MONOTRANSITIVE CONSTRUCTION with a clausal object of the form [NP to-INF] seems more plausible (although an analysis of a metaphorical use of the DITRANSITIVE CONSTRUCTION cannot be ruled out entirely either).

92 A Construction Grammar of the English Language

5.5 Motion constructions

5.5.1 Self-motion and caused-motion

Motion is another central action type that can be expressed by language. Motion involves a 'thing' that is moving, for which the terms THEME or MOVER are often used, as well as a change from one place to another, which is usually expressed linguistically by what we will call a CHANGE-OF-LOCATION CONSTRUCTION as in (38), which contrasts with the POINT-OF-LOCATION CONSTRUCTION (see 5.6.1) in the examples in (39):

| (38) | a. | … it would be fun to go to the Netherlands. | COCA-2016-NEWS |
| | b. | Will you move there? | COCA-2015-FIC |

| (39) | a. | She lives in the Netherlands… | COCA-2013-NEWS |
| | b. | My family lives there. | COCA-2015-SPOK |

One problem in the description of motion constructions is that the slot indicating the change-of-location can have a large number of formal expressions:

(40)	a.	But I don't fly out of airports that start with "P."	TV-2014-Psych
	b.	I'll take you there.	BNC-ANY-1635
	c.	I'm going to where there's sun and sea and sand.	TV-1968-Avengers
	d.	She puts her soiled breakfast things in the sink, already crammed with the relics of last night's supper, and hurries upstairs.	BNC-ANY-650

It thus seems appropriate to make a distinction between different types of CHANGE-OF-LOCATION-CONSTRUCTIONS, depending on the aspect of the motion-event they profile:[75]

i. SOURCE-constructions which indicate the starting point of a motion event, e.g., $[PP_{from}{}^{SOURCE}]$, $[PP_{out of}{}^{SOURCE}]$, etc.

  (41) She came from Penzance, arriving at Paddington by 4 a.m. next morning.
  BNC-GTH-1588

ii. PATH-constructions which highlight the way between SOURCE and GOAL, e.g., $[PP_{via}{}^{PATH}]$, $[PP_{through}{}^{PATH}]$, $[PP_{along}{}^{PATH}]$, etc.

  (42) … the new fibre-optical cable laid across the Atlantic in December 1988 can handle up to 40,000 separate conversations.
  BNC-AN0-211

iii. GOAL-constructions which refer to the endpoint of a motion event, $PP[_{into}{}^{GOAL}]$, $[PP_{onto}{}^{GOAL}]$, $[PP_{to}{}^{GOAL}]$, $[there^{GOAL}]$:

---

75. For the GOAL-bias in English SELF-MOTION constructions see Stefanowitsch & Rohde (2004) and Stefanowitsch (2018).

Chapter 5. Who does what to whom?   93

(43) a. People fly into Newark and all they see is the industrial areas.   COCA-2004-NEWS
b. I think she's gone down there.   BNC-GWB-1254

iv.   DIRECTION-constructions which describe a motion with respect to an endpoint without implying that this endpoint will be reached, e.g., [PP$_{down}$^{DIRECTION}, [PP$_{up}$^{DIRECTION}, [PP$_{toward/towards}$^{DIRECTION}], [down^{DIRECTION}], [up^{DIRECTION}]:

(44)   Was he going towards his house or away from it?   BNC-GW3-666

A second problem in the description of motion-constructions is that various CHANGE-OF-LOCATION CONSTRUCTIONS can occur together:

(45) a. That evening Wycliffe's after-dinner walk took him once more to Newlyn, but it was a fine evening and still light so he continued along the coast road, past the stone quarries, to Mousehole.   BNC-GWB-2596
b. It was impossible to commute from Rummidge to Ipswich or vice versa. BNC-ANY-798
c. I'll take you there.   BNC-ANY-1635

There is a lot of verb-specific idiosyncrasy here – such as, for example, the verb *put* does not easily combine with [PP$_{from}$^{SOURCE}] – which, to some extent at least, can be explained by the semantic properties of the verbs in question, but which we will not go into here (Herbst & Uhrig 2020). At a general level, we can then identify two motion constructions in English – one in which the theme (i.e., the 'thing' undergoing a change of position) is construed as an AGENT or, in our terminology, the ÆFFECTOR, and one in which it is construed as the ÆFFECTED. We will refer to these constructions as the SELF-MOTION CONSTRUCTION (often referred to as "intransitive motion construction") and the CAUSED-MOTION CONSTRUCTION:[76]

SELF-MOTION CONSTRUCTION		
An AFFECTOR-THEME moves from a SOURCE along a PATH in a particular DIRECTION towards a GOAL.		
ÆFFECTOR-THEME		SOURCE/PATH/DIRECTION/GOAL
Subj	V	Obj$_{PP}$
They **flew** from Frankfurt to New York.		

Figure 5.9 The English SELF-MOTION CONSTRUCTION

---

76. We prefer the term "self-motion" over "intransitive motion" because it provides a nicer contrast to "caused motion". The term "self-mover" is used in FrameNet.

94   A Construction Grammar of the English Language

CAUSED-MOTION CONSTRUCTION			
An ÆFFECTOR makes an ÆFFECTED-THEME move from a SOURCE along a PATH or to a GOAL.			
ÆFFECTOR		ÆFFECTED-THEME	SOURCE/PATH/DIRECTION/GOAL
Subj	V	Obj$_{NP}$	Obj$_{PP}$
... he took us to the Guggenheim Museum in New York. COCA-1997-SPOK A new CBS/New York Times poll had put Clinton 13 points ahead of Bush ... COCA-1993-MAG She ... booted the ball into the goal. COCA-2000-FIC This walk takes you on the coastal path [GOAL] around [PATH] to Polkerris [GOAL] and then back [GOAL] to your start point [GOAL] on the Saints' Way [POINT-OF-LOCATION] – a 35-mile route which crosses Cornwall from Padstow [SOURCE] to Fowey [GOAL]. BNC-CME-899			

Figure 5.10 The English CAUSED-MOTION CONSTRUCTION

5.5.2   CAUSED-MOTION and TO-RECIPIENT CONSTRUCTIONS

The CAUSED-MOTION CONSTRUCTION and the DITRANSITIVE CONSTRUCTION offer slightly different construals of the same events and a large number of verbs occur in both constructions (www.patternbank.de) – a fact that has been discussed widely in the literature (e.g., Goldberg 2006: 26–38; Goldberg 2019; Herbst 2014a, b):

(46) a.   The new U.S. trade representative sent a letter to Congress today...   COCA-2017-SPOK
      b.   ... one White House official didn't tell the truth to another White House official.
                                                                                COCA-2017-SPOK

(47) a.   Comey sends Congress a letter correcting his prior sworn testimony regarding emails
           handled by longtime Clinton associate Huma Abedin.   COCA-2017-MAG
      b.   Had Mr. Clinton told Americans the truth – that when the economic boom went bust
           we'd still have to face the challenges of a country concentrating more wealth and
           power in fewer hands – he could have built a long-term mandate for change.
                                                                                COCA-2004-SPOK

If we say that the verbs *send* and *tell* have a participant role SENDEE/TELLEE and then employ the concept of construal (Langacker 2008a; Goldberg 2006), we can argue that this participant is construed as a RECIPIENT in the DITRANSITIVE CONSTRUCTION (as in (47)) and as a GOAL (or a GOAL-ADDRESSEE) in the case of CAUSED-MOTION construction (as in (46)). At the same time, we have to say that such a difference in meaning is best seen as concerning the prototypical descriptions of the constructions, but that the choice of construction in a particular utterance also depends heavily on other factors such as length of constituents, end-weight, etc. (Bresnan & Ford 2010; Goldberg 2006; Herbst 2014b; Uhrig 2015), and even priming (Gries 2005).

Let us just mention in passing that (46) and (47) also illustrate another interesting – and not entirely unproblematic – aspect of the Construction Grammar approach. While at a very high level of abstraction, (46b) can certainly be seen as an instance of the CAUSED-MOTION CONSTRUCTION, with verbs such as *tell* the third argument slot can definitely be narrowed down to PP_{to}^{GOAL}. It would thus be perfectly plausible to postulate a special TRANSITIVE *TO*-RECIPIENT/GOAL construction (see 5.7.3 below).[77]

5.6 Attribute and resultative constructions

5.6.1 SUBJECT-ATTRIBUTE constructions

The surface pattern NP Verb NP can also have another, non-transitive, interpretation. In such cases, the post-verbal argument refers to the Subj-argument and describes or characterizes it:

(48) a. Manhattan is an island...   COCA-2015-MAG
      b. Manhattan is too expensive for a young couple starting out.   COCA-2014-FIC
      c. That was a great debate. Kamala Harris is a great debater ...   COCA-2019-SPOK

The constructs in (48) clearly do not encode a force-dynamic event like the MONOTRANSITIVE CONSTRUCTION does. Instead, we classify this construction as an ATTRIBUTE CONSTRUCTION because the second argument can be characterized as an ATTRIBUTE: the Subj-argument quite clearly is not an ÆFFECTOR that exerts some kind of force, it is best characterized as an entity about which something is said – to which some property is attributed, which is why we will use the term ATTRIBUTEE for the argument role of this Subj slot. Like Aarts & Aarts (1982/1988), but in contrast to CGEL, we also consider cases of POINT-OF-LOCATION as attributes. This includes examples such as the following:

(49) a. President Trump is in the White House.   COCA-2017-SPOK
      b. The White House is in disarray.   COCA-1993-MAG

We can thus identify several attribute constructions:

---

77. Distinguishing between the DITRANSITIVE and the CAUSED-MOTION CONSTRUCTIONS in these cases can help to explain why, as Goldberg (2006: 27) points out, one would not say *send New York a letter*. On the other hand, one could argue that a separate *TO*-RECIPIENT CONSTRUCTION accounts for the fact that the $Obj_{PP:to}$ cannot be replaced by, for example, *there*. For a discussion of this problem see Herbst (2014b).

SUBJECT-ATTRIBUTE CONSTRUCTIONS				
An ATTRIBUTEE is described, identified or located by an ATTRIBUTEE.				
ATTRIBUTEE			ATTRIBUTE	
Subj	V	Attr	NP	*Nancy Pelosi **is** the most powerful Democrat in the House of Representatives* COCA-2017-SPOK
			AdjP	*The lighthouse **is** superb*... COCA-2008-ACAD
			PP	*She **lives** in the Netherlands*... COCA-2013-NEWS
			that_cl	*The problem **is** that both countries are playing a dangerous game.* COCA-2019-MAG

Figure 5.11 English SUBJECT-ATTRIBUTE CONSTRUCTIONS

Note that, in our view, it does not seem appropriate to postulate separate argument structure constructions for those cases that express a state such as (50a) and the ones that express a change of state for sentences such as (50b). Here the difference in interpretation as 'state' or 'change of state' seems to depend on the meaning of the chosen verb:

(50) a. Barack Obama is the 44th president.   COCA-2012-NEWS
      b. Kamala Harris became not only the first woman to serve as vice president ...
                                                                                          NOW-21-05-10-US

The label **ATTRIBUTE** thus comprises any kind of description of the **ATTRIBUTEE**, including indications of their identity, of features they possess, evaluations or of their position in place or time.

5.6.2 OBJECT-ATTRIBUTE constructions

The roles of ATTRIBUTEE and ATTRIBUTE also occur in a combination in which the ATTRIBU-TEE is construed as an ÆFFECTED in a ÆFFECTOR-ÆFFECTED constellation:

(51) a. When President Joe Biden named Kamala Harris as his running mate, there were whispers about her ambition ...   NOW-21-05-24-US
      b. You don't find that disgusting?   TV-2013-HouseofCards
      c. I call that blind, dumb, stupid, awe-inspired luck.   TV-2007-Psych

We will refer to the respective constructions as OBJECT-ATTRIBUTE CONSTRUCTIONS.

Chapter 5. Who does what to whom? **97**

OBJECT-ATTRIBUTE CONSTRUCTIONS				
An ÆFFECTOR assigns an ATTRIBUTE to an ÆFFECTED-ATTRIBUTEE.				
ÆFFECTOR	ÆFFECTED-ATTRIBUTEE		ATTRIBUTE	
Subj	V	Obj	Attr	NP	You sleep with me and you call me Fallon! TV-1988-Dynasty
				AdjP	… he finds people like you and me infuriating. TV-2013-Downton
				PP$_{as}$	I regard that as highly unprofessional. TV-2011-Downton
				to be NP	Well, Einstein considered himself to be a citizen of the world. COCA-2002-MAG
				to be AdjP	Show the world that you regard this to be wrong. COCA-1991-SPOK

Figure 5.12 English OBJECT-ATTRIBUTE CONSTRUCTIONS

5.6.3 A note on resultative constructions

Some accounts (Goldberg 1995; Boas 2003; Goldberg & Jackendoff 2004) identify a special resultative construction to describe cases such as the following:

(52) a. The pond froze solid.   (Goldberg & Jackendoff 2004: 563)
     b. Bill watered the tulips flat.   (Goldberg & Jackendoff 2004: 563)
     c. The truck rumbled into the station.   (Goldberg & Jackendoff 2004: 563)
     d. The ball rolled down the hill.   (Goldberg & Jackendoff 2004: 563)
     e. Bill rolled the ball down the hill.   (Goldberg & Jackendoff 2004: 563)

Although (52c)–(e) can be seen as expressing a 'result', they can equally be analyzed as instances of the SELF- and CAUSED-MOTION CONSTRUCTIONS (as also indicated by Goldberg & Jackendoff 2004: 563). We will subsume examples such as (52c)–(e) and also cases such as (53) as instances of caused motion:

(53) a. You put us on the email list?   TV-2008-Psych
     b. Watch the sun rise. It'll put you in a good mood for the whole day.   COCA-2012-MAG

The case for postulating a separate resultative construction is slightly stronger with examples such as (52a) and (52b). These do not correspond to the prototype of the SUBJECT-ATTRIBUTE and OBJECT-ATTRIBUTE CONSTRUCTIONS because they do not ascribe an ATTRIBUTE to the respective subject or object arguments but describe a 'CHANGE OF STATE' (see also 5.7.7). However, again, it seems that the distinction between resultative and non-resultative cannot really be related to any formal properties, but is primarily a semantic one. The interpretation as resultative sometimes seems to be due to a causative meaning of the verb as (54b) in contrast to (54a):

(54) a. Mom wants her steak well done, Dad prefers his bloody, and the kids like theirs slightly pink? [OBJECT-ATTRIBUTE CXN] COCA-2014-MAG

b. You can cook a steak medium rare in four minutes.

[RESULTATIVE CXN] NOW-21-07-02-GB

In the OBJECT-ATTRIBUTE CONSTRUCTION in (54a), *her steak, his* and *theirs* can be described in terms of an argument role ÆFFECTED-ATTRIBUTEE because they are the elements at which the action of the verb is directed as well as the elements to which the ATTRIBUTEs *well done, etc.* apply. *Her steak* in (54a) itself does not undergo any change by being called *well done.* This is different in the case of *a steak* in (54b), which is cooked until it reaches a certain state, which is why we only label it ÆFFECTED. In other cases, however, a resultative reading arises from the fact that a verb which is not causative as such is interpreted in such a way because no other interpretation makes sense as in the following examples from Boas (2011) – which seems to require a resultative constructional template:

(55) a. Pat ate his plate clean. (Boas 2011: 45)

b. Miriam talked herself blue in the face. (Boas 2011: 44; Goldberg 1995: 189)

Given the productivity of such creative uses, we consider it appropriate to postulate the two resultative constructions described in Figures 5.13 and 5.14 and to envisage them as subtypes of the SUBJECT-ATTRIBUTE and OBJECT-ATTRIBUTE CONSTRUCTIONS (and label them accordingly in construction grids).[78]

SELF-CHANGE-RESULTATIVE CONSTRUCTIONS				
An ÆFFECTOR changes its state into the RESULT.				
ATTRIBUTEE			RESULT	
Subj	V	Attr	NP	*Willem-Alexander* **became** *king of the Netherlands in 2013* ... NOW-20-02-06-GB
			AdjP	*Everything in the house* **froze** *solid — the water in the kettle, even my false teeth in a cup beside my bed.* BNC-BN6-397 ... *Robyn* **became** *deeply involved in a Women's Group at Cambridge* ... BNC-ANY-783

Figure 5.13 The SELF-CHANGE-RESULTATIVE CONSTRUCTION (subtype of SUBJECT-ATTRIBUTE CXN)

---

78. For a more detailed account of resultatives see Boas (2003) and Goldberg (1995). For German see Welke (2019: 225).

Chapter 5. Who does what to whom? **99**

CAUSED-CHANGE-RESULTATIVE CONSTRUCTIONS					
An ÆFFECTOR makes an ÆFFECTED change its state or function into the RESULT.					
ÆFFECTOR		ÆFFECTED-ATTRIBUTEE	RESULT		
Subj	V	Obj	Attr	NP	*It makes conversation rather a hit-or-miss affair* ... BNC-ANY-1021
				AdjP	*Can't we just paint it purple?* TV-2014-Psych

Figure 5.14 The CAUSED-CHANGE-RESULTATIVE CONSTRUCTION (subtype of OBJECT-ATTRIBUTE CXN)

A construction that also expresses a change-of-state involving prepositional objects will be discussed in 5.7.2.

5.7 Constructions with prepositional objects

5.7.1 General characterization

Finally, we have to look at argument structure constructions with prepositional objects. Two points must be made perfectly clear:

i. We are not talking about one construction here, but about a (relatively large) number of constructions whose form can be described in terms of Subj V Obj$_{PP}$. Since there is no common element of meaning that could be generalized across patterns with all the different prepositions, we argue that Subj V Obj$_{PP}$ does not qualify as a single construction. Constructions can only be identified at the level of specific prepositions: thus, prepositional objects with *on* can be described as TOPIC-AREA in sentences such as (56) (cf. 5.7.2):

(56) a. He once lectured on Shakespeare at Yale... COCA-1997-FIC
 b. The seventh Millennium Development Goal focuses on environmental sustainability... COCA-2008-ACAD

ii. Constructions with prepositional objects must be distinguished from constructions with attributes in which Attr can be realized by a prepositional phrase, as in

(57) a. Two weeks ago you were on the Rockefeller Center skating rink ... COCA-2006-SPOK
 b. If you're on the plane, you're on the team. COCA-2017-SPOK

There are a number of differences between the cases in (56) and (57):

i. Prepositional objects (as in (56)) do not characterize or localize Subjs, i.e., they are not attributes.
ii. The choice of preposition in prepositional phrases in attribute constructions is not governed by the constructions, cf.:

(58) a. Did they live in New York? COCA-1991-F
b. Why do you live on a boat? COCA-2002-F
c. ... you don't live there. COCA-2017-SPOK

The prepositional phrases in attribute constructions can often be replaced by a single particle word such as *there* in (58c).

Given the large number of constructions with prepositional phrases, in the following sections we will just provide a few examples of such constructions here (for a more comprehensive account see CASA|Con under www.constructicon.de).

5.7.2 CHANGE-OF-STATE and *INTO*-CAUSATIVE CONSTRUCTIONS

As a further example of constructions with prepositional objects, let us look at constructions with *into*. The cases under (59) are realizations of the CAUSED-MOTION CONSTRUCTION, which applies to situations in which an ÆFFECTOR causes a THEME to move a different location, the GOAL:

(59) a. Any question of taking her into Penzance had to be abandoned... BNC-CDE1336
b. ... anyone can hit a ball into an empty cup. TV-2009-Psych

In (60), the Obj$_{NP}$, however, does not change its location but its nature:

(60) a. ... those protesters will have to turn their street demonstrations against Trump into political action ... COCA-2017-SPOK
b. He translated the book into English ... COCA-2019-SPOK
c. Student A translates a paragraph from L1 into L2. BNC-GoW-3053

These cases can be described in terms of a separate CHANGE-OF-STATE CONSTRUCTION, which, however, is linked to the CAUSED-MOTION CONSTRUCTION and the RESULTATIVE CONSTRUCTION, because we can identify a SOURCE-STATE as well as a GOAL-STATE:

Chapter 5. Who does what to whom? **101**

CHANGE-OF-STATE CONSTRUCTION			
An ÆFFECTOR makes an ÆFFECTED change from one state to another			
ÆFFECTOR		ÆFFECTED	SOURCE-STATE and/or GOAL-STATE
Subj	V	Obj: NP	Obj: PP_{from} and/or PP_{into}
Kennedy reaffirmed his commitment to "translating civil rights from principles into practices." COCA-2013-MAG			

Figure 5.15 The English CHANGE-OF-STATE CONSTRUCTION

A very interesting case is presented by another construction based on the CAUSED-MOTION CONSTRUCTION, namely the *INTO-*CAUSATIVE CONSTRUCTION described by Stefanowitsch & Gries (2003) and Stefanowitsch (2014), exemplified by sentences such as the following:

(61) a. She'd already talked her daughter into making major changes in the wedding plans.

COCA-2012-FIC

b. I still can't believe that you let Shawn talk you into this crazy plan. TV-2009-Psych

c. … he continued to try to press Trump into at least giving him the opportunity to ask a question …

COCA-2017-SPOK

INTO -CAUSATIVE CONSTRUCTION			
An ÆFFECTOR makes an ÆFFECTED take a certain course of action			
ÆFFECTOR		ÆFFECTED	ACTION
Subj	V	Obj: NP	Obj: PP_{into}
But perhaps we can try to… persuade her into returning to the path of truth. TV-2012-Downton *She tricked him into doing it.* COCA-2019-MOV			

Figure 5.16 The English CHANGE-OF-STATE CONSTRUCTION

5.7.3 GENERAL-ISSUE and SPECIFIC-ISSUE: Obj_{PP:about} and Obj_{PP:on}

When speakers wish to mention the topic of a communicative act, they can make use of constructions with Obj_{PP:about} and Obj_{PP:on}. These are not entirely synonymous, however: Firstly, with verbs of communication, *on* tends to be used predominantly to refer to formal occasions, whereas *about* is more neutral. Compare (62) and (63):

(62) a. If Al Gore is speaking, he's speaking about climate change. COCA-2015-MAG

b. He never spoke about his childhood or his parents. COCA-2001-F

c. … no city official has ever spoken about urban renewal and neighborhoods

COCA-1997-NEWS

d. We need to think about things like sea level rise.	COCA-2017-SPOK
e. We always laughed about it.	COCA-2015-MAG

(63) … the President spoke on the economy, violence and education. COCA-1997-F

Secondly, it seems that *on*-prepositional objects express a stronger focus on a particular 'thing' than *about*-prepositional objects:

(64) a. Much of the research in foreign languages has focused on linguistics and the systematic study of phonology. COCA-2001-ACAD

b. Her firm concentrates on kitchens, beds and baths, and floors. COCA-2014-NEWS

The two constructions are not very easy to tease apart, but prototypically we will distinguish the argument roles of $Obj_{PP:about}$ and $Obj_{PP:on}$ by the following labels for the respective argument roles:

– **GENERAL-ISSUE** to denote an area or the scope of 'things' to which the action carried out by the ÆFFECTOR applies,
– **SPECIFIC-ISSUE** to denote a more specific concentration on an area of specialization or a particular topic.

This distinction enables us to postulate the following two argument structure constructions, which does not mean that we do not recognize a considerable amount of overlap between the two:

ABOUT-GENERAL-ISSUE CONSTRUCTION		
An ÆFFECTOR performs an action with respect to a GENERAL ISSUE.		
ÆFFECTOR		GENERAL ISSUE
Subj	V	Obj: PP$_{about}$
*We **worry** about global warming, the vanishing ozone layer, …* COCA-1991-NEWS		

Figure 5.17 The English *ABOUT*-GENERAL-ISSUE CONSTRUCTION

ON-SPECIFIC-ISSUE CONSTRUCTION		
An ÆFFECTOR performs an action with respect to a SPECIFIC ISSUE		
ÆFFECTOR		SPECIFIC ISSUE
Subj	V	Obj: PP$_{on}$
*And if you don't **act** on climate change, it's - inevitably something's going to happen.* COCA-2010-SPOK		

Figure 5.18 The English *ON*-SPECIFIC-ISSUE CONSTRUCTION

Chapter 5. Who does what to whom? **103**

5.7.4 Communication partners: *TO*-RECIPIENT/GOAL and *WITH*-PARTNER

We are faced with a very similar problem of demarcation with *to-* and *with-*prepositional objects: We already pointed out in 5.5.2 that $Obj_{PP:to}$ can clearly be characterized as a GOAL, as in (65).

(65) a. Vice President Gore spoke to reporters at his official residence in Washington.

COCA-2000-SPOK

   b. The British flatly denied it and complained to the White House.   COCA-2017-MAG

We call this role RECIPIENT-GOAL, because, unlike GOAL in the CAUSED-MOTION CONSTRUCTION described above, it is restricted to $Obj_{PP:to}$. $Obj_{PP:with}$ has a similar meaning, but suggests a more reciprocal type of relationship. Look at (66):

(66) a. People can start tweeting with me if they want.   COCA-2009-SPOK
   b. ... or you can tweet to us.   COCA-2015-SPOK

Since (66a) implies an expectation that the person will tweet back, we will refer to this argument role as PARTNER. The reciprocity is particularly obvious in cases such as (67):

(67) a. I'd rather know what he's going to do for the country, I don't care who he sleeps with.

COCA-2015-SPOK

   b. ... he frequently quarreled with his wife who eventually left him ...   COCA-2016-ACAD

Thus, we can identify the following constructions:

TO-RECIPIENT/GOAL CONSTRUCTION		
An ÆFFECTOR performs an action directed towards a RECIPIENT/GOAL.		
ÆFFECTOR		RECIPIENT/GOAL
Subj	V	Obj: PP_{to}
I will immediately write to Congress ... COCA-2005-MAG		

Figure 5.19 The English *TO*-RECIPIENT/GOAL CONSTRUCTION

WITH-PARTNER CONSTRUCTION		
An ÆFFECTOR performs an action together with a PARTNER.		
ÆFFECTOR		PARTNER
Subj	V	Obj: PP$_{\text{with}}$
… they were all arguing with each other… COCA-2015-MAG *I didn't sleep with anybody I didn't want to sleep with…* COCA-2017-SPOK		

Figure 5.20 The English *WITH*-PARTNER CONSTRUCTION

Quite clearly, the constructionist approach relies heavily on an interpretation in terms of prototype category structures, because sentences such as the following only fall under the descriptions provided with a benevolent stretch of imagination:

(68) Other sources of calcium if milk does not agree with you are yoghurt, cheese, shrimps and ice cream. BNC-EX5-2104

More appropriately, however, we could see (68) in terms of an item-specific valency construction of the verb *agree*. One has to bear in mind, in any case, that by no means all occurrences of Obj$_{\text{PP:to}}$ or Obj$_{\text{PP:with}}$ fall into these two categories. In (69), we are simply expressing a relation between Subj and Obj$_{\text{PP}}$:

(69) a. This series corresponds to certain patterns in nature… COCA-2017-ACAD
b. That's a notion both Senate leaders agree with… COCA-2017-NEWS

5.7.5 Instrument and emotion

With-prepositional objects typically also can express the INSTRUMENT with which an action is being carried out, as in (70) and (71):

(70) a. You must show him you can open the door with the key. COCA-2009-FIC
b. And I'll cut my steak with a spoon. TV-2008-Simpsons
c. Cissie was holding her baby with one hand and her book with the other. BNC-GW3-1237
d. … but the man who would later be accused of killing Kennedy with a perfect shot almost never came to the firing range. COCA-1991-ACAD

(71) He writes with a fountain pen. COCA-2008-NEWS

It is, however, not entirely obvious how far a category such as INSTRUMENT can be extended with some cognitive plausibility to the following cases:

(72) He filled the glasses **with exaggerated care.** COCA-1990-FIC

| | | | Chapter 5. Who does what to whom? **105** |

(73) a. … he filled their glasses **with wine from the carafe.**   COCA-2018-FIC
      b. Oh, we're gonna fill the house **with kids.**   TV-1987-Dynasty
      c. Traditional knowledge provides archaeologists **with essential information…**

                                                                                    COCA-2006-ACAD

These examples show the gradual character of the distinctions made: while (70) and (71) definitely qualify as INSTRUMENT, one can just about make a case for analyzing (72) along the same lines. The examples in (73), however, also allow an interpretation in terms of a 'filler or content of a container'. The role CONTENT could also be applied to metaphorical uses such as those of (74), which, however, can also – and perhaps more appropriately – be described by an argument role EMOTION, where the emotion expressed by the PP$_{with}$ acts as a kind of stimulus for the action described by the construction as such:

(74) a. … she is seething with anger about the CIA …   COCA-2014-SPOK
      b. His eyes sparkled with excitement.   COCA-1992-FIC

WITH-EMOTION CONSTRUCTION		
An ÆFFECTOR behaves in a certain way showing an EMOTION.		
ÆFFECTOR		EMOTION
Subj	V	Obj: PP$_{with}$
… she's beaming with love … COCA-2006-MAG		

Figure 5.21 The English _WITH_-EMOTION CONSTRUCTION

5.7.6 The English CONATIVE CONSTRUCTION

In the case of Obj$_{PP:at}$, there is a sense in which the prepositional object can be assigned an argument role TARGET:

(75) a. He looked at her quizzically.   BNC-ANY-1719
      b. He stared at her incredulously.   BNC-ANY-2222
      c. He started yelling at Angela Merkel in a closed meeting that he arrived at late.

                                                                                    COCA-2019-SPOK

The meaning of the construction with [PP$_{at}$^{TARGET}] can easily be worked out by contrasting sentences such as:

(76) a. They shot at the car.   ['shot in the direction of']
      b. They shot at the party leader.   ['shot in the direction of']
      c. They shot the party leader.   ['shot and hit']
      d. They shot the party leader dead. ['shot and killed']

In contrast to the MONOTRANSITIVE CONSTRUCTION in (76c) and the RESULTATIVE CONSTRUCTION in (76d), [PP$_{at}$^{TARGET}] does not necessarily entail a meaning of 'successful achievement' (cf. *They shot at the party leader, but missed.* vs ?*They shot the party leader, but missed.*). This element of 'attempted' meaning is also present in sentences such as

(77) a. She watched a blue jay pecking at a dropped sandwich...   COCA-2013-FIC
      b. ... she sipped at a glass of champagne ...   COCA-2003-FIC

At the same time, some uses of [PP$_{at}$^{TARGET}] do seem to entail a successful attempt:

(78) a. What are you getting at?   BNC-GW3-1828
      b. Then she laughed at herself, with an edge of self-mocking irony.   BNC-A6J-54

How can we capture all of these different event construals of actions (some necessarily successful, others only being attempted)? Tentatively, we suggest a single CONATIVE CONSTRUCTION that contains an Obj$_{PP:at}$ and that expresses the idea of an attempt at establishing contact with a 'thing' – with the question of whether this attempt is successful or not being backgrounded by this construction.[79] Thus, the CONATIVE CONSTRUCTION can construe force-dynamic events in a way similar to the MONOTRANSITIVE CONSTRUCTION, but in contrast to the latter 'zooms in' on the (abstract or physical) force emission from the ÆFFECTOR (backgrounding the effect on the ÆFFECTED participant, which thus becomes interpreted as a 'mere' TARGET):

AT-CONATIVE CONSTRUCTION		
An ÆFFECTOR performs an action directed towards a TARGET		
ÆFFECTOR		TARGET
Subj	V	Obj: PP$_{at}$
They gaped at her as if she was an alien from outer space. BNC-ANY-1731		

Figure 5.22 CONSTRUCTION with [PP$_{at}$^{TARGET}]

5.7.7 DESIRED-THING constructions

There is a certain amount of overlap between the argument roles of TARGET and GOAL, exemplified by (79a) and (79b) respectively, and that of the *for*-prepositional objects in (80):

(79) a. They would sip sherry or port, nibble at the nuts and raisins ...   BNC-GW3-2757
      b. Go to Oxbridge.   BNC-ANY-621

---

79. For a detailed discussion of the conative construction and its meanings see Perek (2015: 90–103).

Chapter 5. Who does what to whom? **107**

(80) a. … And, in fact, just days after global protests calling for action on climate change, there was a special U.N. climate summit today … COCA-2019-SPOK

  b. This president doesn't stand for anything the Republican Party said it stood for. COCA-2019-SPOK

  c. She began to look for a university job outside Cambridge. BNC-ANY-693

We will label this argument role DESIRED THING and characterize the construction underlying (80) as follows:

FOR-DESIRED-THING CONSTRUCTION		
An ÆFFECTOR performs an action directed towards a DESIRED THING		
ÆFFECTOR		DESIRED THING
Subj	V	Obj: PP$_{for}$
I've spent my entire life searching for the impossible. TV-2012-Psych		

Figure 5.23 The English FOR-DESIRED-THING CONSTRUCTION

The same argument role can be used to describe the ÆFFECTED+FOR-DESIRED-THING CONSTRUCTION:

(81) a. He'll ask complete strangers for the time… COCA-2005-FIC

  b. AN RAF plane was searching the Atlantic last night for a missing solo yachtsman. BNC-CEM-2137

ÆFFECTED+FOR-DESIRED-THING CONSTRUCTION			
AN ÆFFECTOR DOES SOMETHING TO AN ÆFFECTED TO GET A DESIRED THING.			
ÆFFECTOR		ÆFFECTED	DESIRED THING
Subj	V	Obj: NP	Obj: PP$_{for}$
I can't ask my friends for money… TV-2016-HouseofCards			

Figure 5.24 The ÆFFECTED+FOR-DESIRED-THING CONSTRUCTION

In the case of (82), the relation between the Obj-NP and the Obj-PP$_{for}$ is quite different and can be described in terms of 'replacement' or 'substitution':

(82) a. I must ask you to exchange your spatula for a phaser rifle. TV-1998-StarTrek

  b. Therefore, we would like to substitute Denver-Carrington for Colbyco in the deal. TV-1985-Dynasty

EXCHANGE-*X-FOR-Y* CONSTRUCTION				
An ÆFFECTOR exchanges an ÆFFECTED for a SUBSTITUTE.				
ÆFFECTOR			ÆFFECTED	SUBSTITUTE
Subj	V		Obj: NP	Obj: PP$_{for}$
She was … too prudent to exchange him for a lover whose interest would probably not last very long. BNC-ANY-743				

Figure 5.25 The English EXCHANGE-*X-FOR-Y* CONSTRUCTION

5.7.8 The nature of prepositional objects

Our discussion of argument structure constructions with prepositional objects has revealed a high degree of polysemy in many prepositions, which has made it necessary to identify more than one construction for a single preposition – with the notable exception of *to*, which always seems to be associated with a RECIPIENT or GOAL sense. Accordingly, the number of verbs occurring in many of these constructions is relatively small. These are, therefore, item-based or item-related argument structure constructions that, unlike say the MONO-TRANSITIVE CONSTRUCTION or the DITRANSITIVE CONSTRUCTION are not fully schematic and also more specific with respect to the scenes they construe.[80]

5.8 Perspectivization of arguments

5.8.1 Actives and passives

There is an obvious connection between active and passive clauses in that they both can be used to describe the same situation.

(83) a. On April 15, the morning after John Wilkes Booth shot Lincoln at Ford's Theatre …

COCA-2009-ACAD

b. … the night Abraham Lincoln was shot by John Wilkes Booth at Ford's Theatre in Washington, D.C.

COCA-2012-BLOG

This relation has been made explicit in traditional teaching grammars by rules saying that you form a passive by making the object of the active clause the subject of the passive clause, etc., or, in Chomsky's (1957, 1965) models by deriving actives and passives from the same deep structure. In a constructionist account, which is non-derivational, we regard active and passive argument structure constructions in their own right, which are connected by horizontal links in the constructicon (which unlike in generative approaches is not a one-way connection from active to passive, but a bidirectional link; cf. Hoffmann 2022b: 199–206).

---

80. Hoffmann (2019, 2021b) consequently calls these 'marginal argument structure constructions'.

Chapter 5. Who does what to whom? **109**

One reason for this is that there is a clear difference in semantic function between them – primarily one that concerns the information structure of the clause, i.e., the way a speaker presents a message (see Chapter 10): The ÆFFECTOR takes a very prominent role as the subject in active clauses, but in the passive it often is not expressed at all, and if it is, then takes the form of a PP$_{by}$.

Furthermore, although active clauses by far outnumber passives in actual language use, there also exist cases of passives which have no active counterpart or where the corresponding active sounds rather awkward:

(84) a. I don't know about you, Gus, but I was born into the wrong family.   TV-2009-Psych
      b. The President is said to be open to taking part in the Paris Agreement if the terms are made more favorable to the U.S.   COCA-2017-SPOK

Nevertheless, it is perfectly clear that the correspondences between active and passives clauses should be indicated. In the CASA approach, this is done at three different levels, namely

i.   corresponding descriptions of the semantic functions of the constructions,
ii.   identical argument roles, and
iii. corresponding labels for the constructions.

In CASA, we treat passive constructs with and without an overt ÆFFECTOR argument as two separate, but obviously related constructions: (85b), e.g., is an instance of the *by*-PASSIVE-MONOTRANSITIVE CONSTRUCTION (in which the ÆFFECTOR is provided in a *by*-PP) and (82c) an instance of the simple PASSIVE MONOTRANSITIVE CONSTRUCTION:

(85) a. He's the one who [ÆFFECTOR] found the body [ÆFFECTED].   TV-2012-Psych
      b. His body [ÆFFECTED] was found by the building manager, a Mr. Lloyd Marr [ÆFFECTOR].   TV-2013-Psych
      c. We have information that you were seen with the victim the day before his body [ÆFFECTED] was found.   TV-2007-Psych

5.8.2 Discrepancies between active and passive expressions of arguments

There are some interesting differences in the formal realization of corresponding active and passive argument structure constructions. For example, arguments that are expressed by a prepositional object in the active construction, have a passive counterpart with a noun phrase subject and a "stranded" preposition (Hoffmann 2011):

(86) a. My car has been tampered with. My trailer has been broken into.   TV-2007-Psych
      b. His bed hasn't been slept in.   BNC-G3E-1614

Clausal realizations of arguments often occur in a construction in which *it* fills the subject slot of the sentence type construction and the clause realizing the Subj-slot of the argument structure construction is expressed in the predicate (cf. also 5.10.6). In traditional terminology, this is often referred to as extraposition:

(87) a. Therefore, it has been argued that adequate language skills are a prerequisite for learning early mathematics (Aiken, 1972; Dehaene, Piazza, Pinel, & Cohen 2003).
COCA-2014-ACAD

b. It is not known whether animals also experience a feeling triumph or elation when they win in a competitive encounter the way humans do... COCA-2018-MAG

5.8.3 Perspectivization

The existence of active and passive constructions allows speakers to make a choice as to which of the participants of the scene described – or, if you like, the frame elements of the respective frame – they wish to refer to explicitly and what kind of prominence they wish to give to them in terms of information structure. For instance, as pointed out above, the verb *bear* is hardly ever used in the active in the sense of 'give birth', as in (88b), whereas the passive as in (88a) is much more common. In present-day English, the passive of *bear* is the established way of referring to a person's birthday or birthplace, while the expression *give birth* is more commonly used in contexts specifying the number of children or the circumstances of birth, or when it is used metaphorically.

(88) a. Queen Elizabeth **was born** on April 21, 1926. NOW-22-05-06-US
b. She **bore** a beautiful daughter, Meg, a year later ... COCA-2019-FIC

(89) a. Incidentally, a similar incident took place in June 2015 at the same hospital when a baby **was given birth** under candle light. NOW-16-10-05-GB
b. Yes, Lady Sybil is in distress. She's about **to give birth.** TV-2012-Downton

These examples show very clearly that there is more to language use than simply relating actives and passives by a rule deriving the one from the other, but that additional factors in terms of Sinclair's (1991) idiom principle (see 11.1.1) or Goldberg's (2019) familiarity of expressions will have to be considered, too. This is also true of the examples in (90):

(90) a. Global warming melts the polar ice caps. NOW-21-01-06-GB
b. ... we now live in a period where the ice caps are being melted by climate change ...
NOW-16-02-01

The reason why (90b) sounds distinctly odd may be seen in the fact that the verb *melt* allows the ÆFFECTED argument to occur as the subject of the SELF-CHANGE-RESULTATIVE CONSTRUCTION as in (91).

(91) a. It's not just the polar ice-caps that will melt as a result. It's also Trudeau's mountain of ice-cream. NOW-16-03-20

b. A tenth of the world's mountain glacier ice will have melted by the middle of this century even if humanity meets the goals of the Paris climate agreement ...

COCA-21-04-29-US

The fact that with some verbs arguments with different semantic roles can occur in the SUBJ-slot of sentence constructions formed a key element of Fillmore's (1968) groundbreaking model of case grammar, which can be seen as an important step towards frame semantics and FrameNet (Fillmore 2014). The term *case* is to be interpreted as a label for what we now call argument roles. Fillmore uses the verb *open* to illustrate the point, as in the examples below (in which we make use of the CASA terms for the respective roles):

(92) a. ÆFFECTOR: Wycliffe opened the door ... BNC-HWP-1998
b. INSTRUMENT: Now, this key opens the door to your buildin' and this key opens the door to your very own penthouse apartment ... COCA-1996-MOV
c. ÆFFECTED: The door opened. BNC-A0N-2475

The choice of which participants of a process are to be expressed in an utterance and how much prominence they are to be given can involve lexical and constructional choices. (93a)–(c), for example, describe the same process, but from rather different perspectives (using the same verb *give* in the active DITRANSITVE CONSTRUCTION, the active CAUSED-MOTION CONSTRUCTION and the passive DITRANSITVE CONSTRUCTION, respectively). Moreover, (93d) can also express the same event, but with a different verb (*receive*) in a different construction (a resultative type of SUBJECT-ATTRIBUTE CONSTRUCTION; see 5.6.3) which again puts a slightly different perspective on the same situation:[81]

(93) a. The teacher **gave** the student a book. (Fillmore et al. 2003: 237)
b. The teacher **gave** a book to the student. (Fillmore et al. 2003: 237)
c. While recovering he **was given** a book of van Gogh's letters ... COCA-2007-NEWS
d. The student **received** a book (from the teacher). (Fillmore et al. 2003: 238)

5.8.4 The mediopassive construction

A construction that is related to the idea of perspectivization is the so-called MEDIOPASSIVE CONSTRUCTION: Like in passive constructions, the subject-slot of the construction is realized by an ÆFFECTED-argument, without, however, being accompanied by the PASSIVE CONSTRUCTION [BE V-en]:[82]

---

81. Observations such as these were originally modelled by Fillmore et al. (2003) in terms of frame semantics. Cf. Petruck (1996: 1): "A '*frame*' is any system of concepts related in such a way that to understand one concept it is necessary to understand the entire system; introducing any one concept results in all of them becoming available." See also Ziem (2008: 97), and for a critique Herbst (2022).

82. There is a certain amount of overlap with THE SELF-CHANGE CONSTRUCTION; compare ... *all doors opened automatically* ... (COCA-2014-FIC) and (94c). Consider also *Don't get me wrong. I love it. But does it sell?* (COCA-2016-TV) where a positive evaluation (in the sense of *sell well*) is implied.

(94) a. This new cream cheese spreads *easily* and has a delicate, airy texture. COCA-2915-MAG
   b. The door opens *easily* but I am at once confronted by another door.COCA-2007-ACAD
   c. The same black velvet gown that sells *well* in London will also play in South Carolina.
                                                                                      COCA-2006-MAG

MEDIOPASSIVE CONSTRUCTION		
An ÆFFECTED has the property specified by the V followed by a modifying element that expresses a degree of difficulty.		
ÆFFECTED		DEGREE OF DIFFICULTY
Subj	V	*well easily* etc.
The menu reads well ... COCA-2001-NEWS		

Figure 5.26 The English MEDIOPASSIVE CONSTRUCTION

5.9 Combining argument structure constructions with sentence type constructions

Constructs are combinations of several constructions. A construct such as (82) can be analyzed in terms of a sentence type construction and an argument structure construction, in this case the DECLARATIVE-STATEMENT CONSTRUCTION and the CAUSED-MOTION CONSTRUCTION:

(95) She puts her soiled breakfast things in the sink...   BNC-ANY-650

The DECLARATIVE-STATEMENT CONSTRUCTION (DECS) contributes the elements SUBJ and PRED and the specification of their order and of concord between the subject and the finite verb in the predicate. The CAUSED-MOTION CONSTRUCTION consists of a verb and three arguments, one of which has the potential of being the subject of a finite clause. There is thus overlap between the two constructions in two points – the verb and SUBJ/Subj. As we have already outlined in previous chapters, we can thus assume a blending operation in the sense of Fauconnier & Turner (1996, see section 15.2) to occur. In the course of this operation the CAUSED-MOTION CONSTRUCTION contributes the ÆFFECTED and the GOAL arguments giving rise to a blended space, which we can represent in a construction grid of the following kind (which also includes the PRESENT-TENSE CONSTRUCTION):

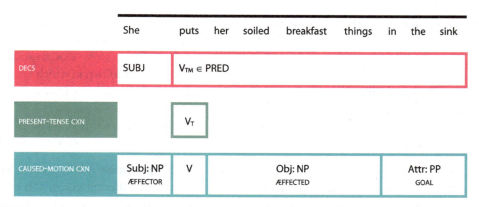

Figure 5.27 Construction grid for *She puts her soiled breakfast things in the sink.* (BNC-ANY-650) showing overlapping elements of three constructions and indicating semantic roles

A construction grid for a construct such as (96) then takes the form of Figure 5.28.

(96) Can I ask you a personal question? TV-2014-Downton

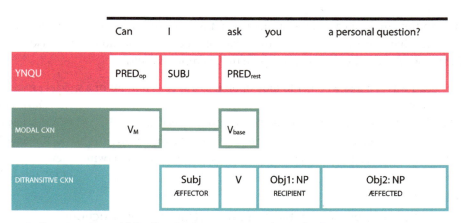

Figure 5.28 Construction grid for *Can I ask you a personal question?*

5.10 Adjectival argument structure constructions

5.10.1 Argument structure constructions across word classes

Although most of the work on argument structure has, for very good and obvious reasons, focused on constructions with verbs, the same relations between 'things' can be expressed using adjectival or nominal constructions. Words such as *parallel(s)* can serve as examples:

(97) a. In short, it may be noticed that Augustine's argument **parallels** the one Socrates makes on behalf of Eros in Plato's Phaedrus: that is, that Eros is a god and hence must be good. COCA-1992-ACAD

b. Significantly, this is not the only moment in A Room of One's Own in which Woolf draws **a parallel** between physical disability and artistic failure. COCA-2016-ACAD

c. We think of science as just fact-based, but the scientific process is **parallel** to the process of making art: asking questions, applying techniques, rethinking and creating again. COCA-2019-NEWS

All of these sentences express essentially the same relationship, namely A ∥ B, even if, from a cognitive point of view, one might make out a good case for different construals of the same facts. The point we wish to draw attention to here, however, concerns the different options of syntactic expression of the same relation between two 'things' outlined in (97). Since the relationship between the phrases printed in orange (ATTRIBUTEE) and brown (ATTRIBUTE) and the **verb** in (97a) *parallels* that between the phrases printed in orange (ATTRIBUTEE) and brown (ATTRIBUTE) and the **noun** *parallel* in (97b) or the **adjective** *parallel* in (97c), we will extend the notion of the term argument structure constructions to such cases.

We can thus make a case for argument structure constructions that are related to word classes other than verbs.[83] This is not only true of adjectives and nouns, but also of multiword expressions such as *at a loss*; compare the examples in (98):

(98) a. ... I was at a loss whether to look upon it as a special honour or a special precaution ... BNC-B1N-676

b. I don't know whether to think this is art or this is life. COCA-2019-SPOK

c. ... he seemed uncertain whether to call himself a capitalist. COCA-2019-SPOK

d. There's some debate whether to call that a Twitter view or a twinterview. COCA-2009-SPOK

5.10.2 General design of adjective argument structure constructions

There is thus a strong case for postulating argument structure constructions for relational uses of adjectives as well: If you consider (99), you can see that using the adjective *friendly* in the ATTRIBUTIVE CONSTRUCTION establishes a relation between two arguments.

---

83. An alternative analysis to the one advocated here is to downplay the differences between the word classes by considering the uses of *parallel* in (97b) and (97c) as parts of the complex verbal expressions *draw a parallel* and *be parallel*. Then the respective noun phrases could be regarded as arguments of a verbal construction just like those in (97a), but sentences such as following show the limitations of such a view: *Moreover, we cannot escape the **parallel** between the supremacy clause in Article XIII of the Articles of Confederation and the one in Article VI of the Constitution.* (COCA-2016-ACAD) *The works of many of the modem artists were seen as **parallel** to the art works of young children.* (COCA-1993-ACAD)

Chapter 5. Who does what to whom? 115

(99) a. Inez was **friendly** with a woman living in Hayle ... BNC-GWB-1907
b. Professors **friendly** with justices, many from Harvard or Yale, early identify star pupils. COCA-1998-NEWS

The expression of the second of these arguments can be described as a special case of a POSTMODIFIER-OF-ADJECTIVE CONSTRUCTION (see 4.2.1.2), the first argument is expressed by an element of another construction. We can thus postulate a construction of the following kind:

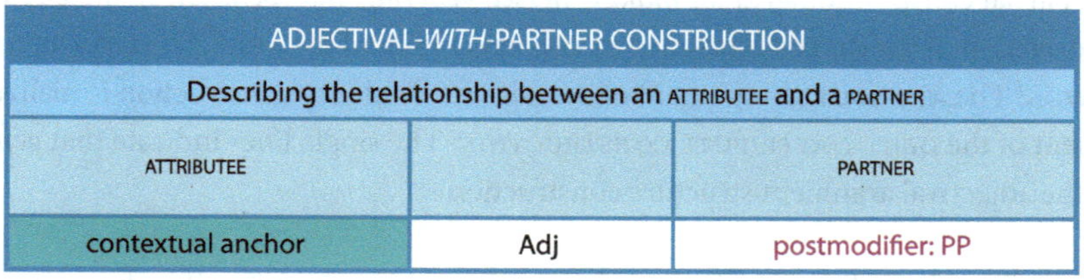

ADJECTIVAL-*WITH*-PARTNER CONSTRUCTION		
Describing the relationship between an ATTRIBUTEE and a PARTNER		
ATTRIBUTEE		PARTNER
contextual anchor	Adj	postmodifier: PP

Figure 5.29 The ADJECTIVAL-*WITH*-PARTNER CONSTRUCTION

Figures 5.30 and 5.31 illustrate how we can imagine an adjectival argument structure construction to combine with other constructions in (99a) and (100):

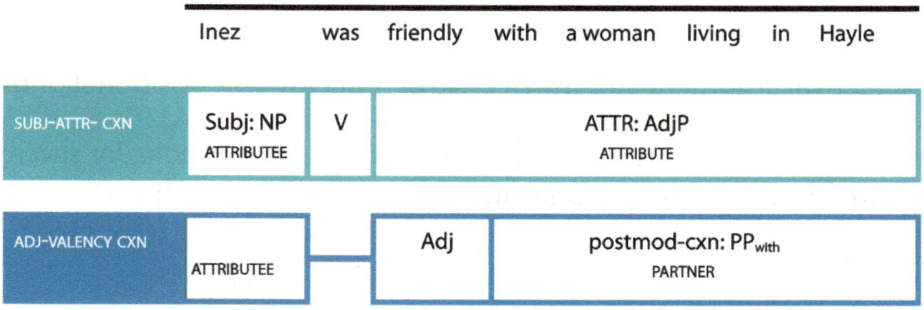

Figure 5.30 Use of the ADJECTIVAL-WITH-PARTNER CONSTRUCTION in combination with the SUBJECT-ATTRIBUTE CONSTRUCTION: The ATTRIBUTEE-argument of the adjectival valency construction is realized by the Subj-argument of the ATTRIBUTE CONSTRUCTION

(100) She was fully stretched preparing her classes, ... marking her essays, ..., and making herself generally indispensable to the Department. BNC-ANY-813

Note that, as with Subj-arguments of verbal arguments structure constructions, a specification in terms of form is difficult because, under the approach taken here, this ATTRIBUTEE-argument

i. is expressed by the element of another construction anyway, which is why its form is not specified in Figures 5.30 and 5.31,

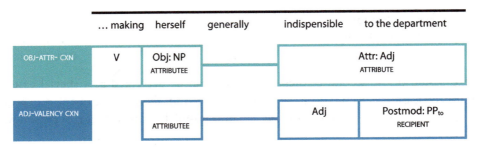

Figure 5.31 Partial construction grid for *making herself generally indispensable to the Department* showing the overlap of the OBJECT-ATTRIBUTE CONSTRUCTION and the ADJECTIVAL TO-RECIPIENT CONSTRUCTION. The ATTRIBUTEE-argument of the adjectival valency construction is realized by the Subj-argument of the OBJECT-ATTRIBUTE CONSTRUCTION. The single lines indicate that *generally* is not part of the adjectival argument structure construction

ii. can be realized by NPs, as in (99) and (100), for example, as well as by certain types of clause, as in (101):

(101) a. Understanding this paradox is crucial to grasping how terror operates in Machen's story.   COCA-2018-ACAD
b. That housing is unequally distributed today is obvious to all.   BNC-FR4-429

5.10.3 Adjectival argument structure constructions with prepositional phrases

We can identify different adjectival argument structure constructions by specifying the semantic role of the postmodifier argument. Let us just list a few examples:[84]

- ADJECTIVAL *TO*-RECIPIENT/GOAL CONSTRUCTION:

    (102) He's been very **kind** to me.   TV-2017-Poldark

- ADJECTIVAL *WITH*-PARTNER CONSTRUCTION:

    (103) a. Eva Geiringer, a Jewish girl who was **friendly** with Anne Frank ...
          COCA-2019-NEWS
    b. ... there's a ton of guys that we're **friendly** with and that we know on that staff.
          COCA-2019-SPOK

---

84. For a much more comprehensive account of adjective complementation in terms of semantic roles in a valency framework see Herbst (1983).

- ADJECTIVAL *ABOUT*-TOPIC-AREA CONSTRUCTION:

(104) a. I'm not very **good** about responding to texts and e-mails or voicemails.
  COCA-2017-SPOK

  b. I don't think they'd be **happy** about that. COCA-2019-SPOK

- ADJECTIVAL *AT*-CAUSER CONSTRUCTION:

(105) a. I am really **surprised** at how many people have jumped on board with this through Instagram, through Twitter. COCA-2019-SPOK

  b. But why are we **surprised** at our surprise? COCA-2019-SPOK

- ADJECTIVAL-*ON*-GOAL CONSTRUCTION:

(106) She doesn't sound too **keen** on the guy. TV-2010-Psych

5.10.4 Adjectival argument structure constructions with *that*- and *wh*-clauses

The postmodifier argument of adjectival argument structure constructions can also take the form of a *that*- or *wh*-clause, as in the following examples:

- ADJECTIVAL-*THAT*-CAUSER CONSTRUCTION:

(107) We're all a little **surprised** that it didn't work out, Carlton. TV-2007-Psych

- ADJECTIVAL-*WH*-TOPIC-AREA CONSTRUCTION:

(108) a. She's **undecided** whether to laugh or cry. COCA-2007-FIC
  b. She is always **uncertain** how to address her Head of Department. BNC-ANY-871

5.10.5 Different types of infinitive constructions with adjectives

In the previous two sections, we only provided a very short outline of some adjectival argument structure constructions with PPs and finite clauses. In this section, which deals with infinitival constructions, we will go into a little more detail – partly because the difference between (109a) and (109b) had received a considerable amount of attention in the generative literature of the 1960s:

(109) a. John is **easy** to please.
  b. John is **eager** to please.

In a constructionist framework, we can describe the different semantic relations exemplified in (109) in terms of different constructions and the semantic roles attributed to the slots identified in these constructions.

5.10.5.1 *DIFFICULT_ETC-TO-INFINITIVE CONSTRUCTION*

There is an interesting parallel between some impersonal infinitive constructions with Obj$_{NP}$ (as in (110)) and adjective constructions such as (111), in which the subject-argument can be seen as an ATTRIBUTEE:[85]

(110) a. It is very **difficult** to answer these questions without exploring our methods of teaching ... COCA-1990-ACAD
b. ... and it's **expensive** to buy advertising on this channel. COCA-2018-SPOK

(111) a. These questions are **difficult** to answer. COCA-2000-ACAD
b. New hardback books are **expensive** to buy ... COCA-2015-MAG

A similar parallel can be drawn in the case of some impersonal constructions with infinitive-constructions containing prepositional objects:

(112) a. It was easy to talk to her, probably too easy because sometimes she said something and he wondered if she were answering a question or telling something he needed to respond to. COCA-2013-FIC
b. ... it's expensive to live in California. COCA-2019-SPOK

(113) a. She is easy to talk to ... COCA-2011-MAG
b. The Atlanta metro area is expensive to live in ... COCA-2002-NEWS

The reason why we classify the subject-arguments of (112) and (113) as ATTRIBUTEES is that the construction as a whole expresses the ease or difficulty with which something can be done. We can thus establish a *DIFFICULT*$_{ETC}$-TO-INFINITIVE CONSTRUCTION:[86]

---

85. Chomsky's (1964: 60–65) drawing attention to the difference between *John is easy to please* and *John is eager to please* has given rise to a considerable amount of discussion within the generative framework, cf., e.g., Chomsky (1965: 162–163; 1970: 187–190) or Rezac (2006). See also Dirven & Radden (1977: 28–31) and Herbst (1983: 126–144).

86. The outline of the constructions in Section 5.10.5 is based on a paper entitled 'Constructionists are not at all easy to please' by Thomas Herbst and Peter Uhrig at the 10th International Conference on Construction Grammar in Paris in 2018.

Chapter 5. Who does what to whom? **119**

DIFFICULT_ETC-TO-INFINITIVE CONSTRUCTION		
EVALUATION of an ATTRIBUTEE in terms of the difficulty, etc. of carrying out an action affecting it		
ATTRIBUTEE	EVALUATION	ACTION
contextual anchor	Adj	postmod to-INF
	difficult easy necessary impossible essential simple cheap expensive good plain fun desirable reasonable terrible wonderful exciting tricky beautiful fast(er/est) costly awkward complex complicated excellent horrible ideal inexpensive interesting nice painful spectacular tough sweet amusing appalling clumsy cost-effective etc	to-infinitive clause whose unrealized object argument is provided by the contextual anchor
Frequency ranges of Adjs: 30 − 35%, 25 − 30%, 15 − 20%, > 5%, 1 − 5%, < 1% BNC		

Figure 5.32 The English *DIFFICULT*$_{ETC}$-*TO*-INFINITIVE CONSTRUCTION

The infinitive-clause must contain an argument structure construction with a slot for an Obj$_{NP}$ or an Obj$_{PP}$. These NPs are not realized in the infinitive clause, however, but form the subject of the larger construction. Figure 5.32 shows the most frequent adjectives occurring in the *DIFFICULT*-ETC-*TO*-INFINITIVE CONSTRUCTION, but a similar construction also occurs with other adjectives if these are premodified by *too* (see 7.2.1.3 for further details).

(114)   We stopped for soup that was **too** hot to eat.   COCA-2003-FIC

Semantically, the construction bears a certain resemblance to the MEDIOPASSIVE CONSTRUC-TION (cf. 5.8.4):

(115)   a.   The foam "wood" cuts easily with plastic tools and attaches neatly together with plas-
          tic screws.   COCA-2010-MAG
        b.   The menu also reads well, with more than a dozen starters ...   COCA-2010-NEWS

5.10.5.2   *WILLING*$_{ETC}$-*TO-INFINITIVE CONSTRUCTION*

Another construction with an adjective and an infinitive clause is the *WILLLING*-ETC-*TO*-INFINITIVE CONSTRUCTION, exemplified by

(116)   a.   Obama was keen to use the economic crisis as an opportunity to jump-start some
          renewable-energy projects.   COCA-2011-NEWS

120 A Construction Grammar of the English Language

b. I thought at the time she sounded a bit over anxious to explain why she hadn't told us before ... BNC-GW3-405

*WILLING*ETC*-TO*-INFINITIVE CONSTRUCTION		
Describing a POTENTIAL ÆFFECTOR'S ATTITUDE towards an ACTION		
POTENTIAL ÆFFECTOR	ATTITUDE	ACTION
contextual anchor	Adj	postmod
	prepared willing keen eager, etc.	*to*-infinitive clause whose unrealized subject argument is provided by the contextual anchor

Figure 5.33 *WILLING*ETC*-TO*-INFINITIVE CONSTRUCTION

In this case, the ÆFFECTOR argument of the infinitive-clause is referentially identical with the POTENTIAL ÆFFECTOR in the Subj slot of the construction.

5.10.5.3 *BRAVE*ETC*-TO-INFINITIVE CONSTRUCTION*

This is the same with the BE-*BRAVE*ETC*-TO*-V CONSTRUCTION, in which the ÆFFECTOR argument of the infinitive-clause is referentially identical with the ÆFFECTOR-subject of the construction. This construction has a different meaning from the previous one in that it does not highlight the subject's attitude towards a potential action, but expresses a speaker's evaluation of an ÆFFECTOR in the light of an action they have carried out. The construction is thus similar to the *NICE*ETC*-OF-YOU* CONSTRUCTION (5.10.6.4), which is also factive in the sense that both the assertive sentence (117a) and the non-assertive one (117b) have the same presupposition (117c) (see Figure 5.34 on the next page):

(117) a. Angela Merkel is wise to reject this Keynesian snake oil. NOW-12-05-21-US
      b. Angela Merkel is not wise to reject this Keynesian snake oil.
      c. Angela Merkel rejects this Keynesian snake oil.

5.10.5.4 *The SURPRISED*ETC*-TO-INFINITIVE CONSTRUCTION*

Another adjective+infinitive construction that we wish to identify is the following one – in which the infinitive-clause can be interpreted as causing a (mental) STATE in an UNDERGOER, as in

(118) a. ... we would of course be very sorry to lose you, you've been a tremendous asset to the Department, even in the short time you've been here. BNC-ANY-952
      b. Mister Trump is proud to pay a lower tax rate. COCA-2016-SPOK

Chapter 5. Who does what to whom? **121**

	BRAVE_ETC-TO-INFINITIVE CONSTRUCTION	
Speaker evaluation of an ÆFFECTOR in the light of an ACTION they have carried out		
ÆFFECTOR	ATTITUDE	ACTION
contextual anchor	Adj	postmod
	great brave wonderful foolish right unwise crazy	to-infinitive clause whose unrealized subject argument is provided by the contextual anchor

Figure 5.34 The English BRAVE_ETC-TO-INFINITIVE CONSTRUCTION

	SURPRISED_ETC-TO-INFINITIVE CONSTRUCTION	
Expression of the emotional state of an ÆFFECTOR in the light of an event		
UNDERGOER	STATE	CAUSE
contextual anchor	Adj	postmod
	happy pleased delighted glad surprised proud	to-infinitive clause whose unrealized subject argument is provided by the contextual anchor

Figure 5.35 The SURPRISED_ETC-TO-INFINITIVE CONSTRUCTION

5.10.5.5   *Adjective+infinitive constructions with quasi-modal meanings*

We can identify two more constructions with the same formal structure, which show a certain parallel to modal constructions in that they assess an event with respect to the subject's ability to performing the action in question and with respect to the speaker's assessment of it happening: The former we will refer to as the BE-ABLE_ETC-TO-V CONSTRUCTION:

(119) a. Whatever it is, he won't be able to get to sleep again.   BNC-ANY-10

b. To Robyn it seemed that critical theory had at last moved to its rightful place, centre-stage, in the theatre of history, and she was ready to play her part in the drama.

BNC-ANY-669

c. I'm inclined to agree with you.   BNC-ANY-1437

122 A Construction Grammar of the English Language

ABLE_{ETC}-TO-INFINITIVE CONSTRUCTION		
Describing a potential ÆFFECTOR's ABILITY to carry out an ACTION		
POTENTIAL ÆFFECTOR	ABILITY	ACTION
contextual anchor	Adj	postmod
	able unable ready entitled ideal unfitted qualified unsuitable well-positioned	to-infinitive clause whose unrealized subject argument is provided by the contextual anchor

Figure 5.36 *ABLE*_{ETC}-*TO*-INFINITIVE CONSTRUCTION

The second of these quasi-modal constructions is the BE-*LIKELY*_{ETC}-*TO*-V CONSTRUCTION:

(120) a. When was the last time we were supposed to have a world-beating aluminium engine? BNC-ANY-260

  b. Cut off from normal social intercourse with the adult world, relieved of inhibition by the ethos of the Permissive Society, the students were apt to run wild... BNC-ANY-588

  c. Well, I am supposed to be an expert on the industrial novel. BNC-ANY-1526

LIKELY_{ETC}-TO-INFINITIVE CONSTRUCTION		
Evaluation of the degree of likelihood/obligation of an event's taking place		
ÆFFECTOR	ATTITUDE	ACTION
contextual anchor	Adj	postmod
	likely supposed unlikely etc.	to-infinitive clause whose unrealized subject argument is provided by the contextual anchor

Figure 5.37 *LIKELY*_{ETC}-*TO*-INFINITIVE CONSTRUCTION

What distinguishes the constructions of 5.10.5.2–5 from the BE-*DIFFICULT*_{ETC}-*TO*-V CONSTRUCTION outlined in 5.10.5.1 is that the subject arguments of these constructions can also be seen as the non-expressed subject argument of the infinitive construction, whereas in the case of the BE-*DIFFICULT*ₑₜ𝒸-*TO*-V CONSTRUCTION the subject of the overall construction corresponds to an Obj$_{NP}$ or the NP of a prepositional object of the infinitive clause.

What we want to illustrate, however, is that despite this structural parallel there is a case to be made on the basis of semantic function and the semantic roles characterizing the various slots to postulate several constructions. It must be understood, however, that we are not suggesting that this is the only possible way of classifying these constructions, of course – for instance, one could imagine subsuming 'willingness' (Figure 5.33) and 'ability' (Figure 5.36) under one the same class.

5.10.6 Impersonal constructions with adjectives

5.10.6.1 *IT-THAT-CLAUSE CONSTRUCTION*

Finally, adjectives frequently occur in so-called impersonal constructions, which contain *it* as an obligatory element, which is realized as the subject of a SUBJECT-ATTRIBUTE CONSTRUCTION or the object of an OBJECT-ATTRIBUTE CONSTRUCTION.

(121) a. It is **indisputable** that climate change is human-caused and will alter ecosystems.
COCA-2019-MAG

    b. I do not consider it **possible** that a single radio host or a single TV host could get rid of a president.
COCA-1994-SPOK

    c. It is a **fact** that the waterways in our region determined the location of the city of Chicago and impacted our history.
COCA-2016-NEWS

In (121a), the construction blends with a SUBJECT-ATTRIBUTE CONSTRUCTION and in (121b), it combines with an OBJECT-ATTRIBUTE CONSTRUCTION. As (121c) shows, there is a parallel construction in which the ATTRIBUTE is an NP. The *that*-clause of this construction can also fill the subject slot of a SUBJECT-ATTRIBUTE CONSTRUCTION, as in sentences such as (122) (and as (122b) shows, the ATTRIBUTE of this construction can also be an NP):

(122) a. That all work here is of a craftsman's standard (and not that of an apprentice) is indisputable.
BNC-J2L-683

    b. That the minutes dragged was not his fault.
COCA-2004-FIC

In traditional accounts, such cases are often treated as extraposition and, accordingly, the *that*-clauses of (121) are often called "extraposed subjects". We consider *it* to be the subject of these clauses, and in order to avoid having two (albeit different kinds of) subjects in one clause, we will refer to the respective *that*-clauses simply as the element expressing the ATTRIBUTEE role. The advantage of this is that we can describe object-attribute constructions in the same way:

(123) At the time, Exxon's own scientists apparently made it clear to leadership that climate change was a threat.
COCA-2016-MAG

124 A Construction Grammar of the English Language

The *IT-THAT* CONSTRUCTION can thus be described as in Figure 5.38:

IT-THAT CONSTRUCTION		
Evaluation of an 'event'.		
CATAPHOR	ATTRIBUTE	ATTRIBUTEE
it	Adj	that-clause
	NP	

Figure 5.38 *IT-THAT* CONSTRUCTION

5.10.6.2 The *IT-BE-IMPORTANT$_{ETC}$-FOR-X-TO-INFINITIVE CONSTRUCTION*

A very similar communicative function to that of the *IT-THAT* CONSTRUCTION can be fulfilled by what we shall call the *IT-BE-IMPORTANT$_{ETC}$-FOR-X-TO-INFINITIVE* CONSTRUCTION as in (124):

(124) a. This is why I demanded that you come. This is why it is so important for you to be here. COCA-2012-FIC

   b. And it's essential for them to keep order, because in a situation like this there's a lot of desperate people. In the last ten minutes that we've been here, this line has pretty much doubled in size. COCA-2010-SPOK

   c. It is usual for a class to consist of between 12 and 16 students divided approximately equally between male and female ... BNC-A06-1317

   d. ...scientists emphasize that it's not enough for each country to carve out its own 30 percent. NYT-13-June-2021

We consider it appropriate to follow the analysis taken in the *Valency Dictionary of English* and to regard the combination of the PP_{for} + CL_{to-inf} as one constituent that corresponds to the *that*-clause in (121a) and, consequently, form an extraposed element. As with the *that*-clauses discussed above, a non-extraposed variant of the construction exists as well:

(125) a. For me to explode would have been absurd. BNC-CKM-411

   b. For a skiing development to win architectural prizes really is extraordinary ... BNC-G2W-772

IT-BE-*IMPORTANT$_{ETC}$-FOR-X-TO-INFINITIVE* CONSTRUCTION		
Evaluation of an 'event'		
CATAPHOR	ATTRIBUTE	ATTRIBUTEE
it	Adj	for NP to-INF

Figure 5.39 *IT-BE-IMPORTANT$_{ETC}$-FOR-X-TO-*INFNITIVE CONSTRUCTION

5.10.6.3 The IT-BE-IMPORTANT_{ETC}-FOR-BENEFICIARY-TO-INFINITIVE CONSTRUCTION

The IT-BE-*IMPORTANT*_{ETC}-*FOR*-X-*TO*-V CONSTRUCTION is not always easy to distinguish from another construction, which consists of the same formal elements, only that the PP_{for} and the infinitive clause can be seen as two separate constituents.

IT-BE-IMPORTANTETC-FOR-BENEFICIARY-TO-INFINITIVE CONSTRUCTION			
Evaluating an action or a potential action with respect to a BENEFICIARY			
CATAPHOR	ATTRIBUTE	BENEFICIARY	ATTRIBUTEE
it	Adj	for NP	to-INF

Figure 5.40 IT-BE-*IMPORTANT*_{ETC}-*FOR*-BENEFICIARY-TO-INFINITIVE-CONSTRUCTION

(126) a. So has it been nice for you to get all this praise?   COCA-1999-SPOK
     b. ... she thought it would be nice for her to get away ...   BNC-KP5-478
     c. Can I ask, do you really think it's good for the Democratic Party to go through hearings like they did, get the negative reaction of the American people. COCA-2006-SPOK
     d. It has also been shown that it is pleasant for children to copy words or rules for different activities ...   COCA-2010-ACAD
     e. It was difficult for the authorities to detect this cumulative process at work.
                                                      BNC-A64-1122

In these cases, the PP_{for} fulfils the function of a BENEFICIARY of the action expressed by the infinitive, which is not necessarily the case of the *IMPORTANT-FOR*-EVENT CONSTRUCTION. We have to say, however, that it is not always possible to keep the two readings strictly apart from one another, as in (127), for example, but the fronting of the PP_{for} as in (128) only allows the BENEFICIARY interpretation:

(127) It is vital **for every pilot** to learn to steer on the ground ...   BNC-A0H-825

(128) For many Communists, it is hard to break with the party that looked after them ...
                                                      BNC-ABG-34

5.10.6.4 The NICE_{ETC}-OF-X-TO-INFINITIVE CONSTRUCTION

Another impersonal adjective construction with a PP is the *NICE*_{ETC}-*OF*-X-*TO*-INFINITIVE CONSTRUCTION (Goldberg & Herbst 2021). In COCA, the most frequent adjective to occur in the construction is *nice*, whereas in the BNC it is *good* that occurs most frequently. Typical examples are:

(129) a. It's nice of you to say so.   COCA-2019-TV
     b. Oh, it was good of you to drop by, son.   TV-1988-Dynasty

c. It's so good of you *to stay*, Mama. It's good of you *to ask me*, Cora.   TV-2015-Downton

The construction provides an assessment of a person on the basis of an action they have carried out.[87] In fact, the *NICE*$_{ETC}$-*OF-X-TO*-V CONSTRUCTION is factive because both (130a) and (130b) presuppose (130c) (Kiparsky & Kiparsky 1971; Herbst 1983; Goldberg & Herbst 2021):

(130) a. ... it's not nice of you *to say that*.   COCA-2001-FIC
      b. Well, it's nice of you *to say that*.   COCA-2007-SPOK
      c. You said that!   COCA-2018-SPOK

Interestingly, the tense of the construction refers to the time when the action was carried out and not to the time of the assessment.

NICE$_{ETC}$-*OF-X-TO*-INFINITIVE CONSTRUCTION			
EVALUATION OF HOW AN ACTION REFLECTS ON ITS ÆFFECTOR			
CATAPHOR	EVALUATION	ÆFFECTOR	ACTION
it	Adj	of NP	to-INF

Figure 5.41 The English *NICE*$_{ETC}$-*OF-X-TO*-INFINITIVE CONSTRUCTION

The *NICE*$_{ETC}$-*OF-X-TO*-V CONSTRUCTION often occurs in the form of fragments such as:

(131) a. Oh! How stupid of me.   TV-2013-Downton
      b. How kind of you *to let me come*!   MyFairLady

5.10.6.5 *Impersonal adjective construction without PPs*

There exists also a plain impersonal adjective construction with a *to*-infinitive, which simply expresses an evaluation of an action or a state in rather general terms (see Figure 5.42 on the next page):

(132) a. It's good *to see you*.   COCA-2019-FIC
      b. Thanks for having me. It's good *to be with you*.   COCA-2019-SPOK
      c. I think when you're talking about infrastructure, it's really easy – it's important, actually – *to talk about some of the things that allow for reduced emissions*," said Ms. Murkowski, who has helped to write climate legislation in the past.   NYT-9-June-2021

5.11 Nominal argument structure constructions

If we look at examples such as (133), it is tempting to apply a similar approach to the one taken for adjectives to nominal argument structure constructions:

---

87. For details of the construction see Goldberg & Herbst (2021).

IMPERSONAL EVALUATIVE CONSTRUCTION		
EVALUATION of an ACTION		
CATAPHOR	EVALUATION	ACTION
it	Adj	to-INF

Figure 5.42 IMPERSONAL EVALUATIVE CONSTRUCTION WITH ADJECTIVE

(133) a. President Biden's meeting with Dr. Anthony Fauci and members of his Covid Response Team   NOW-21-11-17-US

      b. Vice President Kamala Harris met with Emmanuel Macron, the French president ...   NOW-21-11-10-US

It is part of the frame semantic knowledge of speakers that just as one person alone cannot meet, a meeting involves more than one person – which is a parallel between (133a) and (133b). On the other hand, the construal of the situation is quite different in that the verb *meet* describes an activity and the noun *meeting* "an instance of assembling" (OED online s.v. *meeting*, n.). This is even more obvious in cases such as (134):

(134) a. ... this city's plan for a new urban life style ...   NYT-28-Jan-1993

      b. I don't think that Canada will ever forget the will or the wish of Quebecers to leave their nation.   COCA-1995-SPOK

It seems rather likely that (134a) will primarily be interpreted as a plan that the city in question is intending to do rather than as an activity carried out by it.[88] In other words, the POSSESSOR-interpretation typically associated with a GENITIVE NP CONSTRUCTION is more prominent than the evocation of an ÆFFECTOR. We can thus say that the case for interpreting *President Biden* in (133a) or *the city* and *Quebecers* in (134) as identifying an argument of the nouns in question is relatively weak. Irrespective of that, we can identify nominal constructions that have a very similar semantic function to verbal and adjectival argument structure constructions by attributing the corresponding semantic roles to the postmodifier arguments. Constructions with PPs include the following:

–   NOMINAL-*WITH*-PARTNER CONSTRUCTION:

    (135) Trump's meeting with Al Gore   NYT-5-Dec-2016

–   NOMINAL-*TO*-RECIPIENT CONSTRUCTION:

    (136) ... her traditional Christmas address to the nation.   NOW-20-01-08-US

---

88. It is true that (134a) implies that the activity of planning has taken place, but since the plan is the outcome of this planning, the noun *plan* does not necessarily relate to the PLANNER in the same way.

128 A Construction Grammar of the English Language

– NOMINAL-*FOR*-GOAL CONSTRUCTION:

(137) ... eagerness for scientific knowledge ...   COCA-2017-ACAD

Clausal postmodifier constructions often specify the meaning of the noun in a kind of appositional way (see Schmid's (2000) analysis of shell nouns):

– NOMINAL-*TO*-INFINITIVE CONSTRUCTIONS:

(138) Britain's vote to leave the European Union.   COCA-2017-SPOK

– NOMINAL-*THAT*-CLAUSE CONSTRUCTIONS:

(139) the claim that there were millions of fraudulent votes in this election
                                                                 COCA-2017-SPOK

– NOMINAL-*WH*-CLAUSE CONSTRUCTIONS:

(140) the question whether homosexuals could marry   COCA-2008-ACAD

– NOMINAL-*WH-TO*-INFINITIVE CONSTRUCTIONS

(141) the decision whether to rent or buy   COCA-2008-NEWS

What distinguishes these constructions from other POSTMODIFIER-OF-NOUN CONSTRUCTIONS is that they their occurrence is much more closely related to the items that occur in them so that we will refer to them as item-related valency constructions.

5.12 A network of argument structure constructions

Up to this point, we have described argument structure constructions according to whether the non-argument slots are filled by verbs, adjectives or nouns. Nevertheless, and the outline of the previous sections has already shown examples of this, there are also interesting areas of overlap. Thus, and we will give only a few examples here, we find the following kinds of argument structure constructions for all three word classes:

i. constructions containing a [PP$_{to}$^{RECIPIENT}]:

(142) a. verbal: She sent an e-mail to her team ...   COCA-2019-MAG
       b. adjectival: He's very generous to charities.   COCA-1992-MOV
       c. nominal: He plans to make an address to the nation around 10:00 Eastern time
           this morning.   COCA-1996-SPOK

ii. constructions containing a [PP$_{for}^{GOAL}$]:

(143) a. verbal: Kind of makes you long for the good old days. TV-1981-Dynasty

b. adjectival: Those eager for a female candidate may be able to choose between Senator Kamala Harris of California, who is expected to announce a presidential campaign this month, and other potential candidates ... COCA-2019-NEWS

c. nominal: Your desire for a peaceful resolution is blinding you from the truth. TV-2005-Enterprise

iii. constructions containing a [to-INF^{GOAL}]:

(144) a. verbal: And he wants to die in a monsoon of bullets. TV-2014-Psych

b. adjectival: Thomas is keen to be promoted. TV-2012-Downton

c. nominal: ... his ambition to make Scotland a European power. COCA-2013-MAG

These few examples may suffice to give an impression of the immense complexity of the network of constructions that makes up a speaker's constructicon. In the cases illustrated in (142)–(144), the same semantic role can be expressed by the same form across word classes. What this means is that we may be able to identify form-meaning packages, i.e., constructions, that can fill the respective slots in verbal, adjectival and nominal argument structure constructions. This is theoretically interesting in that it shows that the view held in Radical Construction Grammar, that semantic roles can only be defined for specific constructions (Croft 2001, 2013), does not necessarily hold generally. Furthermore, these observations raise the question of whether, and if so, to what extent we can identify argument structure constructions which are not bound to a particular word class. For instance, one could imagine postulating impersonal constructions that evaluate 'propositions' expressed by *that*-clauses and allow for the EVALUATION to be expressed by an adjective or a noun phrase, as shown in Table 5.2:

Table 5.2 Impersonal constructions

It	BE	EVALUATION	EVALUATEE
it	is	no surprise	that his theory is thus more complex than that of his predecessors (COCA-2016-ACAD)
it	comes as	little surprise	that he was a more or less willing accomplice in these activities for much of his career. (COCA-2008-MAG)
it	's	interesting	that you bring that up. (COCA-2017-SPOK)
It	's	stupid	that this has gone on as long as it has. (COCA-2017-SPOK)
		an act of supreme betrayal	

5.13 Argument structure in CASA and other approaches

In this chapter, we outlined a constructionist approach to argument structure constructions – which means that CASA tries to posit constructional templates only if these can be said to have some cognitive plausibility. As far as the purely descriptive side is concerned, it must be pointed out, however, that our approach owes a lot to the extensive description of what is often called English verb complementation. Our analyses are, e.g., heavily informed by the respective chapters of the big reference grammars of present-day English, CGEL (1985) and CAMG (2002) as well as theoretical work, carried out in the frameworks of valency theory, case grammar and FrameNet.

> **Valency theory**: Tesnière's (1959/2015) Dependency Grammar, which has given rise to the development of Valency Theory in Germany and other European countries.[89] Dependency and valency models attribute a central role to the verb in the analysis of sentence structure because, to a certain extent, they see number and type of other elements that occur in the sentence as a property of the verb. In a rather simplified form, the model can be described as follows:
>
> - A verb opens up a certain number of complement (or argument) slots. The number of slots is the verb's valency, correspondingly, one can distinguish between monovalent, divalent and trivalent verbs.
> - The elements that fill the slots, the complements, are determined in their form by the governing verb. These complements can be noun phrases, prepositional phrases, *that*-clauses, *to*-infinitives, etc.
> - Semantically, complements express the participant roles associated with the respective valency slots.
>
> Under this view, *give* in *You're giving Mummy a lovely cuddle ...* (t2_00_18) can be analyzed as a trivalent verb with three noun phrase complements with the participant roles GIVER, GIVEE and THING GIVEN. The valency approach takes a focus on describing individual valency carriers (verbs, adjectives or nouns) and it is thus not surprising that it has resulted in the publication of specialized valency dictionaries such as the *Wörterbuch zur Valenz und Distribution deutscher Verben* (Helbig & Schenkel 1973), VALBU (Schumacher et al., 2004) and the *Valency Dictionary of English* (Herbst et al. 2004). Compared with Goldberg's (2006) model, valency accounts put a stronger emphasis on form and aim at a comprehensive coverage of all valency patterns to be found in a language; cf. the Erlangen Valency Patternbank (www.patternbank.fau.de). However, valency theory does not consider the patterns identified as meaningful in themselves and represents a descriptive, but not a cognitive approach towards language. It thus makes sense to combine the two approaches if we

---

89. For a summary of dependency and valency approaches see Herbst (2020b); for dependency and constituency in a cognitive framework see Langacker (2020: 15–19).

want to account for all the relevant facts (Stefanowitsch 2011a; Herbst 2011a, 2014a, b; Goldberg 2019; see also Welke 2011, 2019).

FrameNet: Another related approach is that of Fillmore's (1968) Case Grammar, which eventually developed into a theory of semantic frames and the specification of frames and valence patterns in the FrameNet project (https://framenet.icsi.berkeley.edu/fndrupal/; see also Boas, Ruppenhofer & Baker 2024). The idea of semantic roles developed by Fillmore (1968) has become central to many theories of syntax, including Valency Theory and Construction Grammar. In many respects, Fillmore's (1968) approach and the notion of valency are perfectly compatible, the main difference being that case grammar and also FrameNet take semantic roles as the starting point and then show how these roles can be expressed at the level of form, whereas valency descriptions first specify the complements of a verb with respect to form and then attribute semantic roles to them (see also Fillmore 2007).

CHAPTER 6

Referring to, describing and evaluating things
Nominal constructions

6.1   Nouns and pronouns in language acquisition

The task that L1-learners face when learning the vocabulary of their language is by no means trivial. This is because not only do they have to identify words and work out and learn the meanings of words, but they also have to abstract from the different word forms (such as *bus, bus's* and *buses*) and relate them to one lexeme as well as detect and remember the constructions and contexts in which the words are being used.

Although nouns have an important function for young children in terms of referring to categorizing the 'things' of the world around them, there is no evidence for the claim that they are easier to learn than verbs (Rothweiler & Meibauer 1999: 15–16; Ambridge & Lieven 2011: 69–70). We cannot go into the details of word learning here, but from the point of view of the end product of this process it is clear that amongst other things children will have to learn is that there are different classes of words which have very similar functions:

1.   Words which – in the particular communicative situation the child finds themselves in – tend to be used for one particular person, animal, place or a toy 'thing'.
2.   Words that can be used to refer to or describe 'things' that are relatively discrete and can be counted.
3.   Words that can be used to refer to or describe 'things' that are construed as substances and cannot be counted because they have such a big extension that one cannot identify their beginning and their end or because they consist of an immense number of small particles.
4.   Words that one can use to refer to different people or 'things' without describing them.

Obviously, these four different categories reflect the centuries-old distinction between proper nouns (i.e., names), count nouns, uncount (or mass) nouns, and pronouns. As we are going to point out in 6.2.4, it is debatable whether these differences are best captured in terms of the meaning associated with individual words or in terms of the meaning of the constructions in which they occur (or possibly both). In any case, within a usage-based approach, the assumption is that children arrive at this kind of knowledge by detecting patterns of use in the input they receive. Thus, they will notice, for instance, whether the words occur after words such as *a/an, the*, after numbers, whether there exist forms with and without an ending such as /s/, /z/ or /ɪz/, whether it is used together with verb forms such as *is* and *goes* or *are* and *go*.

Before we go on to illustrate the various nominal constructions that may give rise to the formation of these categories, we will make a few remarks about the nature of nouns and noun phrases from a cognitive and constructionist point of view.

Chapter 6. Referring to, describing and evaluating things 133

6.2 Characteristics of NP-constructions

6.2.1 NPs can fill the same slots

In the description of argument structure constructions in the previous chapter we characterized many argument slots as noun phrases or NPs, a term that is established in many other models of syntax, too (see Hoffmann 2022b: 114–138). **Noun phrases** or – in Langacker's (2008a) terminology – **nominals** come in quite different forms, as you can see by looking at sentence (1).

(1) What is remarkable about Amsterdam is that while it has one of the largest and most intensely used historic city centers of Europe, its plan to curtail traffic is more radical than that of any other regional capital. NYT-28-Jan-1993

This sentence contains the following noun phrases (NPs), some of which (namely e, f, h and j) are parts of larger noun phrases:

(1) a. what
b. Amsterdam
c. it
d. one of the largest and most intensely used historic city centers of Europe
e. the largest and most intensely used historic city centers of Europe
f. Europe
g. its plan to curtail traffic
h. traffic
i. that of any other regional capital
j. any other regional capital

Why should this panoply of different forms be subsumed under one label? One reason for this is that they are all capable of doing the same job in that they can fulfill the same syntactic function, namely that they can occur as subjects (2a–c), objects or after a preposition in a prepositional phrase.

(2) a. One of the largest and most intensely used historic city centers of Europe was paralyzed by ice.
b. Amsterdam was paralyzed by ice.
c. It was paralyzed by ice.

6.2.2 NPs can be used to refer to 'things'

6.2.2.1 *Reference*

The second reason lies in the semantic function of noun phrases, namely that they can be used to establish **reference**.

Reference is an extremely complex concept that aims to capture the relation between linguistic expressions and the 'things' in the world(s) we associate them with. We use the term 'thing' here in the technical sense introduced by Langacker (2008a), namely as a cover term for objects, people, ideas or concepts. In this sense, 'thing' is a very abstract mental category that construes something as a bounded entity (a metaphorical thing so to speak). In Example (1), *Amsterdam* refers to the capital of the Netherlands, as does *it* (while *its* refers to something that 'belongs to' Amsterdam). While *Amsterdam* or *Europe* are definitely 'things' we would consider to exist in the real world of our experience, linguistic expressions can also refer to 'things' that only exist in a particular conceptual world of our imagination – such as the *Downton Abbey* of the TV series, the *Rummidge* of the university novels by Lodge or the *Westeros* and *Essos* or any of the characters appearing in them. In fact, there is, as Langacker (2008a: 270) points out, no difference between the linguistic means we use for referring to things that exist "in reality" or to things that are part of some imagined world: So a sentence such as (3a), which is taken from the Website of the CALP3 conference, refers to a conference in the real world, whereas (3b), taken from David Lodge's *Nice Work*, refers to a conference in the fictional world of a novel:

(3) a. The conference will take place in the Texas Union (UNB) in the Quadrangle Room and Santa Rita Suite (Level 3). Website of CALP3

    b. 'I had an invitation to a conference in Florida,' says Philip Swallow wistfully.

BNC-ANY-922

These examples demonstrate an important difference with respect to two different types of reference, which linguists label **definite** and **indefinite reference**: Speakers and writers unconsciously keep track of what their hearers/readers (might) know. In (3a) the speaker refers to a particular conference and expects the reader to be able to identify that conference. (If a hearer cannot do this, they might say something like 'Which conference is he talking about?') In (3b), the speaker does not, at this point of the discourse, expect the addressee to identify the specific conference he was invited to – he thus only refers to one of the types of 'things' covered by the expression *conference*. The distinction between definite and indefinite reference is made apparent by speakers through the use of the respective nouns in particular constructions. By using the noun *election* in the construction *the + noun* in (4a), the speaker is establishing definite reference to a 'thing', in this case the 2020 Presidential elections in the United States:

(4) a. President Biden won the election by about seven million votes…

NOW-CNN-21-02-02-US

    b. … you can't win an election without knowing how to raise money. COCA-2018-SPOK

In (4b), this is not the case in quite the same way. The speaker does not necessarily have a particular election in mind but is referring only to one unspecified event of that kind

Chapter 6. Referring to, describing and evaluating things 135

(which, in this case, can be interpreted as being typical of elections in general). As these examples show, from a cognitive point of view we cannot entertain the traditional idea of reference as an act that a speaker performs to identify one particular element out of the set of all 'things' that a word potentially can be used to refer to (called the denotatum in structural theories of semantics).

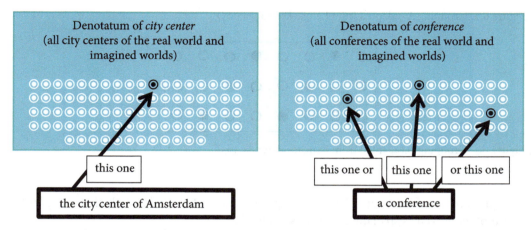

Figure 6.1 Left: City center of Amsterdam ⊙ as referent of the definite noun phrase *the city center of Amsterdam*. Right: Indefinite reference of the noun phrase *a conference*, which refers to one of the elements of the denotatum without specifying to which one

This is also not quite so straightforward with nouns such as *traffic* or *ice* where a distinction between reference and denotatum in the traditional sense of these terms is difficult to draw.[90] Langacker (2008a: 282) shows a way out of this dilemma by focusing on the mental processes of construal that underlie these phenomena. He introduces the notion of "coordinated mental reference, where the speaker and hearer momentarily direct their attention to the same thing instance".

In order to follow Langacker's (2008a: 104–106) line of argument, we can carry out several steps:[91]

i. Human cognition is based on a number of general cognitive processes and mechanisms, which include **grouping** and **reification**.
ii. Grouping can be illustrated by Figure 6.2, which we will perceive as containing a set of three black dots and a set of two black dots rather than one set of five dots.

---

90. See Langacker's (2008a: 279–280) discussion of maximal extension.
91. A classical structuralist position is that a purely semantic approach towards parts of speech does not work. As Langacker points out, however, the above "schematic characterization would seem to have a real chance of being viable" (Langacker 2008a: 106).

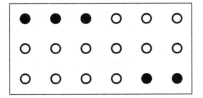

Figure 6.2 Grouping A (adapted from Langacker 2008a: 105)

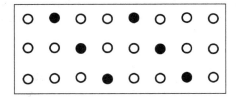

Figure 6.3 Grouping B (adapted from Langacker 2008a: 105)

In Figure 6.3, however, we are likely to recognize two sets of black dots (which are similar to one another as well as spatially congruous or close).

iii. **Reification** describes the process of referring to groups as unitary entities such as when we perceive the dots in Figure 6.3 as parallel because then we are talking about two lines of dots and not the individual dots.

iv. Given the concepts of grouping and reification, a **thing** can be defined "as any product of grouping and reification" (Langacker 2008a: 105) or, in a more general way as "a set of interconnected entities which function as a single entity at a higher level of conceptual organization" (Langacker 2008a: 107).

It is on the basis of such considerations that Langacker (2008a: 106) formulates what he calls a basic proposal of Cognitive Grammar – namely that "**a noun profiles a thing**".

If we apply this definition to those words in sentence (1) that we (and probably all other linguists) consider to be nouns, then this works pretty well: *Amsterdam, city center,* and *Europe* can certainly be seen as bounded entities, which can be identified and pointed at on a map, for instance – even if in cases it may be difficult to define the boundaries of a capital (or even Europe) sharply. Equally, *capital* quite clearly denotes a thing, and so do *plan* and *traffic*: that they are perceived as single entities "at a higher level of conceptual organization" is shown by the fact that, once introduced in the discourse, both can be referred to by *it*. Although a *plan* – like Langacker's (2008a: 106) example *recipe* – does not "exist in space" and although it may involve a number of different measures, these measures must certainly be perceived as forming an interconnected thing if they are to be called a *plan*. Thus, it seems that the idea that nouns profile things is a rather convincing one. As can be

Chapter 6. Referring to, describing and evaluating things **137**

seen in (1), for example, however, it also applies to *what* or *it*, and is thus more adequately seen as a description of a noun phrase (and not just nouns).[92]

6.2.2.2 *Grounding elements*

It is in this context that Langacker's concept of ground is extremely helpful, which he defines as follows (2008a: 259):[93]

> The term **ground** is used in CG [Cognitive Grammar] to indicate the speech event, its participants (speaker and hearer), their interaction, and the immediate circumstances (notably, the time and place of speaking). A grounding element specifies the status vis-à-vis the ground of the thing profiled by a nominal ... Through nominal grounding (e.g., *the, this, that, some, a, each, every, no, any*), the speaker directs the hearer's attention to the intended discourse referent, which may or may not correspond to an actual individual.

If a noun phrase consists of only one word (*Amsterdam, it, conferences*), this word serves as a grounding element as well as establishing a relation to a 'thing'. More typically, perhaps, noun phrases contain a grounding element and a noun, as in (5):

(5) a. What time do you turn those lights on?   TV-2007-Psych
     b. Can I say something about the case, please?   TV-2006-Psych
     c. What's a poetry slam?   COCA-2013-TV
     d. Maybe because you don't have a meteorologist's name.   TV-2007-Psych

We will base our discussion of noun-phrase constructions on the following two basic types:

– phrases that consist of a grounding element (which we will call a **pre-head** or a **determiner**) and a noun (called a **head** in many approaches) such as *what time, those lights, a poetry slam* in (5),
– phrases that consist of only one word (the **head**, if you like) which either is a grounding element per se like *that* in (6a) or encapsulates the grounding element as in (6b):

(6) a. That's not funny, Fallon.   TV-1981-Dynasty
     b. Also, Princeton is increasing its undergraduate scholarship budget by 13 percent.
       COCA-2009-NEWS

More complex noun phrases will be accounted for as combinations of such basic NP constructions with pre- and postmodifier-of-noun constructions (see 6.10.2).

---

92. Langacker (2008a: 122–123) points this out himself and includes pronouns, demonstratives, and articles in the class of nouns, using the term lexical nouns for the more classic cases.

93. Cf. also the discussion in Radden and Dirven (2007: 87–113) and the outline provided by Bierwiaczonek (2016: 27–41).

6.2.3 A family of NP-constructions

It is thus the combination of constructional meaning and the meaning of nouns that enables speakers to create reference – the respective constructions fall under the category of **noun phrase (NP) constructions**, as do constructions such as *what, it*, etc., which share the same properties with respect to syntactic and semantic function. However, given the great diversity of form of noun phrases exemplified by (1), it does not seem appropriate to speak of one single NP-construction. Instead, we see noun phrase as a cover term for a **family of constructions**, all of which have a coherent identity in terms of a form-meaning pairing.[94]

Thus, as we will show below, there are very good reasons for identifying meso-constructions (constructional instances that are partly or fully lexically specified) such as

- NAME-NP CONSTRUCTIONS (*Amsterdam, Prof. Adele E. Goldberg*),
- INDEFINITE-NP CONSTRUCTIONS (*a conference, conferences*),
- DEFINITE-NP CONSTRUCTIONS (*the conference, the conferences*),
- different types of QUANTIFIER-NP CONSTRUCTIONS (*some wine, two cappuccinos*).

Structuralist models tend to have a general template for NPs of the sort: determiner – pre-modifier – head – postmodifier (CGEL 1985: 62; Aarts & Aarts 1988: 105; CAMG: 329–333; and Aarts 2011). This raises the problem that – in the terminologies of these models – some of the units that are classified as NPs do not contain a noun, whereas others do not contain a determiner, which has led to a great deal of discussion about the nature of heads, and the question of whether instead of noun phrases it could be more appropriate to identify determiner phrases (cf., e.g., Hudson 1984: 90–92 (determiners as heads of NPs); Matthews 2007: 61–78; Radford 1993 (co-headedness); CAMG (fused heads); Herbst & Schüller 2008 (nominal head complexes); for recent surveys see Sommerer 2018; Keizer 2020; and also Keizer 2007: 9–21; CAMG: 329–330, further distinguishes between nominals and noun phrases, heads and ultimate heads.)[95]

6.2.4 Proper nouns, count and mass nouns

Noun phrases thus provide a good example of the way the meaning of an expression is the result of combining the semantic function of a grammatical construction and the meaning of a particular noun (in the light of a given context).

For instance, while it is perfectly possible for nouns such as *Amsterdam, traffic* or *wine* to occur as noun phrases of their own, this is hardly conceivable with a noun such as *conference*:

---

94. For a more detailed discussion of noun phrases in a constructionist framework see Hoffmann (2022b: 114–138).

95. For a classification of constructions in terms of heads (i.e. phrase-headed, noun-headed constructions, etc. see Bierwiaczonek 2016).

Chapter 6. Referring to, describing and evaluating things **139**

(7) a. Amsterdam has substantial parking problems... BNC-J35-629
   b. Traffic now accounts for 51 per cent of total nitrogen oxide emissions, compared to 31 per cent in 1980. BNC-J36-522
   c. Wine, free and copious at both lunch and dinner, overcomes language problems.
                                                       BNC-AMW-1085

Furthermore, while the uses of *Amsterdam* in (1) and (7a) constitute a classic case of definite reference, *conference* has to be used in the definite construction with *the* as in (3a) to achieve this effect. In fact, if nouns such as *Amsterdam* or *linguistics* are used in an indefinite NP or definite NP construction, they tend to be used in a rather restricted way, usually made explicit by a postmodifier (see 6.10.2):

(8) a. And the lyrics, whether evoking an Amsterdam where "men dressed up in Gauloise smoke quote Marx right back at you" or the pain of missing life while you're "working your wound," shame the usual Broadway treacle. COCA-2009-MAG
   b. It was the Prague School that ... reformulated Formalist literary theory within the framework of a linguistics which shared most of Saussure's fundamental principles, and to which they attached the label structuralism. BNC-H8V-410

You can test this by assessing the plausibility of the occurrence of the following sentences, for instance:

(9) a. I'd like to read a book about a conference/??an Amsterdam/??a linguistics.
   b. Let's talk about the conference/??the Amsterdam/??the linguistics.

Despite these parallels between *Amsterdam* and *linguistics*, these nouns differ with respect to their occurrence in quantifier constructions:

(10) a. Time for some linguistics. NOW-14-11-19-GB
    b. ??Time for some Amsterdam.[96]

These differences between nouns are, as Langacker (2008a: 128) underscores, **symptomatic** of underlying conceptual differences between the respective nouns, which have long been recognized in grammar writing, where, as mentioned before, it is quite common to make a distinction between the following classes of nouns:

– **count nouns**, which, in the terminology introduced above, can be used to refer to a number of discernible 'things' from a set with the number being anything from 0 (*no conference*), through 1 (*a/one conference*), or several (*two, three, some*, etc. *conferences*) to the totality of the set (*all conferences*);

---

96. As an anonymous reviewer points out, (10b) might, however, be acceptable under certain salience conditions.

- **mass nouns** (or *noncount nouns*), which express the conceptualization of a 'thing' as a whole, and which can be used to refer to the 'thing' as such (*linguistics, wine*) or a certain quantity of the 'thing' (*some linguistics; Would you like some wine?*), but which do not allow for individualization;
- **proper nouns** (names, or proper names), which have a unique referent (*Amsterdam, Goldberg*, etc.).

It has to be understood, however, that the reason why we can call *linguistics* a mass noun and *conference* a count noun is that these words tend to be used exclusively in a way that corresponds to the semantics of the prototypes of count and mass nouns and the constructions associated with them. Very many nouns, however, do not fall so clearly into just one of these categories. Take a word such as *language*, for example, which receives a *count* or *mass* interpretation depending on the construction in which it used:

(11) a. It's Vianessian. – That's not a language. TV-Psych-2009
  b. Yet language was not necessarily designed for the convenience or predilections of the analyst. (Langacker 2008: 13)

And, in fact, *Language* can also be used as a proper noun when referring to the journal of the Linguistics Society of America. We thus very often cannot decide whether a particular interpretation is primarily due to what speakers know about a word or whether it mainly comes from the construction. In a constructionist framework, we expect a speaker's knowledge of words to be inseparably linked to knowledge of the constructions in which they have been experienced anyway. What we have to recognize, however, is that there is a considerable amount of idiosyncrasy involved in that some freely occur in constructions characteristic of a conceptualization in terms of count and mass, whereas others are only established in one of them. We can thus make out a case for referring to nouns which show an almost exclusive preference as mass nouns or count nouns. Nevertheless, even in these cases creative construal cannot be ruled out:

(12) a. And a lot of pie made it up here tonight. COCA-2011-MOV
  b. But, yeah, this is a lot of dog. COCA-2007-SPOK

In other cases, however, such non-prototypical uses are relatively unlikely to occur because the respective meanings can be expressed in established ways already: thus, a potential creative use of the mass noun *furniture* is bound to be pre-empted by the existence of the expression *a piece of furniture*, for example. In any case, what this discussion shows is that it is particular constructions that contribute to an interpretation of a noun phrase in terms of a particular kind of conceptualization. We will thus make use of these labels in the description of NP-constructions in the next sections.

6.3 Indefinite NP-constructions

There are two factors that complicate the description of indefinite and definite NP-constructions. First of all, the contrast between constructions with the indefinite article *a* and the definite article *the* is realized in a different way with plural nouns:

(13) a. … not all the conferences that are going on this summer are concerned with English literature …   Lodge-SmallWorld-233
     b. If you didn't spend so much time going to conferences, Angie, you would have gotten your doctorate by now…   Lodge-SmallWorld-279

Indefiniteness is thus signaled by a construction without an article in the case of plural nouns. The same is true, however, and this is the second complication, of noun senses that have no plural forms such as *wine* or *linguistics*, where sentences such as the ones under (14) have indefinite reference:

(14) a. Wine is not an investment if you drink it as soon as you buy it.   COCA-2019-SPOOK
     b. Linguistics is shifting from a social science to a data science…   COCA-2018-ACAD

We can capture these differences by drawing on the widely-established distinction between **count nouns** (which show a singular-plural contrast) and **mass or non-count nouns** (which do not). It is easy to see the underlying distinction:

On this basis, we can identify three indefinite NP-constructions:

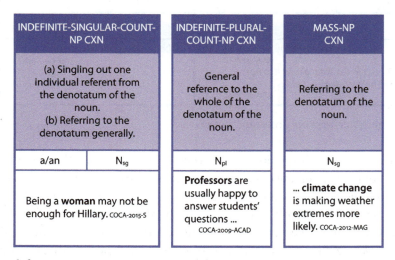

Figure 6.4 Indefinite-count NP constructions and the MASS-NP CONSTRUCTION

There is an obvious parallel both in form and semantic function between THE INDEFINITE-PLURAL-COUNT-NP CONSTRUCTION and the MASS-NP CONSTRUCTION (Langacker 2008a: 130–131; Radden & Dirven 2007: 63–86; Hoffmann 2022b: 114–138):

(15)   … there'll be wine and cocktails too??   TV-2013-Psych

When occurring as the subject of a finite clause, the two constructions differ with respect to concord with the finite verb:

(16)   a.   Wine is culture.   COCA-2009-MAG
        b.   Drinks come free at meals you'll be pleased to know.   BNC-AMV-334

6.4   Definite NP-constructions

6.4.1   *the* + nouns

Definite NP-constructions with nouns are made up of the **definite article** *the* and a noun and have an identifying and referential function.

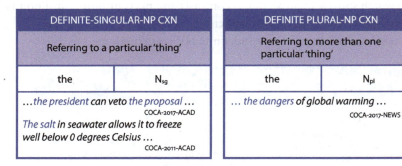

Figure 6.5 English DEFINITE-NP CONSTRUCTIONS

As far as the count/mass-distinction is concerned, it is obvious that the plural is an indication of countability, but arguably in certain contexts constructs such as *the milk, the salt* or *the gossip* also indicate what Radden and Dirven (2007: 64–66) refer to as boundedness in that they are perceived as *gestalts* with identifiable borders just like *the book* or *the coast*. We thus see no need to apply the distinction to definite NP-constructions with singular nouns. The same is true of demonstrative NP-constructions, which will be discussed in the next section (6.3.3).

Definite reference can also be expressed by a number of lexical constructions, namely the following (cf. Hoffmann 2022b: 123–128):

– DEFINITE REFERENTIAL NP-CONSTRUCTIONS
– DEFINITE REFLEXIVE NP-CONSTRUCTIONS
– DEFINITE RECIPROCAL NP-CONSTRUCTIONS.

These constructions are formally realized by pronouns, which means that the categories number (singular – plural), case (nominative – accusative – genitive) and person (1st – 2nd – 3rd) will have to be considered. Since not all pronouns make the same number of distinctions, we find it useful to describe each lexical form (e.g., *I, we, my, mine, me*) as separate constructions, although generalizations across several items are certainly possible. This leads to a rather large inventory of constructions, but since they are all rather frequent it is not unreasonable to assume that they are indeed stored individually as separate constructions in the brain.

6.4.2 Personal pronoun constructions

Definite referential NP-constructions with personal pronouns can be described as follows:

Form: **personal pronoun**
Meaning: Reference to a 'thing' that can only be identified through the linguistic or extralinguistic context

The following definite referential NP-constructions can be distinguished:

Name	Form	Meaning	Explicit description
		Reference to ...	
I-CXN	I	... speaker	DEFINITE-1ST-PERSON NOMINATIVE-SINGULAR CXN
ME-CXN	me	... speaker (non-agent)	DEFINITE-1ST-PERSON-ACCUSATIVE-SINGULAR CXN
WE-CXN	we	... group including speaker	DEFINITE-1ST-PERSON-NOMINATIVE-PLURAL CXN
US-CXN	us	... group including speaker	DEFINITE-1ST-PERSON-ACCUSATIVE-PLURAL CXN
YOU-CXN	you	... person(s) addressed	DEFINITE-2ND-PERSON CXN
HE-CXN	he	... male person or animal	DEFINITE-3RD-PERSON-NOMINATIVE-SINGULAR CXN
HIM-CXN	him	... male person or animal	DEFINITE-3RD-PERSON-ACCUSATIVE-SINGULAR CXN
SHE-CXN	she	... female person or animal (or the moon or a boat)	DEFINITE-3RD-PERSON-NOMINATIVE-SINGULAR CXN
HER-CXN	her	... female person or animal (or the moon or a boat)	DEFINITE-3RD-PERSON-ACCUSATIVE-SINGULAR CXN
IT-CXN	it	... animal or inanimate entity	DEFINITE-3RD-PERSON-SINGULAR CXN
THEY-CXN	they	... more than one thing that is identifiable from the linguistic or extralinguistic context	DEFINITE-3RD-PERSON-NOMINATIVE-PLURAL CXN
THEM-CXN	them	... more than one thing that is identifiable from the linguistic or extralinguistic context	DEFINITE-3RD-PERSON-ACCUSATIVE-PLURAL CXN

Figure 6.6 PERSONAL-PRONOUN-NP CONSTRUCTIONS[97]

6.4.3 Reflexive NP-constructions

Reflexive NP-constructions are used to refer a second time to someone or something that has already been referred to in the same clause. At the level of form, they are realized by **reflexive pronouns.**

(17) a. And Mr. Trump himself said he wants to win all the time. COCA-2017-SPOK

---

97. As an anonymous reviewer rightly pointed out, in addition to this description, many speakers now also have entrenched a *THEY*-CXN as a gender-neutral pronoun.

b. Unfortunately, Trump has shown himself not to be as reflective as Kennedy.

COCA-2017-NEWS

Name	Form	Meaning	Explicit description
		Establishing co-reference in the same clause to …	
MYSELF-CXN	myself	… speaker	DEFINITE-1ST-PERSON-SINGULAR-REFLEXIVE CXN
OURSELVES-CXN	ourselves	… group including speaker	DEFINITE-1ST-PERSON-PLURAL REFLEXIVE CXN
YOURSELF-CXN	yourself	… addressee	DEFINITE-2ND-PERSON-SINGULAR REFLEXIVE CXN
YOURSELVES-CXN	yourselves	… addressees	DEFINITE-2ND-PERSON PLURAL-REFLEXIVE CXN
HERSELF-CXN	herself	… female person or animal	DEFINITE-3RD-PERSON-SINGULAR-REFLEXIVE CXN
HIMSELF-CXN	himself	… male person or animal	DEFINITE-3RD-PERSON-SINGULAR-REFLEXIVE CXN
ITSELF-CXN	itself	… animal or non-animate entity	DEFINITE-3RD-PERSON-SINGULAR-REFLEXIVE CXN
THEMSELF-CXN	themself	… person without specifying gender	DEFINITE-3RD-PERSON-PLURAL-REFLEXIVE CXN
THEMSELVES-CXN	themselves	… things (apart from speaker and addressee)	DEFINITE-3RD-PERSON-PLURAL REFLEXIVE CXN

Figure 6.7 REFLEXIVE NP-CONSTRUCTIONS

6.4.4 Reciprocal constructions

Reciprocal constructions are used to refer to two things previously mentioned in the same clause suggesting some kind of interaction or relation between the two. At the level of form, they are realized by **reciprocal pronouns**.

(18) a. Get endorsements in pairs, with a would-be Clinton voter and would-be Trump voter who know and trust each other teaming up … COCA-2016-MAG

b. … human beings and robots may never be able to understand each other.

COCA-2017-ACAD

c. … people must agree with one another about the meanings of words.

COCA-2017-ACAD

Figure 6.8 table

Name	Form	Meaning
EACH OTHER CXN	each other	Reference to 2 persons or other things previously mentioned specifying a relation between them
ONE ANOTHER CXN	one another	Reference to 2 or usually more persons or other things previously mentioned specifying a relation between them

Figure 6.8 RECIPROCAL-NP CONSTRUCTIONS

6.4.5 Genitive and possessive constructions

Another way of expressing definiteness is presented by genitive constructions, which consist of a slot for a POSSESSOR and one for the REFERENT (i.e., the 'thing' referred to):

(19) a. The vote made official Joe Biden's victory, despite President Trump's attempt to subvert the nation's democratic process, and it put pressure on Republicans to acknowledge the outcome. NYT-14-Dec-2020 (headline)

b. Mr. Biden called for unity while forcefully denouncing the president and his allies for their assault on the nation's voting system. NYT-14-Dec-2020

The role of POSSESSOR can be expressed by a genitive noun phrase (*Joe Biden's, President Trump's, the nation's*) or by the genitive form of a personal pronoun (often referred to as a possessive pronoun: *his, their*). We can thus describe the construction in the following way:

GENITIVE NP-CXN	
Establishing a referential relation between a POSSESSUM and a POSSESSOR	
POSSESSOR	POSSESSUM
N's	
my your his her their whose anyone's everybody's etc.	N

Figure 6.9 GENITIVE NP-CONSTRUCTIONS

Note that the same or a very similar relation can be expressed by other constructions such as a POSTMODIFIER-OF-NOUN CONSTRUCTION with PP_{of} (see 6.10.2.2) as in *of Biden* in (20a) or a PREMODIFIER-OF-NOUN CONSTRUCTION (see 6.10.2.1) as in *electoral college vote* in (20b):

(20) a. We don't want to assume that the election of Biden solves everything. NOW21-01-24-US

b. Electoral College Vote Officially Affirms Biden's Victory NYT-14-Dec-2020 (headline)

Another construction that can express possession is what we can call the POSSESSIVE-NP CONSTRUCTIONS, which comprises the following lexical items: *mine, ours, yours, his, hers* and *their's*.

(21) a. What? This is ours?   COCA-2015-SPOK
 b. … one of the duffel bags was hers …   COCA-2017-ACAD
 c. Four new casinos opened here from 1980 to 2002; three were Mr. Trump's.
                                              COCA-2007-NEWS

6.5 Demonstrative NP-constructions

Demonstrative NP-constructions consist of a **demonstrative** (*this – these, that – those*), which can but need not be followed by a noun. They are deictic in character, i.e., they establish reference by pointing at a 'thing'. If this 'thing' can be identified through the linguistic or non-linguistic context of the utterance, they can make up a DEMONSTRATIVE-NP-CONSTRUCTION on their own, as in the (b) cases below:

(22) a. This president flat-out lied.   COCA-2017-SPOK
 b. "It's not as bad as it sounds. The place we're buying in Fredericksburg is gorgeous. I'm actually looking forward to it." This is a lie …   COCA-2015-FIC

(23) a. It's time to start talking about these issues …   COCA-2017-MAG
 b. These are exciting times in our research community …   COCA-2017-ACAD

The teal-coloured field in Figure 6.19 indicates that (under certain conditions) the referent need not be expressed verbally when it is clear from the linguistic or situational context. We call that a 'contextual anchor'.[98]

(24) Dad, you don't understand. I can't put back one of these. That would be like saying one of these candy bars is less worthy than the others.   TV-2007-Psych

---

98. Note that there are restrictions to the use of a demonstrative on its own; for instance, one would not refer to a person by *this* but by *this one*.

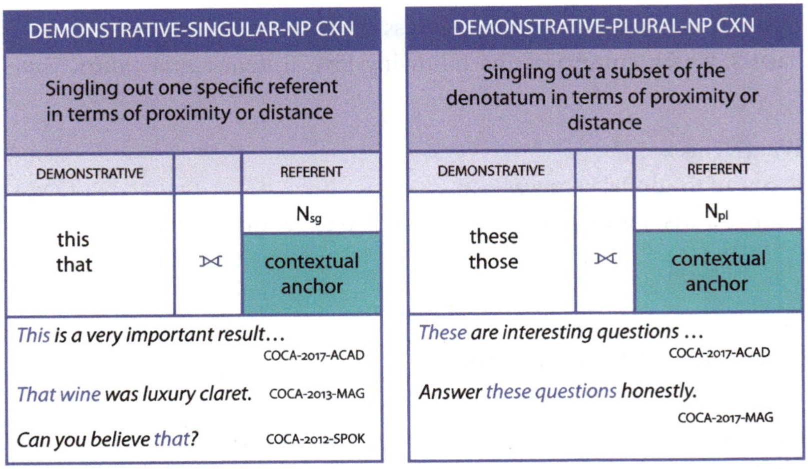

148 A Construction Grammar of the English Language

DEMONSTRATIVE-SINGULAR-NP CXN		
Singling out one specific referent in terms of proximity or distance		
DEMONSTRATIVE		REFERENT
		N_{sg}
this that	⋈	contextual anchor
This is a very important result... COCA-2017-ACAD		
That wine was luxury claret. COCA-2013-MAG		
Can you believe that? COCA-2012-SPOK		

DEMONSTRATIVE-PLURAL-NP CXN		
Singling out a subset of the denotatum in terms of proximity or distance		
DEMONSTRATIVE		REFERENT
		N_{pl}
these those	⋈	contextual anchor
These are interesting questions ... COCA-2017-ACAD		
Answer these questions honestly. COCA-2017-MAG		

Figure 6.10 DEMONSTRATIVE-NP CONSTRUCTIONS

6.6 Quantifying NP-constructions

6.6.1 Numerical NP-constructions

Expressing quantity is very important in language. The distinction between 1 and more than one (or in some languages a distinction between 1, 2 and more than 2) is a very basic one and often expressed in noun and verb morphology (when there are different forms for singular and plural). Furthermore, there are other constructions that express quantification either in the form of stating a precise number or more generally. We see these as a family of quantitative constructions with the following members:

Numerical constructions consist of a **cardinal number** slot and a slot for a REFERENT that can be filled by a plural noun, but this is not necessary if the referent is identifiable from the context (or speakers' general world knowledge):

(25) a. There are six pictures in this photo. What do you expect? Seven. I clearly remember seven photos, Gus. TV-2007-Psych
     b. How old is he? – At least 70. TV-2012-Psych

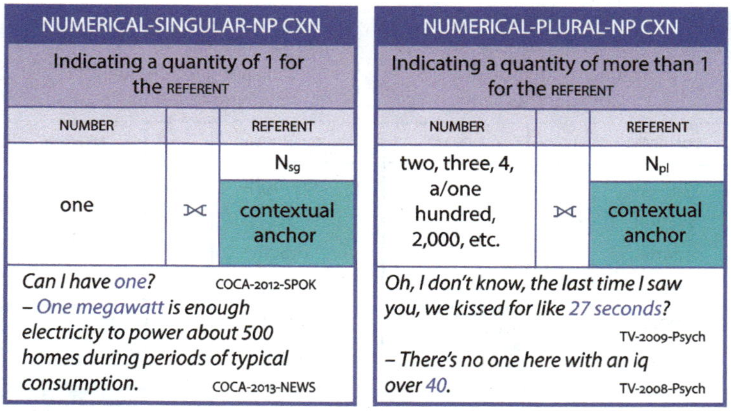

NUMERICAL-SINGULAR-NP CXN			NUMERICAL-PLURAL-NP CXN		
Indicating a quantity of 1 for the REFERENT			Indicating a quantity of more than 1 for the REFERENT		
NUMBER		REFERENT	NUMBER		REFERENT
one	⋈	N_{sg} contextual anchor	two, three, 4, a/one hundred, 2,000, etc.	⋈	N_{pl} contextual anchor
Can I have one? COCA-2012-SPOK *– One megawatt is enough electricity to power about 500 homes during periods of typical consumption.* COCA-2013-NEWS			*Oh, I don't know, the last time I saw you, we kissed for like 27 seconds?* TV-2009-Psych *– There's no one here with an iq over 40.* TV-2008-Psych		

Figure 6.11 Numerical NP-constructions

6.6.2 General quantifier NP-constructions

Whereas mass nouns – for obvious semantic reasons – cannot occur in numerical NP-constructions, both count and mass nouns do occur in general quantifier constructions. The conceptualizations underlying plural count and mass nouns are reflected by the fact that they share a number of quantifiers (like *enough, more, most*), whereas others only occur with either plural count or mass nouns:

(26) a. Could I have some grapes? COCA-1990-MOV

b. Would you like some wine, Mrs Hughes? COCA-201-TV

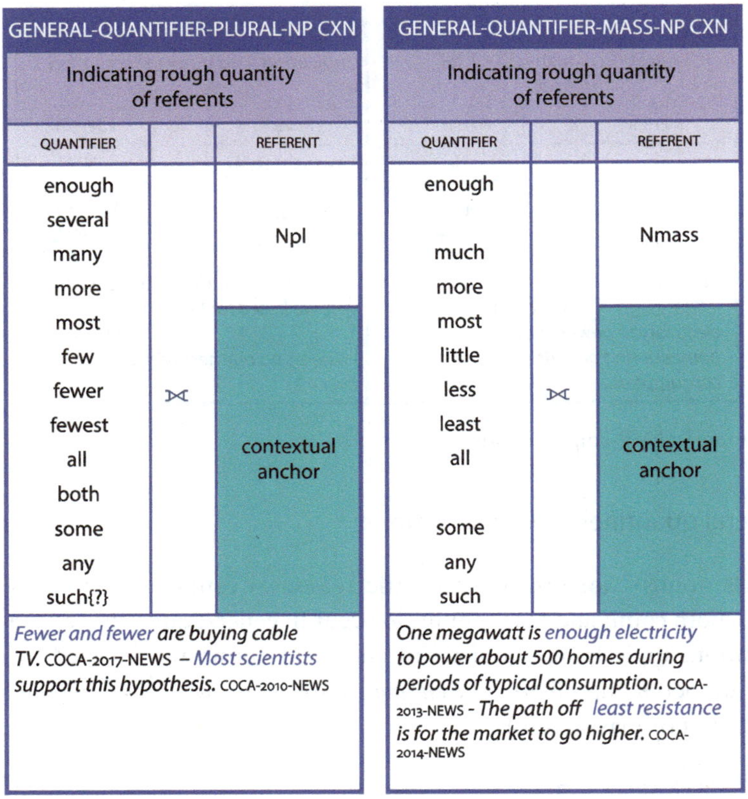

GENERAL-QUANTIFIER-PLURAL-NP CXN			GENERAL-QUANTIFIER-MASS-NP CXN		
Indicating rough quantity of referents			Indicating rough quantity of referents		
QUANTIFIER		REFERENT	QUANTIFIER		REFERENT
enough several many more		Npl	enough much more		Nmass
most few fewer fewest all both some any such{?}	⋈	contextual anchor	most little less least all some any such	⋈	contextual anchor
Fewer and fewer are buying cable TV. COCA-2017-NEWS *– Most scientists support this hypothesis.* COCA-2010-NEWS			*One megawatt is enough electricity to power about 500 homes during periods of typical consumption.* COCA-2013-NEWS *- The path off least resistance is for the market to go higher.* COCA-2014-NEWS		

Figure 6.12 GENERAL-QUANTIFIER-PLURAL-NP CXN and GENERAL-QUANTIFIER-MASS-NP CONSTRUCTION

Furthermore, we can identify a general quantitative singular count NP-construction:

Chapter 6. Referring to, describing and evaluating things   151

GENERAL-QUANTITATIVE-SINGULAR-COUNT-NP CXN		
Indicating range of referents		
QUANTIFIER		REFERENT
every no		N_{sg}
any each	⋈	
		contextual anchor
anybody/anyone/anything somebody/someone/something everybody/everyone/everything nobody/no one/nothing/none		

That's all **any man** can do.
TV-1959-Bonanza

And that favors someone like Barack Obama who doesn't
have a lot of experience...   COCA-2008-SPOK

Figure 6.13 GENERAL-QUANTITATIVE-SINGULAR-COUNT-NP CXN

6.7   Ranking NP-constructions

Rankings are typically expressed by **ordinal numbers.**

RANKING-NP CXN	
Indicating the place of the REFERENT in an order of 'things'	
ORDINAL	REFERENT
first	[N]
second	
15th	
etc.	contextual anchor
last	

Joseph Robinette Biden, Jr. is the 46th president of the United
States.   NOW-21-02-24-US

Figure 6.14 RANKING-NP CXN

6.8 Wh-NP-constructions

The following sentences all contain noun phrases with a *wh*-element:

(27) a. Who is this man? TV-2014-Psych
b. With whom am I speaking? TV-2014-Psych
c. What do you think? TV-2006-Psych

(28) a. The final 232–197 tally was a stark departure from Trump's first impeachment which played out along partisan lines. NOW-21-01-14CA
b. Do you have any idea who'd want to shoot you? TV-2009-Psych

(29) a. But, to be clear, it was the White House who released that call transcript. COCA-2019-SPOK
b. What I need is a miracle, or a facsimile of one. TV-2006-Psych

These uses are typical of interrogative-'question' constructions (27), relative clause (28), cleft- and pseudo-cleft constructions (29) (see 9.3 and the discussion there). Since the (semantic) function a particular wh-word has in a construct is dependent on the construction in which it is used, we see no point in making the kind of distinction that you find in many traditional grammar books between, for example, interrogative pronouns and relative pronouns, but rather take them to be WH-NP-CONSTRUCTIONS (n.b., the individual wh-words vary considerably with respect to their distribution; see Sag 2010 for more details):

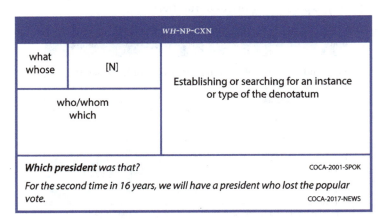

Figure 6.15 WH-NP CONSTRUCTIONS

6.9 Name and title constructions

In 6.2.4 we already pointed out that words such as *Amsterdam, Shawn* or *Harris* belong to the special category of proper nouns, which is generally characterized as having unique reference. This, however, only applies within the mental situational or cultural space: In very

Chapter 6. Referring to, describing and evaluating things **153**

many contexts, *Amsterdam* can be taken to refer to the capital of the Netherlands; it could, however, also refer to one of the many other places in the world called *Amsterdam*, a ship or a person of that name.

It would be incorrect to say that names are completely devoid of any meaning. Some personal names tend to be used almost exclusively for women, men or non-binary persons, some can be used for any gender, but would not usually be used for animals or places. Some people may choose to give a child a particular name on the basis of religious or other cultural reasons, but this does not, in fact, necessarily correspond to any particular properties of the actual referent. Place names can also be motivated in many ways: *Amsterdam*, in Dutch, is clearly related to the Amstel river; there is also a reason why places are called New Amsterdam, New York, New Hampshire, etc. or, in a slightly different way, Newcastle, Newbridge, etc. Nevertheless, it makes sense to say that proper nouns do not have meaning in the sense of a denotatum as a set of all the items that share particular properties. Ronald Reagan and Ronald Langacker presumably do not have very much in common apart from being men and being called Ronald, and there is nothing to set apart the millions of men not called Ronald from those that are.

This special status of proper nouns also shows in the combinations they enter with other nouns. Referring to people alone, there is a wide range of schematic constructions, and the following list is by no means exhaustive:

Name	Form	Meaning	Example
		Reference to	
FIRST-NAME CXN	$N_{first\ name}$	... person (familiar relationship)	Adele
LAST-NAME CXN	$N_{last\ name}$	... person (neutral relationship or formal context)	Goldberg
FULL-NAME CXN	$N_{first\ name}\ N_{last\ name}$	... person (formal, official)	Adele E. Goldberg
TITLE+FULL-NAME CXN	$N_{title}\ N_{first\ name}$ $N_{last\ name}$	... person	Prof. Elena Lieven Dr. Peter Uhrig
TITLE+LAST-NAME CXN	$N_{title}\ N_{last\ name}$	... person	Prof. Uhrig Mr. Trump
TITLE+FIRST-NAME CXN	$N_{first\ name}\ Num$	... monarch	Elizabeth II

Figure 6.16 Selected PERSONAL-NAME CONSTRUCTIONS of English

Apart from PERSONAL-NAME NP CONSTRUCTIONS, there are constructions denoting places (*Amsterdam, New York*), squares and streets (*Times Square, Piccadilly Circus, High Street*), buildings (*The Empire State Building, Big Ben*), institutions (*The European Court of Justice, the University of Oxford*), firms (*Facebook, AmTrak*), products (*Fanta, Airbus 310*), works of art (*Two Piece Reclining Figure*), etc.

6.10 Noun phrases

6.10.1 Basic NP-constructions

At the beginning of this chapter, we argued that it is best to speak of a family of NP-constructions, and the outline of the NP-constructions in the previous chapter has shown a considerable degree of variation between them both in terms of form and semantic function. In fact, we consider all the constructions outlined in Sections 6.2 to 6.8 as somehow basic in that they represent the minimal linguistic forms we can use to establish reference.

In this section, we will illustrate how these basic constructions can be expanded to form larger noun phrases such as, e.g., *one of the largest and most intensely used historic city centers of Europe* from sentence (1). We can do this by using what we call premodifier- and postmodifier constructions.

6.10.2 Modifier-of-noun constructions

6.10.2.1 *Premodifier-of-noun constructions*

Whereas the prime function of basic NP-constructions is to establish the scope of reference of the noun in the sense that they make clear whether it is one particular 'thing' (*the conference, one conference*), a certain number of 'things' (*three conferences, several conferences*) or all 'things' (*conferences, all conferences*) covered by the denotatum of the noun that is being referred to, the constructions described in this section do not primarily have such an identifying or quantifying function, but provide further information about the referent, i.e., their function is mainly a descriptive or evaluative one, as in (30) and (31) respectively.

(30) a. It points to the fact that green ideas have too often become a virtue signal for the carbon-heavy bourgeoisie... NOW-17-03-18-GB
   b. The idea of doing research and pursuing an academic career was common ground to both of them... BNC-ANY-619

(31) a. What a splendid idea! COCA-2019-FI
   b. Wasn't that a nice conference? COCA-1996-FIC

That modifier constructions can also narrow down the scope of reference of the noun in question is pretty obvious, thus (32a) refers only to certain conferences and (32b) only to a particular one (giving it a kind of name status):

(32) a. … the administration used the occasion to lay down a set of formal rules governing reporters' behavior at future White House news conferences, a highly unusual step.

NYT-19-Nov-2018

 b. Tenth International Conference on Construction Grammar

Website-ICCG10

PREMODIFIER-OF-NOUN CONSTRUCTIONS consist of a slot for an adjective, a present participle, a noun functioning as the premodifier and the noun being modified.

PREMODIFIER-OF-NOUN CXN		
Providing description or evaluation of 'thing' referred to by noun		
premodifier	noun	
Adj	N	*American presidents* *golden daffodils* *brand-new streetcar* *very pretty tulips*
V-en	N	*needed information* *tossed salad*
V-ing	N	*graduating class* *attending physician* *leaning tower*
N	N	*railway network* *canal system* *communications breakdown* *Birmingham corpus*

Figure 6.17 The English PREMODIFIER-OF-NOUN CONSTRUCTION

Note that the PREMODIFIER-OF-NOUN CONSTRUCTION in Figure 6.17 can in some cases give rise to fully entrenched compounds such as *greenhouse* or *barman*.[99]

6.10.2.2 *Postmodifier-of-noun constructions*

With postmodifier-of-noun constructions one can make a distinction between those that can generally function as postmodifiers of nouns and those that are related to the valency of the nouns, i.e., those cases which in valency theory are classified as complements of a noun (Herbst et al. 2004; Herbst & Schüller 2008; see also 5.11). General modifiers can occur with any noun. This applies to certain types of prepositional constructions and to relative clauses, for instance:

---

99. For compounds see Schmid (2005: 121–123) and Ungerer & Schmid (2006: 271–275), who discuss compounds in terms of conceptual blending.

156   A Construction Grammar of the English Language

(33) a. Democrats and Republicans in congress have long sparred on the subject of gun regulation in America ...   COCA-2017-SPOK

   b. Hurricane Irma continues to be a threat that is going to devastate the United States in either Florida or some of the Southeastern states.   COCA-2017-SPOK

The *that-* and *to-*infinitive clauses in (34), however, are specifically related to the nouns *conviction* and *desire* and their valency:

(34) a. Wittgenstein's understanding of spontaneity does not express the conviction that concept-formation is an act of a community.   COCA-2017-ACAD

   b. ... the president's desire to integrate our economies more closely to that of Europe ...
                                                                          COCA-2013-NEWS

We can thus identify the following two types of POST-MODIFIER-OF-NOUN CONSTRUCTIONS:

GENERAL-POSTMODIFIER-OF-NOUN CXN		
Providing description of noun		
N	PP	*the canals of Amsterdam* COCA-2010-MAG
	RELATIVE–CLAUSE CXN	*air pollution which may reasonably be anticipated to endanger public health or welfare.* COCA-2006-ACAD *President-elect Donald J. Trump, who has called climate change a hoax perpetrated by the Chinese, ...* NYT-5-Dec-2016
	V-ing_CL	*the person driving the stolen car* COCA-2015-NEWS
	V-en_CL	*the fourth-youngest person elected president* COCA-2014-NEWS

Figure 6.18 GENERAL POSTMODIFIER-OF-NOUN CONSTRUCTION

The latter construction Figure 6.19 on the next page represents an abstraction over a large number of item-related noun-valency constructions, which differ both with respect to their formal realization and semantic function.

6.10.2.3   *Discontinuous modifier-of-noun constructions*

If we look at a sentence such as (35), we can identify a third type of MODIFIER-OF-NOUN CONSTRUCTION, namely a discontinuous modifier (Aarts & Aarts 1988):

(35) ... he's not a good enough player to be on this team   COCA-2011-NEWS

Here, the infinitive clause *to be on his team* is structurally and semantically dependent on *good enough.*

Chapter 6. Referring to, describing and evaluating things 157

		VALENCY-RELATED POSTMODIFIER-OF-NOUN CXN	
		Providing argument of noun	
N	PP	*Trump's meeting with Al Gore*	NYT-5-Dec-1016
	that_CL	*the claim that there were millions of fraudulent votes in this election*	COCA-2017-SPOK
	wh_CL	*the question whether homosexuals could marry*	COCA-2008-ACAD
	to_INF	*Britain's vote to leave the European Union.*	COCA-2017-SPOK
	wh_to_INF	*the decision whether to rent or buy*	COCA-2008-NEWS

Figure 6.19 VALENCY-RELATED-POSTMODIFIER-OF-NOUN CONSTRUCTION

6.10.3 A simplified, integrated view of NP-constructions

As explained above, we see pre- and postmodifier-of-noun constructions as constructions that combine with basic NP-constructions to modify the noun of those constructions to form a larger expression. The area of overlap between the respective constructions is presented by the noun N, which belongs to both constructions. We would thus say that *a nice evening* constitutes a blend of the INDEFINITE-SINGULAR-COUNT-NP CONSTRUCTION with the PREMODIFIER-OF-NOUN CONSTRUCTION, which can be represented in a construction grid of the following kind:

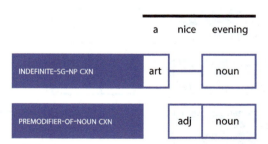

Figure 6.20 Construction grid for *a very nice evening* showing the layers of constructions making up the expression. Since *nice* is not part of the INDEFINITE-SG-NP CONSTRUCTION, we use a line to connect the two slots of the construction

What Figure 6.20 is supposed to illustrate is that the construct *a nice evening* can be analyzed as a blend of two constructions – the basic INDEFINITE-SG-COUNT-NP CONSTRUCTION and a PREMODIFIER-OF-NOUN CONSTRUCTION. An alternative representation could take the form of Figure 6.21: The fact that the whole construct can be regarded as one NP is indicated by the fact that the box for the NP-construction is larger than that of the premodifier construction.

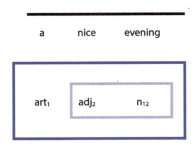

Figure 6.21 Construction grid for *a very nice evening*. All items indexed as 1 belong to the INDEFINITE- SINGULAR-NP CXN, all items indexed as 2 to the PREMODIFIER-OF-NOUN CONSTRUCTION. The fact that cxn$_2$ is "surrounded" by cxn$_1$ indicates the order of the elements and shows that the scope of the determiner extends to *nice evening*

(36), which contains an NP-construction with a premodifier and a postmodifier construction, can be represented as in Figure 6.22 below:

(36) Each new quarter of the city became linked to (not separated from) the older quarters by canals... NYT-15-Oct-2002

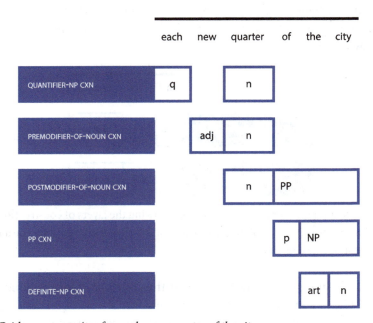

Figure 6.22 Grid representation for *each new quarter of the city*

6.10.4 Shortcut representations

Figures 6.21 and 6.22 show the internal composition of NP constructs of some complexity. This type of representation, while cognitively plausible in our view, is rather clumsy to handle when it comes to analyzing sentences in the form of construction grids. We will thus introduce the following shortcut notation:

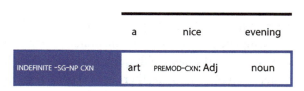

Figure 6.23 Shortcut representation of *a nice evening*

This shortcut representation looks suspiciously like – and, in fact, is largely compatible with – the description of noun phrases provided in other models of syntax and in reference grammars such as CGEL or CAMG:

Table 6.2 The structure of the (prototypical) noun phrase in standard reference grammars

determinative	premodification		head	postmodification[*]	CGEL 1985: 62
determiner	premodifier		head	postmodifier	Aarts & Aarts 1988: 105
	discontinu-			-ous modifier	
pre-head dependents			head	post-head dependents	CAMG: 329–333
determiner	pre-head modifier			post-head modifiers complements	
determiner	pre-head adjunct		head	post-head adjunct complement	Aarts 2011
pre-head	PREMODIFIER-CXN(s)		head	POSTMODIFIER-CXN(s)	CASA[**]

[*] Including complementation of premodification, corresponding to the discontinuous modifiers of Aarts & Aarts (1988).
[**] See also Herbst & Schüller (2008).

It may thus be necessary to point out where the differences lie: most importantly, the cognitive approach we are taking regards this kind of template as the result of a combination of constructions. This will usually involve one of the basic NP-constructions identified above and one or more modifier constructions. For this reason, we explicitly speak of modifier constructions and indicate them as separate constructions whenever there is more than one of a particular type, as in Figure 6.24 as a representation of (37):

(37)   The canals never gave the port city enough room to lay out great classic squares…

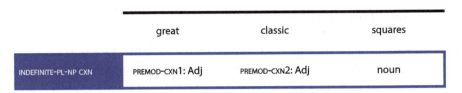

Figure 6.24 Shortcut representation of *great classic squares*

It has to be said, however, that even from a cognitive point of view there is nothing to stop us from assuming that a template such as the one illustrated in Figure 6.24 can emerge in (some) speakers' constructicons on the basis of frequent exposure to such constructs. In fact, in some cases, this is rather likely. All the same, there are two reasons supporting an analysis in terms of a combination of constructions, namely (i) that premodifier constructions can be combined with NP-constructions recursively, as in (37) above, and (ii) that the relatively large number of pre- and postmodifier constructions (see the examples below) opens up such a wide range of combinations that an account in terms of storage of all of these seems less plausible.

(38) a. the inevitable framed inscribed photograph of mother BNC-GWB-1731
 b. conventional municipal statutory local plan-making BNC-BN8-743
 c. an intelligent unmarried Edwardian middle-class young woman BNC-GTH-230
 d. White white white white white white white white white white white white white BNC-KE3-7409

In 6.2.4, we established a distinction between count nouns, mass nouns and proper nouns – and this distinction is fairly established in most theories of syntax and grammars. This is not the case in the same way for the "non-nouns" that can function as heads or pre-heads in noun phrases. In view of the many item-specific properties of these words, we think that it is most appropriate to use the relatively traditional labels for small groups of words that we introduced in the context of the constructions in which they occur. The following table provides a summary of these categories:

Table 6.3 Word classes other than nouns occurring in NP-CONSTRUCTIONS

Word class label	Items	Uses	In construction
indefinite article	a, an	pre-head	INDEFINITE NP-CONSTRUCTION
definite article	the	pre-head	DEFINITE-NP CONSTRUCTION
personal pronoun	I, she, it, etc. your, their, etc.[*] me, them, etc.	head (of subject-NPs)[**] pre-head head (of non-subject-NPs)	DEFINITE-1/2/3 PERSON SG/PL-NP CXN

Chapter 6. Referring to, describing and evaluating things   **161**

Table 6.3 *(continued)*

Word class label	Items	Uses	In construction
possessive pronouns	*mine, hers, his, yours, theirs, etc.*	head	DEFINITE-1/2/3 PERSON SG/PL-NP CXN
reflexive pronoun	*herself, themselves, etc.*	head (of non-subject-NPs)	DEFINITE-REFLEXIVE-NP CXN
reciprocal pronoun	*each other, one another* *each other's, one another's*	head (of non-subject-NPs) pre-head	DEFINITE-RECIPROCAL-NP CXN
demonstrative	*this, that, these, those*	pre-head and head	DEMONSTRATIVE-NP CXN
cardinal numeral	*one, 2, 4, 410, a hundred, etc.*	pre-head and head	NUMERICAL-NP CXN
quantifier	*all, many, enough, etc.* *everything, somebody, anyone, none, etc.* *no* *anyone's, everybody's, etc.*	pre-head and head head pre-head pre-head	GENERAL-QUANTIFIER CXN
ordinal numeral	*first, second, third, etc.*	pre-head and head	RANKING-NP CXN
wh-pronouns	*who, whose, what, whom, etc.*		WH-NP CXN

* Note that the genitives of personal pronouns are sometimes included under possessives.
** More precisely: subjects of finite clauses.

Note that words that can function as pre-heads are often called determiners in many approaches. However, the term is sometimes also used to refer to a word class (as in CGEL), sometimes for the phrase-internal function we call pre-heads (CAMG). Furthermore, subsuming all words that can function as pre-heads under one word class (i.e., the determiners of CGEL, and, respectively the determinatives of CAMG) entails an analysis in terms of multiple word class membership for those words that can also function as heads of NPs (which then belong to the word class of determiner and the word class of pronouns).

CHAPTER 7

Using adjectives to evaluate, describe and compare

7.1 Adjectives and adverbs

7.1.1 Uses of adjectives

If we accept the tagging systems of the respective corpora, then about every 8th word in the British National Corpus and every 16th word in the Corpus of Contemporary American English is an adjective. There is a considerable difference in the use of adjectives with respect to text types, as one can see from Table 7.1, which shows the top 20 adjectives for each subcorpus:

Table 7.1 Adjectives in the subcorpora of COCA (1990–2019)[*]

TV/MOV	SPOK	FIC	NEWS	MAG	ACAD
4.5%	5.7%	6.2%	7.3%	8.1%	9.8%
good	good	good	new	new	new
sorry	new	old	good	good	social
little	great	little	American	American	American
great	big	new	high	great	political
sure	American	long	national	big	different
right	right	small	big	small	important
big	little	big	public	high	national
new	different	sure	great	best	high
fine	sure	black	best	black	public
nice	important	white	federal	national	significant

[*] Percentages relate to the number of items in the respective genres. *other, others,* - – and _y* (punctuation marks) were excluded. For TV/MOV no figures for _y* were available. The query was ADJ (all adjectives).

These data show that the percentage of adjectives in the spoken component of COCA is considerably lower than in the academic subcorpus and that some adjectives tend to occur with high frequency in the various genres (the adjectives in black in Table 7.1 are the ones that only occur amongst the top 10 in only one genre). But they also give us an indication of the semantic functions that adjectives are frequently being used for, namely

i. to express evaluations (*good, great, fine, nice, important, significant,* etc.),
ii. to provide descriptions of 'things' with respect to size (*big, small, little, high,* etc.), age (*new, old,* etc.), colour (*black, white,* etc.),

iii. to relate 'things' to a particular group, area or domain (*American, national, public,* etc.),
iv. to express a degree of certainty (*sure,* etc.).

7.1.2 The ADJECTIVE CONSTRUCTION

As pointed out earlier, in Construction Grammar all words are considered to be constructions. In the case of adjectives, the constructional template, as we see it, consists of two elements – the adjective in the semantic role of an ATTRIBUTE, and a slot for the ATTRIBUTEE, because adjectives (almost) always need a point of reference to be used meaningfully (the 'thing' that is *good, old, public,* etc.). For reasons that will become apparent in Chapter 15, we will refer to this kind of basic construction simply as the **ADJECTIVE CONSTRUCTION**:

Name	ADJECTIVE CONSTRUCTION	
Meaning	Ascribing an ATTRIBUTE to an ATTRIBUTEE	
Semantic roles	ATTRIBUTE	ATTRIBUTEE
Form	Adj	provided by another construction (with Adj slot)
		contextual anchor point

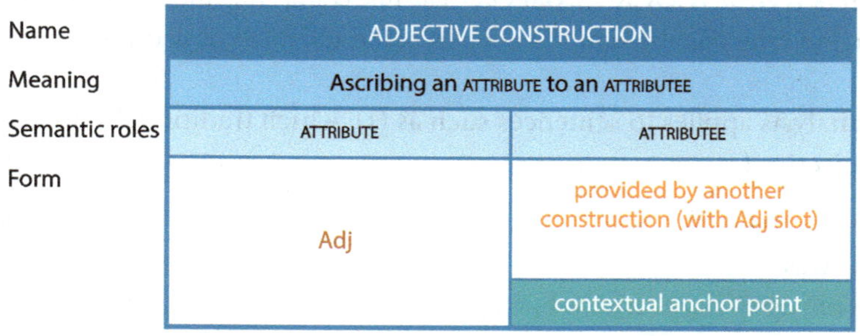

Figure 7.1 ADJECTIVE CONSTRUCTION

By taking this view of adjectives as constructions, we can explain how adjectives combine with other constructions to form utterances: For instance, in Chapter 5, we identified the SUBJECT-ATTRIBUTE CONSTRUCTION as containing an ATTRIBUTEE slot (expressed by the Subj), a verb, and an ATTRIBUTE slot (expressed formally as an Attr). The overlap between the two constructions is obvious:

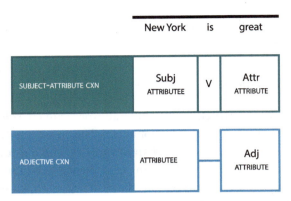

Figure 7.2 Combination of the SUBJECT-ATTRIBUTE CXN and the ADJECTIVE CONSTRUCTION in the sentence *New York is great.* (COCA-2015-SPOK) The line connecting the two slots of the ADJECTIVE CONSTRUCTION indicates that the verb V is not part of the adjective construction

This kind of analysis applies to sentences such as (1), which traditionally are called **predicative uses** of adjective (ATTRIBUTEES are given in orange, ATTRIBUTES in brown):

(1) a. New York is great. COCA-2015-SPOK
    b. That was nice. BNC-A89-2193
    c. You're busy. Things are confusing. NYT-26-Sept-2020

Sentences such as (2a) combine an ADJECTIVE CONSTRUCTION with the OBJECT-ATTRIBUTE CONSTRUCTION as in Figure 7.3, (2b) represents a use of an ADJECTIVE CONSTRUCTION in the RESULTATIVE CONSTRUCTION.

(2) a. Vice President Biden considers another 9/11 type attack unlikely. COCA-2010-SPOK
    b. Last year, my father painted the kitchen apple green for Mama. COCA-2016-FIC

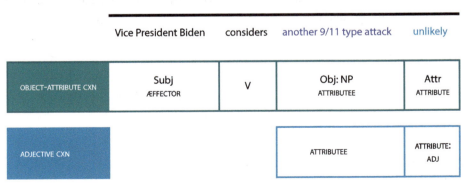

Figure 7.3 Combination of the OBJECT-ATTRIBUTE CONSTRUCTION and the ADJECTIVE CONSTRUCTION in the sentence *Vice President Biden considers another 9/11 type attack unlikely*

Chapter 7. Using adjectives to evaluate, describe and compare   **165**

In construction grid representations of actual sentences, we will not normally go into this much detail, but only specify the respective slot filler of the argument structure construction as Adj. Figures 7.2 and 7.3 thus only serve as an illustration of how the adjective construction combines with argument structure constructions.

7.1.3   The PREMODIFIER-OF-NOUN CONSTRUCTION

In (1) and (2) the adjective constructions fill a slot of a verbal argument structure construction. Another typical use is that in PREMODIFIER-OF-NOUN CONSTRUCTIONS (see 6.10.2) illustrated by the sentences in (3):

(3)   a.   They had a nice meal in a posh restaurant.
     b.   The misleading notion that Mr. Biden is too addled for the presidency has been driven by Mr. Trump since 2018, when he first started referring to the former vice president as Sleepy Joe.

           NYT-27-Sept-2020

In traditional grammar, these uses are called **attributive uses.** In a constructionist framework, we can account for them as a combination of the ADJECTIVE CONSTRUCTION with the PREMODIFIER-OF-NOUN CONSTRUCTION (see 6.20).

7.1.4   Item-relatedness in attributive and predicative uses

It is worth noting that not all adjectives can occur in both attributive and predicative uses. For instance, most of the so-called *a*-adjectives (*afraid, asleep, aground, etc.*), which go back to Old English participles, tend not to occur in the PREMODIFIER-OF-NOUN CONSTRUCTION, as in (4bc), while others are not normally used in the predicative SUBJECT-ATTRIBUTE CONSTRUCTION, as in (5bc):

(4)   a.   On March 24, 1989 the oil tanker Exxon Valdez ran aground on Bligh Reef in Prince William Sound...
           BNC-J3D-636
     b.   ??an aground oil tanker
     c.   ??an afraid person, an asleep cat, etc.

(5)   a.   She felt like a complete and utter fool.
           COCA-2016-FIC
     b.   ??The fool was utter.
     c.   ??The fool was complete.

Furthermore, there are set phrases in which the adjectives are restricted to the PREMODIFIER-OF-NOUN CONSTRUCTION, e.g., *an old friend* is not necessarily "a friend that is old" and *friendly fire* is not "fire that is friendly".

7.2 Expressing degree

7.2.1 Modifier-of-adjective constructions

7.2.1.1 *Premodifier constructions*

Many adjectives are **gradable**, which means that the quality expressed can be seen as being applicable to a higher or lower degree. There are various ways of indicating the point or area on a scale that seems appropriate to the situation expressed. One is by making use of a PREMODIFIER-OF-ADJECTIVE CONSTRUCTION, containing an adverb or a quantifier:

(6) a. They had a very nice meal.
  b. I'm a little nervous, to be honest. COCA-2019-SPOK
  c. Good to see you, it's a bit strange... COCA-2019-SPOK

This **PREMODIFIER-OF-ADJECTIVE CONSTRUCTION** is not restricted to adverbs of 'degree'. However, if adjectives such as *fundamentally, triumphantly* or *stupidly* are used in the construction, they receive a 'degree' interpretation to a certain extent, which is a nice example of the blending processes of the meaning of lexical items and the meaning associated with a construction:

(7) a. The tax returns that Mr. Trump has long fought to keep private tell a story fundamentally different from the one he has sold to the American public. NYT-27-Sept-2020
  b. Depression hits people who are triumphantly successful... COCA-1991-SPOK
  c. Apple's famed AirPods are undeniably cool, but they're also absurdly expensive. COCA-2018-MAG

The PREMODIFIER-OF-ADJECTIVE CONSTRUCTION can thus be described as follows:

PREMODIFIER-OF-ADJECTIVE CONSTRUCTION	
Intensifying or modifying an ATTRIBUTE	
PREMODIFIER	ATTRIBUTE
Adv	Adj

Figure 7.4 The English PREMODIFIER-OF-ADJECTIVE CONSTRUCTION

7.2.1.2 *Postmodifier constructions*

A very similar function can be fulfilled by the **POSTMODIFIER-OF-ADJECTIVE CONSTRUCTION**, which is often expressed by a prepositional phrase:

(8) a. This statement is true to a large degree. COCA-1999-ACAD
  b. Scholarships are available on a first come first serve basis. COCA-2013-NEWS

Chapter 7. Using adjectives to evaluate, describe and compare   **167**

  c. She blames the shelter facility, calling it inadequate in many ways.   COCA-2012-WEB
  d. As one who thinks of himself as Catholic in a Calvinist rather than Roman way...

      COCA-2006-MAG

GENERAL POSTMODIFIER-OF-ADJECTIVE CONSTRUCTION	
Intensifying or modifying an ATTRIBUTE	
ATTRIBUTE	POSTMODIFIER
Adj	PP

Figure 7.5 The GENERAL-POSTMODIFIER-OF-ADJECTIVE CONSTRUCTIONS

As with nouns, a distinction can be made between postmodifiers that can be used with more or less any adjective, and others which are specific to particular adjectives (and their valency) (Herbst 1983, 1984). Such postmodifiers of adjectives not only include prepositional phrases, but also *to*-infinitive clauses (see 7.5), *that*- and *wh*-clauses:

  (9) a. She doesn't sound too keen on the guy.   TV_2010-Psych
      b. We're all a little surprised that it didn't work out, Carlton.   TV-2007-Psych
      c. She's undecided whether to laugh or cry.   COCA-2007-FIC
      d. She is always uncertain how to address her Head of Department.   BNC-ANY-871

They are best characterized in terms of adjectival valency constructions (see, e.g., 7.5, 5.10).

7.2.1.3 *Discontinuous modifier constructions*

In addition to pre- and postmodifier constructions, a third type of modifier construction can be identified, in which a certain premodifier presupposes the presence of a particular postmodifier.

  (10) This tendency is **so** strong **that it can override the animacy preference of the verbs.**

    COCA-2019-COCA

Following Aarts and Aarts (1988:118–119), we will refer to this as a **DISCONTINUOUS-MODIFIER-OF-ADJECTIVE CONSTRUCTION.**

7.2.2 Expressing maximum degree

If one wants to refer to the absolute maximum or absolute minimum of the gradability scale, one can use one of the following constructions (see Hoffmann 2022b: 81–86):

– the SUPERLATIVE CONSTRUCTION: adjective + {-est} suffix or

(11) a. Mr. Trump mocked his opponent for wearing "the biggest mask I've ever seen…"

NYT-30-Sept-2020

b. "You're the worst president America has ever had," he said to Mr. Trump.

NYT-30-Sept-2020

– the *MOST-/LEAST*-CONSTRUCTION:

(12) a. Mr. Trump made no effort to address his most obvious political vulnerabilities, from his mismanagement of the pandemic to his refusal to condemn right-wing extremism…

NYT-30-Sept-2020

b. It is no accident that the country that's least affected by this is Germany.

COCA-2017-MAG

c. And I consider myself most fortunate to have been able to do so. COCA-2019-SPOK

d. What is remarkable about Amsterdam is that while it has one of the largest and most intensely used historic city centers of Europe, its plan to curtail traffic is more radical than that of any other regional capital.

NYT-28-Jan-993

The two constructions differ with respect to the adjectives that occur in them (which is mostly a matter of shorter adjectives preferring the SUPERLATIVE CONSTRUCTION and long adjectives preferring the *MOST-/LEAST*-CONSTRUCTION), but they also share a number of properties:

i. They both refer to an endpoint of the scale denoted by the respective adjective.

ii. As outlined in 7.1.2, the ATTRIBUTEE of the adjective can either be the noun of the PREMODIFIER-OF-NOUN CONSTRUCTION, as in (11) and (12a), the subject of a SUBJECT-ATTRIBUTE CONSTRUCTION as in (12b), or an object of an OBJECT-ATTRIBUTE CONSTRUCTION as in (12c).

iii. Both constructions can either be used to denote the absolute degree of the quality by the adjective as such, as in (12c), or single out one ATTRIBUTE from a set of ATTRIBUTEES of the same kind as having this quality more than the others (*the biggest mask I've ever seen*). The scope of these ATTRIBUTEES can be made clear by postmodifier-of-noun constructions, as, for example, in (11) or (12d).

We can thus describe these constructions in the following way:

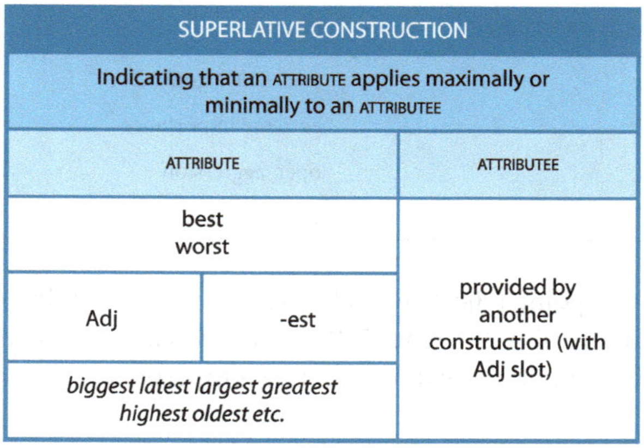

Chapter 7. Using adjectives to evaluate, describe and compare   **169**

SUPERLATIVE CONSTRUCTION		
Indicating that an ATTRIBUTE applies maximally or minimally to an ATTRIBUTEE		
ATTRIBUTE		ATTRIBUTEE
best worst		provided by another construction (with Adj slot)
Adj	-est	
biggest latest largest greatest highest oldest etc.		

Figure 7.6 The SUPERLATIVE CONSTRUCTION

MOST-/LEAST-CONSTRUCTION		
Indicating that an ATTRIBUTE applies maximally or minimally to an ATTRIBUTEE		
ATTRIBUTE		ATTRIBUTEE
most least	Adj	provided by another construction (with Adj slot)
	important likely recent popular common powerful famous effective etc.	

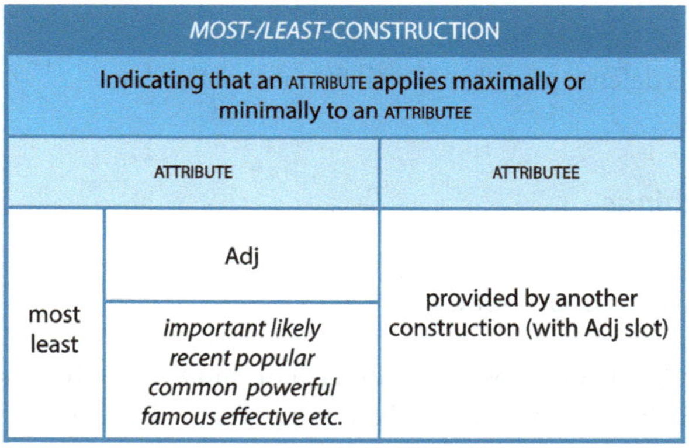

Figure 7.7 The *MOST-/LEAST*-CONSTRUCTION

The distinction between the SUPERLATIVE CONSTRUCTION and the *MOST-/LEAST*-CONSTRUC-TION corresponds to the distinction between a synthetic morphological superlative form and a periphrastic superlative construction in traditional grammars (see CGEL 1985: 458).

7.3 Collocational parallels between adverb-adjective and adjective-noun patterns

There are obvious parallels between combinations of adjectives and nouns and the combination of certain adverbs and adjectives, compare, e.g., the columns in Table 7.2:

Table 7.2 Adverb-adjective and adjective-noun combinations

statistically significant	statistical significance
extremely important	extreme importance
openly aggressive	open aggression
clearly visible	clear visibility

This shows that, up to a point, adjectives and certain adverbs can fulfill the function of pre-modifiers in a similar way. The difference is that adjectives usually relate to 'things', whereas adverbs can be used to provide a qualification to a 'property', as in (13), or a 'process', as in (14).

(13) a. ... it's very smart of Joe Biden to be doing this.   COCA-2019-SPOK
    b. I think this is incredibly important.   COCA-2019-SPOK

(14) a. "Thank you," she said politely.   COCA-2019-FIC
    b. The Ravens defense played very well for most of the day...   COCA-2018-NEWS

7.4 Comparing things

7.4.1 The COMPARATIVE CONSTRUCTION

The COMPARATIVE CONSTRUCTION has a similar communicative function to the SUPERLA-TIVE CONSTRUCTION, but it draws an explicit comparison between two (or more) ATTRIB-UTEES (see also Hoffmann 2022b: 81–86). ATTRIBUTEE2 can either be expressed in a construction slot after *than* or it is implied:

(15) a. ... this is ... worse than Watergate.   COCA-2019-SPOK
    b. Speaking on the cell phone while driving is much riskier than keeping both hands on the wheel.   COCA-2001-MAG
    c. Things will be better this term.   BNC-ANY-1051

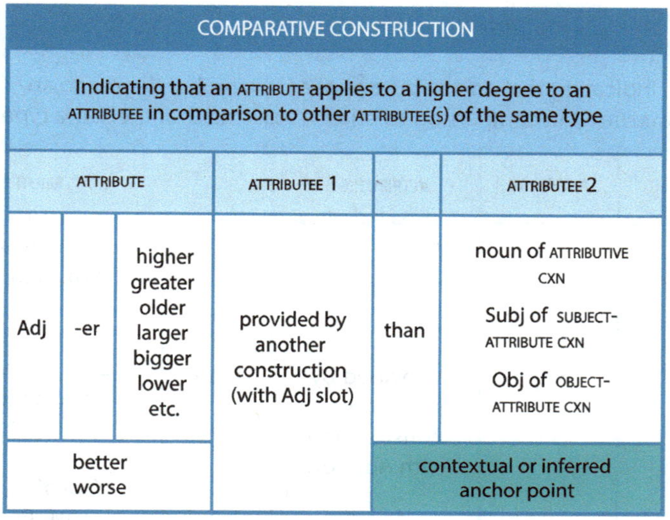

Chapter 7. Using adjectives to evaluate, describe and compare 171

COMPARATIVE CONSTRUCTION					
Indicating that an ATTRIBUTE applies to a higher degree to an ATTRIBUTEE in comparison to other ATTRIBUTEE(s) of the same type					
ATTRIBUTE			ATTRIBUTEE 1		ATTRIBUTEE 2
Adj	-er	higher greater older larger bigger lower etc.	provided by another construction (with Adj slot)	than	noun of ATTRIBUTIVE CXN Subj of SUBJECT-ATTRIBUTE CXN Obj of OBJECT-ATTRIBUTE CXN
	better worse			contextual or inferred anchor point	

Figure 7.8 The COMPARATIVE CONSTRUCTION

7.4.2 The *MORE-THAN*-COMPARISON CONSTRUCTION

Just as we have split up what traditional grammars call superlative into the SUPERLATIVE CONSTRUCTION and the *MOST-/LEAST*-CONSTRUCTION, we will not treat cases such as the ones under (16) as instances of the COMPARATIVE CONSTRUCTION discussed in the previous section:

(16)   a.   The boundary matrix ... is more useful than the adjacency matrix.   COCA-2019-MAG
     b.   Listening is usually more appreciated than giving advice...   COCA-2009-MAG
     c.   Trump's motives could not be more transparent.   NYT-29-Oct-2020

Instead, we cover these by the following constructional template:

MORE-THAN-COMPARISON CONSTRUCTION				
Indicating that an attribute applies to a higher degree to an ATTRIBUTEE 1 in comparison to other ATTRIBUTEE(S) 2 of the same type				
QUANTIFIER	ATTRIBUTE	ATTRIBUTEE 1		ATTRIBUTEE 2
more	Adj	provided by another construction (with Adj slot)	than	NOUN OF ATTRIBUTIVE CXN
				Subj of SUBJECT-ATTRIBUTE CXN
				Obj of OBJECT-ATTRIBUTE CXN
				contextual or inferred anchor point

Figure 7.9 The MORE-THAN-COMPARISON CONSTRUCTION (type 1) as in Examples (15)

The reason for identifying a separate MORE-THAN-COMPARISON CONSTRUCTION is even more compelling than in the case of the superlatives, because the MORE-THAN-COMPARISON CONSTRUCTION also covers cases such as the following, which are not adjectival:

(17) a. ... year after year, Mr. Trump appears to have lost more money than nearly any other individual American taxpayer ... COCA-2019-MAG

b. She owed me more money than I made in a year. COCA-2019-SPOK

(18) a. "In 47 months I've done more than you have in 47 years," Mr. Trump shot back... NYT-30-Sept-2020

b. Bilingual spelling patterns in middle school: It is more than transfer. COCA-2019-ACAD

c. The seeking of relatedness is more than seeing similarities in objects across media... COCA-2007-ACAD

This is partly due to the many uses of the word *more*, which all have in common the comparative element discussed above. Traditionally, these uses of more can be accounted for in terms of different parts of speech – e.g., as an adverb in (16), as a determiner in (17), or a pronoun in (18). What may be far more important from a cognitive point of view is the recognition of the pattern *more (adj/noun) than*. We attempt to do this by describing all of these patterns in terms of MORE-THAN COMPARISON CONSTRUCTIONS (which all three can be subsumed under one MORE-THAN COMPARISON hyper-construction, of course):

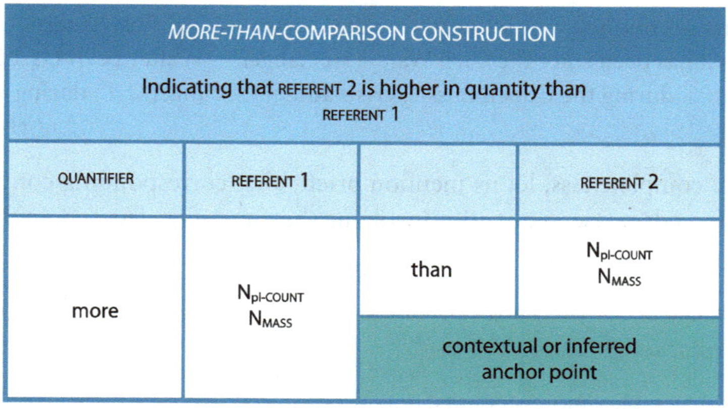

Chapter 7. Using adjectives to evaluate, describe and compare   173

Figure 7.10 The *MORE-THAN*-COMPARISON CONSTRUCTION (type 2) as in Examples (17)

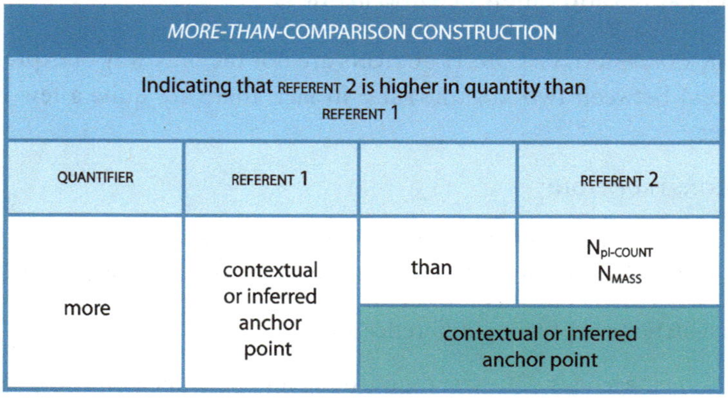

Figure 7.11 The *MORE-THAN*-COMPARISON CONSTRUCTION (type 3) as in Examples (18)

That any differences as to the part-of-speech classification of *more* may not be psychologically relevant in such cases is shown by examples of coordination such as (19), which is not unusual (as shown by more than 700 instances of *more and better/etc. noun* in COCA):

(19)   It also says it will provide more and safer locations to park and repair bicycles to encourage cyclists.   NYT-28-Jan-1993

Incidentally, some of the uses of what we call the *MORE*-COMPARATIVE CONSTRUCTION, rely quite heavily on the interpretative skills of the hearer or reader, as shown by the following two versions of essentially the same text, published on the day of the first Presidential debate in the 2020 campaign, (20a) being a kind of sub-header, (20b) part of the text:

(20)   a.   Our democracy is in terrible danger – more than since the Civil War, more than after Pearl Harbor, more than during the Cuban missile crisis.   NYT-29-Sept-2020

b. I can't say this any more clearly: Our democracy is in terrible danger – more danger than it has been since the Civil War, more danger than after Pearl Harbor, more danger than during the Cuban missile crisis and more danger than during Watergate.

NYT-29-Sept-2020

For the sake of completeness, let us mention briefly that corresponding constructions can be postulated for a decrease in quantity, involving the quantifiers *less* and, in the case of $N_{pl\text{-}count}$, *fewer*, as in (21) and (22):

(21) a. Schizoaffective disorder is less common than schizophrenia... COCA-2015-MAG
b. Two plus seven is less than ten. COCA-2019-MAG

(22) We should be taking more students, not fewer. BNC-ANY-2051

7.4.3 Ways of expressing difference and likeness

The MORE-THAN-COMPARATIVE CONSTRUCTIONS are not the only way of expressing a difference (or likeness) between two ATTRIBUTEES. In fact, there are quite a few ways of doing this, for instance:

i. the AS-AS CONSTRUCTION:

(23) a. They look alike but they're as different as chalk and cheese. BNC-GW3-1379
b. And having a bilateral deal is not as good as a trilateral deal. COCA-2018-SPOK

ii. verbal constructions expressing difference:

(24) a. ... their agendas differ from those of their opponents only by degrees.
COCA-2019-MAG

b. Cesarean delivery rates vary tenfold among US hospitals... COCA-2019-MAG

iii. adjectival constructions:

(25) a. The street looked very different from its Sunday image... BNC-GWB-1002
b. He walked back by a different route which took him along the waterfront.
BNC-GW3-712

iv. noun constructions

(26) a. ... the difference between structuralism and poststructuralism ... BNC-ANY-668
b. It wasn't hard to see talent discrepancy between the teams... COCA-2019-MAG

Chapter 7. Using adjectives to evaluate, describe and compare   **175**

In very much the same way, speakers can express similarity and equalness:

i.   using particular verbs in verbal constructions such as the SUBJECT-ATTRIBUTE CONSTRUCTION:

(27) a. So one plus one **is** two, two plus one is three, three plus two is five. COCA-2019-TV
       b. It's getting both sides of the Air France KLM group to be more effective, so that gets one plus one **equals** three or four.   COCA-2019-SPOK

ii.   using particular adjectives expressing identity or similarity:

(28) a. Jessica's eyes moved to Elizabeth's – eyes identical to Elizabeth's. COCA-2019-FIC
       b. And I want them to have exactly the same opportunities that I had.
                                      COCA-2019-SPOK

iii. using particular nouns:

(29) a. If you're looking for a parallel to baseball in Detroit and in Michigan to match 1968, forget it.   COCA-2018-NEWS
       b. Oh, no, there's no physical resemblance.   COCA-2007-TV

It must be underscored that the list of constructions discussed in this chapter is by no means exhaustive. However, what the discussion of the different ways of expressing difference, similarity, etc. has shown is that we can achieve the same or a very similar communicative effect in a large variety of different ways – some of which are predominantly lexical in character, while others involve constructions with a greater degree of schematicity. We have also seen that even some of the more schematic constructions contain fixed lexical elements such as *more, than, as*, etc., whereas others, like the COMPARATIVE CONSTRUCTION and the SUPERLATIVE CONSTRUCTION, are based on morphological elements such as {-er} or {-est}. It is observations such as these that make construction grammarians and cognitive linguists reject a strict dividing line between lexis and grammar.

CHAPTER 8

Where, when and how
Specification of circumstances

8.1 Going beyond "who does what to whom"

Argument structure constructions have received considerable attention in the construction-ist literature because they fulfill a basic need of human communication in that they allow speakers to express "who did what to whom" (Goldberg 2019: 65). However, speakers also relate facts and events to other facts and events, and, in particular, to their own experience of the real world or an imaginative world (such as the world of a film, a novel, etc.). This involves talking about when, where, why or how a particular event takes or took place.

In English, there is a wide range of constructions that can be used to provide information that goes beyond saying "who does what to whom". It would be impossible to cover all such constructions here, but in this chapter we would like to identify the most important types of such constructions and will provide a few examples of these types.

8.2 Constructions situating an event with respect to location and time

8.2.1 Different ways of expressing similar meanings

Let us start by looking at some aspects of the following passage from a Cornish detective novel:

(1) [a] Wycliffe, unsettled in his mind, made a broad detour on the way back to his hotel. [b] He walked as far as the beaches and along the deserted sea front. [c] Wavelets swished idly over white sand and the broad plain of the sea stretched away into darkness. [d] To his left, St Anthony lighthouse flashed at intervals, and far away to his right the sky was lit now and then by an arc of light from The Lizard.

(W. J. Burley, Wycliffe and the Winsor Blue, 2010)

You will have noticed that the passage contains quite a few references to locations. These are often expressed by prepositional phrases such as *along the deserted sea front* or *to his left* (marked in green). Some of these locational references related to geographical points (*St Anthony lighthouse, the Lizard*) of the so-called real world, others depend for their interpretation on the mental space evoked by the story (*the way back to his hotel*). In particular, expressions such as *to his left* or *far away to his right* are relational in character in that they can only be worked out taking the protagonist, *Wycliffe*, as a point of orientation.

Furthermore, this short passage relates the actions described to one another with respect to time. In addition to the verbs marked for tense and aspect (*made, walked, swished,* etc.), it is again prepositional phrases (*at intervals*) and adverb phrases (*now and then*) that

Chapter 8. Where, when and how **177**

express time relations; furthermore, even without knowing any of the preceding text, the noun *darkness* and the fact that one can see the beams of two lighthouses provide a clear indication of the time of the day. Less obvious, but definitely worth noting, is the fact that as readers we will expect the sequence of events described to correspond to the order in which they are presented here.[100]

In sentence [b], we must interpret the walk to the beaches as occurring before walking along the sea front. The next two sentences show, however, that it is by no means always the case that we interpret coordinated events in terms of a natural sequence, because our knowledge of the world allows us to see the events as going on simultaneously. In other words, we will arrive at a sequence-of-events-interpretation only if (a) there is a reason to assume that the two events could not occur simultaneously and independently from one another, and if (b) there is no explicit indication of a different sequence as, for example, in (2):

(2) a.   Before going out Wycliffe again studied the map ...   BNC-GW3-1711
     b.   Things got a little crazy after you left last night.   TV-2013-Psych

What this short analysis shows is that both place and time relations can be expressed in a number of rather different ways, and that our knowledge of the world and the inferences we can make on its basis interact in arriving at an interpretation of how we situate the events described in a text with respect to location in space and time.

8.2.2   Point of location

There are various constructions in English that can be used to describe the position of a 'thing' (in the technical sense of person, object, event, etc.) with respect to another 'thing'. We refer to these as POINT-OF-LOCATION-CONSTRUCTIONS:

(3) a.   In some places, the sea level relative to the land rose more than eight inches between 1960 and 2020.   NYT-12-May-2021
     b.   It was available on the agency's website but was not kept current.   NYT-12-May-2021
     c.   That's where I saw you!   BNC-ANY-1899
     d.   Where shall I sit?   BNC-ANY-2732

Different prepositions can express different locational relations, as, for instance, in (4):

(4) a.   I wasn't in Santa Barbara. I was in New York.   TV-2013-Psych
     b.   ... when they were all students at Santa Barbara University.   TV-2008-Psych

In (4a) the locational PP fills the Attr slot of a SUBJECT-ATTRIBUTE CONSTRUCTION. (4b) also contains a SUBJECT-ATTRIBUTE CONSTRUCTION, but here the Attr slot is filled by the NP *all students* and the PP functions as additional, extra information. This is a difference that we will explore in more depth below.

---

100. For iconic sequencing see, e.g., Ungerer & Schmid (2006: 301).

8.2.3 Time

In English, talking about time and time relations often happens in terms of what one could see as a metaphorical extension of the ways in which people talk about physical space. With respect to time, we can identify constructions such as the following:

- POINT-IN-TIME-CONSTRUCTIONS

  (5) a. The new data notes that the extent of Arctic sea ice cover in 2020 was the second-smallest on record. NYT-12-May-2021
  b. The new flowers caused a sensation in the 17th century and soon became the rage. NYT-24-Oct-1993

- TIME-SPAN-CONSTRUCTIONS

  (6) a. Since taking office, President Biden has made climate action a top priority across the federal government. NYT-12-May-2021
  b. At 14 of 15 sites, permafrost temperatures rose between 1978 and 2020 NYT-12-May-2021
  c. Until 2016, the E.P.A. regularly updated its climate indicators. NYT-12-May-2021

- TIME-DURATION-CONSTRUCTIONS

  (7) It had gone on for some time, she couldn't say how long. BNC-HWP-1191

- TIME-FREQUENCY-CONSTRUCTIONS

  (8) a. Somewhere out to sea the beam of the lighthouse appeared intermittently as a misty glow in the sky and the fog-horn was sounding. BNC-GW3-3404
  b. ... St Anthony lighthouse flashed at intervals ... BNC-HWP-2529
  c. Out to sea the beam of the lighthouse swept a great arc every fifteen seconds ... BNC-GW3-24

- TIME-SEQUENCE-CONSTRUCTIONS

  (9) a. 'And afterwards?' BNC-GW3-2997
  b. A car with headlights on came towards him, cautiously negotiated the hairpin bend, and for some time afterwards he could hear it grinding up the hill to Albert Terrace. BNC-GW3-2516
  c. She knew she was good, and it wasn't long before she privately concluded that she was better than most of her colleagues – more enthusiastic, more energetic, more productive. BNC-ANY-716

Apart from the constructions listed here, there are a number of other ways to relate 'things' to time – most importantly, of course, the tense and aspect constructions discussed in Chap-

Chapter 8. Where, when and how   **179**

ter 4, but also by lexical means. For instance, the elements of the meaning of a verb some-times discussed under the label of *Aktionsart* are clearly related to time. Thus the meanings of verbs such as *knock* or *hop* entail an element of repetition of the same action (such verbs are called iterative); durative verbs such as *read* or *drive* describe an action of some dura-tion, punctual verbs such as *explode* or *collapse* in contrast refer to actions that are rather short, and yet other types of verb, the so-called terminative verbs, imply a point of begin-ning or end (e.g., *start, drown* or *die*).

8.3 Constructions detailing the way the action described is carried out

Just as – to a greater or lesser degree – verb meanings entail a temporal dimension, the meaning of some verbs contains an element of manner:

(10) The fog-horn on the lighthouse moaned at intervals, a surpassingly dismal sound like a cow in labour.   BNC-GW3-270

(11) a. Why would someone shoot and stab the first victim and then just stab the second one?   TV-2013-Psych

  b. I found this body a couple of hours ago in my living room, stabbed to death with a knife from my kitchen.   TV-2014-Psych

  c. It was so impressive the way you just attacked that mad woman with a knife.
                                                                                   TV-2009-Psych

More commonly, though, constructions such as the following are used to describe the way an action is carried out:

− MANNER-CONSTRUCTIONS

  (12) a. 'Is that you?' she says drowsily ...   BNC-ANY-102

    b. ... but she deals with them in a rational, orderly manner.   BNC-ANY-559

− INSTRUMENT/MEANS-CONSTRUCTIONS

  (13) a. Cissie was holding her baby with one hand and her book with the other.
                                                                                   BNC-GW3-1237

    b. ... Robyn made her way back to the car park by going round the outside of the building ...   BNC-ANY-2876

    c. They don't know quite how to react.   BNC-ANY-439

180   A Construction Grammar of the English Language

8.4 Constructions that situate the event described within the domain of causation and interrelatedness of 'things'

Another group of constructions addresses the need of speakers to show how one 'thing' is related to other 'things':

– BENEFICIARY-CONSTRUCTION

(14) a. I have some important information for you.   BNC-ANY-2858
     b. It must be a worrying and distressing time for you ...   BNC-GW3-487
     c. 'Call for you, sir – Dr Franks.'   BNC-HWP-3051

– PURPOSE-CONSTRUCTIONS

(15) a. Scientists say the world needs to prevent average global temperatures from rising more than 3.6 degrees Fahrenheit (2 degrees Celsius) above preindustrial levels to avoid irreversible damage to the planet.   NYT-12-May-2021
     b. To mark the event, the Netherlands begins a yearlong tulip quadricentennial.
                                                               NYT-24-Oct-1993

– REASON-CONSTRUCTIONS

(16) a. That's especially useful because many Americans tend to view climate change as a problem affecting other people or more remote parts of the world ...
                                                               NYT-12-May-2021
     b. Since they were featured in so many of the paintings of the Dutch masters, these tulips became known as the Rembrandt tulips.   NYT-24-Oct-1993

– CONDITION-CONSTRUCTIONS

(17) If you're coming to Amsterdam and are enamored of architecture, the canal belt is where you will be spending much of your time.   NYT-20-June-2010

– CONTRAST-CONSTRUCTIONS

(18) a. Records also show that shortly thereafter a single bulb was sold for 4,500 guilders or $ 2,250 plus a horse and carriage. But prices have settled down and today tulip bulbs are about 50 cents each.   NYT-24-Oct-1993
     b. It runs well, though the battery is getting feeble.   BNC-ANY-730

– COMPARISON-CONSTRUCTIONS

(19) a. Away to his right the lighthouse stood on its rocky island like a picture in a story book ...   BNC-GW3-131
     b. ... the dark side of Rummidge, as foreign to her as the dark side of the moon.
                                                               BNC-ANY-1555

– REPLACEMENT-CONSTRUCTIONS

Chapter 8. Where, when and how **181**

(20) a. But you called him "Clay" instead of "dad" or "father". TV-2009-Psych
b. She was too honest to deceive him and too prudent to exchange him for a lover whose interest would probably not last very long. BNC-ANY-743
c. Well, she was sick and tired of the place, tired of its beautiful architecture housing vanity and paranoia, glad to exchange its hothouse atmosphere for the real if smoky air of Rummidge. BNC-ANY-805

– ROLE-CONSTRUCTIONS

(21) a. … you work as a psych… TV-2009-Psych
b. I didn't mean it as a compliment. TV-1965-Bewitched

8.5 Constructions that express an assessment of the event described by the speaker

Some constructions also allow speakers to express how likely they think the event described in an argument structure construction actually is:

– LIKELIHOOD-CONSTRUCTIONS

(22) a. She probably knows more about the nineteenth-century industrial novel than anyone else in the entire world. BNC-ANY-833
b. He most likely used an EMP device. TV-2010-Psych
c. So I think, in all likelihood, the Mueller investigation goes beyond the election. COCA-2019-SPOK

Other ways of indicating likelihood include MODAL CONSTRUCTIONS (4.2) and constructions with adjectives (*It was not very **likely** that the cuts of asteroids have survived.* (TV-2009-The Universe)) or nouns *There's a high **probability** of tears.* (TV-2017-Grey's Anatomy)).

Similarly, COMMENT-CONSTRUCTIONS can be added to argument structure construction to express a speaker's stance on an event:

– COMMENT-CONSTRUCTIONS

(23) a. Luckily he was in. BNC-ANY-2123
b. 'Frankly, no, but as you say, it is necessary.' BNC-GW3-3167
c. To be honest, we were just expecting a phone call. TV-2010-Psych
d. No, really, it's very kind of you, but – BNC-ANY-1612

8.6 Constructions that situate the event described within the text

A final group of constructions that we would like to mention here is related to what Halliday (1970:143) calls the "textual function" of language. These allow speakers to indicate the domain for which they think an event is true:

– SCOPE-CONSTRUCTIONS

    (24) a.   This is obviously true with respect to the Senate ...   SupremeCourt-22318-2016
          b.   But remember this, as far as Steed is concerned, I do not exist.   TV-1969-Avengers

– STRUCTURING-CONSTRUCTIONS

    (25) a.   Um, where do I start? First of all, you're not a psychic.   TV-2013-Psych
          b.   And furthermore, it's completely irrelevant to these proceedings. TV-1984-Dynasty

8.7 The gradient character of these distinctions

It is important to understand that, in some cases at least, the boundaries between these constructions are by no means clear-cut – something that is perfectly in line with the overall take on the nature of categories in cognitive models. As Langacker (2008a:13) emphasizes, it is an open question "whether the basic discreteness commonly assumed by linguistic theorists has been **discovered in** language or **imposed on** it". It has long been recognized that in many cases linguistic categories are best described in terms of gradience (CGEL 1985:90 or Aarts 2007) or family resemblance (Wittgenstein 1953). Penguins, e.g., cannot fly, and are, therefore, considered less prototypical examples of the category bird than say robins (which can fly). Since penguins share more properties with the category bird than any other category, they are, consequently, still classified as birds. Category membership is, therefore, not categorical but gradient in nature, with some members showing more prototypical features than others. The same gradience of membership can also be observed with constructions. A case in point are constructions with PP_{for}:

  (26) a.   Do you want them alive for questioning, sir?   TV-1969-Avengers
        b.   Sorry to disturb you. Which platform for the 08:10 to Liverpool?   TV-1967-Avengers
        c.   Now, put that gun down. On the bench. For Mrs Peel's sake.   TV-1965-Avengers
        d.   But I'll make it easy for you.   TV-1989-Dynasty
        e.   Well, I brought something for you.   TV-2013-DoctorWho
        f.   Mr Steed, I have been a lawyer for Mrs Peel's family for years.   TV-1966-Avengers
        g.   I know you think this is easy for me, but I do go through a mental process.
                TV-2007-Psych

        h.   I'm waiting for someone.   TV-1967-Avengers
        i.   I'm actually here for some police advice.   TV-2010-Psych

j. I'm just looking for some sunscreen. TV-2010-Psych
k. Well, no, I'm not gonna pay for it. TV-2006-Psych

(26a) presents a clear case of a PURPOSE-CONSTRUCTION, and a certain element of 'purpose' can also be detected in (26b)–(d). (26e) and (26f) might be seen as prototypical instances of a BENEFICIARY-CONSTRUCTION, although (26e) can be related to 'purpose' in a way (namely the purpose of doing something from which the other person benefits), which is less plausible in the case of (26f). Despite the similarity to (26d), (26g) seems to be neither describing a 'purpose' nor a 'beneficiary', but is rather to be interpreted in terms of a STANDARD characteristic of the person in question. In a very benevolent kind of analysis, (26h) and (26i) could be given a 'purpose' interpretation, but a category such as 'thing desired or aimed at' might be more appropriate, which presumably also matches (26j). In (26k) we might see the relationship as exchanging one 'thing' for another. What this short and by no means exhaustive analysis is supposed to illustrate is simply that – especially in cases such as that of the notoriously polysemic preposition *for* – there is considerable overlap between the various meanings we can identify for such constructions.

This, of course, is not a new insight nor one that is restricted to cognitive research. Just as you will hardly find two dictionaries agreeing on how many – let alone *which* – senses to identify for semantically complex words, it is rather unlikely that any two linguists will arrive at the very same classification of, say, the examples under (26). To a certain extent it is unavoidable that by analyzing such cases we impose certain categories on the material analyzed, but this does not in any way mean to ignore the considerable amount of overlap between them, as indicated in Figure 8.1.

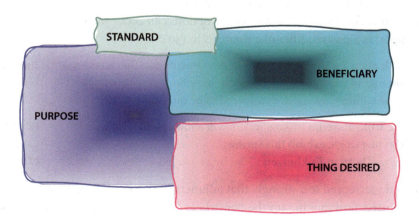

Figure 8.1 The overlap of semantic meanings of *for* constructions in the constructional network

8.8 The syntactic status of adjunct constructions

8.8.1 Integration in sentences and utterances

Constructions such as the POINT-OF-LOCATION CONSTRUCTION, the TIME-DURATION CONSTRUCTION, or the CONDITION CONSTRUCTION all presuppose an event, action or process to which they apply. We consider this to be a part of a speaker's knowledge of a construction, which we subsume under the **usage conditions** of the respective constructions.

In some cases, the constructions we have called adjunct constructions can fill slots of argument structure constructions, as in the case of (27), or occur as a fragment construction that takes up an argument slot of another construction in the context, as in (28):

(27) a. I was in New York.   TV-2013-Psych
      b. She puts her soiled breakfast things in the sink ...   BNC-ANY-650

(28) a. 'Nobody believes that, Mr Wycliffe.' — 'Then why do they say it?' — 'Because it makes a good story, something to talk about in the pubs.'   BNC-GW3-580-582
      b. 'When did you get back to the house?' — 'Just before one.'   BNC-GW3-3071-3072

These cases are special in that their occurrence is dependent on the presence of an argument structure providing a slot for the respective adjunct — in German linguistics, these elements are often referred to by terms such as *Adverbativergänzungen* (see VALBU 2004: 34; Herbst & Uhrig 2020).

More typically, adjuncts can combine with a clause in a number of different places (CGEL Ch. 8), depending on whether they modify a particular element of a clause or the clause as a whole. For instance, adjunct constructions can occur sentence-initially, as in (29), or, for example, as a postmodifier of a noun, as in (30):

(29) a. With many colleges facing falling enrollments and financial pressure, the decision whether to require vaccinations can have huge consequences.   NYT-22-May-2021
      b. On the Enterprise I was considered to be quite amusing.   TV-1998-StarTrek

(30) a. The **Rijksmuseum** in Amsterdam will showcase most of its works by Rembrandt van Rijn in a single exhibit this spring ...   COCA-2019-MAG
      b. He was born in **Enkhuizen** in northern Holland.   COCA-2010-MAG

It cannot be underscored too strongly that adjuncts of this latter type are not "required" by any other construction making up the construct.[101] Whether, strictly speaking, one should consider them to be part of the predicate or not may be debatable, but is, in our view, relatively irrelevant. What is relevant from a constructionist point of view is solely that the predicate in the DECLARATIVE-STATEMENT or YES-NO-QUESTION CONSTRUCTIONS does not contain slots for adjunct constructions.

---

101. The only exception is presented by wh-quesstion constructions.

Chapter 8. Where, when and how   **185**

8.8.2   Adjunct constructions

The term adjunct is a theoretically 'loaded' one, which is why we need to discuss it in a bit more depth. Traditionally, the term is used in very much the same way as the term adverbial (or, as in CGEL, optional adverbial). Typical adjuncts in the traditional and structuralist sense refer to clause constituents that

i.   are not determined in their form by the main verb of the clause,
ii. can be left out without making a sentence ungrammatical.

Both these criteria are not entirely unproblematic, because there are constituents to which criterion (i) applies, whereas criterion (ii) does not – hence the slightly contradictory category obligatory adverbials in CGEL).

From a frame-semantic (Fillmore 2014; FrameNet; Goldberg 2019; Herbst 2022) or cognitive point of view, it may be easier to approach the problem from the other side: Frames are mental spaces or knowledge structures associated to a particular situation or process, frame elements are the 'things' immediately involved in the actions or processes described as well as the circumstances under which they can happen. Some frame elements are more central to particular frames than to others – for instance, a frame element such as PRICE is more likely to be activated in the brain when you speak about buying or selling something, where PATH is not particularly relevant, which, however, is relevant in the context of *walking* or *travelling*. This is why PATH is listed as a frame element in FrameNet in the Self_motion and Ride_vehicle frames, but not in the Commercial_transaction frame. The opposite is true of MONEY, although it is perfectly possible that someone will talk about the price of, say, flying to New York from Nuremberg via Amsterdam. It is thus perfectly clear that the frame elements that are of greater relevance to a frame will be activated more often when the central verbs belonging to the frame are being used. We can thus reasonably expect such frame elements to be captured by the corresponding argument structure constructions of these verbs.

While a frame element such as PRICE is very specific and only serves to describe a relatively small number of frames, others such as POINT OF LOCATION or POINT IN TIME can be applied to the description of almost any 'process'. Thus, there is no particularly strong association between the constructions expressing these frame elements and most verbs. The only exception is presented by cases in which one of these frame elements is crucial to the characterization of a particular frame, say, the frame element POINT OF LOCATION in the Residence frame. This is why it comes as no surprise that this frame contains verbs which have slots for a POINT-OF-LOCATION argument such as *live, reside* or even *inhabit*. When applied to other situations, for which POINT OF LOCATION is not a characteristic, we cannot expect there to be verbs that provide a corresponding argument slot. These are the cases when information such as this has to be supplied by an adjunct construction.

The semantic function of adjunct constructions can be captured in a very general way by saying that they provide further information about the process described by situating it within the dimensions outlined in this chapter, i.e., with respect to TIME, MANNER, etc.

186   A Construction Grammar of the English Language

At the level of form, they can be characterized as consisting of two slots – one for type of adjunct (which entails specification of form and meanings in terms of constructions as the ones specified above) and one for the argument structure construction to which it attaches and that expresses the process described.

ADJUNCT CONSTRUCTION	
Providing further information about a state or process	
CIRCUMSTANTIAL INFORMATION	PROPOSITION
Adjunct	Argument structure cxn

Figure 8.2 The English ADJUNCT CONSTRUCTION

The adjunct construction as such does not specify the order of elements, as can be seen from (31), which contains one adjunct before and one after the argument structure construction:

(31)   ... Fascinated by the boldness of Piet Mondrian's work, he created the Mondrian dress in 1965 ...   COCA-2008-MAG

Under this view, we thus get overlap between the adjunct constructions, which we can show in a construction grid of the type represented in Figure 8.3:

	he	created	the Mondrian dress	in 1965
DECS	SUBJ	$V_{TM} \in PRED$		
MONOTRANSITIVE CXN	Subj	V	Obj: NP	
ADJUNCT CXN	PROPOSITION			PP

Figure 8.3 Construction grid for *He created the Mondrian dress in 1965* showing that the adjunct construction has a slot for the argument structure construction it refers to

As with pre- and postmodifier constructions of nouns, adjectives and adverbs, we will, however, refrain from explicitly showing this overlap in most grids, resulting in simpler grids such as Figure 8.4 on the next page.

Adjunct constructions in our model are thus similar to modifier constructions in that they describe a rather general function and are not specified for a specific form as such. Rather, adjunct constructions do not "exist" (in the model) as a single abstract constructional template but can be seen as creating a slot in sentence structure for more specific

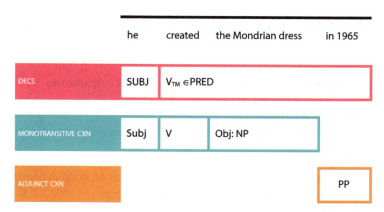

Figure 8.4 Construction grid for *He created the Mondrian dress in 1965* (simplified graph)

constructions of the meso-construction types (i.e., mid-level partially filled constructions) outlined above, e.g., for a POINT-IN-TIME or a PURPOSE-CONSTRUCTION.

In the kind of analysis that we propose for the purposes of this textbook, we thus suggest describing all of the instances marked in colour as adjunct constructions at the most schematic (macro-)level of analysis and using the far more specific constructional labels identified above for discussions at the micro-level, taking up a distinction introduced by Traugott (2008: 236):

(32) [meso-level: POINT-IN-TIME CXN – macro-level: ADJUNCT CXN]
    a. We talked about it last night.   TV-2012-Downton
    b. Last night he looked so well.   TV-2010-Downton

(33) [meso-level: PURPOSE CXN – macro-level: ADJUNCT CXN]
    a. Until now, it has been necessary to maintain secrecy in order to protect the character of my client's design.   TV-1966-Bewitched
    b. Well, in order to distinguish between the two, people inevitably refer to one as "big" and the other as "little."   TV-1966-Bewitched

Examples (32) and (33) also illustrate another typical aspect of adjunct constructions, namely that they can occur in different places in a clause – which is often seen as an indication of a rather peripheral role in the clause. It must be noted that it is a feature of the individual micro-constructions in which positions in a clause they can occur and whether they can occur as arguments or postmodifiers.

Note that the distinction between argument structure constructions and adjunct constructions reflects distinctions made in most theories of syntax in one form or another – e.g., between *complements* and *adjuncts* in Valency Theory, which goes back to the famous stage metaphor employed by the founder of Dependency Grammar, Tesnière (1959/2015: 97). Tesnière drew a comparison between a clause and a theatrical performance, in which the *actants* "are the beings or things ... that participate in the process ..." and the *circumstants* "express the circumstances of time, place, manner, etc.". Numerous structural criteria have

188 A Construction Grammar of the English Language

been suggested to establish the distinction, but no criterion or no combination of criteria has been established that would reliably do that.[102]

8.8.3 POINT IN TIME and POINT OF LOCATION as adjuncts or arguments

The distinction between argument structure constructions and adjunct construction is not always as clear-cut as we would like it to be for the purposes of syntactic analysis. Take a look at the following examples:

(34) a. Queen Elizabeth II was born on April 21, 1926, the eldest child of King George VI and his wife, the Queen Mother Elizabeth Bowes-Lyon. NOW-21-04-25-AU
    b. Harris was born in Oakland. COCA-2019-SPOK
    c. William Shakespeare was born in 1564 in Stratford-upon-Avon. COCA-1999-MOV

Since having been born is not a particularly good criterion to distinguish one individual from another, it is not surprising that uses of *was born* without indicating a point in time or a place are not very frequent, unless there is some other "newsworthy" item:

(35) I mean, a star was born. COCA-2019-SPOK

The question is to what extent occurrences such as (35) should influence the analysis of (34): Does (35) show that the entrenched pattern is a lexically filled SUBJECT ATTRIBUTE CONSTRUCTION and that the TIME- and PLACE-constructions in (34) must, consequently, be classified as adjuncts that specify the circumstances under which the action took place? One could also argue, however, that the high frequency of patterns such as (34) indicates that speakers have entrenched PP^{TIME} and PP^{PLACE} as integral constructional parts of this argument structure. In this case, we can analyze (34a) and (34b) as representing a PASSIVE ATTRIBUTE CONSTRUCTION in which the Attr slot is filled by a POINT-IN-TIME or a POINT-OF-LOCATION construction. This, however, still leaves us with the problem of how to analyze (34c) – as

i. an attribute construction in which the Attr slot is taken by a PP^{PLACE} (and the PP^{TIME} is an adjunct), or
ii. an attribute construction in which the Attr slot is taken by a PP^{TIME} (and the PP^{PLACE} is an adjunct), or
iii. a combination of two attribute constructions in which the Attr slot is taken by a PP^{TIME} in the one and a PP^{PLACE} in the other.

From a cognitive point of view, options (i) and (ii) do not make much sense. If we expect speakers to have formed strong associations of the phrase *was born* with temporal and locational phrases that is all we need to know – and describe.

---

102. See Haegeman (1991: 37) for a government-binding theory approach to the argument-adjunct distinction.

Chapter 8. Where, when and how   **189**

In a syntactic analysis, one will have to make an informed decision of some kind. In our view, there are good arguments for either the two-adjuncts or the two-arguments solution – but whichever "solution" one decides on, it must be clear that it is based on a linguist's desire to provide a consistent and unambiguous analysis rather than something that was "discovered" in the language (Langacker 2008a: 37). (For it is very well possible that individual speakers also differ as to how they have stored these patterns: some might have entrenched the two-argument construction, others might have created the construct on-the-fly by adding two adjuncts.)

What makes the situation even more complicated is that constructs that look rather similar to those in (34) might nevertheless lend themselves to a different analysis. While (36a) and (36b) definitely qualify as an ATTRIBUTE CONSTRUCTION on very much the same grounds as (34a), in (36c) one can make out a strong case for a time adjunct (supported by the different word order in 36d).

(36) a. She lives in Hoorn. COCA-2005-MOV
b. Shakespeare lived from 1564 to 1616. NOW-18-02-15-US
c. Ai Weiwei lived in New York from 1983 to 1993. NOW-15-11-27-AU
d. From 1969 to 1975 he lived in Paris where he collaborated closely with luminaries such as Karl Lagerfeld, Kenzo, Yves Saint Laurent … COCA-1992-MAG

As you can see, CASA analyses are open to the fact that it is not always possible to provide a single, 'correct' analysis. It is important to always remember that some constructs can be explained by the blending of different constructions – and that it is very well possible that individual speakers follow different paths to arrive at the same construct.

8.8.4   CHANGE-OF-LOCATION constructions and multiple realization

We are faced with similar kinds of problems with CHANGE-OF-LOCATION CONSTRUCTIONS, which we discussed in the context of the SELF-MOTION and CAUSED-MOTION CONSTRUCTIONS in 5.5. This is mainly because the verbs occurring in these constructions are so closely related to the idea of motion and the indication of the change of location that characterizing the locational information as circumstantial seems inappropriate. Even a verb such as *tiptoe*, which profiles the manner of walking rather than the change of location, almost always occurs together with some change-of-location expression in the BNC:

(37) Catherine tiptoed over the polished parquet floor to the bed … BNC-ANL-3257

As already pointed out (8.2.3), there are different types of CHANGE-OF-LOCATION CONSTRUCTIONS, each of which can serve as slot fillers on their own, as, e.g., in (38), or in combination with others, as in (39):

(38) a. We sailed from Edinburgh's port of Leith, on the RMS St Ninian, … BNC-AS7-250
b. The trawler went down after sailing from Falmouth in February 1991. BNC-K5D-825

(39) a. FIRE broke out yesterday on a cross-Channel ferry sailing from Dieppe to
Newhaven. BNC-CBF-6868

b. Drake sailed back to Plymouth in 1581 ... BNC-FS3-88

In 5.5, we adopted an approach that does not prioritize one of these constructions, say the PP_{from}^{SOURCE} in (39a), over another, the PP_{to}^{GOAL} in this case, and to say that one of them fills the CHANGE-OF-LOCATION slot of the construction and the other one does not and is therefore an adjunct. A more sophisticated analysis of individual verbs, however, might lead one to do precisely that, however.

Take a verb such as *put*, for example. *Put* definitely has an inherent GOAL-orientation, and hardly ever occurs with a SOURCE-, let alone a PATH-construction (with the exception of phrases such as *put it from your mind* in (40)). And even in a less extreme case, *come*, we can observe this GOAL-orientation even when the GOAL-argument is not explicitly expressed, as in (41):

(40) The big question is whether they have mastered the complicated job of putting bugs from a laboratory inside a useful battlefield weapon. BNC-ABE-2958

(41) a. He walked to Newlyn, where the paintings and the pilchards came from in the old days ... BNC-GWB-973

b. The only sound came from the ticking of a clock. BNC-GWB-1021

(41b) has an implicit GOAL-orientation in the form of the place at which the protagonist is at this particular place in the narration. (41a) allows a similar, though more general interpretation in terms of the community that used to buy the fish. A further indication of this GOAL-orientation of *come* is the fact that, as a response to (42a), (42b) is far less odd than (42c):

(42) a. Pa, he came, but he didn't stay. TV-1960-Bonanza

b. When did he come?

c. ??Where did he come?

One could take such a line of reasoning as the basis for classifying the SOURCE-constructions in (40) and (41) as adjuncts and the GOAL-construction in (40) as an argument because only the former two provide "additional" information. However, in the light of the gradience character of the distinction between arguments and adjuncts it seems rather pointless to apply it here.

Similarly, it would be odd to treat one of the PPs as a pre- or postmodifier of the other. We advocate a solution here that allows THE CHANGE-OF-LOCATION slot of the SELF-MOTION CONSTRUCTION and the CAUSED-MOTION CONSTRUCTION to be realized in principle by any and any number of the CHANGE-OF-LOCATION CONSTRUCTIONS identified above (Herbst & Uhrig 2020). This means that we will allow for what we can call **multiple realizations** of one argument slot by various subconstructions that fit the respective argument role.

Chapter 8. Where, when and how

8.8.5 The (ir)relevance of the argument vs. adjunct distinction

The distinction between arguments (or, in other terminologies, complements) and adjuncts (peripheral elements, optional adverbials, etc.) is a textbook example of the purpose-drivenness of certain aspects of linguistic analysis.

For lexicography and language teaching it is important to distinguish between elements that are closely related to and possibly determined in form by a particular verb, the arguments, and elements that can occur in sentences independently from particular verbs. In this respect, the distinction between arguments and adjuncts is a very useful one (despite its gradience character) because it helps to elicit the constructions that should be learnt, taught and presented in dictionaries together with the respective verbs.

Taking a cognitive perspective, the current state of the art suggests that frequency of co-occurrence and in particular **transitional probabilities** play a much more crucial role in the production and perception of utterances alongside the way that certain recurrent constellations of linguistic units come to form the clusters we call constructions. Although we would expect argument structure constructions – especially those with a high degree of schematicity such as CAUSED-MOTION or the DITRANSITIVE CONSTRUCTION – to emerge and become entrenched in speakers' mental constructicons, any debate about whether particular borderline cases ought to be subsumed under an argument structure construction or be treated as an adjunct are relatively futile.

8.8.6 Vocatives

Finally, in this section on adjuncts, let us include a category that usually does not play any great role in sentence structure – vocatives (CGEL 1985: Ch. 10.51–53). We will identify as a VOCATIVE CONSTRUCTION any personal name or other identifying noun phrase that does not fill a slot of any argument structure construction in the sentence and has the semantic function of catching the addressee's attention.

(43) a. You said it yourself, Jules. It's torrential out there.   TV-2009-Psych
     b. 'Dr Penrose,' he said, 'I think you've got the wrong idea about your position here.

                                                                          BNC-ANY-2803

     c. Friends, Romans, countrymen, lend me your ears ...   Shakespeare-JuliusCaesar

CHAPTER 9

Joining ideas and clauses

9.1 Compression through blending

Language use tends to be economical. This shows in various ways: Words that are used frequently tend to be reduced phonetically (*She is* > *She's, I do not know* > I *dunno*) or become shortened (*circumstances* > *circs*) or abbreviated (*Woman Police Constable* > *WPC*). For the same reasons of language economy, you are very unlikely to come across a sentence such as (1):

(1) The authors of this book met at a cognitive linguistics conference in Edmonton and the authors of this book met at a cognitive linguistics conference in Newcastle and the authors of this book met at a cognitive linguistics conference in Paris and the authors of this book met at a cognitive linguistics conference in Eichstätt and the authors of this book met a cognitive linguistics conference in Osaka.

Rather, a speaker might choose the following form for expressing the same content:

(2) The authors of this book met at cognitive linguistics conferences in Edmonton, Newcastle, Paris, Eichstätt, and Osaka.

This kind of compression is a characteristic of the cognitive process of blending (see 1.5).

9.2 Coordination

9.2.1 Asyndetic and syndetic coordination

It is common practice to distinguish between two types of coordination. In the case of **asyndetic coordination**, the coordinated items are simply listed, separated by commas, with the last item having a falling tone and the preceding items a rising tone.

(3) Ron Langacker gave keynotes at the construction grammar conferences in Edmonton, Newcastle, Juiz de Fora.

With **syndetic coordination**, there is an explicit verbal marker like *and*:

(4) Ron Langacker and Adele Goldberg have delivered many keynote speeches at international conferences.

If there are more than two items being coordinated, one usually finds a combination of asyndetic and syndetic coordination:

(5) Ron Langacker delivered keynote speeches in Edmonton, Newcastle, Juiz de Fora, and Erlangen.

Chapter 9. Joining ideas and clauses

9.2.2 Levels of coordination

Coordination can take place at all levels of linguistic analysis:

i. word + word, or, more precisely, phrase + phrase

> (6) a. In and out, down and up. BNC-ANY-376
> b. She put this calmly and rationally to Charles one day, and calmly and rationally he accepted it. BNC-ANY-762

> (7) All over Rummidge and its environs, people are at work – or not, as the case may be. BNC-ANY-1080

ii. predicate + predicate

> (8) Robyn straightens the sheet on the bed, shakes and spreads the duvet. BNC-ANY-671

iii. subject + subject

> (9) She and Charles worked hard and, despite the fact that they were pursuing the same course, without rivalry. BNC-ANY-614

iv. clause + clause

> (10) She knew she was good, and it wasn't long before she privately concluded that she was better than most of her colleagues – more enthusiastic, more energetic, more productive. BNC-ANY-716

v. sentence + sentence

> (11) Well, she was sick and tired of the place, tired of its beautiful architecture housing vanity and paranoia, glad to exchange its hothouse atmosphere for the real if smoky air of Rummidge. And to make the break with Cambridge somehow entailed breaking finally with Charles. BNC-ANY-805-6

Note that, in most cases, the effect of coordination is to create a new unit with the same syntactic function as that of the items coordinated. (Exceptions are the cases under (iv) and (v), which, however, is related to the distinction between clause and sentence in the case of (iv). (For (v) see 13.3.5.1 below.)

9.2.3 Additive coordination constructions

The elements that are being coordinated tend to share either formal properties (i.e., either *phrase + phrase* or *clause + clause*) or have the same syntactic function (e.g., *subject + subject*, *predicate + predicate*, etc.). We can thus identify two coordination constructions; COORDINA-TEE is the term we use for the semantic function of the elements being coordinated in the construction.

Name	ASYNDETIC-COORDINATION CONSTRUCTION			
Meaning	Listing two or more 'things'			
Semantic roles	COORDINATEE 1	COORDINATEE 2	...	COORDINATEE N
Form	X	X		X
Intonation	rising tone	rising tone	+	falling tone
Punctuation	, or ;	, or ;		

Figure 9.1 The English ASYNDETIC-COORDINATION CONSTRUCTION

Name	ADDITIVE-COORDINATION CONSTRUCTION			
Meaning	Listing two or more 'things'			
Semantic roles	COORDINATEE 1	COORDINATEE 2	COORDINATOR	COORDINATEE n
Form	X	X		X
Intonation	rising tone	rising tone	and	falling tone
Punctuation	, or ;	, or ;		

Figure 9.2 The English ADDITIVE-COORDINATION CONSTRUCTION

In the ADDITIVE-COORDINATION CONSTRUCTION there is an overt coordinator (which we simply provide in the COORDINATOR slot; *and* in Figure 9.2). The ASYNDETIC-COORDINATION CONSTRUCTION has no coordinator – we indicate this by a '+' sign in the COORDINATOR slot (Figure 9.1).

Note that additive coordination, although combining items with the same "status", may imply a (temporal or logical) sequence, as in (8) above or in (12):

(12) She puts her soiled breakfast things in the sink, already crammed with the relics of last night's supper, and hurries upstairs. BNC-ANY-650

9.2.4 Alternative coordination constructions

In the case of alternative coordination constructions, the coordinated items represent a choice rather than an addition:

(13) All the men in the University seemed to be married or gay or scientists, and Robyn had no time or energy to look further afield. BNC-ANY-812

Note that this also applies when the alternative coordination construction is combined with the asyndetic construction:

(14)   Was he polite, bantering or aggressive?   BNC-GW3-2060

ALTERNATIVE-COORDINATION CONSTRUCTION			
Listing two or more 'things'			
COORDINATEE 1	COORDINATEE 2	COORDINATOR	COORDINATEE n
X	X	or	X

Figure 9.3 The English ALTERNATIVE-COORDINATION CONSTRUCTION

9.3   Connectors and connection constructions in general

9.3.1   Connectors as a word class

We will use the term **connector** (CGEL 1985: 921) to refer to the word class of *and, or* and words with a similar function in constructions. Another additive coordinator is *as well as*, but in contrast to *and* it can also occur before the coordinated items and cannot be combined with the asyndetic construction:

(15)   As well as the additional healing properties, they are biodegradable, so are an environ-
        mentally friendly alternative to conventional dressings ...   COCA-2019-MAG

Other coordinators can be seen as discontinuous, e.g., *both+and, either+or* or *neither+nor*:

(16)   a.   Both Republicans and Democrats are claiming victory here.   COCA-2019-SPOK
        b.   Either you're insane or I am...   COCA-2019-TV
        c.   Neither Washington nor Moscow have provided a reason for the delay in that meet-
             ing.   COCA-2019-NEWS

As so often, it is notoriously difficult where to draw the line. We define as a connector any construction ranging from a single word, usually an adverb in the traditional sense, to larger units such as prepositional phrases or to-infinitive clauses

i.   that presupposes the existence of another expression in the same or a neighbouring sentence, and

ii.   that is not a subject, an object, or an attribute or a part of it.

This rather wide view of connectors has the advantage that it covers many of the lexico-grammatical means that establish cohesion in texts. We will discuss this in more detail in 9.5.

9.3.2 Connection constructions

Connection constructions are constructions like coordination constructions, which contain a connector and several elements which can be characterized as the items that are being connected, e.g., the COORDINATEE.

COORDINATEES are a special case of CONNECTEES, if we take CONNECTEES as the label for the semantic function of the elements being connected. However, as we will show below, in many cases the semantic function of the respective slots in the construction can be specified in more detail so that the CONNECTEE will only be used for one of the constructional slots, usually that part of a clause to which the more specific description applies.

Let us take a look at two connection constructions in the following extracts from an article in the *New York Times*:

(17) a. A day of dueling appearances laid out the stark differences between the two candidates, an incumbent president who has long scorned climate change as a hoax and rolled back environmental regulations and a challenger who has called for an aggressive campaign to curb the greenhouse gases blamed for increasingly extreme weather. ...   NYT-15-Sept-2020

   b. But Wade Crowfoot, California's secretary for natural resources, pressed Mr. Trump more bluntly. "If we ignore that science and sort of put our head in the sand and think it's all about vegetation management, we're not going to succeed together protecting Californians," he told the president.   NYT-14-Sept-2020

(17a) is an example of a coordination construction, as represented in Figure 9.4:

general	CONNECTEE	CONNECTOR	CONNECTEE
specific	COORDINATEE	CONNECTOR	COORDINATEE
	an incumbent president who ... environmental regulations	and	*a challenger who ... extreme weather*

Figure 9.4 General and specific semantic roles in the Coordination Construction (17a)

(17b) is an example of a condition construction, as in Figure 9.5:

general	CONNECTEE	CONNECTOR	CONNECTEE
specific	CONDITION	CONNECTOR	CONNECTEE
	we're not going to succeed together protecting Californians	if	*we ignore that science and sort of put our head in the sand and think it's all about vegetation management*

Figure 9.5 General and specific semantic roles in the CONDITION CONSTRUCTION (17b) (not indicating word order)

The two types of connecting constructions are distinguished by the lexical connectors occurring in them, as will become apparent below.

9.3.3 Connection constructions with only one expressed CONNECTEE

As with verbs and in other cases, we find instances of connective constructions in which the CONNECTEES (one or even both) are not expressed explicitly. We would still want to argue that these are instances of the construction, because semantically the constructional slots must be interpretable from the context as in (18):

(18) It's not either or. It's both and all-of-the-above.   COCA-2019-SPOK

9.4 Reasoning in discourse

9.4.1 Discourse organization

9.4.1.1 *More on addition*

Our wide definition of connectors also covers constructions that would not traditionally be seen as coordination, which tends to be restricted to the levels of clauses, phrases and sentences. However, words such as *also, too, as well*, etc. link one element of a sentence to an element of the same or a preceding sentence.

(19) a. YAMICHE-ALCINDOR: The president stopped short of all-out rejecting the bipartisan plan. He also hinted that he doesn't want to allow government funding to run out this Friday. DONALD-TRUMP: I don't think you're going to see a shutdown. I wouldn't want to go to it, no. If you did have it, it's the Democrats' fault. YAMICHE-ALCINDOR): Mr. Trump also left open the possibility that he might still declare a national emergency.   COCA-2019-SPOK
      b. Almost every Friday for the past year, and Wednesdays too, some weeks.
                                                                                                    BNC-GW3-2781

Since the semantic function of constructions such as <in addition (to)>^{CONNECTOR}, <additionally>^{CONNECTOR} or <furthermore>^{CONNECTOR} is very similar indeed, we include those under connectors, too.

(20) a. Furthermore, these results suggest that mental state prior to the start of a tennis match plays a crucial role in overall success or failure...   COCA-2004-ACAD
      b. Most gratins, additionally, lose very little by being made in advance.COCA-2014-NEWS

9.4.1.2 Sequence

In 9.2.3 we already pointed out that coordination constructions may indicate a sequence of events. This can be expressed by a number of different constructions:[103]

– Constructions expressing temporal sequence such as $CL_{\text{fin-after}}^{\text{SEQUENCE}}$, $CL_{\text{fin-before}}^{\text{SEQUENCE}}$ or constructions containing words such as <*first, second* (etc.)>

(21) a. Mr. Trump did not argue the point. "Absolutely," he said, and then turned the floor over to another briefer. NOW-20-09-15-US

b. In the first stage, beginning this year, the plan aims to curtail traffic and to make life as unpleasant as possible for motorists who insist on nudging their way around the city's inner ring of canals. ... In the final stage, all non-vital traffic is to be banned. NYT-28-Jan-1993

– Constructions expressing textual sequence such as <*first/firstly, second/secondly* (etc.), *last/finally*>, <i, ii (etc.)>, <A, B (etc.)>

(22) a. There are two problems with this. Firstly, you are hardcoding an assumed processor speed. # Second, plenty of real-world compilers are smart enough to simply optimise that loop away ... COCA-2012-BLOG

b. As for the projectile impact analyses, three approaches are commonly adopted, (i) field medium to large caliber projectile impact tests and the corresponding fitted empirical formulae; (ii) semi-empirical formulae based on the cavity expansion or constant resistance models; (iii) numerical simulations with various constitutive models of concrete. COCA-2019-ACAD

9.4.2 Contrast

A contrast between two CONNECTEEs, sometimes referred to as concession, can be expressed by a number of different constructions such as $PP_{\text{despite}}^{\text{CONTRAST}}$, $PP_{\text{in-spite-of}}^{\text{CONTRAST}}$ or $CL_{\text{although-fin}}^{\text{CONTRAST}}$:

(23) a. Despite these findings, bacterial serpins remain poorly studied and data about their origin and functions need to be established. COCA-2019-ACAD

b. Although the low-achieving spellers relied on' sounding out' words, this strategy was not always executed accurately. COCA-2019-ACAD

---

103. Despite the inappropriatness of talking about finite verb forms in English pointed out earlier, we will use the subscript "fin" to refer to clauses that have a subject and a predicate containing a verb that can be interpreted as instantiating a tense or a model construction.

9.4.3 Why: Cause

A different kind of relation between CONNECTEES is being established when speakers want to make clear why something is the case. We distinguish between two different types of constructions in this respect:[104]

– Constructions with a slot with the semantic function of REASON, which can be used to explain why a particular process or state has come about, which include $PP_{because-of}^{REASON}$, $CL_{fin-because}^{REASON}$, $CL_{fin-since}^{REASON}$, CL_{V-ing}^{REASON} or, e.g., <with NP Attr>:

(24) a. WHO estimates that 160,000 people die annually because of the effects of climate change. COCA-2004-MAG
   b. Displaying a thin grasp of science, President Donald Trump questioned the reality of global warming because it was cold outside. COCA-2018-NEWS
   c. Since potatoes will grow well at a pH in this range, all the grower needs to do is keep the pH below 5.3. COCA-1998-MAG
   d. Being a businessman, I think, he knows how to sell something... COCA-2018-MAG
   e. With Republicans in control of both chambers, the bills are moving forward rapidly. COCA-2015-NEWS

– Constructions with a slot with the semantic function PURPOSE, which can be used to explain the motivation behind an 'action', which are usually expressed by $PP_{for}^{PURPOSE}$, $CL_{to-inf}^{PURPOSE}$ or <in order CL_{to-inf}>^{PURPOSE}, etc.:

(25) a. ... we're just doing it for fun. COCA-2009-NEWS
   b. To get there park at the Glyn Collwn car park... BNC-CHJ-1244

9.4.4 Conditions

Finally, speakers can link two statements by making one the condition for the other:

(26) a. If you live in the West, the connection between climate change and fire is unavoidable. NYT-16-Sept-2020
   b. I don't go in with her, not unless she wants me to. BNC-ANY-165

Condition constructions are a very good example of the appropriateness of describing language in terms of a Construction Grammar approach, because of the interdependency of verb forms to express different meanings, which can be indicated as follows:

---

104. See Huddleston & Pullum (2002: 726–727) for the distinction between REASON and PURPOSE as types of CAUSE and the overlap between these categories.

REALISTIC-CONDITION CONSTRUCTION		
Expressing a CONDITION that may be met and under which the CONNECTEE would happen		
CONNECTOR	CONDITION	CONNECTEE
if	$CL_{fin\text{-}present\text{-}tense}$	CL_{fin}

Figure 9.6 The English REALISTIC-CONDITION CONSTRUCTION

HYPOTHETICAL-CONDITION CONSTRUCTION		
Expressing a CONDITION that is not met and the degree of likelihood of the CONNECTEE happening in case it could be met		
CONNECTOR	CONDITION	CONNECTEE
if	$CL_{fin\text{-}past\text{-}tense}$	$CL_{fin:\ would/could/might}$

Figure 9.7 The English HYPOTHETICAL-CONDITION CONSTRUCTION

The difference between these two constructions is by no means clear-cut, but often signals the speaker's assessment of how likely it is that a condition can be fulfilled, as is obvious from (27a) and (27b).

(27)   a.   If that were the case, the putative Planet Nine could well be a black hole, too, in a distant orbit around the sun.   NYT-11-Sept-2020
       b.   If her findings are correct, that would mean that Planet Nine orbits the sun about once every 17,117 years.   NYT-20-Oct-2016

If we are not talking about the present or the future, but about past time, we can use the following construction:

UNREALISTIC-CONDITION CONSTRUCTION		
Expressing a CONDITION that was not met and the degree of likelihood of the CONNECTEE happening in case it had been met		
CONNECTOR	CONDITION	CONNECTEE
if	$CL_{fin\text{-}past\text{-}tense+perfective}$	$CL_{fin:\ would/could/might}$

Figure 9.8 The English UNREALISTIC-CONDITION CONSTRUCTION

Chapter 9. Joining ideas and clauses 201

(28) If women had had the same power, status, and conditioning that men have had over the centuries, we might see parallels in female group behavior. COCA-2005-MAG

There are some variants of condition constructions. For example, the so-called "putative *should*" can be used to express a tentative realistic condition, as in (29a):

(29) a. Should she have any trouble, I'm sure she'll set pen to paper and let you know. COCA-2016-FIC

b. If there should be a vacancy and he were nominated to be chief justice, would you vote for him? COCA-2002-SPOK

Furthermore, CONDITION can be expressed by a number of constructions such as the "subjunctive" as in (30), inversion as in (31) or lexical constructions such as <in case>CONDITION as in (32):

(30) a. If Congress were to vote down the measure, either President Bush or Obama would have to exercise a veto to get the money. COCA-2009-NEWS

b. If this be treason, make the most of it. COCA-1997-FIC

(31) Had the president not vetoed those bills, the spending might have been higher, the deficit higher. COCA-2009-SPOK

(32) In case you missed it, here is a sample. COCA-2018-SPOK

9.4.5 SCOPE

Other types of construction can be used to restrict or widen the SCOPE of a message; this can be done by:

- Lexical constructions containing a deictic element such as <in this respectSCOPE>:

(33) ... and I think I may be in a minority in this respect... COCA-2019-SPOK

- Lexical constructions containing an open slot such as <with regard to XSCOPE>, <as far as X is concernedSCOPE>:

(34) a. As far as acquisition of language is concerned, it seems clear that reinforcement, casual observation, and natural inquisitiveness (coupled with a strong tendency to imitate) are important factors ... BNC-CG6-114

b. ... no significant differences were detected with regard to sex, skin color or marital status. COCA-2019-ACAD

- Lexical constructions ending in -*ly*:

(35) Neurologically, there's nothing wrong with you. COCA-2015-TV

9.5 Linguistic implications

The rather wide definition of connectors established in 9.3 has enabled us to subsume a great number of constructions under the label of connection constructions that contribute to creating textual cohesion (Halliday & Hasan 1976).

Furthermore, this wide notion of connectors touches upon the traditional distinction between coordination (all of the cases discussed in 9.2 fall under this label), and subordination, where one clause, the subordinate clause, is considered to be a constituent of another clause, the superordinate clause. Interestingly, the conventional practice to see words such as *because* or *if* as part of a subordinate clause was questioned by Sinclair & Mauranen (2006: 13–14). They outline four ways of analyzing the relationship of clauses connected by, e.g., *because*, which we present in a slightly different form below:

(36) Trump has ignored climate change because it's been politically easy to do so.
NYT-16-Sept-2020

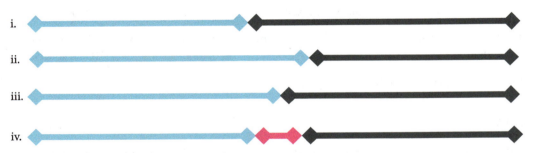

Figure 9.9 Four ways of analyzing (36): (i) main clause + subordinate clause (including *because*), (ii) main clause (including *because*) + subordinate clause, (iii) two clauses (both including *because*), and (iv) two clauses (*because* belonging to *neither*)

In a way, the approach taken in CASA combines (iii) and (iv) but it offers yet another solution because although connection constructions have, as outlined in 9.3.2 above, three slots, but in contrast to (iv), these slots together form a meaningful construction:

Figure 9.10 A fifth way of analyzing (36). (The pink box represents a construction.)

CHAPTER **10**

Information structure constructions

10.1 Information structure and construal

An important cognitive process is our ability to look at a single event from different perspectives. The constructions that speakers use thus also tell us something about how they view a scene (how they construe it in their minds; Croft 2012: 13–19). In Chapter 5., e.g., we have already seen how different argument structure constructions can sometimes be chosen to describe the same event. Take a situation where a relationship ends, and one partner is deeply sorry about this. Drawing on a conventionalized metaphor, English speakers often describe such events as 'heart breaking':

(1) Her heart broke when he married her cousin and she's yet to recover from it.
https://roseisreading.home.blog/2020/03/19/her-wicked-duke-lisa-torquay/

(2) Harry breaks Ginny's heart ...
He broke her heart and the sad thing about it was that he had no clue he had just done it. With three simple words he broke her heart into a trillion little pieces.
Harry Potter Fan Fiction: Dancing in the Moonlight https://www.siye.co.uk/siye /viewstory.php?sid=134

(3) Ms Mountford, an artist, moved from her home in Sydney to a cave in the Blue Mountains after her heart was broken by her Canadian lover.
https://www.telegraph.co.uk/news/worldnews/australiaandthepacific/australia /5773220/Australias-Miss-Havisham-died-heartbroken-in-a-cave.html)

The blue part in (1) is an instance of the INTRANSITIVE CONSTRUCTION and thus focuses on the undergoer of the emotion (*her heart* being a metonymy for the person being left and *broke* a metaphor for their emotional experience). In (2), the first two blue clauses describe a similar event, but this time the writer draws on the MONOTRANSITIVE CONSTRUCTION and, consequently, presents the scene as an "ÆFFECTOR (*Harry / he*) causing the emotion in the ÆFFECTED" (*Ginny's heart / her heart*). In addition to this, (2) also has an ATTRIBUTE (RESULTATIVE) CONSTRUCTION that does not just mention the "ÆFFECTOR (*he*) and the ÆFFECTED" (*her heart*), but also an ÆFFECTED-ATTRIBUTE (*into a trillion little pieces*). Finally, as discussed in Chapter 5, active argument structure constructions that express a force-dynamic relationship of an ÆFFECTOR and ÆFFECTED often have a corresponding passive argument structure construction that assigns a more prominent role to the ÆFFECTED. (3) is an example of such a construction, namely the PASSIVE-MONOTRANSITIVE CONSTRUCTION, in which the "ÆFFECTED (*her heart*) is the Subj and the ÆFFECTOR (*her Canadian lover*)" is realized a by PP_{by}.

In cognitive linguistics, we have labelled the choice between these constructions the result of 'construal'. Note that while this term brought a cognitive perspective to the different ways of presenting the same proposition, the linguistic phenomenon itself had already been

A Construction Grammar of the English Language

described by traditional linguistics. Leech (1981:19), e.g., covered such alternations by the term 'thematic meaning', by which he meant the information of "what is communicated by the way in which a speaker or writer organizes the message, in terms of ordering, focus, and emphasis". The study of these thematic meanings is sometimes referred to as 'information structure': 'the means by which the speaker intends the sentence to inform the hearer, in the context of previous discourse' (Jackendoff 2003:408; Halliday 1970:162–164).[105]

Now, so far, we have focused on how constructions enable a speaker to express various perspectives on a single event. However, when we talk or write, we do not just consider our own individual perspective. We are also very well aware that other people might not know everything we do. Besides, other people might choose to view the exact same situation from a different perspective. This cognitive ability to take into account the mental states of interlocuters is known as "theory of mind" (Tomasello 2003:277). Theory of mind is an important prerequisite for learning a language. The first crucial steps of acquiring a language require **joint attention** of child and caretaker ('Are we both talking about the same things and events right now?') as well as **intention-reading** ('What is the other person trying to achieve right now?'). Both, joint attention and intention reading, enable us to understand what exactly our interlocutors are talking about and what their intentions are.

10.2 Reference: Which 'thing' are we exactly talking about?

In Chapter 6.1 on NP-constructions, we discussed how the choice of reference constructions depends on what we think our interlocutors does or does not already know (Lambrecht 1994; Leino 2013:335; see also Hoffmann 2022b:115–123). Let us illustrate this with an example from the Thomas corpus. In (4), the mother tells Thomas (who is 2 years, 8 months and 3 days at this stage) the following story about a snowman (apparently, she is reading from an interactive picture book that makes a squeaky sound if the child presses on the snowman):

(4) a. once upon a winter's day when snow lay down around
    b. three elves made a magical snowman who sang with a squeaky sound
    c. just once
    d. that's right
    e. when Mummy says squeaking or squeaky or squeaked or squeak you can press it then

---

105. Halliday (1970) makes a distinction between 'thematic structure' and 'information structure'. Thematic structure refers to the organization of a message in terms of a 'theme', the starting point of a message, and a 'rheme' – concepts that had been introduced by the Prague School (see Halliday 1970:161); information structure is described by Halliday in terms of 'given' and 'new'. For an application of the concepts of theme and rheme to the description of sentences in the framework of functional grammar see Halliday (1994). For a discussion of various approaches to information structure see Brown & Yule (1983:153–189) and Kaltenböck (2020).

> f. at first the snowman's squeaky song was just a touch off key
> g. but once he'd coughed and cleared his throat he squeaked most tunefully
> h. the story spread around the town about the snowman's tune
> i. they marvelled at his clever squeak   t2_08_03m

During the reading, posture, gaze and gestures will tell the mother whether there is joint attention (whether the child is looking at the book or not). With this particular book, she will also be able to track the child's attention by checking that Thomas clicks on the snowman whenever a word form of SQUEAK is uttered. Now, take a closer look at how the snowman is introduced in the story and how it is referred to from that point onwards: In (4b), the mother uses the INDEFINITE-SINGULAR-COUNT-NP CONSTRUCTION (*a magical snowman who ...*) for her first mention of the snowman. This construction signals that she is 'singling out one individual referent from the denotatum of the noun' (she is going to talk about one, not two or more snowmen). In addition to that, this construction also has information structural meaning. You use the construction in cases where you introduce a referent into the discourse that you assume the hearer or reader has not activated in their mind at this point. When the mother then mentions the snowman again in (4f) and (4h), she can safely assume that at this point it is already activated information in the mind of the child. In such cases, speakers can employ the DEFINITE-SINGULAR-COUNT-NP CONSTRUCTION (*the snowman's...*). Using this construction, the speaker is 'referring to a particular 'thing'' (cf. Section 6.3.1) and implicitly tells the hearer 'I am expecting you to know which 'thing' I am talking about'. Alternatively, a 'thing' that has been activated by the INDEFINITE-SINGULAR-COUNT-NP CXN can later also be picked up by a PERSONAL-PRONOUN CONSTRUCTION (6.3.2) such as the HE-CXN (4g) or a GENITIVE-NP CXN with a pronoun such as *his throat* (4g) or *his clever squeak* (4i).

The particular choice of NP-construction thus depends on whether the speaker can assume that the hearer will be able to identify a 'thing' or not. As we have seen above, in many cases the first instance of a 'thing' will therefore be via the INDEFINITE-SINGULAR-COUNT-NP CXN. In addition to that, however, hearers can be expected to have activated particular 'thing'-s because of their encyclopedic frame-based knowledge. Take the following variant of the bar joke:

(5) **A ghost** walks into **a bar, the bartender** says, "Sorry, we don't serve spirits."[106]

The basic structure of jokes such as (5) is always INDEFINITE-SINGULAR-COUNT-NP CXN *walks into a bar* <something happens there>.[107] Since neither the ghost nor the bar can be expected to be activated in the mind of a hearer when you start telling the joke, you will

---

106. https://thoughtcatalog.com/january-nelson/2019/08/33-hilarious-man-walks-into-a-bar-jokes-that-will-have-you-rolling/
107. https://en.wikipedia.org/wiki/Bar_joke

need to use the INDEFINITE-SINGULAR-COUNT-NP CXN when you first introduce them (5). Note, however, that when the bartender is then mentioned this happens via the DEFINITE-SINGULAR-COUNT-NP CXN. How is that possible if this 'thing' has not already been mentioned earlier? The reason the DEFINITE-SINGULAR-COUNT-NP construction works here has to do with the way meaning is stored in our minds. Our mental concept of bars is frame-based and encyclopedic. When you mention *a bar*, hearers do not just activate an abstract meaning like 'place to buy a drink'. Instead, they will picture a rich scene of a bar, including a counter at which you can buy (mostly) alcoholic drinks as well as the kind of participants you expect to find in a bar, i.e., waiters, customers and bartenders.

These insights into how our knowledge of the world influences our linguistic behavior goes back to ideas developed by Charles Fillmore under the name of **frame semantics** (see Chapters 5.8.3 and 8.8.2). Put simply, the idea is that a so-called frame-evoking element such as *a bar* activates in speakers' minds all sorts of 'things' associated with that element. In the context of describing a situation in which people are boarding a plane, for example, it is perfectly possible to use a definite construction to refer to *the flight attendant(s)* or *the pilot* even if these persons have not been mentioned before (Ungerer & Schmid 2006) because you expect there to be flight attendants and pilots on a plane, i.e., these 'things' form a part of your 'flight'-frame.[108] Thus, once you have introduced the concept of a bar, you can expect the idea of a bartender to be activated in the hearer's mind, which is why the DEFINITE-SINGULAR-COUNT-NP CXN is used in (5) (and, in fact, using the INDEFINITE-SINGULAR-COUNT-NP CONSTRUCTION *a bartender* in (5) would suggest that there was more than one bartender).

10.3 Topic: What are we talking about? – Focus: What's new?

The choice of reference constructions is only one of many phenomena addressed in information structure studies. Throughout discourse, speakers also need to (unconsciously) keep track of information that is new to the addressee (known as 'focus' or 'rheme')[109] and information that can be considered given at a certain point of the conversation (the 'presupposition' in the sense of Jackendoff 2002: 409). As we will see in this section, English has many constructions that allow speakers to mark information as new, i.e., in focus.

One obvious sign that a speaker has to provide new information is if a hearer asks for it: Let us illustrate this with another example from the Thomas corpus:

---

108. For the development of the frame approach in artificial intelligence research see Minsky (1975). Compare Brown & Yule (1983) for this and related approaches such as Schank & Abelson's (1977) concept of scripts.

109. See Jackendoff (2002: 409). See also Halliday (1994); Brown & Yule (1983); Lambrecht (1994); Leino (2013), Hilpert (2019: 106–112).

(6) a. Mother: you had some little trains.
     b. Mother: **who** did you have?
     c. Thomas: Gordon.
     d. Mother: Gordon.
     e. Thomas: James.
     f. Mother: James.
     g. Thomas: Thomas.
     h. Thomas: a ...
     i. Mother: Thomas.
     j. Thomas: a Percy.
     k. Mother: and Percy.
     ...
     l. Thomas: a the Thomas the tank engine.
     m. Thomas: Thomas play em a Percy.
     n. Mother: yes.
     o. Mother: you were playing with Thomas Gordon and Percy, weren't you?   t2-07-06

In (6), the mother asks Thomas (who is two years, seven months and six days at this point) about a game they played with toy tank engines (from a show called 'Thomas the Tank Engine'). The mother, obviously, knows fully well which toy trains her son had, but she uses the exchange to create rapport and practice Thomas's language skills. In (6b), she uses the WH-QUESTION CONSTRUCTION *who did you have?* to ask for information. Normally, this type of question is used to elicit information that will be new to the person asking the question. Thomas replies with a simple NAME CONSTRUCTION (*Gordon*). The mother then repeats this name, (6d), to indicate that this is the information she was looking for and thus reassures Thomas that he made the correct linguistic choice.

A simple NP construction can thus be used to present new, focused information. In such situations, the NP is marked as new information by a particular intonation: It is marked by a high-fall accent, i.e., a high tone on the stressed syllable of **GOR**don that falls steeply on the following unstressed syllables to a low tone (see Wells 2006: 262). We can, consequently, describe this construction as follows:

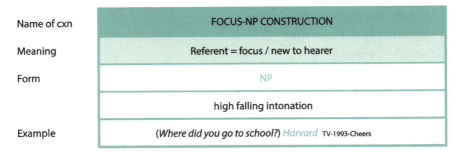

Figure 10.1 The English FOCUS-NP CONSTRUCTION

In spoken language, the FOCUS-NP CONSTRUCTION is often the expected choice in question-answer adjacency pairs. As you can see, it can either appear on its own (7a) or it can be blended with a DECLARATIVE-STATEMENT CONSTRUCTION (7b):

(7) a. All right, what do you want from me?
   A fight. A fair fight.   TV-1958-Hitchcock
   b. Well, what do you want?
   I want a fight.   TV-1958-Hitchcock

This, however, is not the only construction that can be used to highlight new/focused information. Another construction that can be used in these situations is the IT-CLEFT CONSTRUCTION (8):

(8) I don't give a damn about your money. – It's you that I wanted in my life.   TV-Dynasty-1986

(7b) and (8) express a similar proposition of a speaker wanting something (using the WANT-MONOTRANSITIVE CONSTRUCTION in a DECLARATIVE-STATEMENT CONSTRUCTION). However, since the 'thing' that they want constitutes new information it is marked by the FOCUS-NP CONSTRUCTION in (7a) and (7b). In addition to intonation, the construction in (8) also has a specific constructional template to highlight that the desired 'thing' is in focus: The IT-CLEFT CONSTRUCTION (8) has an *it* subject, a form of BE as its main verb, an element that is in FOCUS and finally a finite clause with the rest of the predication (excluding only the element that is in the FOCUS position, so with respect to its propositional meaning (8) is equivalent to *I wanted you in my life.*; Hoffmann 2022b: 224).

As you can see in Figure 10.2, in addition to its word order, the IT-CLEFT CONSTRUCTION also highlights the FOCUS element by a high falling intonation. The dependent clause that follows the FOCUS position is a construction-specific element of the IT-CLEFT CONSTRUCTIONS. At first glance, it might appear to be a relative clause.[111] Unlike a relative clause, however, it does not restrict the semantics of the preceding FOCUS slot: *You are [the person [that I always wanted]*RELATIVE CLAUSE*]* confines the number of potential persons to only the

---

111. In some cases, *who* can appear instead of *that* in the dependent clause (Aarts and Aarts 1988: 76).

Chapter 10. Information structure constructions   209

IT-CLEFT CONSTRUCTION			
Highlight focused / new information to hearer			
		FOCUS	
SUBJ	V	OBJ/ATTR	dependent clause
it	BE	NP AdvP etc.	that who whom whose where when rest of clause
high falling intonation			
It's you *that I wanted in /my life.* TV-1986-Dynasty *It was* then *that Afrobeat was born.* Movie-2014-FindingFela *Catherine, it was* because I loved you *that I disappeared that night.* Movie-1948-AWomen'sVengeance1948 *I suppose it was* you who arranged that meeting ... TV-1985-Dynasty *It's* here where she has done groundbreaking neuroimaging research ... COCA-2014-SPOK			

Figure 10.2 *IT-CLEFT CONSTRUCTION*[110]

one that the speaker has always desired. In contrast to this, the reference of the pronoun *you* in the cleft sentence *It's you that I wanted in my life* (TV-1986-Dynasty) is obviously not restricted by its *that* clause (for further details and related constructions see Hilpert 2019:116; Hoffmann 2022b:224–225).

A construction that is closely related to the IT-CLEFT CONSTRUCTION in (8) is the WH-CLEFT CONSTRUCTION (9) (which is also known as the PSEUDO-CLEFT CONSTRUCTION):[112]

(9)   Like what? It's what you want. What I want is a little smile.   TV-2012-Mentalist

As (9) shows, the focused element of WH-CLEFT CONSTRUCTIONS (*a little smile*) is placed in sentence-final position. The rest of the proposition is found in the subject slot of the construction, which must be realized by a *who-* or *what-clause* (*What I want*). Finally, the main verb of the construction has to be a form of BE. In many situations, speakers can choose either an IT-CLEFT CONSTRUCTION or a WH-CLEFTS to express a similar meaning. There are, however, processing factors that might affect this choice (Hilpert 2019:115): if the focused element contains a lot of words, it is considered 'heavy'. In these situations, due to the prin-

---

110. See CGEL (1386–1387), Herbst & Schüller (2008:152) and for the phrasal and clausal realization of the FOCUS slot see also Kim and Michaelis (2020:304).

112. Aarts and Aarts (1988:98); Herbst and Schüller (2008:156); Lambrecht (2001); Hilpert (2019:113–118); Hoffmann (2022b).

ciple of end weight, speakers might prefer WH-CLEFTS since the heavy phrase then appears clause-finally. Since its focused element is a complex clause, the WH-CLEFT CONSTRUCTION in (10) might, therefore, sound more natural than the corresponding *IT*-CLEFT CONSTRUCTION in (11), (following Hilpert 2019, we use '#' to indicate that a sentence is pragmatically odd):

(10)   What I wanted was to see this thing that people were drawn to in such a singular and powerful way.   Movie-2002-Adaptation

(11)   #It was to see this thing that people were drawn to in such a singular and powerful way that I wanted

There are a couple of further differences between WH-CLEFT CONSTRUCTIONS and *IT*-CLEFT CONSTRUCTIONS, which are, however, beyond the scope of this book (for details see Hilpert 2019: 115–118; Hoffmann 2022b: 224–227). Figure 10.3 provides the CASA template for WH-CLEFT CONSTRUCTION:

WH-CLEFT CONSTRUCTION		
Highlight focused / new information to hearer		
		FOCUS
SUBJ		ATTR
wh-clause	V: BE	NP AdjP PP V-ing to-INF wh-cl
high falling intonation		
What I want is a little smile TV-2012-Mentalist ... and I hope *who you want to be is* better than me. TV-2016-Scandal *What you want to be is* on time for school. TV-2009-Medium *What you want is* to do good. TV-2016-MastersofSex *What you want to know is* whether I did it with one of them and which one. MOV-2007-Closing		

Figure 10.3 *WH*-CLEFT CONSTRUCTION[113]

WH-CLEFT CONSTRUCTIONS and *IT*-CLEFT CONSTRUCTIONS have the function to emphasize the new, focused information. In addition to this, they also structure what we talk about.

---

113. The phrasal and clausal realization of the FOCUS slot are taken from Kim and Michaelis (2020: 304).

Chapter 10. Information structure constructions   211

In information structure terms, they have a topic-comment structure. A topic is 'that which the sentence is about' (Lambrecht 1994:118). In a DECLARATIVE CONSTRUCTION, the topic of a proposition is normally found in the subject slot (Hoffmann 2022b:226). In contrast to this, the predicate normally encodes the 'comment', "that which is asserted about the subject" (CGEL 1985:79; see also Croft 2012:183). Note that both new (focus) and old (presupposed) information can be topics. In the IT-CLEFT CONSTRUCTION, we can say that the FOCUS slot indicates to the hearer what the sentence is about. Thus, in addition to encoding new information, the FOCUS element in the IT-CLEFT CONSTRUCTION also gives us the topic that the speaker wants to tell us something about, while the dependent clause provides a (presupposed) comment on it. In WH-CLEFT CONSTRUCTIONS (*What I want is a drink.* (TV-2016-Lucifer)), the topic (= *What I want*) is the *wh*-clause and the comment (= *a drink*) is in the focus slot (see also Hoffmann 2022b:226–227).

English has several constructions that allow speakers to change the topic (Hoffmann 2022b:227):

(12)   His first task was to assess Londons old sewers. These had been designed only to carry off surface water.   TV-2003-SevenWondersoftheIndustrialWorld

(13)   Shut up! Thuggish behaviour will not be tolerated. You disgrace that uniform, you disgrace all of us, and you know that. As for Mr Edwards, he will be dealt with by the proper authorities in due course.   TV-2010-SeaPatrol

(14)   You won't be the one dictating terms here. I will. And regarding your laundry, you have my word that Danny won't be involved, but you need to keep that man on a leash.   TV-2012-Suits

(12) illustrates a typical instance of thematic progression: What was introduced as a FOCUS (sometimes also labelled 'rheme', here *London's old sewers*) in the first clause becomes the topic (often referred to as 'theme') of the subsequent clause. In (12), this is achieved by using an anaphoric pronoun (here *these*) in the subject slot. In (13), a new TOPIC (*Mr Edwards*) is introduced by the AS-FOR-X CONSTRUCTION is used (Hilpert 2019:110). Similarly, a new TOPIC (here *your laundry*) is established in (14) by *regarding* X (like *about X*, or *concerning* X,). Prosodically, topic phrases in English are marked by a rising accent (e.g., **THE**se, *As for* Mr **ED**wards, *Regarding your* **LAUN**dry, Hoffmann 2022b:227).

Three very frequent constructions for topic management are provided in (15–17; Hoffmann 2022b:227–229):

(15)   Topicalization: The Muppets I like.   TV-2012-TheNeighbors

(16)   Left-Dislocation: Jalapenos I like them, but they don't like me.   MOVIE-2009-Sarah'sChoice

(17)   Right-Dislocation: I like them these ladies.   MOVIE-1967-TheFlim-FlamMan

The TOPICALIZATION CONSTRUCTION in (15) has the TOPIC (*The Muppets*) in clause-initial position (in contrast to the final position it would take in a declarative construct *I like the Muppets.*). In the LEFT-DISLOCATION CONSTRUCTION (16), the TOPIC phrase is also in clause-initial position, but additionally the construction requires the presence of a so-called resumptive pronoun (*them*) that is co-referential with the TOPIC phrase. The RIGHT-DISLOCATION CONSTRUCTION (17) also exhibits such a clause-final pronoun (*them*), but this pronoun is used cataphorically, i.e., the co-referential TOPIC phrase (*these ladies*) follows it.

Why does English have so many different constructions that all share the same function of introducing topics (see also Hoffmann 2022b: 227–229)? Now, Goldberg claims that languages follow the Principle of No Synonymy (Goldberg 1995: 67–68) – i.e., we should not find two or more constructions that are identical in meaning (though see Uhrig 2015). Once we look at the usage constraints of the above topic constructions, we do, in fact, find subtle differences in their discourse functions (Gregory and Michaelis 2001; Hilpert 2019: 119–120; Lambrecht 2001): The TOPICALIZATION CONSTRUCTION tends to continue an existing topic (which explains why it is often realized by a pronoun; e.g., *The muppets were on TV ... Them, I like.*) that might soon be discontinued. The RIGHT-DISLOCATION CONSTRUCTION, on the other hand, takes a current topic and indicates that the speaker wants to continue talking about it. Finally, the LEFT-DISLOCATION CONSTRUCTION introduces a new topic for the following discourse. Moreover, there are also formal differences between the three constructions: TOPICALIZATION CONSTRUCTIONS, e.g., display a variety of different types of Topic phrases (e.g., NPs, AdjPs, AdvPs and PPs). LEFT-DISLOCATION and RIGHT-DISLOCATION CONSTRUCTION, on the other hand, are predominantly used with NP topics (Sag 2010: 513). Summarizing the above similarities and differences, Figure 10.4 to 10.6 provide the CASA templates for these three topic management constructions:

TOPICALIZATION CONSTRUCTION	
Continuing / ending an activated TOPIC	
TOPIC	
NP AdjP AdvP PP	rest of clause
rising intonation	
There were three rifles in there, two I passed away, and the other one I kept. MOVIE-1997-LittleDieterNeedstoFly	
And happy I am to think, sir, that I had some small hand in saving young Master Hawkins... MOVIE-1950-TreasureIsland	
Old MacDonald had a farm Ee I ee I oh And on his farm he had a penguin... MOVIE-2016-Mother'sDay	

Figure 10.4 TOPICALIZATION CONSTRUCTION

As mentioned above, the TOPIC slot of the TOPICALIZATION CONSTRUCTION (Figure 10.4) can be filled by various phrasal fillers that, with respect to their meaning side, express a topic that will not be continued for very much longer.

The LEFT-DISLOCATION CONSTRUCTION looks fairly similar to Figure 10.4:

LEFT-DISLOCATION CONSTRUCTION		
introducing a new TOPIC		
TOPIC		
NP$_1$	rest of clause	PRON$_{resumptive1}$
falling intonation		
the prisoners-- I captured them! Well, Major, you will be a hero. TV-1970-Hogan'sHeros		

Figure 10.5 The English LEFT-DISLOCATION CONSTRUCTION

While the TOPICALIZATION CONSTRUCTION signals the end of a topic, the LEFT-DISLOCATION CONSTRUCTION introduces a new topic for the upcoming discourse (and, on the formal side, includes a resumptive pronoun (PRON$_{resumptive}$) in the REST-CLAUSE that is coreferential with the initial Topic phrase; NP$_1$ and PRON$_{resumptive1}$)

Finally, the RIGHT-DISLOCATION CONSTRUCTION in (17) continues an active topic NP$_1$ that appears clause-finally after a coreferential cataphoric pronoun (**PRON**$_{cataphoric1}$):

RIGHT-DISLOCATION CONSTRUCTION		
continuing an active TOPIC		
		TOPIC
REST-CLAUSE	PRON$_{cataphoric1}$	NP$_1$
		rising intonation
You want it the bomb ship? I let you right to it. MOV-2010-HunterPrey		

Figure 10.6 RIGHT-DISLOCATION CONSTRUCTION

10.4   Summary

As the current section has illustrated, constructions are not only used to express referential or propositional meaning. The function of the various constructions covered in this section mainly lies in information management – they help speakers organize the flow of information in a way that takes into account the knowledge states of their interlocutors. In addition to this, they allow speakers to direct their hearers' attention to the topics they want to talk about. Sometimes these constructions have, therefore, been called 'information structure constructions', and vice versa. However, this label is somewhat misleading (Lambrecht 1994: 16–17; cit. in Leino 2013: 341): Not only IT-CLEFT CONSTRUCTIONS or TOPICALIZATION CONSTRUCTIONS have such pragmatic usage-constraints. As we have seen, the subject of the DECLARATIVE CONSTRUCTION is also prototypically a topic. In fact, all sentence-type constructions can be seen as 'information structure constructions'. The only difference between sentence-type constructions (Chapter 3) and the constructions we discussed in this section is that the former are used more frequently and that the latter exhibit certain distinct formal properties (such as a different word order), which have attracted more explicit scholarly attention.

CHAPTER 11

Speaking idiomatically
Prefabricated chunks as low-level constructions

11.1 Idiomaticity

11.1.1 The idiom principle

One of the most important insights into the nature of language acquisition was formulated by Michael Tomasello (2003: 99–100 & 101–102) when he said:

> ... children do not first learn words and then combine them into sentences via contentless syntactic 'rules'. Rather, children learn simultaneously from adult utterances meaningful linguistic structures of many shapes and sizes and degrees of abstraction, and they then produce their own utterances on particular occasions of use by piecing together some of these many and variegated units in ways that express their immediate communicative intention.
>
> It turns out that, upon inspection, a major part of human linguistic competence–much more than previously believed–involves the mastery of all kinds of routine formulas, fixed and semi-fixed expressions, idioms and frozen collocations. Indeed one of the distinguishing characteristics of native speakers of a language is their control of these semi-fixed expressions as fluent units with somewhat unpredictable meanings ...

Learning item-based constructions is no doubt an important step in language acquisition (Lieven 2014). One of the key findings of corpus linguistic research on adult language of the last fifty years or so is that there is a much stronger interaction between the syntactic structure of an utterance and the words used than previously assumed. As it turns out, in actual language use, adult speech also contains a large proportion of recurrent fixed as well as semi-fixed chunks. The British corpus linguist John Sinclair (1991: 110) drew attention to this by formulating his famous idiom principle:[114]

> The principle of idiom is that a language user has available to him or her a large number of semi-preconstructed phrases that constitute single choices, even though they might appear to be analysable into segments. To some extent, this may reflect the recurrence of similar situations in human affairs; it may illustrate a natural tendency to economy of effort; or it may be motivated in part by the exigencies of real-time conversation. However it arises, it has been relegated to an inferior position in most current linguistics, because it does not fit the open-choice model.

In very much the same vein, Langacker (2008a: 28) speaks of the "countless units representing normal ways of saying things" – and, in fact, right from the beginning, this kind of idiomaticity has been a central concern, if not a driving force, in the development of Con-

---

114. See also Sinclair (2004).

struction Grammar (Croft & Cruse 2004: 225). Fillmore, Kay & O'Connor (1988: 504) have shown how the use of expressions such as *the Xer the Yer* or *let alone* requires a wide array of formal, semantic and pragmatic knowledge that is tied to these particular expressions, thus underscoring the importance of "knowledge that will account for speakers' ability to construct and understand phrases and expressions in their language which are not covered by the grammar, the lexicon, and the principles of compositional semantics, as these are familiarly conceived" (see 1.3.5 and 11.5.3). Through questioning the wisdom of drawing a strict dividing line between syntax and lexis – something that has been argued for equally by Sinclair (2008) and by Langacker (2008a), for example – Construction Grammar provides a framework that is equally suitable for the description of units of a relatively low level of abstraction such as *let alone* and the more abstract constructions we have been dealing with in the previous chapters of this book.[115]

11.2   Idioms as constructions

Idioms are the classic case of expressions that traditional (and generative) approaches tend to treat as exceptions which do not form part of the analysis of core grammar (Chomsky 1995). Idioms are often defined as expressions that consist of several words but have a meaning that does not arise from the component parts. At best, these criteria serve to describe some kind of prototype. It is true that some idioms are devoid of semantic interpretability if you don't know them (such as *double-dutch* 'incomprehensible', or *get on like a house on fire*, which learners might at first take to mean something quite negative, but which actually has the rather positive meaning of 'get on very well with another person'; others, like many proverbs, however, can easily be worked out (take *a stitch in time saves nine* or *the early bird catches the worm*, for example). Furthermore, idioms tend to be restricted in terms of formal variation, but creative uses of the type illustrated by (1b) or (2bc) are by no means uncommon:[116]

(1)	a.	They say a stitch in time saves nine.	COCA-2018-MOV
	b.	A Stitch In Time Saves $ 900.	COCA-2012-WEB

(2)	a.	The early bird gets the worm, right?	COCA-2014-NEWS
	b.	In an epicurean dreamland like Portland, the early bird gets the brunch ...	
			COCA-2017-NEWS

---

115. See Herbst (2015). For the role of idiomatic expressions in Construction Grammar see Croft & Cruse (2004: 225–256), Gries (2008) or Ungerer & Schmid (2006). For a discussion of the corresponding GESCHWEIGE-DENN CONSTRUCTION in German see Habermann (2023).

116. Compare, however, drunkonyms, i.e. the fact that almost any participle can – given the right contextual cues – be used in the pattern *be/get* + intensifier + V-ed to express a state of drunkenness; see Sanchez-Stockhammer & Uhrig (2023) for details.

> c. The early bird gets the worm, but the early worm gets eaten.   COCA-2012-WEB

As pointed out in 1.3.4, in Construction Grammar, idioms can quite simply be seen as constructions since knowing a construction entails knowledge of meaning as well as knowledge of its potential for formal expression. It is not even necessary – maybe not even possible – to identify a special type of idiom construction, because even the gradient character of "[w]hat is and what is not an idiom" (Palmer 1981:81) has long been recognized and because the concept of construction per se includes assemblies of varying degrees of specificity, or, vice versa, schematicity.[117]

THE-EARLY-BIRD-CATCHES-THE-WORM CONSTRUCTION						
An ÆFFECTOR acts early enough to gain an advantage over others .						
ÆFFECTOR				ÆFFECTED		
SUBJ: NP			V	Obj: NP		
The	early	bird / etc.	gets / catches / eats / etc.	the		worm / etc.

Figure 11.1 Constructional description of *the early bird gets the worm* (on the basis of COCA). Low frequency of occurrence (23 instances of *gets*, 14 of *catches* and 1 of *eats*) does not allow any more precise indication of creative variation

It should be noted that idioms such as *a stitch in time saves nine* or *the early bird gets/catches the worm* are relatively rare in actual language use: in the BNC (98 million words) we found a total of 4 instances of the canonical form of the former and only one of the latter, in COCA (1 billion words) 15 of the former and 38 of the latter – compared with 1860 for *drive* (all forms) *me crazy* in COCA.[118]

---

117. For this reason (and for the purposes of this book), there seems to be little point in going into the various attempts of defining idioms or certain types of phraseological units such as proverbs, etc. See, however, Cruse (1986:37), Gläser (1990), or Granger & Paquot (2008).

218 A Construction Grammar of the English Language

Nevertheless, such units quite clearly represent constructions that have a meaning of their own (even if that meaning can sometimes be worked out on the basis of the meanings of its parts). One indication of this is that with the fragment uses in (3), which evoke the meaning of the whole expression, this would not be possible (Herbst 2015):

(3)	a.	A stitch in time, so to speak.	COCA-2004-MOV
	b.	Be the early bird.	COC-2012-WEB

The intended meaning of (3b), e.g., is not to literally act like a bird but to advise the hearer to 'act early enough to gain an advantage over others'. In order to understand (3b) the hearer, therefore, has to access the idiomatic construction in Figure 11.1. As the example shows, constructs that only partially realize constructions are still interpretable (as long as the realized fragment still allows the activation of the full construction; Bauer and Hoffmann 2020). What is particularly relevant in the context of a book on syntax is that idioms are syntactically transparent enough to allow an analysis in syntactic terms that may give rise to creative uses and deviations from the canonical form of the idiom.

11.3 Constructions involving particles

11.3.1 Verb-particle constructions

The double-sided character of syntactic analyzability and semantic unity is also typical of structures that are highly frequent in English. Compare the sentences in (4) and (5)/(6):

(4)	a.	James takes the ball up the side	MOVIE-2008-MoreThanaGame
	b.	You'd better come in.	BNC-GW3-885

(5)	a.	… and she quickly gave up the idea that there was anything she could do or say …	COCA-2014-FIC
	b.	Is it true you've given in and let Mr Barrow get away with it?	TV-2012-Downton

(6)	a.	… she gave the whole idea up.	COCA-2013-FIC
	b.	The cartridges on the back seat fell on to the floor. Philip leant back and picked them up.	BNC-ABX-1352

While the examples under (4) can be analyzed as straightforward examples of the CAUSED-MOTION CONSTRUCTION (4a) and the SELF-MOTION CONSTRUCTION (4b), this is not the case

---

118. The low frequency of some idioms makes it very difficult to establish collo-profiles (i.e., frequency-based lists of slot-fillers) on a sufficiently large empirical basis. A very detailed description of the lexical fillers of slots of idiom constructions can be found in the pioneering lexicographical descriptions provided in the two volumes of *the Oxford Dictionary of Current Idiomatic English* (Cowie & Mackin 1975; Cowie, Mackin & McCaig 1983).

with the sentences in (5) and (6), even if at first glance they might appear similar: the CAUSED-MOTION CONSTRUCTION (4a) has an ÆFFECTOR Subj (*James*), an ÆFFECTED-THEME Obj (*the ball*) and a PATH PP (*up the side*) (see 5.5.1). (5a) also might appear to have a Subj (*she*), an Obj (*the whole idea*) and a PP (*up*), but *give up* clearly does not express motion in space in the way that (4a) does (meaning 'to resign, surrender; to hand over, part with' instead; OED online s.v. *to give up*). Similarly, just like (4b), in addition to the V, the form part of (5b) has a Subj (cf. *you* in ((4b and (5b)) and a simple particle *in* (in both examples). Yet, while (4b) expresses the directional movement meaning of the SELF-MOTION CONSTRUCTION, *give in* in (5b) means 'to yield; to give up the contest; to acknowledge oneself beaten' (OED online s.v. *to give in*) and thus, also does not encode motion in space. Treating (5a) as an instance of the CAUSED-MOTION CONSTRUCTION or ((5b) as an instance of the SELF-MOTION CONSTRUCTION would mean making the examples match the theory rather than the other way round. While the word order of the examples in (5) is the same as that of the motion-constructions in (4), those in (6) exhibit a different word order.

Traditionally, combinations such as *give in, give up,* etc. are classified as **phrasal verbs**, which means that they are treated as lexemes in their own right in dictionaries and many grammars. Under this view, which represents a lexical perspective, phrasal verbs are multiword units that typically consist of a verb and a particle, where the term particle is used to refer to a small number of words that can enter such combinations with verbs and that fall under the category of prepositions in our framework – words such as *about, around, down, in, off, on, out, over, through, under* or *up*.

As far as their semantic characterization is concerned, there are clearly different degrees of idiomaticity ranging from the completely idiomatic to the fully transparent: *give up* clearly does not involve an act of 'giving', and *up* does not refer to an upward movement but rather expresses a development towards an endpoint, a meaning that we also find in *eat up* or *finish up. Pick up* in (6b), on the other hand, is fully transparent semantically, but *pick up* also occurs in more idiomatic uses:

(7)   a.   He picked up the Radio Times and glanced through the evening's programmes.

BNC-GW3-229

       b.   I have to pick her up at the airport.   TV-2013-Psych

       c.   ... the long, north-bound train began slowly to move forward, gradually picking up a little speed, before moving out and away along the curving stretch of line that led to Banbury.

BNC-HWM-2052

From a Construction Grammar point of view, however, what is more important than the degree of idiomaticity of particular combinations is whether, like the examples in (4), they can adequately be captured in terms of the SELF-MOTION and the CAUSED-MOTION CONSTRUCTION or not. We thus have to find a way of dealing with the problem that the more idiomatic types of combinations do not fit the descriptions of the semantic function of the two MOTION-constructions, although they have the same or a similar formal structure (and

220 A Construction Grammar of the English Language

in many cases can be seen as the result of a historical development similar to that of the grammaticalization of, say, the *BE-GOING-TO*-v construction; see 4.3.3.2).

Since the relation between the arguments and the verbs can be captured in terms of ÆFFECTOR and ÆFFECTED, and since they consist of a verb and a particle, we will deal with such cases as those under (5)–(7) in terms of low-level lexical constructions such as a *GIVE-UP*-INTRANSITIVE-VERB-PARTICLE CONSTRUCTION and a *GIVE-IN*-TRANSITIVE-VERB-PARTICLE CONSTRUCTION. Note that we do not claim the existence of a generalized, completely schematic verb-particle construction, because the meaning of each of these constructions crucially depends on the combination of a particular verb and a particular particle.

In order to qualify as a **verb-particle construction**, a combination must fulfill the following criteria:

i. Despite formal similarities, the meaning expressed by the construction does not comply with the 'motion'-characteristics of the INTRANSITIVE-MOTION and CAUSED-MOTION CONSTRUCTIONS:

> (8) a. Well, this is my office, so fire away.   TV-2008-Psych
>   b. Couple guys tried to chat her up, but she just blew them off.   TV-2015-Longmire
>
> (9) a. Wycliffe walked along the deserted waterfront. [SELF-MOTION CXN]BNC-GW3-3403
>   b. Wycliffe went up the steps to the verandah ...   BNC-GWB-1546
>   c. He walked back by a different route which took him along the waterfront.
>   [CAUSED-MOTION CXN]   BNC-GW3-712

ii. The construction consists of a verb and a particle in which the particle can be stressed:

> (10) a. He's showing OFF.   TV-2010-Psych
>   b. So we give UP?   TV-2016-Poldark
>
> (11) a. Did they FLY or DRIVE up? [SELF-MOTION CXN]   COCA-2017-SPOK
>   b. Oh, which island did you deCIDE on? [*DECIDE-ON*-TRANSITIVE CXN]
>   COCA-2019-TV

iii. In the case of monotransitive particle constructions, the particle follows pronominal Obj-NPs and can precede or follow all other Obj-NPs.

> (12) a. She gave it up.   COCA-2013-FIC
>   b. ... Shawn called me up and told me you guys were working on a case ...
>   TV-2011-Psych
>   c. The cartridges on the back seat fell on to the floor. Philip leant back and picked
>   them up.   BNC-ABX-1352
>
> (13) a. Maybe we should just give up the whole idea.   TV-1988-Dynasty
>   b. ... she gave the whole idea up.   COCA-2013-FIC

The CASA template for the GIVE-UP-VERB-PARTICLE CONSTRUCTION can be summarized as follows:

GIVE-UP-MONOTRANSITIVE-VERB-PARTICLE CONSTRUCTION				
An ÆFFECTOR decides not to continue something they have been doing for quite some time or not to pursue an action they had planned any longer				
ÆFFECTOR			ÆFFECTED	
	V	part	Obj	part
Subj	give	up	NP (≠ pron) V-ing-cl	
			NP V-ing-cl	up

Figure 11.2 The *GIVE-UP*-VERB-PARTICLE CONSTRUCTION

Other monotransitive uses of phrasal verbs can be described in a similar way; an example of an SELF-MOTION-PHRASAL-VERB CONSTRUCTION is presented in (14) and Figure 11.3.

(14)   … every time a plane takes OFF, the pilots do the calculation …   COCA-2014-SPOK

Name of cxn:	TAKE-OFF-SELF-MOTION-VERB-PARTICLE CONSTRUCTION		
Meaning	An ÆFFECTOR carries out an action.		
Argument roles	ÆFFECTOR	ACTION	
	Subj	V	part
	NP	take	'off

Figure 11.3 *TAKE-OFF*-SELF-MOTION-VERB-PARTICLE CONSTRUCTION

In a grid presentation, we suggest treating the particle as an attribute and indicating the idiomatic status of the phrasal verb in an extra column so that (8a) could be analyzed as in Figure 11.4:

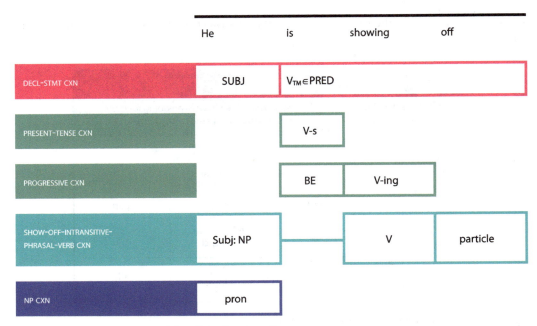

Figure 11.4 Construction grid for *He is showing off*

It is obvious that there is no sharp dividing line between the motion constructions and verb particle constructions. In (15a), for instance, *look up* suggests that someone had been looking in a downward direction on a desk or was reading, etc., and raised their head to look at the person(s) in the room, and (15b) *drive up* means 'stop the car on the side of the road':

(15) a. He looked up as though the question had startled him.   BNC-GW3-629
      b. He drove up, got out of his car and went in – '   BNC-HWP-2329

Whether their meaning is a sufficient reason to classify these cases as verb-particle constructions may be debatable, but it must be understood that this does not really affect the issue of the mental representation of these constructions. In an understanding of grammar that attributes a crucial role to factors such as frequency and transitional probability, there is, in fact, very little point in arguing about the classification of borderline cases when it is obvious that we are faced with a gradient of idiomaticity.

Verb-particle constructions must be kept apart from constructions that appear to have the same or a very similar structure, but do not have any idiomatic meaning as, e.g., in *They walked up the hill side by side* (BNC-F9R-2808) or *All right, now I want you to look to your left, and look up the wall.* (TV-2011-Unforgettable). Similarly, in a sentence such as *We just went to the Hamptons for the weekend* (COCA-2014-TV), *to the Hamptons* is a prepositional phrase, which realizes the Attr-slot in a SELF-MOTION CONSTRUCTION. It could be replaced by *there, where* or a *where*-clause, but the preposition *to* could not be placed after the NP.

Furthermore, verb-particle constructions are different from MONOTRANSITIVE CONSTRUCTIONS with an Obj-PP: *And almost everyone agrees on the solution.* (COCA-2000–

Chapter 11. Speaking idiomatically 223

NEWS). Here, *on the solution* cannot be realized by one word, nor can the preposition follow the NP (also in cases in which it is realized by a pronoun: ...*all of us agree on it* (COCA-1991-SPOK)). (Note that these cases are referred to as *prepositional verbs* in grammars such as CGEL and that many phrasal verb dictionaries subsume them under *phrasal verbs*.)

11.3.2 Constructions with two particles

In addition to the verb-particle constructions with one particle, there are also such constructions with two particles. This type is exemplified by (16):

(16) a. 'Let's get on with it!'   BNC-GWB-1120
      b. 'It's up to you.'   BNC-GWB-2798
      c. I don't want to put up with Mary's pity any longer than I have to.   TV-2014-Downton

This type of verb-particle construction consists of a verb, a particle in the sense defined above, and a prepositional phrase. Since the final particle can be seen as forming a part of the idiomatic meaning of the construction, we will describe these cases as in Figure 11.5 below:[119]

PUT-UP-WITH-VERB PARTICLE CONSTRUCTION				
An ÆFFECTOR accepts or tolerates a 'THING' DISLIKED.				
ÆFFECTOR	ACTION			THING DISLIKED
Subj	V	particle	particle	Obj
NP	put	up	with	NP

Figure 11.5 The *PUT-UP-WITH*-VERB-PARTICLE CONSTRUCTION

---

119. Admittedly, this kind of representation deprofiles the fact that the second particle and the Obj-NP constitute a prepositional phrase (which is the reason why CGEL, 16.9, employs the term phrasal-prepositional verbs). However, we wish to give prominence to the fact that it is the combination of the verb with the two particles that gives rise to the specific meaning of these multi-word expressions. In these constructions, the preposition is less instrumental in establishing a semantic role (contrast (16a)–(c) with *Callaghan, therefore, decided against an early election.* (BNC-A66-295) as opposed to *Eden began his premiership in a businesslike fashion even though he had decided on an instant election.* (BNC-BoH-333).

11.4 Collocation

We will now turn to another aspect of idiomatic language use. Idiomatic use of a language has nothing to do with the frequent use of idioms (which very often are not all that frequent after all, as we have just seen). What is far more important is the phenomenon described by the founder of British contextualism, J.R. Firth with the catchphrase "You shall know a word by the company it keeps". Since Firth was a little unclear about what he meant by company, the term collocation has been applied to pairs of words

- that occur together more frequently than one would expect on the basis of the individual frequency of each of the two items in a corpus,
- whose co-occurrence cannot be strictly predicted on the basis of semantic considerations.

The first use of the term collocation is typical of much corpus linguistic work, whereas the latter interpretation is relevant to foreign language teaching. Interestingly, the views with respect to unpredictability and frequency as determining factors of a collocation find an interesting parallel in the definition of constructions given by Goldberg in 1995, which only attributes construction status to non-compositional units, and her 2006 definition, which also includes highly frequent items.[120]

If we take semantic transparency as a criterion for classifying a combination of words as a collocation (as opposed to an idiom), collocations do not present any problems in terms of language perception. This is quite different in language production, because – depending on your definition – all or some collocations are not predictable, which is why some scholars such as Makkai (1972) and Fillmore, Kay & O'Connor (1988:505) classify them as "encoding idioms".

That speakers of a language tend to have rather strong associations between certain words has been known for quite some time. For instance, Greenbaum & Quirk (1970) found that when asked to complete a sentence beginning with *I entirely* and *I badly*, the majority of the British English subjects taking part in the experiment used one of three verbs (*agree* 78%, *disagree* 19% and *forget* 3%) with *entirely* and either *need* (69%) or *want* with *badly* (28%). These results were confirmed with slighter tendencies towards these verbs for speakers of American English by Greenbaum (1974), but in a similar experiment with German learners of English only 23% opted for *agree* and 11% for *need* (Herbst 1996).

Learners of English with L1 Dutch or German must learn that in English the verb that is commonly used with *teeth* is *brush* (not *clean*, which in other contexts corresponds to Dutch *poetsen* and German *putzen*), that a group of sheep is referred to as a *flock* and not a *herd* (whereas Dutch and German use the same nouns to refer to groups of sheep and cattle). Similarly, learners with L1 French have to learn that *make a decision* is far more frequent in

---

120. For different approaches to collocation see Hausmann (1984, 1985, 2007); Gilquin (2007); Nesselhauf (2005); Schmid (2003); Herbst (1996, 2011b, 2018b); Cantos & Sanchez (2001).

English than *take a decision* (*prendre une décision*), etc. (Gilquin 2007). Like many things in the historical development of languages, there is no particular reason why particular words should be established in one language to express a certain meaning. But precisely because there is no way of knowing or predicting, these combinations of words have to be learnt: collocations belong to the uncountable mass of constructions speakers learn when they learn a language.

Concerning the issue of how collocational knowledge is stored in the speakers' minds, it is still an open question whether they are represented as complex constructions (e.g., a single *brush one's teeth* construction) or whether individual words have stronger links to other words in the constructicon that they frequently co-occur with (e.g., *brush* could be strongly associated with the word *teeth*). This is an empirical question that cannot be decided theoretically but must be investigated using psycho- and neurolinguistic experiments (Hoffmann 2020). Regardless of which of these analyses turns out to be the more plausible one, however, both involve symbolic form-meaning parings and, as a consequence, are perfectly compatible with a Construction Grammar approach.

11.5 Small-scale constructions

As Croft and Cruse note, "construction grammar grew out of a concern to find a place for idiomatic expressions in the speaker's knowledge of a grammar of a language" (2004: 225). This early work on idioms and collocations quickly made it clear that the traditional dichotomy of a meaningful lexicon on the one hand and contentless syntactic rules on the other hand could not be upheld (cf. also Schönefeld 2020). As we have seen throughout this book, symbolic pairings of form and meaning, constructions are the central units of grammar and exist on a lexicon-syntax cline. In this last section, we now illustrate this with phenomena that are clearly located at the syntax end of this gradient, but which also exhibit idiomatic and idiosyncratic properties.

11.5.1 The *let-alone* construction

We pointed out at the beginning of this chapter that the article 'Regularity and Idiomaticity in Grammatical Constructions: The Case of *let alone*', published by Fillmore, Kay and O'Connor in 1988, was rather instrumental in developing the constructionist approach. *Let alone* is indeed a very good example of how rather complex semantic and pragmatic properties can become associated with a fairly innocent looking combination of two words that involves the larger syntactic context.

Formally, *let alone* can be seen as a multi-word conjunction that can be used to coordinate different kinds of phrases and clauses:

(17) a. On the subject of marriage, I have no right to give advice, let alone orders. [coordination of nouns within an NP] TV-2014-Downton

b. ... it was no longer clear that existing nuclear reactors, let alone new ones, made economic sense. [coordination of two noun phrases within an NP] COCA-1994-NEWS

c. That everyone knew journalists and the police were engaged in petty barter does not make it acceptable, let alone legal. [coordination of two adjectives phrases within an AdjP] COCA-2011-NEWS

d. It is not your place even to have opinions of my acquaintance. Let alone express them. [coordination of two infinitive clauses] TV-2015-Downton

e. He won't even look at me. Let alone have sex the way we used to. [coordination of two infinitive clauses] COCA-2016-FIC

What is interesting about the semantics of the *LET-ALONE* CONSTRUCTION is that the two coordinated elements cannot be exchanged, because the second part (almost) always expresses a higher degree or extent of something than the first on a scale (though see Cappelle, Dugas & Tobin 2015 for exceptions to this pattern). This explanation also holds in cases such as (18b) in the context of a sentence such as (18a) (Fillmore, Kay & O'Connor 1988:519):

(18) a. I doubt I have enough material here for a week.

b. You've got enough material there for a whole SEMESTER, let alone a WEEK.

(18b), e.g., would sound odd if we exchanged the two NPs (?*You've got enough material there for a WEEK, let alone a whole SEMESTER.*)

Although *let alone* can be classified as a conjunction, or, in our terminology, a connector, it differs from other coordinating conjunctions in a number of ways. A case in point is the phenomenon Fillmore, Kay & O'Connor (1988:518) call "VP ellipsis":

(19) a. Louis won't eat shrimp and (Sarah) will/won't eat squid.

b. *Louis won't eat shrimp let alone (Sarah) will/won't eat squid.

For obvious reasons, we cannot list all the properties of the *LET-ALONE* CONSTRUCTION discussed by Fillmore, Kay & O'Connor (1988), let alone discuss them in detail, but these examples may suffice to illustrate how Fillmore, Kay & O'Connor (1988:534) arrive at a conclusion that was to instigate a lot of linguistic thought into the direction of Construction Grammar:

> Those linguistic processes that are thought of as irregular cannot be accounted for by constructing lists of exceptions: the realm of idiomaticity in a language includes a great deal that is productive, highly structured, and worthy of serious grammatical investigation.

In other words, we do not just need constructions to explain idiomatic lexical phenomena, but also to account for syntactic patterns that seem regular and productive at first glance, but which, on closer inspection, turn out to also possess idiosyncratic properties.

11.5.2 The *GOD-KNOWS* CONSTRUCTION

Another example of an idiomatic construction that is difficult to analyze in a non-constructionist framework is the *GOD-KNOWS* construction. The construction shows a certain degree of schematicity, as is illustrated by the examples in (20):

(20) a.   This is the first time I've been down here since God knows when.   BNC-GWB-1543
   b.   ... I shall be satisfied just to stop worrying about schedules, cargoes, ... port dues and God knows what else.   BNC-HWP-2308
   c.   I feel guilty though God knows why I should.   BNC-HWP-1378
   d.   And for the rest of the winter until only the Bundesbank knows when.   BNC-CH2-5097

The difficulty for a conventional analysis of (20a) lies in the fact that *God knows* functions as a kind of premodifier to *when* – after all, *since then* would be perfectly "normal" in this context. (20b) and (20c) show that the construction is not restricted to *when* and that a full clause can realize the last wh-slot as in (20c). The N-slot seems to be restricted to a very small number of lexical items, but it does allow for ironic extensions such as in (20d). This is a pattern for which we, therefore, also have to postulate a constructional template (cf. Herbst 2016):

GOD-KNOWS-WHAT CONSTRUCTION			
Expressing one's puzzlement about (some detail of) an ACTION by (seemingly) referring to a higher AUTHORITY as the only source of precise information			
AUTHORITY		ACTION DISCUSSED	
NP	V	WH	
God goodness heaven lord	knows	what how why where when who which whom whether	rest of clause contextual anchor
Typically, the noun in the first slot is stressed.			

Figure 11.6 THE *GOD-KNOWS-WHAT* CONSTRUCTION (Size of typeface providing a rough idea of the frequency of items in the BNC: *God* almost 70%, *goodness* 20%, *what* ca. 50%, *how* 12%; all other items under 10%)

11.5.3 The COMPARATIVE-CORRELATIVE CONSTRUCTION

Finally, let us look at a highly schematic construction that spans two clauses but also turns out to exhibit many idiosyncrasies with respect to its form as well as its meaning:

(21) a. The longer you're a suspect,[clause 1]
the more you become an object of public curiosity.[clause 2]　　　TV-1999-Law&Order

b. The more you lie,[clause 1]
the easier it will be to make you on a murder charge. [clause 2]　　　TV-1999-Law&Order

c. the longer the rain lasted,[clause 1]
the more quickly the ramparts melted.[clause 2]　　　BNC-EFW-690

(21) are instances of the COMPARATIVE-CORRELATIVE CONSTRUCTION (Hoffmann 2019a; Hoffmann, Horsch & Brunner 2019; Hoffmann, Brunner & Horsch 2020; Fillmore, Kay & O'Connor 1988 called it the *THE-X-ER-THE-Y-ER* CONSTRUCTION). Similar to WH-QUESTION (***How much longer** will you be a suspect?*) and WH-RELATIVE CLAUSE CONSTRUCTIONS (*the time **for which** you will be a suspect…*), COMPARATIVE-CORRELATIVE CONSTRUCTIONS are introduced by phrases (e.g., *the longer* and *the more* in (21a)) that in DECLARATIVE CONSTRUCTIONS are part of the clause-internal predicate (*You are no longer a suspect. / You more and more become an object of public curiosity.*). There are, however, also crucial differences between COMPARATIVE-CORRELATIVE constructions and WH-QUESTION- / WH-RELATIVE-CLAUSE CONSTRUCTIONS: Unlike the latter, COMPARATIVE-CORRELATIVE constructions comprise two clauses (in (21a) clause C1 = *the longer you're a suspect* / clause C2 = *the more you become an object of public curiosity*). Each of these two clauses specifies a time frame during which something increases or decreases (in (21a) clause C1: the period during which you are considered a suspect increases / clause C2: the degree to which you are an object of public curiosity increases). Moreover, the initial clause C1 is construed as the 'protasis' that causes the second 'apodosis' clause C2 (i.e., *the longer you're a suspect → the more you become an object of public curiosity*). Note also that the two clause-initial *the*-s are not instances of the determiner *the* (cf. 13.2.8; in (21a) *longer* and *more* are AdvPs that normally do not take determiners). The *the*-s in the COMPARATIVE-CORRELATIVE construction have a meaning of 'as… so…' – (21a) consequently means 'as you are a suspect for a longer amount of time, so you more and more *become an object of public curiosity*'). In light of these construction-specific properties, a Construction Grammar analysis of COMPARATIVE-CORRELATIVE constructions (Hoffmann 2019a) needs to treat them as a bi-clausal template that contains fixed clause-initial elements ([ðə …]$_{C_1}$ [ðə …]$_{C_2}$). These clause-initial elements are then followed by a schematic slot that has to be filled by a comparative phrase (cf. *the {more/more often/less} you lie, the {easier/more difficult/more fun} it will be to make you on a murder charge.*). After the comparative phrase, the subject and the rest of the predicate follow (cf. *the **more** <u>you lie</u>, the **easier** <u>it will be to make you on a murder charge</u>.*). Figure 11.7 provides a constructional template for this construction:

COMPARATIVE-CORRELATIVE CONSTRUCTION WITHOUT VERB									
As the degree of Comparative Phrase1 increases/decreases with respect to NP1					so the degree of Comparative Phrase2 increases/decreases with respect to NP2				
	CompP 1					CompP 2			
the	Adj-er Adv-er		(Subj: NP₁)	(Pred)	the	Adj-er Adv-er		(Subj: NP2)	(Pred)
	more	Adj				more	Adj		
	less	Adv				less	Adv		
	more fewer					more fewer			
Well, the more expensive the lawyer, the longer the trial. Movie-1999-TheHuntfortheUnicornKiller									

Figure 11.7 The abstract COMPARATIVE-CORRELATIVE CONSTRUCTION template

The template in Figure 11.7 is already pretty complex, but on closer inspection, comparative correlatives exhibit further idiosyncratic properties:

(22) a. The stronger economic growth is,
the higher wages, and therefore benefits, are. COCA-2000-MAG
  b. The better the preparation,
the stronger the memory … COCA-2000-MAG

(22b) represents a variant of the construction without a verb in either slot, although the relationship between the adjective and the noun phrase that follows still can be described in terms of ATTRIBUTE and ATTRUBUTEE.[121]

In fact, one occasionally finds a mixture of the two constructions, as in (23):

(23) a. The older you are the greater the chance of you having shingles. BNC-A0J-971
  b. As with all animals, the colder the climate the bigger the body becomes.
BNC-BMG-1508

However, corpus data show quite clearly that speakers have a strong preference for using a verb in both or in neither slot, as represented in Figure 11.7 (Hoffmann 2019a; Hoffmann, Horsch & Brunner 2019; Hoffmann, Brunner & Horsch 2020).[122]

Note that under certain circumstances the COMPARATIVE-CORRELATIVE CONSTRUCTIONS even can be truncated down to the comparative phrase:

(24) a. … the more data, the more information … BNC-FA8-1024

---

121. This can be seen as a construction-specific property since there is no other SUBJECT-ATTRIBUTE CONSTRUCTION without a verb in English.

122. See Culicover and Jackendoff (1999: 554) for details.

b. Oh, the more, the merrier. MOV-2017-Bigfoot

As you can see, some of these truncated patterns such as (24b) are strongly lexicalized (Croft and Cruse 2004:234; Fillmore, Kay and O'Connor 1988:506). Much more could be said about COMPARATIVE-CORRELATIVE CONSTRUCTIONS (for details; cf. Hoffmann 2019a). What we wanted to emphasize by the above discussion is that in addition to abstract constructions (such as Figure 11.7), empirical evidence suggests that speakers have also entrenched (probably a vast amount of) semi-schematic or fully substantive constructional patterns (such as 24b).

11.6 Outlook

Speakers of a language, obviously, have many constructions that are highly frequent and highly schematic in language use (such as the DECLARATIVE-STATEMENT CONSTRUCTION, the PROGRESSIVE CONSTRUCTION, or certain argument structure constructions). At the same time, as we have seen in this chapter, they also possess a great number of idiosyncratic constructions. In the terminology of construction grammarians, the constructicon of native speakers can be said to comprise fully schematic as well as partially productive open choice as well as phonologically-filled idiomatic construction. Constructions exist on a lexicon-syntax cline and for some constructions empirical evidence (such as idiosyncratic properties or high frequency) indicates that speakers have detailed knowledge of abstract constructional templates as well as of partially-filled item-based constructions.

CHAPTER 12

Solving problems with Construction Grammar

12.1 Ligature

In this chapter, we would like to draw your attention to a number of problems of grammatical analysis which, from a cognitive point of view, have not been accounted for in a particularly satisfactory manner in previous accounts. One has to do with the fact that the phenomenon of ligature, which, as we outlined in 1.3.4, can be seen as key to constructionist approaches, can be applied to many cases which traditionally are often described as complex or multi-word units. Like graphic symbols such as ⟨æ⟩ or ⟨œ⟩, a ligature construction is a construction that can be perceived and analyzed as a whole and as consisting of several parts at the same time. It is easy to see that this dual nature of ligature constructions is psychologically real if you think of the fact that speakers of English will process an idiom such as *spill the beans* as a semantic unit, but nevertheless recognize *spill* as a verb and combine it with modal and tense constructions accordingly:

(1) He spilled the beans.   COCA-2019-SPOK

Similarly, although the senses of *deal* and *lot* as nouns that gave rise to chunks such as *a great deal of* and *a lot of* may not be apparent to all speakers of present-day English, we can analyze these as multi-word units functioning as determiners:

(2) a. I've given this a great deal of thought.   TV-2006-Psych
     b. Honestly, Gus, I haven't given it a lot of thought.   TV-2007-Psych
     c. I've given it much thought and consideration.   TV-1996-Dynasty

In a construction grid, this dual character can be shown as in Figure 12.1:

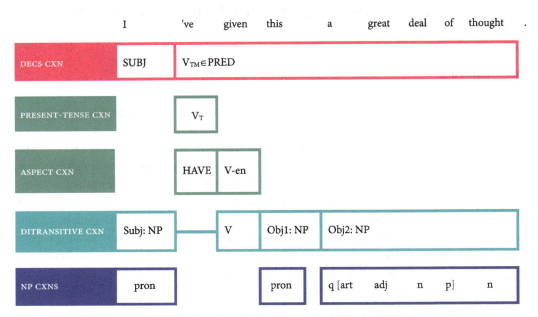

Figure 12.1 Construction grid for *I've given this a great deal of thought*. The elements in square brackets give an indication of the internal structure of the quantifier *a great deal of*

This type of analysis seems to us more plausible than a structuralist analysis that would take *deal* as the head of an NP and the PP as a postmodifier.

12.2 Reporting what other people have said

12.2.1 The quotative construction

Another example of a construction that is rather special and for which conventional wisdom does not necessarily offer the most appropriate analysis is the QUOTATIVE CONSTRUCTION.

(3) a. 'No,' said Robyn. BNC-ANY-1721
 b. 'O brave new world,' said Robyn, 'where only the managing directors have jobs.' BNC-ANY-2322
 c. 'I don't like making men redundant,' he said, 'but we're caught in a double bind. ...' BNC-ANY-2324
 d. 'You British!' said Penny Black, shaking her head in despair. BNC-ANY-1517

This construction consists of a QUOTE, which repeats what another person has said, and a reporting clause, which identifies the originator of the QUOTE and describes the way the utterance is made:

Chapter 12. Solving problems with construction grammar **233**

(4) a. 'What are you suggesting?' asked Lewis, vaguely. BNC-HWM-1488

 b. 'Well,' she shrugged, 'that's the trouble with capitalism, isn't it?' BNC-ANY-2529

What marks the QUOTATIVE CONSTRUCTION as special with respect to form is that

i. the reporting clause can introduce the QUOTE, interrupt or follow it,
ii. reporting clauses that interrupt or follow the quote are flexible in terms of word order (subject verb or verb subject).

From a constructionist point of view, it is also worth noting that the verb in the reporting clause need not necessarily express verbal communication as such, but that other verbs – like *shrug* in (4b) – can receive such an interpretation on the basis of being used in the QUO-TATIVE CONSTRUCTION.

12.2.2 REFERRING-TO-SOURCE CONSTRUCTION

While in (3) and (4), the QUOTE-clause can be analyzed as an object of the verb in the reporting clause, cases such as the following do not lend themselves to such an analysis in quite the same way:

(5) a. ... Morse himself would then address the group and tell them as much or as little as he wanted to tell them, believing, he admitted, that Rumour had probably lost little of her sprinting speed since Virgil's time, and that most of the tourists already had a pretty good idea of what had happened. BNC-HWM-569

 b. What reflection on the experience of internal soliloquy actually shows, Derrida argues, is that there is neither a unitary "self" nor any eternally present "ideas" for it to contemplate. COCA-1995-ACAD

Semantically, the reporting clause in these cases has a function that is more like that of a comment reminding the reader of the originator of the ideas presented. The clause surrounding this type of reporting clause is presented at the level of the main line of argument of the text. This is a more important characteristic of this construction than the fact that formally the "surrounding" clause cannot be seen as an object of the verb of the reporting clause in all such cases. However, this makes the reporting clause rather special in that the Obj-argument of the *ARGUE-* and *ADMIT-*MONOTRANSITIVE CONSTRUCTIONS has no formal realization, although the "surrounding" clause can be seen as its referent.

 This is very similar to the uses in (6), in which the particle *as* functions as a kind of pro-form for that Obj-argument:

(6) a. The tendency of the access is, as Heidegger puts it, "simply original," and "this simplicity is constantly secured." COCA-2017-ACAD

 b. This was also tree for the FSP intervention. However, as pointed out above, the odds ratio failed to reach significance (i.e., $p > .05$). COCA-2001-ACAD

12.2.3 Indirect speech

The so-called INDIRECT SPEECH CONSTRUCTION provides another way of relating an utterance, belief or insight to its originator. Formally, it consists of a reporting clause and a dependent clause, which fills an argument slot of the reporting verb.[123] The latter can be introduced by *that* or a *wh*-word:

(7) a. Why don't you tell us where the next race is? TV-2010-Psych
     b. Well, you said you wanted to be the mascot for the Milwaukee brewers ...
         TV-2007-Psych
     c. He said he'd been back for over a year. TV-2006-Psych
     d. Einstein showed that mass is equivalent to energy. ... COCA-2004-ACAD

One reason why the constellation of reporting and dependent clause qualifies as a construction is that there is some interdependency between them in terms of tense. If the reporting clause is present tense as in (7a), the tense of the dependent clause tends to correspond to the tense of the original utterance – or, to be more precise, the tense of a hypothetical utterance not introduced by a reporting clause. However, if the reporting clause is past tense, past tense use in the reported clause may well correspond to the use of present tense in a corresponding clause in direct speech as (7b) and (7c). The constellation of past tense in the reporting and present tense in the dependent clause as in (7d) is supposed to underscore the fact that the 'process' reported on still holds at the moment of speaking.

12.3 Tag constructions

So-called tag-constructions are extremely common in spoken English. They are placed after an instance of the DECLARATIVE-STATEMENT CONSTRUCTION and include an operator verb (i.e., a modal or a form of *be, do* or *have*). The semantic function associated with the tag depends on the nature of the preceding clause; the examples in (8) are associated with the idea that the speaker regards the statement as uncontroversial, whereas those in (9) signal some kind of disagreement between speaker and hearer:

(8) a. 'He does love acronyms, doesn't he,' Philip murmurs. BNC-ANY-1356
     b. 'It's not proper cooking, is it? BNC-ANY-23
     c. 'Anyway, you couldn't put all this in a report, could you?' BNC-GW3-3286

(9) a. 'Oh, it's my fault, is it?' she said, and her lower lip began to tremble. BNC-ANY-31
     b. 'You don't believe the gossip, do you?' BNC-GW3-692

---

123. We prefer the term dependent clause over the term reported clause (e.g., Leech & Svartvik 1975) because the latter carries a stronger implication of the reported clause being derived from an actual utterance in direct speech, which, however, need not be the case.

These tag-constructions can be described in the following way:

Name of cxn	AFFIRMATIVE-TAG CONSTRUCTION	
Meaning	Emphasizing the content of a statement as uncontroversial	
Form	DECLARATIVE-STATEMENT CXN (positive polarity) (negative polarity)	op pron (positive polarity) (negative polarity)
		falling intonation

Figure 12.2 The English AFFIRMATIVE-TAG CONSTRUCTION (op: Operator verb; pron: Personal pronoun)

Name of cxn	CONTROVERSIAL-TAG CONSTRUCTION	
Meaning	Emphasizing the content of a statement as controversial	
Form	DECLARATIVE-STATEMENT CXN (positive polarity) (negative polarity)	op pron (positive polarity) (negative polarity)
		rising intonation

Figure 12.3 The English CONTROVERSIAL-TAG CONSTRUCTION (op: Operator verb; pron: Personal pronoun)

12.4 Constructions with *it* and *there*

12.4.1 Existential *there*

In English, there are a number of constructions which can be used to say that something exists. The EXISTENTIAL-*THERE* CONSTRUCTION is an attribute construction in which the first position is taken by unstressed *there*:

(10) a. There was a knock on the door. COCA-2015-FIC
b. There were signs of improvement ... COCA-2008-NEWS

It may be a matter of debate whether this *there* should be given subject status in such clauses since concord of the verb is determined by the number feature of the Attr argument. In a constructionist model, which takes a holistic view of constructions, this is not particularly

236   A Construction Grammar of the English Language

important. We will nevertheless treat *there* in such cases as the subject of the respective clauses, partly because it can occur in the position typical of Subj-arguments in non-finite clauses:

(11)   ... I don't for a minute expect there to be any complications.   BNC-JY0-161

12.4.2   Other constructions with *there* and *here*

Arguably, *there* in (10) and (11) can be attributed a locative meaning, too (Langacker 2008a: 496), but a locative interpretation is even more plausible in the following cases, which were discussed in terms of a family of deictic-*there* constructions by Lakoff (1987: 483–485) in one of the early analyses carried out in a cognitive approach (Croft & Cruse 2004: 240–241)

(12)   a.   There comes a point when you get tired of the chaos ...   COCA-2018-NEWS
      b.   "Here comes the maestro," he whispered.   COCA-2018-FIC

12.4.3   Constructions with impersonal *it*

12.4.3.1   *Weather verbs*

Impersonal *it*-constructions – or, if you like, constructions with impersonal *it* – are used in cases in which the *it* has no referential properties, i.e., in which it does not function as a pro-form for another noun phrase. This is typically the case with some so-called meteorogical verbs:

(13)   a.   All around us, as it rains or snows, one might, upon close inspection, find such collections of life – bacteria, algae, and fungi – falling toward us in great densities. It is not raining cats and dogs, but it is, more often than not, snowing bacteria.
                                                     COCA-2009-ACAD
      b.   The bottom line is, it's snowing Styrofoam and I'm stuck here.   TV-2010-Psych

If used metaphorically, subjects other than *it* can occur as well:

(14)   a.   And ash was raining down both to the north and east on that particular day ...
                                                COCA-1998-SPOK
      b.   Particles forged in the heart of a nearby supernova are still raining onto Earth today
                                                NOW-16-04-22-US
      c.   Red, blue, green, white balloons were raining down from the ceiling by the thousands ...   COCA-2000-MAG

The same kind of quasi-existential use of *it* can be found with expressions such as the following:

(15)   a.   ... it was dark outside ...   BNC-GW3-2552

b. What time is it? It's almost 1:00. *TV-2010-Psych*

12.4.3.2 *Impersonal constructions with verbs, adjectives and nouns*

A related, though not entirely similar, use of *it* can be found in impersonal constructions with adjectives and nouns used in argument structure constructions with slots for *to*-infinitive, *that-* or *wh*-clauses (see 5.6):

(16) a. It's simply impossible to deny that rhyme has provided countless poems with a musical richness ... *COCA-2009-ACAD*

b. It is indicative of the particular local society in Sheffield that this gesture had to be made. *BNC-B2L-1196*

c. ... it depends on what you are writing whether a piece of information is useful or relevant. *BNC-FU3-2130*

In these cases, the *it*-subject can be seen as referring to the clause at the end, which is why these clauses are sometimes called postponed subjects (CGEL 1985: 1391–1393 for an account in terms of extraposition). The motivation for using such constructions lies in the theme-rheme structure of the clause: by putting a long constituent at the end it receives more prominence than in the examples in (17):

(17) a. To deny it is therefore impossible. To break it down is extremely difficult. *BNC-A6J-787–788*

b. That anyone who logged on to Reddit at the specified time could ask questions of a high-status astrophysicist is indicative of the participatory phenomenon of social media. *COCA-2015-ACAD*

c. Whether to use the three-step cycle or an alternate strategy depends solely on which composition needs the most demanding musical concentration. *COCA-2001-ACAD*

On the whole, such uses with a clausal subject tend to be less frequent than the corresponding impersonal constructions (Uhrig 2018: 217–221; CGEL 1985: 1392); in some cases only the impersonal construction is possible:

(18) a. It appears that my call to Madrid cost me 8 pounds, 10 shillings. *TV-1963-Avengers*
b. It seems that the little hut at Trebyan meant a lot to your brothers. *BNC-GWB-2260*
c. "He was trying." "So it seems." *COCA-2018-FIC*

It thus seems inappropriate to treat the clauses in (16) as postponed subjects, also because the idea of postponing suggests a change to a hypothetical structure of the clause, which goes contrary to the basic assumptions of a constructionist account. We would rather argue that the corresponding examples in (16) and (17) represent different argument structure constructions, and, consequently, we treat *it* as the Subj-argument of the examples in (16) and the "postponed" clauses as clausal Attr. This must not be taken to deny the fact that these clausal Attr represent the same argument role as the Subj-arguments in sentences such as (17).

The reason why we consider the *it* as an element without a semantic role of an argument structure construction is, quite simply, because these *it*-s do not necessarily occur as subjects of a clause, as shown by (19):

(19) a. 'You thought it unreasonable that he should exploit the property to his advantage – is that it?'
BNC-GWB-1768
  b. I consider it a mistake to limit planting choice to our indigenous flora. BNC-AoG-1009

CHAPTER 13

Words as constructions in a constructional network

13.1 Words

13.1.1 Word-lemmata and word-forms

Provided you have read this book through right from the beginning, you will have come across 183 instances (or tokens) of one linguistic term without being provided with a proper definition for it – namely the term *word*. You probably didn't notice this, because *word* is used in everyday language to refer to a particular linguistic unit, and even in the linguistics literature its use is by no means unambiguous, as becomes clear when you consider whether *cat* and *cats* represent the same word or two different words or whether *white wine* should be counted as one word or two. The problem is complicated further by the fact that compounds do not necessarily have to be spelt as "one word" or with a hyphen, but at the same time corpus analyses count "words" such as *washing machine* or *of course* as two words (cf. Herbst 2010: 95–98; Sanchez-Stockhammer 2018).[124] On the whole, this does not matter greatly, because linguists tend to know how to interpret the word *word* in a given context. Nevertheless, there is no harm in trying to be more precise.

From a cognitive point of view, our prime interest lies in modelling possible mental representations within what we may call a multidimensional constructional space without a sharp division between grammatical and lexical constructions.[125] We would like to do justice to these different uses of *word* by distinguishing between *word-lemma* and *word-form*. If the distinction is clear from the context, both *word-lemma* and *word-form* can simply be referred to as *word*.

W1.   A word-lemma is a lexical construction, i.e., it has a stable form component combined with a certain meaning potential. The word-lemma *cat* thus has the written form <cat>, the spoken form /ˈkæt/, and a meaning of the type 'a small feline animal that chases mice and is often kept as a pet'.

W2.   A word-form is either (i) identical with the form of the word-lemma or (ii) a combination of a word-lemma with an inflectional suffix combining forms and meanings of the word-lemma and the suffix. The different word forms of English nouns, verbs and adjectives are listed in Table 13.1. below:

---

124. For a discussion of the problem of word classes in structuralist frameworks see Crystal (1967); Allerton (1990), and for an outline of an alternative framework see Herbst & Schüller (2008: 31–75).

125. For a discussion of other word classes within Cognitive Grammar see Langacker (2008a); Radden & Dirven (2007); and Hollmann (2014).

Table 13.1 Word forms of the major English word classes

nouns	cat	child	singular (not genitive)
	cats	children	plural (not genitive)
	cat's	child's	genitive singular
	cats'	children's	genitive plural
adjectives	nice	good	positive
	nicer	better	comparative
	nicest	best	superlative
verbs	persist	give	base form
	persists	gives	3rd person singular present tense
	persisted	gave	past tense
	persisted	given	past participle
	persisting	giving	present participle

Whether we consider word forms such as *cats* or *persisted* constructions or not depends on whether they occur frequently enough to be stored as wholes or whether we expect them be created by speakers on the fly – an issue which cannot be resolved generally because it clearly depends on the individual language experiences of different speakers.

13.1.2 Words as nodes in networks

Knowing a word does not only entail knowledge of the phonological (and, with literate speakers, also of the orthographic) form of the word-lemma but also knowledge of the constructions in which it occurs. As shown above, some of these constructions (like 3rd person singular) combine with verb lemmata in the form of word-forms (*persists*), whereas in other cases the lemma is linked with a construction in the form of an itecx, i.e., an item that occurs in a particular slot of, say, an argument structure construction in established use.

Furthermore, a speaker's knowledge of a word comprises what Goldberg (2019: 15) refers to as "lossy compression": the "meaning" of a word is an abstraction over the usage events in which it has been experienced. In fact, following recent accounts, it is probably more appropriate to speak of the "meaning potential" of a word or another construction (Hanks 2000), because, as Diessel (2019: 15) puts it with respect to Langacker's (2008a: 39) concept of a semantic network, "linguistic signs do not 'have' meaning but serve to 'create' meaning in communicative interactions".[126]

In other words, imagining a word to be a static combination of a form and a meaning in the sense of de Saussure's linguistic sign is probably not entirely adequate from a cognitive

---

126. For a more detailed account of a dynamic view of meaning see Diessel (2019: 93–109).

point of view. Rather, we would argue that words are best envisaged as nodes of mini-networks within constructional space, as indicated in various forms by, e.g., Elman (2004) or Diessel (2019). Goldberg (2019:17) characterizes words in the following way:

> Individual words are represented by a cluster of abstracted sequences of sounds and structured context-based semantic representations. The cluster emerges on the basis of similarities and parallels within representations, and from differences between other existing clusters. Thus, a "word" is in fact a cluster of partially overlapping structured representations within our hyper-dimensional conceptual space.

13.1.3   A note on polysemy

The network conception of words can also be a good way of looking at the phenomenon of polysemy. If we look at a word in terms of its connections with other words and more abstract constructions, we can either see an area that can plausibly be interpreted as one coherent area or subspace or, alternatively, several such subspaces. Let's take a very simple example and look at the word *table*: a search for the collocates of *table* in the 1-billion-word COCA corpus produces the following result:

Table 13.2 Top collocates for *table* in COCA (1 billion words 1990–2019)

+ NOUN		NEW WORD	?	+ ADJ		NEW WORD	?	+ VERB		NEW WORD	?	+ ADV		NEW WORD	?
4788	5.05	kitchen		1343	4.89	round		9077	3.90	sit		807	2.75	below	
3876	4.84	coffee		827	2.57	additional		5850	2.50	show		288	2.87	respectively	
3099	4.33	chair		810	3.36	mean		3089	3.84	present		161	2.03	across	
2943	4.08	dinner		768	4.14	wooden		3056	2.44	set		124	2.54	statistically	
2761	2.00	room		658	5.70	descriptive		1168	3.81	list		65	2.35	neatly	
2623	2.39	result		596	2.22	following		1127	5.87	summarize		41	2.93	eg	
2516	6.10	dining		526	4.27	demographic		1001	2.30	indicate		24	4.00	pairwise	
2407	3.10	figure		525	5.88	periodic		981	2.42	contain		16	2.36	elegantly	
2051	2.02	food		503	2.40	empty		899	2.14	lay		14	2.38	opposite	
1858	2.04	data		403	2.15	standard		837	5.25	seat		13	2.91	elaborately	

None of these columns forms a coherent lexical set. However, if we make a distinction between two different senses of *table* – one denoting a piece of furniture, the other a table in the sense of "Table 13.2" above – it is easy to find words in each column that fits the respective sense:[127]

1.   *kitchen, coffee, chair, dinner; wooden; sit, set, lay; opposite.*
2.   *result, figure, data; mean, following, demographic, periodic; show, list, summarize; below, statistically.*

---

127. Of course, we do not claim that there are only two senses of *table*; e.g., *cards* will be related to the idiom *put one's cards on the table* and *round table* can have a sense relating to discussions, etc.

In a much more sophisticated way, such links between words are being exploited for the analysis of meaning in the vector approach of distributional semantics (Lapesa & Evert 2014; Jurafsky & Martin 2023). If we interpret such approaches in terms of the network within constructional space, then we can visualize the fact that the word-lemma *table* shares properties with many other nouns as in Figure 13.1 (such as the PLURAL-COUNT NP: *tables*, DEFINITE-NP CONSTRUCTION: *the table*, the DEMONSTRATIVE-NP CONSTRUCTION: *this/that table*, etc.) and that there are also links that lead us to an analysis in terms of two senses:[128]

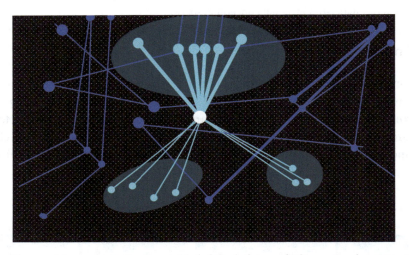

Figure 13.1 The word-lemma construction *table* (white dot) in multidimensional constructional space showing strong links to constructions which can be combined with both senses of *table* (green area above lemma) and weaker links to constructions which occur with only one of these senses (below left and right)

In a case such as the (clearly simplified) one discussed above, one can speak of polysemy. The term polysemy has been used for a long time to refer to cases where one form is related to different meanings (Palmer 1981; Herbst 2010) and has been applied in Construction Grammar with respect to, e.g., the DITRANSITIVE CONSTRUCTION (Goldberg 1995: 38), lexical items (Goldberg 2006: 170), or frozen metaphors (Diessel 2019: 109).

---

128. Obviously, there will be individual differences with respect to issues such as how far separate senses identified for a word-lemma are apart from one another, to what extent there is overlap between them, and whether distinct senses can be identified at all. In traditional accounts, the issue of polysemy (one sign: one form – more than one sense) is usually contrasted with homonymy (two signs with identical form but different meanings). Synchronically, this distinction is very hard to draw anyway, and it remains to be seen whether in a network model of linguistic meaning it is helpful at all. Nevertheless, there are cases in which no semantic overlap can be found although the forms of the constructions can be analyzed as being identical – take the third person singular {S} of present tense verbs and the "regular" {S}-plural form of nouns, for example. Note, however, that in the way we have analyzed these constructions, namely as V-s and N-s, the issue does not arise in these cases.

13.2 From words to word classes: Similarities between words

13.2.1 Aspects of word learning

The above conception of words in terms of constructional networks that comprise knowledge about word forms, uses of words and meaning potentials may also be helpful in understanding how children learn words. In L1-learning, it is certainly helpful to assume that not all properties of a construction – be it a word or a larger construction – are idiosyncratic, i.e., specific to that one construction. Once children have begun to learn words, one would expect them to look for similarities of any new word they encounter with words they have learnt previously. Imagine a child coming across the words *waiter, approaching* or *rotors* for the first time in sentences such as the ones under (1):

(1) a. Did the waiter come with a beautiful big chocolate cake?   t2-05-28
    b. I think the flashing lights, Thomas, are probably as the fire engine is approaching the fire.   t2-10-27
    c. ... his rotors were completely bent and fire engines quickly approached.   t4-00-09

It is more than reasonable that the child will group these new words together with words they already know such as (a) *baker, butcher* or *postman*, (b) *singing, bringing* and *asking*, and (c) *wheels, trains* or *cars*. In fact, this kind of association may be instrumental to the learning process. Let us take this a step further and imagine a child that has come across the forms marked in blue in Table 13.3, but not the ones in green:

Table 13.3 Hypothetical input encountered by a young L1-learner

1	a dog	a cat	a donkey	a budgy
2	the dog	the cat	the donkey	the budgy
3	another dog	another cat	another donkey	another budgy
4	this dog	this cat	this donkey	this budgy
5	my dog	my cat	my donkey	my budgy

We can assume that the child may produce forms such as *my donkey* and *the budgy* because there is a sufficient likeness between *donkey* (concerning 1, 2 and 4) and *budgy* (with respect to 1) with *dog* and *cat*. So, there is a point in grouping words together on the basis of similarities between them – be they semantic or distributional.[129]

It is important to note, however, that the emergence of a generalization (such as that nouns combine with plural forms ending in /s/, /z/ or /ɪz/) must go hand in hand with finding out whether the generalization holds for a newly-learnt item or whether it is pre-empted

---

129. Of course, such expectations may turn out to be wrong. On the basis of *cats, dogs, budgies* and *donkeys*, language learners might well expect there to be a plural form *sheeps*.

by an established form that does not correspond to the general pattern (such as *sheep, mice* or *oxen*). Nevertheless, the formation of classes may facilitate the learning of new words by at least resulting in hypotheses about their potential properties.

13.2.2 Plausibility

Seen in this way, assigning a word to a particular word class is not to say that it shares a certain number of semantic or formal properties with all other members of that class. Rather such an assignment should be seen in terms of a best-match approach, i.e., that a particular word shares more properties with the other members of a class than with those of any other class. In other words: in a cognitive approach, word classes are not Aristotelean categories, but prototypes (Taylor 1989:22–24 & 173–196) – a view which is perfectly in line with the emphasis on gradience in earlier approaches (CGEL; Aarts 2007).

Thus, on the basis of sentences such as

(2) a. You fell asleep during your own show.   TV-2013-Psych
     b. Jules is asleep.   TV-2013-Psych

in which *asleep* occurs in the ATTR-slot of a RESULTATIVE CONSTRUCTION (2a) and an ATTRIBUTE-CONSTRUCTION (2b) respectively, we will classify *asleep* as an adjective even though it does not appear in the PREMODIFIER-OF-NOUN CONSTRUCTION as other adjectives normally do (expressions such as *an asleep baby* or *very asleep* do not occur).[130] It is important to bear in mind, however, that while for descriptive purposes it may be sufficient to classify such *a*-adjectives as marginal members of the category (CGEL: 408–409), for speakers of the language it is not. Speakers of English know in which constructions they can use *asleep* and similar adjectives beginning with *a*-, and in which constructions (in which other adjectives occur) they cannot. Whether this means that speakers first form hypotheses about possible uses, as suggested in the previous section, which then get pre-empted for lack of evidence, or whether learners store words such as *asleep* as attributive adjectives right from the start (and revise such specific kinds of storage when encountering evidence for the need to do so) is difficult to say.

13.2.3 Dual class membership

A-adjectives and similar cases are problematic because a word such as *asleep* does not occur in all the constructions in which adjectives typically appear. The opposite case is presented by a word such as *love*:

---

130. It may be noticed in passing that Boyd and Goldberg (2011) have shown that the cause for these restrictions on *a*-adjectives can be traced back to their origin as prepositional phrases in Old English participles, see also Goldberg (2019).

Chapter 13. Words as constructions in a constructional network 245

(3) a. We would **love** to join you and your lovely wife for a six-course dinner. TV-2014-Psych
   b. Oh, my God, I **love** those shoes. TV-2011-Psych

(4) a. He was, you know, truly one of the **loves** of my life and he always will be.
   COCA-2019-SPOK
   b. Well, she still has the same **loves** that I do. COCA-2019-SPOK
   c. And they have to have a **love** of correct grammar ... TV-2008-Psych
   d. I believe that **love** travels at varying speeds TV-2014-Psych

Is *love* a verb in (3) or a noun in (4)? Since it is frequently used and thus firmly established in verb-typical and noun-typical constructions, this question does not really make that much sense. Cognitively, even the question of whether there are one or two words *love* in English is not particularly relevant. What is more important is that there are a large number of verbs and nouns which are identical in their base forms and which fall into both categories and that speakers are able to exploit this fact and make creative use of words established in one of these two word-classes by using them in the other. Interestingly, however, this is only possible if the noun is not marked morphologically as a noun by a suffix such as *-ery* or *-ness*:

(5) a. I want to thank you for helping me out in the surgery today ... COCA-2005-TV
   b. ???I want to thank you for helping me out surgerying today

13.2.4 The CASA category of particles

13.2.4.1 *Particles and the traditional distinction between prepositions, adverbs and conjunctions*

Analyzing words in terms of more than one word class only makes sense if they share a substantial number of properties with prototypical members of each of those classes, as in the case of *love, bridge* or *garden*. Some of the traditional word classes are problematic in this respect: For instance, subordinating conjunctions are traditionally distinguished from prepositions by the criterion that subordinating conjunctions are followed by a clause as in (6):

(6) a. Well, it's good to see that you're still working. TV-2010-Psych
   b. Look, he took your jewelry because he's trying to figure out your ring size.
   TV-2007-Psych

Prepositions, in contrast, are defined as being followed by a noun phrase:

(7) ... I worked at the Hampton Inn for that three-day weekend in Austin ... TV-2006-Psych

This looks like a fairly clear-cut distinction, but it is problematic in a number of respects: First of all, some but not all conjunctions can also be followed by non-finite V-ing clauses, as can some but not all prepositions:

A Construction Grammar of the English Language

(8) a. Although studying and admiring Tchaikovsky's methods of composition, Stravinsky felt he could break away from the stereotyped dance forms demanded by nineteenth-century balletmasters ... BNC-A12-166

b. Her Facebook wall has a link to a site about dating inanimate objects. TV-2011-HowIMet

Secondly, words such as *after* can be followed by finite clauses, NPs or a V-ing clause (so that you cannot decide whether in (9c) it is a preposition or a conjunction, see CGEL 1985: 660):

(9) a. After he'd gone, did you hear anything? BNC-GW3-3446

b. She had forgotten how nice it was, after so long an interval. BNC-ANY-519

c. ... could he have driven the car to Exeter after disposing of his wife? BNC-GWB-1940

Thirdly, some words can be followed by a clause, a noun phrase, and can occur on their own (i.e., without any complement):

(10) a. Shawn, we have to solve this case before he leaves. TV-2007-Psych

b. I never met Mr. Hale before that night. TV-2007-Psych

c. Have you seen either of these two guys here before? TV-2007Psych

Instead of assigning *before* to three word classes – (a) conjunction, (b) preposition, and (c) adverb – we consider it by far more appropriate to think of *before* as one single word with different uses.[131] This is perfectly in line with the conception of words outlined at the beginning of this chapter because under this view, knowledge of a word explicitly entails knowledge about the uses of a word. In this spirit, we will use the term **particle** (instead of preposition) for a word class that comprises traditional subordinating conjunctions and prepositions. Note that we will not assign such words to a different word class if they occur on their own as in (10c).

What all particles have in common is that they express a relation between two things.[132] These things can either both be expressed linguistically as in (6)–(10b) or one is expressed by the element preceding the particle and the second one can be inferred from the context, as in (10c).

Particle (phrase) constructions, which we abbreviate as PP, thus consist of the following elements (taking (10a) as an example):

– an anchor point which is not expressed by the construction itself (*we have to solve this case*),

---

131. This has indeed been proposed in the recent reference grammars by Huddleston & Pullum (CAMG 2002) and Aarts (2011), who extend the term preposition to cover all of these cases, and, in a similar form, by Herbst & Schüller (2008), where subordinating conjunctions are also subsumed under this category. We will differ from these approaches, however, by not subsuming words such as *here* or *then* under this category (see 13.2.4 and 13.2.5). See also Radford (1988) and Emonds (1976).

132. Up to a point, this is also true of connectors (coordinating conjunctions; see I.3.1) and verbs in argument structure constructions (see also Langacker 2008a: 115–118).

Chapter 13. Words as constructions in a constructional network **247**

– a reference point (*we leave*), which (depending on the particle) is either expressed explicitly or can be identified from the context, and
– the particle which specifies the position or role of the reference point.

Based on sentences such as the ones under (11) we can describe the particle construction with the particle *at* as in Figure 13.2:

(11) a. Didn't teach you much at Oxford, did they?   BNC-AoU-514
     b. You guys are terrible at cleaning up after yourselves.   TV-2009-Psych

Name of cxn	AT-POINT-OF-LOCATION-CONSTRUCTION		
Meaning	Relating the ANCHOR POINT to the THING INDICATED		
	ANCHOR POINT	particle	THING INDICATED
Form	contextual anchor	at	NP V-ing CL

Figure 13.2 The English AT-POINT-OF-LOCATION CONSTRUCTION as an example of a particle construction

We will refer to the formal side of this particle construction as a particle phrase (PP) – depending on the particle, particle phrases can take the following form:

– particle on its own or particle with PREMODIFIER-OF-PARTICLE CONSTRUCTION:

(12) a. And we've actually met before.   TV-2009-Psych
     b. She backtracked and ended up in a small square where she had been a few minutes before.   COCA-2019-FIC

– particle followed by a noun phrase, a V-ing clause or an adverb:

(13) a. I think he's been waiting in there since Thursday.   TV-2009-Psych
     b. Wipe your shoes before entering.   TV-2008-Psych
     c. Miss York was highly trusted, despite being the lowest-ranking member of the diplomatic team.   TV-2011-Psych
     d. Since then she has published three dozen books ...   COCA-2019-NEWS

Since the type of particle phrase exemplified by (13a)–(c) is identical with what is commonly called a prepositional phrase, the latter term is equally appropriate.

–   particle + finite clause or *to*-infinitive construction

(14) a. I've been worried about you since you were three years old ...   TV-2007-Psych

b. I haven't decided whether to put the fern on the right or the left side

TV-2011-HowIMet

Particles can thus be seen as a word class all members of which have a slot that can be filled by a noun phrase or a clause. Some particles (such as *since*) can leave the slot unexpressed if the THING INDICATED is identifiable from the context. However, words such as *here* or *then*, which cannot appear in constructions with such a slot, we will still classify as adverbs. This seems justified in the light of Langacker's (2008a: 116) account of the difference between prepositions and adverbs, which is based on the idea that adverbs have only one focal participant, whereas prepositions (which fall under the category of particles in CASA) have two. This is very much a matter of degree, however. Compare, for example, (15a) and (15b):

(15) a. She moved to Durango in 1973 to ski and has been here since.   COCA-2004-NEWS

b. I moved to Sydney and I'm still here now and enjoying life.   NOW-2019-AU

While the interpretation of *since* is clearly dependent on the point-in-time explicitly mentioned in the previous clause (*in 1973*), that of *now* is independent of any previously mentioned point-of-time because *now* always refers to the present time, or, to be precise, to the time of speaking. As such, *now* has a greater degree of "auto-semanticity" than *since*. Although both expressions are deictic in a way, what Langacker calls the second focal participant is integrated into the meaning of *now*, but has to be expressed explicitly. We can thus justify classifying *before* as a particle and *here* as an adverb. Nevertheless, this remains a borderline case, which we will come back to in 13.2.5 (see also CAMG: 598–616; Aarts 2011; and Herbst & Schüller 2008: 59–67).

13.2.4.2   *Complex particles*

There are a number of recurrent multi-word sequences which we can subsume under the category of particles. Combinations such as *out of* in (16) or *onto* in (17a) are good examples of ligature constructions (see L1), because quite clearly they are form-meaning pairings in the sense of constructions, but at the same time can easily be recognized as being made up of two components.

(16) a. Robyn got out of the car.   BNC-ANY-1710

b. What they didn't eat or steal, they burned or ruined out of pure spite.   COCA-2015-FIC

(17) a. Robyn sank down on to a chair.   BNC-ANY-2170

b. She dropped down onto the chair beside his desk.   COCA-2012-FIC

Spellings such as *onto* or *into* are indication of the holistic interpretation of such combinations. On the other hand, by no means all occurrences of, say, *on* and *to* can be analyzed as one chunk; see, for example:

Chapter 13. Words as constructions in a constructional network   **249**

(18)   We're moving on to Oklahoma.   COCA-2016-MAG

13.2.5   Adverbs

Adverbs can then be defined as words that occur in adjunct constructions, as in (19), or PREMODIFIER-OF-ADJECTIVE, PREMODIFIER-OF-ADVERB and PREMODIFIER-OF-PARTICLE CONSTRUCTIONS as in (19a)–(c), respectively:

(19)   a.   Read any good books lately, Vic?   BNC-ANY-1485
       b.   Get out of here.   TV-2006-Psych
       c.   Would you like to have lunch with us? Perhaps afterwards you could give us a little
            tour.   TV-2008-Psych

(20)   a.   Don't be too late.   BNC-ANY-308
       b.   A character who, rather awkwardly for me, doesn't herself believe in the concept of
            character.   BNC-ANY-533
       c.   We've been close ever since.   TV-2009-Psych

The problem with the adverb class is that it is extremely heterogeneous and does not deserve the name class at all; in fact, it could be seen as a dustbin category for many words that cannot be assigned to any of the more homogeneous word classes. To come back to the case of *now* and *here* discussed in the previous section (15): Using the term adverb for these words and including them in the same class as *very, too, rather, etc.* must appear far from ideal when one considers that (i) *here, there* or *afterwards* do not occur in the PREMODIFIER-OF-ADJECTIVE CONSTRUCTION, whereas *now* and *then* do, as in (21), that (ii) *now* and *then* also occur in the PREMODIFIER-OF-NOUN CONSTRUCTION, as in (22), which is rather untypical of adverbs, and that (iii) all of these words can occur in the equally untypical POSTMODIFIER-OF-NOUN CONSTRUCTION, as in (23):

(21)   a.   the now infamous Trump Tower meeting in New York   COCA-2019-SPOK
       b.   ??the here situation

(22)   a.   the now President-elect   COCA-2016-SPOK
       b.   the then-director of the CIA   COCA-1991-SPOK

(23)   a.   Looks like the situation here is still a mess.   NOW-16-12-19-GB
       b.   ... not only on September 11, and in the days and the months afterwards, but still
            today ...   NOW-21-09-25-GB

One solution to the heterogeneity of the adverb class would be to distinguish between *-ly*-adverbs or manner adverbs on the one hand and time and place adverbs on the other, or to identify a larger number of more specific classes, but even such approaches show a great deal of overlap.[133] For the purposes of assigning a word class label to words in construction

---

133. Compare, for instance, Greenbaum (1969) and CGEL (1985: 441–663).

grids, we will make use of adverb (adv) as a class based on family resemblance (see 8.7). Cognitively, it probably makes sense to assume that parallels between the adverbs ending in -*ly* may be exploited in the process of learning, but that a lot of the knowledge speakers have in their constructicons about the uses of words such as *now, then, there, etc.* is related to those particular items.

13.2.6   Determiners and pronouns

A similar problem of classification is presented by cases such as the following:

| (24) | a. | Things will be better this term. | BNC-ANY-1051 |
| | b. | This is Dr Robyn Penrose, of Rummidge University,' he said. | BNC-ANY-2735 |

| (25) | a. | Do have some cake. | TV-2014-Downton |
| | b. | Pineapple upside-down cake. Would you like some? | TV-2007-Psych |

Basically, there are two ways of classifying *this* and *some* here. One is to focus on the differences in syntagmatic context in the (a) and (b) cases and make a distinction between determiners and pronouns, depending on whether *this* and *some* are followed by a noun or not. The other is to base the classification on semantic considerations and identify classes such as demonstratives (13.3.2.3) and quantifiers (13.3.2.5). As in the case of particles such as *before*, we think there is a strong case for not assigning a word such as *some* and similar words to two different word classes. Rather, we tend to see knowledge as to whether a word can function as a determiner and a pronoun as part of the knowledge about the uses of a word, as outlined in 16.1. The strong association between words and the constructions in which they occur form the basis of the classification of these items outlined in Chapter 13.

In fact, it can be doubted whether there is much room for generalization in this area of English grammar. The fact that there are only four words in the English language that can function as determiners only and not as pronouns (the articles *a/an, the, no* and *every*) is at best anecdotal, but the knowledge about these uses is much more item-specific. *Would you like some* in (25b) clearly refers to the *cake* mentioned before, but although the demonstrative *that*, for instance, also has a determiner- and a pronoun-use, they are by no means equivalent in the way that they are with *some*: Reference to the *song* in Examples (26b) has to take the form of *that one* because *that* on its own tends to refer to a proposition rather than a 'thing' so that (26c) sounds distinctly odd:

(26)	a.	If I could produce the same effect on other people as Louis Armstrong does with that song, then I'd be really happy.	BNC-AB3-1186
	b.	But then again, my favourite song in the world is 'Wonderful World" by Louis Armstrong. If any song really chokes me up, it's that one.	BNC-ANY-1184
	c.	??If any song really chokes me up, it's that.	

| (27) | Armagnac on the terrace? How charming! I like that! | BNC-AoL-3877-3879 |

Chapter 13. Words as constructions in a constructional network   **251**

13.2.7   *Wh*-words

The difficulties of classification also show with respect to the words *who, whose, whom, which, what, where, when, why, how,* and *whether.* From a certain perspective, they can be taken together as a class because they share a number of interesting properties, but they also differ in important respects.

–   What all wh-words have in common is that they can occur in wh-clause and wh-to-infinitive slots of other constructions:

> (28) a.   And there is serious doubt as to *whether* you're really even psychic.
>   COCA-2006-Psych
>   b.   I still can't understand *how* they would do all of that just for money.
>   COCA-2012-Psych
>   c.   I don't care *whose* smoothie it is.   TV-2006-Psych
>   d.   Do you have any idea *who*'d want to shoot you?   COCA-2009-Psych

> (29) a.   I don't know *whether* to drink this or use it to take the rust off my patio furniture.
>   TV-2007-Psych
>   b.   I don't even know *where* to begin.   TV-2013-Psych

–   All the words in the series except *whether* can occur in WH-QUESTION CONSTRUCTIONS:

> (30) a.   *Which* one is hers?   TV-2006-Psych
>   b.   *Whose* is it?   TV-2012-Psych
>   c.   *Why* does everyone talk as if we don't live in the modern world? TV-2019-Downton

–   With the exception of *whether* and *what,*[134] wh-words can occur in RELATIVE-CLAUSE CONSTRUCTIONS:

> (31) a.   What about the Paris Agreement on climate change *which* commits the country to very significant cuts in carbon emissions ...   COCA-2016-SPOK
>   b.   Now is the point *where* you tell me what the hell we're doing here.
>   COCA-2010-Psych

–   *What, who, where* and *when* can occur in PSEUDO-CLEFT CONSTRUCTIONS:[135]

> (32) a.   *What* Robyn likes to do is to deconstruct the texts, to probe the gaps and absences in them, to uncover what they are not saying ...   BNC-ANY-836
>   b.   Here is *where* Big Data and Big Data technologies have opportunities and challenges, but also risks.   COCA-2018-ACAD

---

134. What can occur as a relative element in some varieties of English.

135. For details see CGEL (1985: 1387–1389).

252   A Construction Grammar of the English Language

– Like demonstratives and quantifiers, *whose, which* and *what* can occur in noun phrases
   with or without an accompanying noun in questions:

(33) a.   What type of store generally has separate entrance and exit points?   BNC-B2U-44
      b.   ... some are made with added butter, others with vegetable oil. Which is better?
                                                                          BNC-H06-275–276

In the case of wh-words, the class character emerges largely from an element of formal similarity (*wh-*) and overlapping syntactic and semantic functions. Obviously, knowledge of each of these highly frequent but rather idiosyncratic words entails knowing in which constructions they can occur, but there is little point in going any further than that and attaching word class labels to them if you want the label to allow predictions about the possible uses of such words. In the construction grids to be outlined in Chapter 15, we will just use *wh* instead of a subclassifying word class label.[136]

13.2.8   The limits of classification

The problem of word classes has also been touched upon by Fillmore, Kay and O'Connor (1988: 508) in their discussion of the COMPARATIVE-CORRELATIVE CONSTRUCTION (11.5.3) when they address the question of whether we "have the right to describe the *the* here as the definite article". Clearly, the use of *the* in expressions such as *the sooner the better* does not correspond to a definition of the definite article as a category that has emerged from its use in DEFINITE-NP CONSTRUCTIONS. In fact, from a cognitive point of view, it does not matter at all how we classify the *the* in *the sooner the better*, although descriptively one could make out a case for calling it an adverb because it occurs in a PREMODIFIER-OF-ADVERB CONSTRUCTION AND THE PREMODIFIER-OF-ADJECTIVE CONSTRUCTION (which is, in fact, what many dictionaries do) (see 13.2.8).

A similar point can be made with respect to uses of demonstratives such as the following:

(34) a.   The trouble is, I don't believe it's that simple.   BNC-HWP-1757
      b.   ... most of the books are not all that rare.   BNC-GWB-314

Analyzing *that* as an adverb, however, is also problematic since *all* frequently occurs in combination with the definite article and demonstratives:

---

136. Of course, there may be situations in which you may want to take a prototype approach to word class assignment and classify a word as a member of a class if it meets many but not all of the defining criteria of the class, as CGEL (1985: 404) does when it distinguishes between central and peripheral adjectives, for instance. The point is, however, that this depends on the purpose of word class labelling. In a learners' dictionary, for example, the prototype approach might result in errors because users would expect a word to have all the features associated with the class.

(35) a. Well, we'll probably be running into each other all the time. TV-1967-Jeannie

b. How can all that knowledge be condensed into a fifty-minute lecture to students who know almost nothing about it? BNC-ANY-834

It seems we will just have to accept the fact that some words resist any kind of discrete classification in that they may have all – or almost all – of the properties that characterize one word class but have additional properties that are not shared by other members of that class.

13.2.9 Summary

Our approach to word classes in the English language can be summarized as follows:

1. There is a strong case for establishing three major word classes – nouns, adjectives and verbs, because these word classes can be captured by relatively clear conceptual and structural criteria, and also because they contain a large number of items. Nevertheless, we regard these classes as prototypes in the sense that some properties are shared by many, but not necessarily all members of the category.
2. Word classes are categories that emerge from language use.
3. As a consequence, word classes must be seen as language-specific (Croft 2001, 2016).
4. As far as function words are concerned, we are faced with a considerable amount of idiosyncrasy and we consider it an open question whether or to what extent speakers of English form far-reaching generalizations in terms of word-classes at all. It seems to be possible to identify a few very small word classes such as the articles or demonstratives, and one with an infinite number of items, namely numerals, but these category labels do not capture what the items of these specific classes have in common. Cognitively, one might argue that item-related knowledge is more relevant here than any kind of class membership in the sense that speakers simply know in which constructions a word can be used, i.e., that they relate the word to the relevant constructions in their mental constructicon – and that is it.

Figures 13.3 and 13.4 may serve to illustrate the situation as we see it. As you can tell from the discussions in the previous sections, Langacker (2008a: 13) is perfectly right when he says that "language was not necessarily designed for the convenience or predilections of the linguist". Quite obviously, word classes do not fall into clearly defined categories as in Figure 13.3:

Figure 13.3 Parts of speech as distinct classes

Figure 13.4 seems to paint a more realistic picture. The orange fields are meant to represent relatively abstract constructions such as the DEFINITE-NP CONSTRUCTION or argument structure constructions, the dots stand for words, and the lines connect the words with the constructions in which they occur. The three green dots stand for a relatively large number of items that occur in the same four constructions. Thus, we can assign them to a class. However, there are also words that occur in some, but not all of these four constructions (lime-coloured), just as there may be words that predominantly occur in one of them. The word in teal, however, shows stronger links to other constructions and is thus not a very good example of the constructions typical of the green class and a construction in which members of the green class do not occur (in light green). It is a more or less arbitrary decision whether one subsumes the lime and light green words under the green class or not.

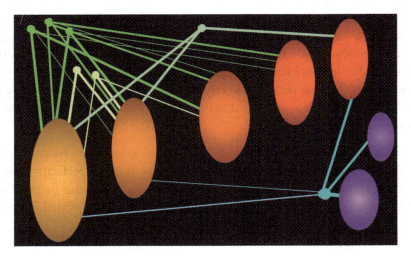

Figure 13.4 Word classes in constructional space

13.3 CASA word classes

13.3.1 Survey

Based on the considerations outlined above, we will make use of the following word class labels. Some of these word classes are best defined in terms of the items that occur in them, others are schematic in character.[137]

13.3.2 Words that play a part in establishing reference to a 'thing'

13.3.2.1 *Nouns*

Table 13.4 Definition of nouns

Noun [n]	*Amsterdam, Paula, Tregenza, canal, jersey, query, sea, salt, wine ...*	Chapter 6
Semantic function:	Denoting a 'thing', which can be (i) an element of a class or the whole class of 'things' that share common properties (like *a canal, these canals*) (ii) an unbounded 'thing' (like *the sea, pepper*), (iii) a unique 'thing' (like *Vaughan, St. Ives*).	
Occurrence:	Noun slots in NP-CONSTRUCTIONS	
Word forms:	Different word forms when used in: PLURAL-NP CONSTRUCTIONS (*canals, boats, women, mice*) GENITIVE-NP CONSTRUCTIONS (*Amsterdam's, canals'*)	
Comment:	Cases (i), (ii) and (iii) indicate semantic constellations that are often described in terms of **count nouns, mass** (or noncount/uncountable) **nouns** and **names** (or proper nouns). In a constructionist account, it seems more appropriate to see these differences as the result of the meaning potentials of the nouns and the constructions in which they are used.	

13.3.2.2 *Pronouns*

Table 13.5 The personal pronouns of the English language

Personal pronoun [pron_personal]	*I, my, me – he, his, him – she, her – it, its – you, your – we, our, us – they, their, them*	Chapter 6
Semantic function:	Denoting a 'thing' which is identifiable from the linguistic or extra-linguistic contexts	
Occurrence:	NP-slots	
Form:	Different word forms according to person, case, and number.	

---

137. This reflects the traditional distinction between closed and open word classes.

A Construction Grammar of the English Language

Table 13.6 English possessive pronouns

Possessive pronoun [pron_possessive]	*mine, yours, hers, ours, theirs*	Chapter 6
Semantic function:	Denoting POSSESSOR of a 'thing' which is identifiable from the linguistic or extra-linguistic contexts	
Occurrence	ATTR slots in PREDICATIVE-CONSTRUCTIONS	
Comment:	Note that we use the term possessive pronoun only for the five items listed above and not for the uses of personal pronouns in GENITIVE CONSTRUCTIONS.	

Table 13.7 English reflexive pronouns

Reflexive pronoun [pron_reflexive]	*myself, yourself, himself, herself, themselves, itself ourselves, yourselves, themselves*	Chapter 6
Semantic function:	Referring back to a 'thing' that has already been mentioned, usually in the same clause, expressing identity	
Occurrence	NP-slots	
Usage:	Reflexive pronouns are typically used in argument structure constructions in which the referent is expressed in a preceding NP-slot (*Yeah, well, I've Googled myself, too, and there's a lot of stuff missing.* (TV-2009-Psych)) or an adjunct construction with emphasizing effect (*You said it yourself, Jules.* (TV-2009-Psych))	

Table 13.8 The English reciprocal pronouns

Reciprocal pronoun [pron_reciproca]	*each other, one another*	
Semantic function:	Referring to two (*each other*) or more (*one another*) members of a group of persons that interact.	
Occurrence	NP-slots	

13.3.2.3 Demonstratives

Table 13.9 English demonstratives

Demonstrative (dem)	*this, that, these, those*	Chapter 6
Semantic function	Referring to a thing that is identifiable from the context in relation to its position in relation to the speaker	
Typical occurrences	Slot filler of NP-slots in argument structure constructions Determiner-slot in NP-constructions	
Comment	Given the formal identity and the semantic function of these words, we do not make a distinction between demonstrative pronouns for cases in which the demonstrative establishes reference directly and demonstrative determiners for cases in which the demonstrative is followed by a noun. *This* and *that* also occur as premodifiers in PREMODIFIER-OF-ADJECTIVE and PREMODIFIER-OF-ADVERB CONSTRUCTIONS.	

Chapter 13. Words as constructions in a constructional network **257**

Table 13.9 *(continued)*

Demonstrative (dem)	*this, that, these, those*	Chapter 6
Examples	*Now, I thought you might want these.* (COCA-2011-MOV) – *... look at the tops of those trees over there.* (COCA-2005-SPOK) – *Rose, it's not that funny.* (TV-1990-GoldenGirls) *I never thought we'd be here again, or at least not this soon.* COCA-2019-FIC	

13.3.2.4 *Numerals*

Since the mathematical conception of figures is that of an infinite set, numerals, the words that express figures in language, are infinite as well. Funnily enough, of word classes with a large number of elements, it is the numerals that form the most coherent word class.

Ordinal numbers express an order of 'things' specified.

Table 13.10 Ordinals

Ordinal numeral [numeral$_{ordinal}$]	1st, 2nd, 3rd, ... fifth, ... twelfth, ... twenty-first, one millionth
Semantic function	Specifying the order of one thing with respect to others, or the denominator of a fraction
Typical occurrences	Determiner-slot in NP-constructions, ordering adjuncts
Examples	*First impressions?* (TV-2010-Psych) – *That was fifth season, episode eleven.* (TV-2008-Psych) – *Not if I get there first.* (TV-2007-Psych)

Cardinal numerals refer to the numbers as such:

Table 13.11 English cardinal numbers

Cardinal numeral [numeral$_{cardinal}$]	1, 2, 3, ... 1066, ... 506,786,98, ... one, two, ... twenty-six, ... 3 million 1/3rd, 0.537, – 48
Semantic function	specifying quantity, order, or the numerator in a fraction
Typical occurrences	Slot filler of NP-slots in argument structure constructions Determiner-slot in NP-construction
Example	*Can I have two please?* (COCA-2000-SPOK) – *... four glasses of wine.* (COCA-2015-FIC) – *That was fifth season, episode eleven.* (TV-2008-Psych)

In COUNT-NP CONSTRUCTIONS, cardinal numbers can be used to specify the exact quantity of things referred to. In this sense, they could be included in the class of quantifiers, but since they have other uses as well, we reserve the term quantifier for items that indicate quantity in a more general way (see next question):

(36) a. four glasses of wine (COCA-2015-FIC) [numeral$_{ordinal}$: ordinal numeral]
      b. a few glasses of wine (COCA-2019-FIC) [quant: quantifier]

13.3.2.5 *Quantifiers*

As outlined above, we use the term quantifier – or general quantifier – as a semantically motivated label for all words that indicate a quantity of the referent. It cannot be underscored too strongly that quantifiers in this sense do not form a coherent class with respect to the constructions in which they can be used. The typical occurrences listed below thus do not apply to all members of the category:

Table 13.12 Quantifiers

Quantifier (quant)	*enough, a few, few, many, more, some*
Semantic function	Giving a general indication of the quantity of the thing(s) referred to
Typical item-related occurrences	E.g., slot filler of NP-slots in argument structure constructions E.g., determiner-slot in NP-constructions
Example	*a few glasses of wine* (COCA-2019-FIC) – *I haven't made many friends here.* (TV-1993–NYPDBlue) – *Well, it can't be much fun.* (TV-1979-TheWaltons)

13.3.2.6 *Articles*

The semantic function of the definite article (*the*) and the indefinite article (*a/an*) coincides with that of the constructions in which they occur, namely DEFINITE-NP CONSTRUCTIONS (*the*), and the INDEFINITE-SINGULAR-NP CONSTRUCTION (*a, an*).

With only two members, articles can hardly be regarded as a class. Uses of *the* such as those under (37) we do not see as being covered by the term article, but as item-specific properties of *the* (which will always be marked by capitalized THE in construction grids; see 11.5.3):

(37) a. the sooner the better   COCA-2019-TV
      b. That danger is all the more present in an era of populist leaders who disregard expert advice from diplomats, intelligence communities, and scholars in favor of sound bites.   COCA-2019-ACAD

13.3.3 Words that refer to relationships situated in time

13.3.3.1 *Verbs*

Table 13.13 Properties of verbs in English

Verb [v]	*go, laugh, be, do, walk, adjust ...*	Chapter 4
Semantic function	Describing a process or a relation between two things (with the potential of relating them to time)	
Typical occurrences	In V-slots of other constructions, e.g.:	
	MODAL CONSTRUCTIONS	
	TENSE CONSTRUCTIONS	
	PERFECTIVE CONSTRUCTIONS	
	PROGRESSIVE CONSTRUCTIONS	

13.3.3.2 *Modals*

Table 13.14 The English modals

Verb [v]	*can, could, may, might, must, shall, should, will, would*	Chapter 4.2.3
Semantic function	Epistemic or root modification of the proposition expressed by the verb and its participants	
Typical occurrences	MODAL CONSTRUCTIONS	

Furthermore, typical properties of modals are

a. that they are followed by an infinitive (without *to*) in modal constructions,

> (38) That very well may **be** the most humiliating moment of your life. TV-2008-Psych

b. that they do not occur with the *DO*-SUPPORT CONSTRUCTION in negated or interrogative clauses:

> (39) a. May I help you? TV-2008-Psych
> b. Does all this have anything to do with why these two shouldn't be married?
> TV-2006-Psych

c. that they do not take 3rd person singular {S}:

> (40) She must be a very good friend. TV-2019-FIC

260 A Construction Grammar of the English Language

Verbs such as *dare, need* or *ought* express a meaning similar to the modals, but have some item-related formal properties, especially with respect to the three properties mentioned above – infinitive, negation, and {S}:[138]

(41)	a.	How dare you accuse my brother of murder.	TV-2010-Psych
	b.	And who'd dare to try?	COCA-2019-FIC
	c.	He ought to resign and move on …	COCA-2019-NEWS
	d.	??He ought resign …	

(42)	a.	Don't you dare stop this car, Lassie!	TV-2009-Psych
	b.	He dared not argue the point here and now …	COCA-2017-FIC
	c.	A story ought not to refer to itself; it ought not to let slip that it is only a story.	COCA-2017-MAG

(43)	a.	Would she dare live here in the country?	COCA-2014-FIC
	b.	She dares not make a mistake.	COCA-2018-NEWS

13.3.4 Words that have a descriptive or evaluation function

13.3.4.1 *Adjectives*

Table 13.15 Properties of English adjectives

Adjective (adj)	*good, new, great, nice, smart, beautiful, friendly …*
Semantic function	Assigning a property to a 'thing'
Form	Slot filler of ATTR-slots in ATTRIBUTE and RESULTATIVE CONSTRUCTIONS
	Premodifier slot in PREMODIFIER-OF-NOUN CONSTRUCTION

The category of adjectives can be defined relatively well in terms of semantic function.

13.3.4.2 *Adverbs*

Table 13.16 Adverbs in CASA

Adverb (adv)	*beautifully, cleverly, well …*
Semantic function	(i) modifying an action or the description of a 'thing'
	(ii) evaluating a proposition
	(iii) structuring a message
	(iv) indicating the place or time of an event
Form	Slot filler of ADJUNCT CONSTRUCTIONS
	Premodifier slot in PREMODIFIER-OF-ADJECTIVE CONSTRUCTION

---

138. For the historical development of modals and semi-modals see Krug (2000).

As pointed out above (13.2.5), the adverb category is problematic in a number of respects. We'd like to draw your attention to the fact that we treat words such as *here, then* or *afterwards* as adverbs, although they depend on their interpretation on information provided by the context in a way similar to uses of *before* and *up* in (44) that we classify as particles:

(44) a. 'You're not going shopping with her **afterwards**?'   BNC-ANY-168
      b. I've never seen you **before**.   BNC-GW3-1363

(45) a. 'Still **here**', he said, lifting an eyebrow.   BNC-ANY-2889
      b. 'Is the super still **in**?'   BNC-GUD-4113

Only in the case of (45) can the information also be given explicitly in the form of a longer particle phrase. (46)

(46)   He's in the office but he's busy.   BNC-GW3-475

13.3.5   Words that refer to atemporal relationships

13.3.5.1   *Particles*

Table 13.17 Particles

Particles [p]	*after, at, before, by, concerning, for, in, into, on, up*	Chapter 9.2
Semantic function	Introducing a 'thing' and establishing its relation to another 'thing'	
Typical occurrences	In particle-phrase constructions of the kind specified below	

We identify the following PARTICLE-PHRASE CONSTRUCTIONS:

–   particle (or prepositional) phrases only consisting of a particle p with the information required being provided by the context of utterance:

(47) I had this dream before, Shawn.   TV-2009-Psych

–   particle (or prepositional) phrases of the type [p NP]:

(48) Tell me you're not excited about pancakes.   TV-2006-Psych

–   particle (or prepositional) phrases of the type [p V-ing]:

(49) I congratulate you on using a metaphor that has not yet been used in Washington.
                                                                                 COCA-1993-SPOK

–   particle (or prepositional) phrases of the type [p Adv]:

(50) I think I need to get away before then ...   COCA-2019-FIC

- particle (or prepositional) phrases of the type [p NP V-ing]:

  (51) She had to rely on him reading it in her smile. COCA-2001-FIC

- particle phrases of the type [p V$_{base}$] (traditionally called infinitive clauses):

  (52) Huge tidal barriers are designed to protect Amsterdam and Rotterdam from 1-in-10,000-year floods. NOW-12-12-17-US

- particle phrases of the type [p CL$_{fin}$] (traditionally subsumed under subordinate clauses)

  (53) a. Scientists have long warned that global heating is causing extreme weather events to become more frequent and intense. NOW-21-02-19-US
  b. He said he did not know whether climate change was man-made, though the same report said "there is no convincing alternative" posed by the evidence. ... COCA-2018-NEWS

The semantic function of particle-phrase constructions can be determined by the meaning of the respective particles, as in (54), or the semantic role attributed to them by the argument structure construction in which they occur, as in (55):

(54) a. ... it was a fine evening and still light so he continued along the coast road, past the stone quarries, to Mousehole. BNC-GWB-2596
b. ... by the time he returned to the coast road at Newlyn it was quite dark. BNC-GWB-2611

(55) After all, she worked on the nineteenth-century industrial novel for something like ten years... BNC-ANY-831

Furthermore, some particles can be used in adjunct- and premodifier constructions:

(56) a. The winner of this competition can just about choose his university. TV-2006-Psych
b. Wow. That is about as orange as you can get. TV-2006-Psych
c. This was about 18 months ago. TV-2006-Psych

13.3.5.2 Connectors

Table 13.18 Connectors

Connectors [con]	And, or, but, nor, let alone neither–nor, either–or	9.2
Semantic function	Combining two words, phrases, clauses, or sentences	
Typical occurrences	Syndetic co-ordination constructions	

Chapter 13. Words as constructions in a constructional network **263**

In the CASA grid representations, we represent co-ordination constructions by the lexical item that functions as a connector.

13.3.6 Interjections

Table 13.19 Interjections

Interjections [i]	Oh, yeah, hello	Chapter 2.2
Semantic function	Short way of expressing an emotion or greeting	
Typical occurrences	Used in adjunct conjunctions	

13.3.7 Items defying further classification

13.3.7.1 *Who, whose, whom, which, what, why, where, when, and how*

Who, whose, whom, which, what, why, where, when, and *how* are often seen as a class on the basis of the letters *wh*. Wh-words occur in the WH-QUESTION CONSTRUCTION (3.3.2), RELATIVE-CLAUSE CONSTRUCTIONS (6.10.2.2), WH-CLEFT CONSTRUCTIONS (10.3), as well as WH-NP CONSTRUCTIONS (6.7), but, as shown in 13.2.7 above, by no means all *wh*-words occur in all of these constructions. We will thus not treat *wh*-words as forming a word class of their own but rather as items with very specific constructional properties. (In construction grids, we will indicate this by a capitalized 'WH'.).

13.3.7.2 *So*

Another item that shows a variety of uses is *so*. In (57ab) it is used as a premodifier, in (57c) it introduces a conclusion, and in (57de) it can be analyzed as a pro-form referring to a proposition:

(57) a. Not **so** fast, Mr. Spencer. TV-2006-Psych
   b. What's **so** funny? TV-2008-Psych
   c. **So** somebody at that house did pay a ransom. TV-2006-Psych
   d. Is that **so**? BNC-GWB-64
   e. 'Apart from all that, if somebody heard him scream, why did they wait till now to say **so**?' BNC-GW3-232

In all of these cases, *so* has a deictic element of meaning, which can be made explicit in discontinuous modifier constructions:

(58) The drizzle was **so** fine **that it amounted to fog and he had to drive slowly.** BNC-GW3-203

In CASA grids, we will only render all these instances as 'SO' and take the specific function of the word to follow from the construction it is embedded in.

13.3.7.3 As

The situation with *as* is similar to *so*. It can occur in comparison constructions (see 8.4) as in (59a), where the term of comparison can either be expressed explicitly or be retrievable from the context of utterance:

(59) a. She was about as friendly **as** you'd expect ...   BNC-GW3-1860
  b. She's as active **as** you or me and a damn sight tougher.   BNC-GW3-2285
  c. I hope some day it will make you just **as** happy.   TV-1986-Dynasty

Cases such as (59c) have to be distinguished from (60):

(60) Did he seem just **as** usual?   BNC-ANY-675

Furthermore, *as* can introduce clauses, where an implied comparison can be detected in the expression of likeness or simultaneity:

(61) a. Though urged by the school to apply for a place at Oxbridge, she chose instead to go to Sussex University, **as** bright young people often did in the 1970s, because the new universities were considered exciting and innovatory places to study at. BNC-ANY-574
  b. these are the things that are worrying Robyn Penrose **as** she drives through the gates of the University ...   BNC-ANY-828

Finally, particle phrases with *as* can fill slots of argument structure constructions, as in (62), and *as* can serve as a kind of deictic pro-form, as in (63):

(62) a. Stoltenberg said he regarded the Capitol storming "**as** an attack on the core democratic institutions of the United States and therefore also on core values of NATO."
                                                                                      NOW-21-11-21-US
  b. Only 13 percent of congressional Republicans see global warming **as** a human-caused issue, compared to 95 percent of Dems.   NOW-20-01-17-US

(63) a. Just get on my tail and stick to it, **as** the bee said to the pollen.   BNC-ANY-1694
  b. But having no wish, **as** Virginia Woolf put it, 'to dabble her fingers self-approvingly in the stuff of other souls' and believing in the stick and carrot philosophy of human conduct, she joined the police.   BNC-HWP-1183

Similar to *so*, all these uses will be marked as 'AS' in the CASA grids with the specific function being inferable from the constructional slot in which the *as* is used.

13.3.7.4 Not

Not is another word that does not fall into any of the traditional word classes and which will thus be labelled 'NOT' in construction grids.

CHAPTER 14

Word order

14.1 The functions of word order in English

14.1.1 Meaning, textual organization, and processing

Language is organized in a largely linear way, i.e., when speakers utter or hear a sentence, they produce or perceive a sequence of speech sounds, and, similarly, written language consists of sequences of letters. This means that the order of elements can be relevant with respect to meaning: Just as *bat* has a different meaning from *tab*, the different orders of the verb and the subject in (1a) and (1b) indicate a difference in meaning:

| (1) | a. | Nuclear power is carbon-free, which is a huge benefit. | NOW-21-11-12-AU |
| | b. | Is nuclear power the answer? | NOW-19-12-23-AU |

The semantic difference between (1a) and (1b) is reflected by the fact that they represent different constructions – the DECLARATIVE-STATEMENT and the YES-NO-QUESTION CONSTRUCTION. In a language such as English, which is poor in inflexions, word order also plays an important role in expressing semantic relations of the who-does-what-to-whom type:[139]

| (2) | a. | The president blames the Congress. | COCA-1992-SPOK |
| | b. | The Congress blames the president. | COCA-1992-SPOK |

Another difference in meaning caused by the order of the words in a clause is related to the position of adverbs as in (3) and (4):

| (3) | a. | This really is a problem ... | COCA-1998-NEWS |
| | b. | I think this is really a problem for the media and a problem for this country ... | COCA-2005-SPOK |

| (4) | a. | I don't think this comes as a surprise | COCA-2018-NEWS |
| | b. | But I think this is not a surprise. | COCA-2012-SPOK |

The difference in meaning between these pairs can be related to the scope of the qualifying adverbs (*really, not*), which extends to those elements of the sentence that follow the adverb in question. While in the cases above the sentences of each pair may be interchangeable for most communicative purposes, in other cases a different position of *not* leads to quite different meanings:

| (5) | a. | ... and he didn't say he was going to run at the time. | COCA-1999-SPOK |
| | b. | ... he also said he was not going to answer questions ... | COCA-2017-SPOK |

---

139. In case languages such as German or Dutch argument roles can also be expressed by inflectional cases, which in English only shows in pronouns: *He adores her and she adores* him (COCA-2003-SPOK).

A Construction Grammar of the English Language

In the three cases discussed so far, the position of an element in a clause has a semantic function that is associated with a particular construction. To be distinguished from these are cases in which meaning arises from the fact that the order of elements in a clause does not correspond to what one may consider a normal (or canonical) structure, as in the following examples:

(6) Citicorp, for example, gives more than $ 23 million to charity each year. To Planned Parenthood it gave $ 24,500 in 1989.
COCA-1990-ACAD

(7) (He then removed from his pocket two mobile phones – his own iPhone, and the one lifted from the same apartment where he'd taken the boxed wine. His phone he set on the table. The other he scrolled through clumsily ...
COCA-2013-SPOK

Deviating from what speakers know to be the established or most frequent word order may give prominence to a particular part of the message (which may also be marked by special phonetic prominence) as in the second sentence of Example (6) or in cases of contrast such as (7). This phenomenon is closely linked to the ways in which information can be presented in sentences, i.e., to the information structure constructions outlined in Chapter 10.

Examples (6) and (7) can also be seen as a way of providing textual structure which is easy to work out for the reader or hearer. This is also the case in situations in which speakers wish to facilitate the processing of a sentence by putting a longer constituent at the end of a clause as in (8b) (referred to as the "end-weight" in CGEL 1985:1395):

(8) a. Do I need to explain the law to you, Shawn?
TV-2009-Psych
   b. ...I will try to explain to you the rationale and the reasoning that went into that decision.
COCA-2017-SPOK

Also related to processing is the fact that the order of elements plays a key role in the identification of constructions and their constituents.

We can thus identify five functions of word order:

– distinguishing between different sentence type constructions as in (1),
– expressing semantic relations between arguments of argument structure constructions as in (2) (see also 14.3),
– indicating the scope of, for example, negation or other qualifications of a proposition (cases 3 to 5 and 14.4),
– giving prominence to certain units within a sentence (Examples (6) and (7) and 14.5)
– supporting and facilitating the processing of running text by providing cues as to which elements can occur after one another in very much the same way as knowledge of phonotactics is useful to the decoding of running speech at the phonetic (or phonological) level (Example (9) and Section 14.2),

14.1.2 Word order in Construction Grammar

Dealing with word order is perhaps one of the biggest challenges of Construction Grammar. It is true that word order forms an integral part of the description of some constructions, as in the case of what we call sentence type constructions. However, in cases in which the order of elements is determined by factors such as the length of constituents and ease of processing effort, it seems less straightforward to cover the facts satisfactorily in terms of form-meaning pairings. Let us come back to Example (9) above: One could argue, for instance, that (9a) and (9b) represent two different constructions, which can be distinguished at the level of form:

(9)   a.   Subj V NP$_{short}$ PP$_{to}$
       b.   Subj V PP$_{to-short}$ NP$_{long}$

What speaks against such an analysis is that sentences such as (9b) can also be found with verbs such as *send*, which also occur in the DITRANSITIVE CONSTRUCTION, because the ditransitive allows speakers to place a long constituent at the end, as in (10b):

(10)   a.   She had sent me a text about the menu that we were going to have for Easter.

                                                         COCA-2018-SPOK

       b.   ... he sent to us a laminated card with his telephone number and those of several senior officers with a notation if you can't get the right word from my subordinates call me directly.   COCA-1990-SPOK

This could be taken as an argument for seeing the (b)-cases as a variant (or allostruction)[140] of an Subj V NP PP$_{to}$-construction. However, the same phenomenon can be observed with other constructions as well (see also Uhrig 2015). Compare, e.g., the following instances of the OBJECT-ATTRIBUTE CONSTRUCTION:

(11)   a.   Calling me a stubborn ostrich was presumably not an attempt at biological classification but rather an instance of metaphor.   (Langacker 2008: 41)
       b.   Yet he calls arrogant the desire of lawyers to maintain these standards of conduct from encroachment as a result of MDP.   COCA-1999-NEWS

The most obvious generalization is to see these cases as the fronting of the shorter elements or the moving to the back of the longer ones. In contrast to the generative notion of movement which is based on a postulated underlying structure arising from the inborn Universal Grammar, a constructionist account of such movement would have to be related to a frequency-based knowledge of the more common form of the realization of the construction. Nevertheless, it remains doubtful whether an account in terms of a mental opera-

---

140. For uses of the term allostruction see, e.g., Cappelle (2006), Herbst & Uhrig (2009–); for a critical assessment of this notion, see Hoffmann (2022a).

tion affecting the positioning of elements can be termed a construction.[141] This might be seen as in conflict with the constructionist claim that "it is constructions all the way down" (Goldberg 2006: 18), "that knowledge of language can modelled exhaustively and exclusively as a network of symbolic form-meaning pairings" (Hilpert 2020: 107; see also Stefanowitsch 2011b: 200).

One possible solution to this problem is to consider word order to be part of the dimension of "shared contextual knowledge" of Goldberg's (2019: 7) definition of constructions, i.e., in our terminology, to be part of the usage conditions of the constructions in question. It is in this spirit that we will address issues of word order in this chapter.

14.2 Word order and language processing

14.2.1 Noun phrases

An example of absolutely fixed word order in the English language is that definite and indefinite articles always precede nouns in NP-constructions. The occurrence of *the* or *a/an* thus provides a strong cue for processing running text in that it signals the beginning of a new unit with a high degree of probability (except for cases such as *all the* or *such a*). However, this does not necessarily mean that the noun is directly adjacent to the article since PREMODIFIER-OF-NOUN CONSTRUCTIONS may result in, say, an adjective phrase taking a position between the article and the noun, as in Examples (12b), (12c) or (12d):

(12) a. the bus
      b. the European capital
      c. the global climate crisis   COCA-2016-MAG
      d. an extraordinarily difficult position   COCA-2017-SPOK

Nevertheless, this kind of structuring principle can be imagined to be relevant to the process of sentence comprehension. We know that on encountering a word hearers build up expectations as to which word is going to follow. *The* or *a/an* can thus be imagined to make a hearer expect the corresponding noun as the next item (or one of the next items). This could take roughly the following form:

i. The occurrence of an article triggers the expectation of a noun. In a case such as (12a), the expectation is met by the immediately following word.

---

141. This is highly reminiscent of the discussion of whether a vowel change in words such as *foot* and *feet* can be seen as a morpheme in structuralist morphology (Palmer 1971: 116).

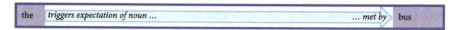

Figure 14.1 Expectation of the occurrence of a noun after the occurrence of *the*

In the BNC, for instance, ca. 70% of all occurrences of the definite article *the* are followed by a noun.

ii. The same expectation is triggered by *the* in (12b), where, however, it is not met by the next word since the article is followed by an adjective. This is unproblematic since speakers know that adjectives frequently follow articles, but they also know that if an adjective follows *the*, it belongs to a PREMODIFIER-OF-NOUN CONSTRUCTION. The expectation of a noun is thus maintained, and, in a way, the adjective is a kind of detour on the way to the noun.

Figure 14.2 Processing of a case where the expectation of a noun is backgrounded by the occurrence of an adjective (symbolized by the pink arrow), which also triggers an expectation of a noun

Again, we can interpret BNC data to support such a view: *the* is followed by an adjective in 19% of all cases, adjectives are followed immediately by a noun in 66% of all cases, but the combination *the* + adjective is followed immediately by a noun in 80% of all occurrences.

iii. In cases such as (12d), we can imagine a similar process – only that the detour is more complex since an adverb such as *extraordinarily* cannot directly be followed by a noun. So, when the word *extraordinarily* has been processed in the brain, there will be two separate expectations – one for an adjective to follow the adverb and one for the noun (triggered by the initial *an*).

Figure 14.3 Processing of a case in which the expectation of a noun is backgrounded by the occurrence of an adverb (symbolized by the pink arrow), which triggers an expectation of an adjective, which in turn triggers an expectation of a noun

In this way, we can combine speakers' knowledge of transitional probabilities, i.e., the expectations they have about the kind of word (such as a noun or an adjective) that is likely to occur after a particular word (e.g., *the*), with their knowledge of constructions: if, as in Example (12d), *the* is followed by an adverb such as *very* or *extraordinarily*, speakers know that this adverb must be the premodifier of an PREMODIFIER-OF-ADJECTIVE CONSTRUCTION, which in turn is most likely to be part of a PREMODIFIER-OF-NOUN CONSTRUCTION. Obviously, this is a very simplified account, because one would also have to consider more specific factors such as the transitional probabilities between individual words.

14.2.2   Verbs in finite clauses

The order of verbs in declarative and the various types of interrogative clauses also allows a number of generalizations that are important with respect to the processing of sentences. As pointed out in 4.7, the order of constructions is as follows:

MODAL OR TENSE CXN ➜ PERFECTIVE CXN ➜ PASSIVE CXN ➜ PROGRESSIVE CXN

In terms of the expectations that are being raised by the occurrence of a particular word, this means that, for example,

– if the first verb is a modal, it must be followed by an infinitive (without *to*),
– if the first verb is a form of *HAVE* and not immediately followed by a noun phrase, it will be followed by an *en*-participle (i.e., expressing perfective aspect), etc.

14.3   Word order in argument structure constructions

We have characterized argument structure constructions in such a way that they do not contain any explicit specification of the order of the elements. This is to allow for the fact that certain information structure constructions as in (13a) or relative clause constructions as in (13b) may lead to a special order of elements:

(13) a. To him she said, "I'll tell your mom what you just said."   COCA-2007-FIC
      b. But the A form, to which she gave most of her attention, does not signal the spiral form of the molecule nearly as clearly as does the B form.   COCA-2010-NEWS

In "normal", i.e., unmarked cases in which an argument structure construction is combined with a DECLARATIVE-STATEMENT CONSTRUCTION, the order in which the arguments occur corresponds to that in which they are represented in the outline of the constructions as given in Chapter 5, i.e.:

– The Subj-argument precedes the verb; all further arguments follow it:

   (14) Wilcox gave this noun a solemn emphasis.   BNC-ANY-2469

– Attr-arguments follow the verb if they refer to the Subj-argument and the object if they refer to an NP-Obj:

Chapter 14. Word order **271**

(15) a. She was a popular and conscientious teacher ... BNC-ANY-719
b. ... let's consider this an isolated episode, okay? TV-2011-Psych

– Obj1 (indirect objects) precede Obj2 (direct objects):

(16) She gave him a suspicious look. BNC-GW3-1826

– NP-objects precede PP-objects and clausal objects:

(17) a. You put us on the email list? TV-2008-Psych
b. I ask you to think of the traditions of our county. TV-2016-Poldark

– Clausal objects follow NP- and PP-objects:

(18) a. Biden told CNN's Kaitlan Collins that she was in "the wrong business" after a question about Russian President Vladimir Putin. NOW-21-08-17-US
b. it can also demonstrate to parents how school ought to be and how teachers support children in cognitive and psychosocial ways. COCA-2004-ACAD

However, as pointed out above, we will have to allow for some variation: firstly, if there is more than one argument in the predicate, their length may affect the order in which they occur; and, secondly, the arguments may appear in a different order in certain types of information packaging constructions (see Chapter 10). Furthermore, there will be a difference in the order of the participants depending on whether an active argument structure construction is used (in which the ÆFFECTOR is the subject-argument) or a passive one (in which the ÆFFECTED is the subject argument and the ÆFFECTOR can be expressed by a *by*-PP, which is usually placed at the end). The only case in which variation of word order does not seem to occur is when two noun phrases occur immediately adjacent to one another, as in the DITRANSITIVE CONSTRUCTION (Hoffmann & Herbst forthc.).

14.4 The position of adjunct constructions

The position of adjunct constructions depends both on their form and their semantic function. If we take a look at a single adverb such as *really*, we can see that it occurs in a large number of different positions in a clause:

i. front position, i.e., before the subject in a declarative-statement construction:

(19) Really, I'm totally fine. TV-2006-Psych

ii. before the verb (in clauses without auxiliaries):

(20) And I really believed you. TV-1988-Dynasty

272   A Construction Grammar of the English Language

iii.   before the first auxiliary:

   (21)   I really can't say.   TV-2007-Psych

iv.   after the first or only auxiliary:

   (22)   You can't really blame the cat.   TV-2007-Psych

v.   final position in the predicate:

   (23)   It's disgraceful, really.   COCA-2008-Psych

vi.   on its own in sentence-fragment constructions:

   (24)   Really?   BNC-ANY-852

As pointed out at the beginning of this chapter, the position of an adverb determines its scope. Thus, in (25a), the position of the adverb *suddenly* before the subject can be taken to refer to the event, whereas in (25b) it refers to a process affecting *cars* (which are presented as given information):

(25)   a.   ... and suddenly everyone gets suspicious.   TV-2007-Psych
       b.   More importantly, cars don't suddenly blow up on their own.   TV-2010-Psych

Such differences in scope may go hand in hand with differences in meaning. In (26a), *frankly* represents a separate tone unit, and it characterizes the speaker as being frank, whereas *frankly* in (26b) characterizes the way the referent of the subject-NP performs the action of admitting. Such uses of adjuncts are not really different in character from PREMODIFIER-OF-ADJECTIVE CONSTRUCTIONS as in (26c).

(26)   a.   Frankly, it's an embarrassment.   TV-2013-Psych
       b.   ... many participants frankly admitted that they had very low expectations at the out-
            set ...   BNC-ALP-197
       c.   Prince Philip was frankly disappointed in his first born and took no pains to hide his
            feelings.   BNC-AH7-211

MANNER-adjuncts such as (26b) could thus be analyzed in terms of PREMODIFIER-OF-VERB or POSTMODIFIER-OF-VERB CONSTRUCTIONS (which in the light of the gradience between this and other types of adjuncts we will not do, however):

(27)   a.   In cool climates' Mrs. Dudley Cross' can be grown beautifully in a large container
            and kept in a greenhouse over the winter.   COCA-1991-MAG
       b.   And yet it's grown in a beautiful way, you know?   COCA-2011-SPOK

A further difference between (26a) and (26b) can be seen in the fact that only the former use has infinitival equivalents of the following type:

(28)   a.   To be frank, there wasn't a shortage ten years ago.   BNC-ASD-821

b. So do we, sir, to be frank. BNC-B20-973

(29) a. To be honest I couldn't make up my mind about him and I'd like you to see him
yourself. BNC-GWB-959
b. Honestly, I don't know. TV-2014-Psych

In fact, the use of adjuncts in English allows some large-scale generalizations, but also entails a great deal of knowledge related to particular items or small groups of items. We will not go into any detail here, but the following tendencies may serve as examples of this kind of knowledge:

– location constructions tend to precede time constructions:

(30) a. German Foreign Minister Annalena Baerbock said she would travel to Moscow
next week for talks on the Ukraine crisis. NOW-22-01-14-US
b. U.S. climate envoy John Kerry told reporters in Glasgow on Wednesday that the
joint declaration builds on statements made by both countries in April.
NOW-21-11-25-US

– long adjunct constructions tend to occur after short ones

(31) a. The Met Office has also issued a yellow warning for 'dense fog patches' starting
from 10pm tonight until 12pm tomorrow in central and southern England, as
well as parts of Wales. NOW-22-01-12-GB
b. When it opened in 2012 on Broadway, where it would win five Tony Awards ...
COCA-2014-NEWS

– structuring constructions such as *firstly, secondly*, etc. tend to occur before the subject of
a DECLARATIVE-STATEMENT CONSTRUCTION

(32) a. Um, where do I start? First of all, you're not a psychic. TV-2013-Psych
b. And furthermore, it's completely irrelevant to these proceedings. TV-1984-Dynasty

Word order is thus a very good example of the complex interplay of the meaning to be associated with the position of an adjunct in a clause as well as the meaning – and the form – of particular adjuncts or small meaning-based groups of adjuncts. This is also apparent from the extensive descriptions of the uses of adjuncts in English as provided by Quirk, Greenbaum, Leech and Svartvik (CGEL 1985: 490–501), Greenbaum (1969) or Buysschaerts (1982), for example. As pointed out in 8.8, we consider knowledge about the positional options of the various constructions to be part of the usage conditions of constructions.

14.5 Inversion

In a few cases, the subject-verb word order that is typical of most English sentence type constructions is deviated from in that an operator verb (i.e. a modal or a form of *be, have* or *do*) precedes the subject. A case in point is presented by the YES-NO-QUESTION CONSTRUCTION (3.3.2). However, this word order (often referred to as **inversion**) can also be triggered by particular words such as *never, rarely, neither, nor* or the *NEITHER-NOR* CONSTRUCTION (Herbst 2024):

(33) a. Only rarely can these concepts or theories be applied to the relatively short time scales considered in the context of land use impacts in riverine ecosystems.

COCA-2002-ACAD

 b. Never has she told anyone.

COCA-2015-FIC

 c. Still doesn't mean I'm gonna put you on this case. Nor would I even want to.

TV-2008-Psych

 d. She took no new live-in lover, and as far as she was aware, neither did Charles.

BNC-ANY-791

CHAPTER 15

Putting it all together
Blending constructions

15.1 From constructions to constructs

Now that we have looked at all the levels of constructional knowledge, from words to complex syntactic constructions, we can come back to one of the first examples presented in this book:

(1) Do you want tea or coffee?   TV-2004-MalcomintheMiddle

As pointed out in 1.5, we analyze (1) as a construct that arises from a combination of the following constructions:

a. YES/NO-QUESTION CONSTRUCTION (see Chapter 3)
b. *DO*-SUPPORT CONSTRUCTION (see Chapter 4.8)
c. MONOTRANSITIVE CONSTRUCTION (see Chapter 5.4)
d. *OR*-COORDINATION CONSTRUCTION (see Chapter 9)
e. *you, want, tea, coffee* word constructions

As pointed out in 1.3.1, the term 'construct' is used to refer to actual utterances, which can be combinations of several constructions. Remember that constructions are form-meaning pairings that are stored in the long-term memory. Constructs, on the other hand, are created in the working memory by activating and combining constructions (Cowan 2008; Diamond 2013; Hoffmann 2017, 2020, 2022b). There are, of course, utterances in which a single construction is used to create a construct (cf., e.g., routine, entrenched greetings such as *Good afternoon!*, or sayings such as *Actions speak louder than words.* – as mentioned in Chapter 1, even (1) can become an entrenched construction for a flight attendant that has to ask this question several times during every flight). In most other cases, however, a number of different constructions will be used to 'construct' a construct in the working memory (Hoffmann 2018, 2020, 2022b: 277). So how can we model the combination of constructions in the working memory using insights from cognitive linguistics?

15.2 Combining constructions

15.2.1 Juxtaposition and superimposition

In a study of questions in the language of children between 2;0 and 3;0 years of age, Dąbrowska & Lieven (2005) argue that the way in which children combine constructions to form constructs can be explained in terms of only two different mental operations – juxtaposition and superimposition.

Juxtaposition "involves linear composition of two units, one after the other" (Dąbrowska & Lieven 2005: 442). So, children apparently combine units such as *Daddy* and *Why are you holding me* to new expressions such as:

(2) a. Daddy, why are you holding me?
     b. Why are you holding me, Daddy?

Superimposition they define as the process whereby one unit "elaborates a schematically specified subpart of another unit" (Dąbrowska & Lieven 2005: 443), in other words, when a unit fills a slot of another construction. Since, as Bybee (2010: 66) says, the "operations proposed by Dąbrowska and Lieven – juxtaposition and superimposition – are equally available to adults producing continuous speech", they play an important role in the CASA model as well. When, for instance, an NP-CONSTRUCTION is used to specify the ÆFFECTOR-slot of an argument structure construction, this is a case of superimposition, and the occurrence of adjuncts can best be explained in terms of juxtaposition. A third operation that we postulate in CASA is the combination of constructions through overlap, i.e., combining an argument structure construction with a sentence-type construction is possible because there is overlap between them with respect to the SUBJ-slot and the V-slot of the sentence-type construction. All three of these operations can be subsumed under the heading of conceptual blending, which we will address in the next section.

15.2.2 Conceptual Blending as the cognitive process of construction

From a cognitive perspective, we argue that Conceptual Blending offers the best explanation of constructional combination in the working memory (Fauconnier & Turner 2002; Turner 2018; Herbst & Hoffmann 2018; Hoffmann 2019b; Hoffmann 2022b: 277–281). Conceptual Blending is a domain-general process that has been used to account for the fact that in logical reasoning, music, dance and virtually all other domains of human cognition, humans can combine and modify existing knowledge to create novel and innovative thoughts and ideas (http://blending.stanford.edu). Conceptual Blending takes two or more input spaces and selectively blends these into a new, emergent space. We assume that, in a similar fashion, Conceptual Blending is the domain-general process that combines constructions in the working memory. Note that this not only explains how constructs such as (1) are created. As several studies have shown, this approach also explains multimodal communication (e.g., Steen and Turner 2013; Turner 2018; Hoffmann 2017, 2021a, 2022b: 277–281; Uhrig 2020, 2021): Gesture and verbal information are often combined spontaneously to produce complex semiotic packages (such as sarcastically saying *Yeah, right!* and shaking one's head at the same time). Since Conceptual Blending is required for and can successfully explain complex, multimodal constructs, we argue that it should also be considered the sole domain-general process that combines constructions into constructs.

15.3 CASA construction grids

As we have shown throughout this book, authentic constructs are very often the result of blending several different constructions. Now, constructions are, obviously, always form-meaning pairings with complex functions and usage-conditions. It is, consequently, impossible to provide a full analysis of a construct that includes all form and meaning properties of the blended constructions. Instead, CASA analyses provide partial representations of all the constructions that are used to create a construct. CASA analyses should, thus, be seen as prompts for the full constructional descriptions found at, e.g., constructicon.de.

We, currently, do not have any neurological evidence that would allow us to specify in what order constructions become activated in the working memory (very often, they will most likely be activated simultaneously). For the sake of simplicity, however, we will always order constructions from top to bottom using the order given in Figure 15.1:

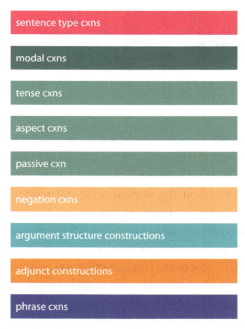

Figure 15.1 The CASA grid template (COORDINATION CONSTRUCTIONS are to be added in the appropriate places)

Concerning the placement of adjunct constructions in CASA analyses, there are, of course, those that act as slot-fillers of a wh-question construction or an argument structure construction. Most other adjuncts, however, can occur relatively freely in a sentence (CGEL ch. 8), and for these, we consider it irrelevant whether construction grids show such adjunct constructions under the scope of the predicate or not. In the following, it is simply for reasons of convenience that sentence-initial adjuncts are not subsumed under the predicate in the grids, whereas post-verbal adjuncts will be appear within the scope of the predicate.

15.4 Sample analysis

In this section, we will now give full-fledged CASA analyses of a couple of authentic, natural sentences. A sentence such as (3) can be analyzed in the way illustrated in Figure 15.2:[142]

(3) I will always love you. (Whitney Houston, song title | CASA-Ch.15 ex-1)

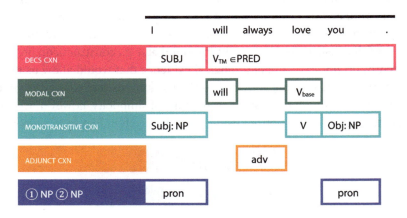

Figure 15.2 Construction grid for *I will always love you*

Figure 15.2 should be interpreted as follows: The DECLARATIVE-STATEMENT CONSTRUCTION has two slots, one for a subject (SUBJ) and one for a predicate that needs to include a modal or a tensed verb ($V_{TM} \in PRED$). The MODAL CONSTRUCTION provides the modal verb corresponding to the V_{TM} slot and, at the same time, it introduces a new V-slot. This is the point of overlap between the MODAL CONSTRUCTION and the MONOTRANSITIVE ARGUMENT STRUCTURE CONSTRUCTION, which introduces a new object argument. The subject argument of the MONOTRANSITIVE CONSTRUCTION overlaps/blends with that of the MODAL-*WILL* CONSTRUCTION and the SUBJ-slot of the DECLARATIVE-STATEMENT CONSTRUCTION.

Horizontal lines are used to connect elements that belong to the same construction if in the linear order of the construct elements belonging to other constructions intervene.

Sentence (4) can be represented as in Figure 15.3:

(4) Don't worry, be happy! (Bobby McFerrin, song title | CASA-CH15-ex-2)

---

142. For further examples see Hoffmann (2023).

Chapter 15. Putting it all together 279

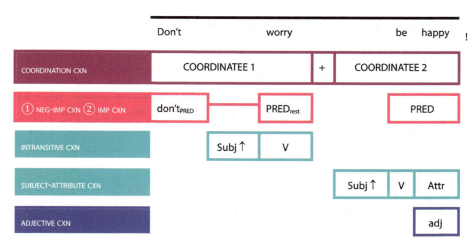

Figure 15.3 Construction grid for *Don't worry, be happy!*

The + sign serves to indicate an ASYNDETIC-COORDINATION CONSTRUCTION (Chapter 9.2.3). What is special about cases such as (4) is that the subject argument of the argument structure construction is not explicitly expressed. The upward arrow ↑ indicates that it can be identified from the context.

In Example (5), a NAME CONSTRUCTION, *Luke Skywalker*, fills a verb slot (for a detailed analysis of this type of constructional creativity; see Hoffmann 2022a: 272):

(5)   He Luke Skywalkered himself.   (Reddit[143] | CASA-CH15-ex-3)

(5), which only contains constructions that have already been used in the figures above, can be represented as follows:

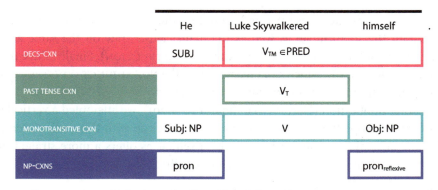

Figure 15.4 Construction grid for *He Luke Skywalkered himself*

---

143. Source: https://www.reddit.com/r/marvelstudios/comments/8redh4/was_odins_death_scene_in_thor_ragnarok_a/) [last accessed 13 March 2022].

A slightly more complex sentence is analyzed in (6) (which draws on an analysis by Hoffmann 2022a: 275):

(6) You're not you when you're hungry   (Snickers Mr Bean TV advert[144] | CASA-CH15-ex-4)

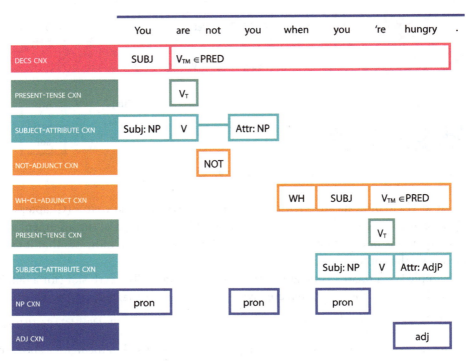

Figure 15.5 Construction grid for *You are not you when you are hungry*

(6) contains a subordinate clause that is licensed by the WH-CL-ADJUNCT CONSTRUCTION. Moreover, both the subordinate as well as the main clause draw on the same argument structure construction (i.e. the SUBJECT-ATTRIBUTE CONSTRUCTION). Finally, since the main clause contains the verb BE, which can take negation, the NOT-ADJUNCT CONSTRUCTION can simply be added without the requirement for DO-support.

In an earlier publication (Herbst & Hoffmann 2018: 201), we attempted a vertical CASA analysis of (7). We hope the readers who compare Figure 15.6 with this earlier attempt will agree that the current horizontal grid analysis of sentences offers a more straightforward representation of all the constructions that blend into the construct:

(7) She puts her soiled breakfast things into the sink,...
                    (BNC-ANY-650 | Herbst & Hoffmann 2018: 201 | CASA-CH15-ex-5)

---

144. Source: https://youtube/qIVDxL2lgN4 [last accessed 14 March 2022].

Chapter 15. Putting it all together

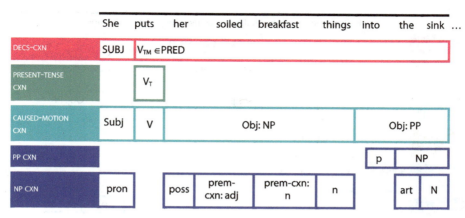

Figure 15.6 Construction grid for *She puts her soiled breakfast things into the sink*

The same is true for (8), which was originally analyzed in a vertical format in Herbst & Hoffmann (2018: 204–205):

(8) Grinding her teeth, Juliette pushed her way through the crowd until she was at the edge of the fountain. (COCA-FIC-2010 | Herbst & Hoffmann 2018: 204–5 | CASA-CH15-ex-6)

In the case of such long constructs, it may make sense to break the construction grid up into two or more parts. Three dots at the end or the beginning of the chart indicate that the grid is being continued, as in Figure 15.7 below:

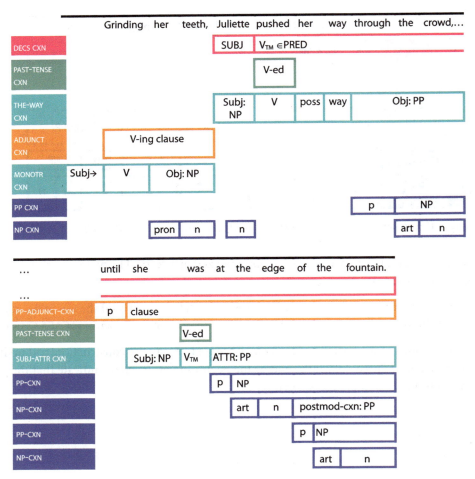

Figure 15.7 Construction grid for *Grinding her teeth, Juliette pushed her way through the crowd, until she was at the edge of the fountain*

(8) starts off with an adjunct clause that is licensed by the V-ING CLAUSE CONSTRUCTION. This non-finite construction does not offer a subject slot, and the Subj slot of the embedded arguments structure construction (the MONOTRANSITIVE CONSTRUCTION) is instead interpreted as co-referential with the subject of the main clause (*Juliette*). As Figure 15.7 shows, in CASA, we indicate this co-referentiality by a right arrow (Subj→) that indicates that the relevant subject argument is to be identified by the main clause subject.

Similarly, (9) is also too long to be analyzed in a single grid, so Figure 15.8 again breaks it up into two grids:

(9) IJburg is going to be crisscrossed by canals, and when completed it will have 43 bridges, all different. (NYT-15-Oct-2002 | CASA-CH15-ex-7)

Chapter 15. Putting it all together   283

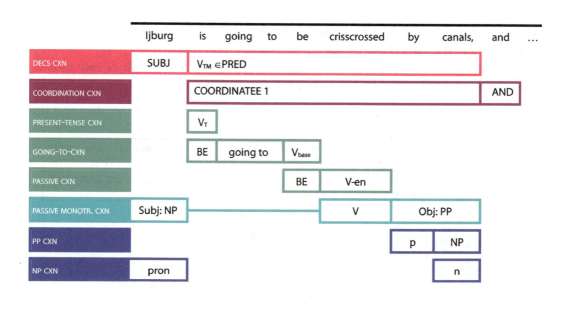

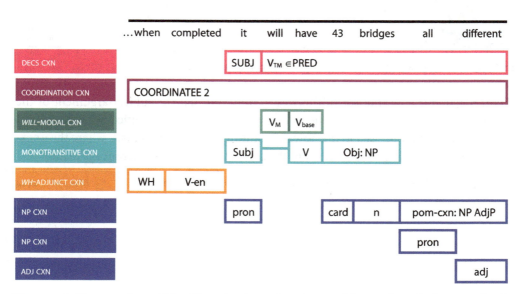

Figure 15.8 Construction grid for *IJburg is going to be crisscrossed by canals, and when completed it will have 43 bridges, all different*

The top part of Figure 15.8 illustrates how the PRESENT-TENSE CONSTRUCTION and the GOING-TO-V CONSTRUCTION overlap and blend with the PASSIVE CONSTRUCTION to produce the construct *is going to be crisscrossed*. The full sentence is also licensed by the SYNDETIC COORDINATION CONSTRUCTION, which in the grid above we simply indicate by the word *and* on the clause-level. The second coordinated clause is introduced by a WH-ADJUNCT CON-STRUCTION and the main clause contains a WILL-MODAL CONSTRUCTION.

Finally, sentences (10) and (11) illustrate how multi-word units such as collocations, phrasal verbs and idioms can be made explicit in construction grids:

(10) She got up and began clearing the table.   BNC-HNJ-2275

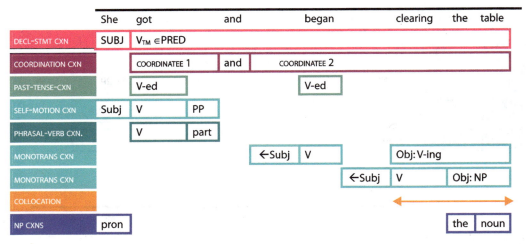

Figure 15.9 Construction grid for *She got up and began clearing the table*

In Figures 15.9 and 15.10, the leftward arrow ← indicates that the subject-argument of the respective argument structure construction is not expressed but is identical with the subject of the main clause (as opposed to the upward pointing arrow in Figure 15.3, where the unexpressed argument has to be retrieved from the context in which the utterance is made).

(11) Both are trying to present the disagreement as a storm in a teacup.   BNC-ABE-2444

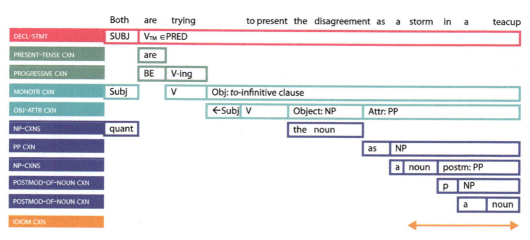

Figure 15.10 Construction grid for *Both are trying to present the disagreement as a storm in the teacup*

The current chapter concludes the presentation of our CASA approach. As we have pointed throughout the book, CASA grids should be seen as a shorthand notation of all the constructions that are involved in creating a construct. Our main goal was to familiarize foreign language teachers and students with a Construction Grammar approach to language that will enable them to identify the many different constructions that overlap and blend to create authentic constructs. We believe that a pedagogical syntactic theory must enable students the analyze even the most complex, naturally occurring utterances – and we hope that we have succeeded in illustrating how the CASA model can be used for this purpose.

Beyond that, however, CASA is also theoretical model that foregrounds the importance of the major tenets of cognitive linguistics in general and Construction Grammar in particular that students should know: The central unit of language are form-meaning pairs, constructions, that are stored in the long-term memory. These constructions are activated and combined into new constructs by the domain-general process of Conceptual Blending (see, e.g., Hoffmann 2020, 2022b). Moreover, we have argued that it is important to remember that often there will not necessarily be only a single possible CASA grid analysis for an authentic utterance. Different speakers can draw on different constructions to create an identical construct (take, e.g., (1), which some speakers might produce using the various constructions listed at the start of the chapter, while flight attendants might have entrenched it as a single, holistic construction due to its high frequency of use).

Finally, while this concludes our textbook, this should only be seen as the starting point of our CASA project. We will continue to expand the accompanying constructicon (www.constructicon.de) by adding more and more constructions. The CASA project is, therefore, one that is 'under construction'.

References

Aarts, Bas. 2007. *Syntactic Gradience: The Nature of Grammatical Indeterminacy*. Oxford: Oxford University Press.

Aarts, Bas. 2011. *Oxford Modern English Grammar*. Oxford/New York: Oxford University Press.

Aarts, Jan & Flor Aarts. 1988. *English Syntactic Structures* (2nd edition). New York & Leyden: Prentice Hall & Martinus Nijhoff. (1st edition 1982 Pergamon Press)

Allerton, David. 1990. Language as form and patterns: Grammar and its categories. In N. E. Collinge (ed.), *An Encyclopaedia of Language*, 68–111. London & New York: Routledge.

Altenberg, Bengt. 1998. On the phraseology of Spoken English: The evidence of recurrent word-combinations. In Anthony P. Cowie (ed.), *Phraseology: Theory, Analysis, and Applications*, 101–121. Oxford: Clarendon Press.

Ambridge, Ben & Elena V. M. Lieven. 2011. *Child Language Acquisition: Contrasting Theoretical Approaches*. Cambridge: Cambridge University Press.

Bauer, Eva-Maria & Thomas Hoffmann. 2020. *Turns out* is not Ellipsis: A Usage-based Construction Grammar view on reduced constructions. *Acta Linguistica Hafniensia* 52(2), 240–259.

Bauer, Laurie. 1983. *English Word-formation*. Cambridge: Cambridge University Press.

Behrens, Heike. 1999. Was macht Verben zu einer besonderen Kategorie im Spracherwerb? In Jörg Meibauer & Monika Rothweiler (eds.), *Das Lexikon im Spracherwerb*, 32–50. Tübingen/Basel: Francke.

Behrens, Heike. 2007. The acquisition of argument structure. In Thomas Herbst & Katrin Götz-Votteler (eds.), *Valency: Theoretical, Descriptive and Cognitive Issues*, 193–214. Berlin/New York: Mouton de Gruyter.

Behrens, Heike. 2009a. Usage-based and emergentist approaches to language acquisition. *Linguistics* 47(2), 383–411.

Behrens, Heike. 2009b. Konstruktionen im Spracherwerb. *Zeitschrift für Germanistische Linguistik* 37, 427–444.

Behrens, Heike. 2011. Grammatik und Lexikon im Spracherwerb: Konstruktionsprozesse. In Stefan Engelberg, Anke Holler & Kristel Proost (eds.), *Sprachliches Wissen zwischen Lexikon und Grammatik*, 375–396. Berlin/Boston: de Gruyter.

Bierwiaczonek, Boguslaw. 2016. *An Introductory English Grammar in Constructions*. Częstochowa: Academia.

Boas, Hans C. 2003. *A Constructional Approach to Resultatives*. Stanford: CSLI Publications.

Boas, Hans C. 2011. Zum Abstraktionsgrad von Resultativkonstruktionen. In Stefan Engelberg, Kristel Proost & Anke Holler (eds.), *Sprachliches Wissen zwischen Lexikon und Grammatik*, 37–69. Berlin/Boston: de Gruyter.

Boas, Hans C. 2013. Cognitive Construction Grammar. In Thomas Hoffmann & Graeme Trousdale (eds.), *The Oxford Handbook of Construction Grammar*, 233–252. Oxford: Oxford University Press.

Boas, Hans C. 2022. From Construction Grammar(s) to Pedagogical Construction Grammar. In Hans. C. Boas (ed.), *Directions for Pedagogical Construction Grammar. Learning and Teaching (with) Constructions*, 3–43. Berlin/Boston: Mouton de Gruyter.

Boas, Hans C., Benjamin Lyngfelt & Tiago Timponi Torrent. 2019. Framing constructicography. *Lexicographica* 35, 15–59.

Boas, Hans C., Joseph Ruppenhofer & Collin Baker. 2024. FrameNet at 25. *International Journal of Lexicography* XX, 1–22.

Booij, Geert. 2013. Morphology in Construction Grammar. In Thomas Hoffmann & Graeme Trousdale (eds.), *The Oxford Handbook of Construction Grammar*, 255–273. Oxford: Oxford University Press.

Boyd, Jeremy K. & Adele E. Goldberg. 2011. Learning what not to say: The role of statistical preemption and categorization in 'a'-adjective production. *Language* 81(1), 1–29.

Bresnan, J. & M. Ford. 2010. Predicting syntax: Processing dative constructions in American and Australian varieties of English. *Language* 86, 168–213.

Brown, Gillian & George Yule. 1983. *Discourse Analysis*. Cambridge: Cambridge University Press.

Burgschmidt, Ernst. 1977. Strukturierung, Norm und Produktivität in der Wortbildung. In Herbert Ernst Brekle & Dieter Kastovsky (eds.), *Perspektiven der Wortbildungsforschung*, 39–47. Bonn: Bouvier Verlag.

Buysschaert, Joost. 1982. *Criteria for the Classification of English Adverbials*, Brussel: Paleis der Academiën.

Bybee, Joan. 1995. Regular Morphology and the Lexicon. *Language and Cognition Processes* 10(5), 425–455.

Bybee, Joan. 2010. *Language, Usage and Cognition*. Cambridge: Cambridge University Press.

Bybee, Joan. 2013. Usage-based theory and exemplar representations of constructions. In Thomas Hoffmann & Graeme Trousdale (eds.), *The Oxford Handbook of Construction Grammar*, 49–69. Oxford/New York: Oxford University Press.

Bybee, Joan. 2015. *Language Change*. Cambridge: Cambridge University Press.

Bybee, Joan & Joanne Scheibman. 1999. The effect of usage on degrees of constituency: The reduction of don't in English. *Linguistics: An Interdisciplinary Journal of the Language Sciences* 37(4), 575–596.

Cantos-Gomez, Pascual & Moises Almela Sánchez. 2001. Lexical constellations: What collocations fail to tell. *International Journal of Corpus Linguistics* 6(2), 199–228.

Cappelle, Bert. 2006. Particle placement and the case for 'allostructions'. *Constructions* SV 1–7: 1–28. www.constructions-journal.com

Cappelle, Bert, Edwige Dugas & Vera Tobin. 2015. An afterthought on *let alone. Journal of Pragmatics* 80, 70–85.

Casenhiser, Devin & Adele E. Goldberg. 2005. Fast mapping between a phrasal form and meaning. *Developmental Science* 8(6), 500–508.

Chomsky, Noam. 1957. *Syntactic Structures*. The Hague: Mouton.

Chomsky, Noam. 1964. *Current Issues in Linguistic Theory*. The Hague: Mouton.

Chomsky, Noam. 1965. *Aspects of the Theory of Syntax*. Cambridge/Mass: MIT Press.

Chomsky, Noam. 1970. Remarks on nominalization. In R.A. Jacobs & P.S. Rosenbaum (eds.), *Readings in English Transformational Grammar*, 184–221. Blaisdell.

Chomsky, Noam. 1986. *Knowledge of Language*. New York: Praeger.

Chomsky, Noam. 1995. *The Minimalist Program*. Cambridge/MA/London: MIT Press.

Clark, Herbert E. & Eve V. Clark. 1979. *Psychology and Language*. San Diego: Harcourt Brace Jovanovich.

Colleman, Timothy. 2011. Ditransitive verbs and the ditransitive construction: A diachronic perspective. *Zeitschrift für Anglistik und Amerikanistik* 59(4), 380–410.

Cowan, Nelson. 2008. What are the differences between long-term, short-term, and working memory? *Progress in Brain Research* 169, 323–333.

Cowie, Anthony P., Ronald Mackin & Isabel R. McCaig. 1983. *Oxford Dictionary of Current Idiomatic English. Vol 2: Phrase, Clause and Sentence Idioms*. Oxford: Oxford University Press.

Cowie, Anthony P. & R. Mackin. 1975. *Oxford Dictionary of Current Idiomatic English. Vol. 1: Verbs with Prepositions and Particles*. London: Oxford University Press.

Croft, William. 2001. *Radical Construction Grammar: Syntactic Theory in Typological Perspective*. Oxford: Oxford University Press.

Croft, William. 2012. *Verbs: Aspect and Causal Structure*. Oxford. Oxford University Press.

Croft, William. 2013. Radical Construction Grammar. In Thomas Hoffmann & Graeme Trousdale (eds.), *The Oxford Handbook of Construction Grammar*, 211–232. Oxford: Oxford University Press.

Croft, William. 2016. Comparative concepts and language-specific categories: Theory and practice. *Linguistic Typology* 20, 377–393.

Croft, William & Alan. D. Cruse. 2004. *Cognitive Linguistics*. Cambridge: Cambridge University Press.

Cruse, David A. 1986. *Lexical Semantics*. Cambridge: Cambridge University Press.

Crystal, David A. 1967. English. *Lingua* 17, 24–56.

Culicover, Peter W. & Ray Jackendoff. 1999. The view from the periphery: The English comparative correlative. *Linguistic Inquiry* 30, 543–571.

Dąbrowska, Ewa. 2014a. Recycling utterances: A speaker's guide to sentence processing. *Cognitive Linguistics* 25(4), 617–653.

Dąbrowska, Ewa. 2014b. 'Words that go together': Measuring individual differences in native speakers' knowledge of collocations. *Mental Lexicon* 9, 401–418.

Dąbrowska, Ewa & Elena Lieven. 2005. Towards a lexically specific grammar of children's question constructions. *Cognitive Linguistics* 16(3), 437–474.

Dąbrowska, Ewa & Marcin Szczerbinski. 2006. Polish children's productivity with case marking: The role of regularity, type frequency, and phonological diversity. *Journal of Child Language* 33(3), 559–597.

Deacon, Terrance. 1997. *The Symbolic Species: The Co-evolution of Language and the Human Brain*. London: Penguin.

Diamond, Adele. 2013. Executive functions. *Annual Review of Psychology* 64, 135–68.

Diessel, Holger. 2013. Construction Grammar and first language acquisition. In Thomas Hoffmann & Graeme Trousdale (eds.), *The Oxford Handbook of Construction Grammar*, 347–364. Oxford: Oxford University Press.

Diessel, Holger. 2019. *The Grammar Network: How Linguistic Structure Is Shaped by Language Use*. Cambridge: Cambridge University Press.

Dirven, René & Günter Radden. 1977. *Semantische Syntax des Englischen*. Wiesbaden: Athenaion.

Ellis, Nick C. 2003. Constructions, chunking & connectionism: The emergence of second language structure. In Catherine J. Doughty & Michael H. Long (eds.), *The Handbook of Second Language Acquisition*, 63–103. Malden: Blackwell.

Ellis, Nick C. 2006. Selective attention and transfer phenomena in L2 acquisition: Contingency, cue competition, salience, interference, overshadowing, blocking, and perceptual learning. *Applied Linguistics* 27(2), 164–194,

Ellis, Nick C. & Stefanie Wulff. 2015. Usage-based approaches to SLA. In Bill Van Patten & Jessica Williams (eds.), *Theories in Language Acquisition: An Introduction*, 75–93. Florence: Taylor and Francis.

Elman, Jeffrey L. 2004. An alternative view of the lexicon. *Trends in Cognitive Science* 8(7), 301–306.

Emonds, Joseph. 1976. *A Transformational Approach to English Syntax*. New York: Academic Press.

Esser, Jürgen. 1992. Neuere Tendenzen in der Grammatikschreibung des Englischen. *Zeitschrift für Anglistik und Amerikanistik* 40(2), 112–123.

Evert, Stefan. 2005. *The Statistics of Word Co-occurrences: Word Pairs and Collocations*. Stuttgart: University of Stuttgart Dissertation.

Evert, Stefan, Peter Uhrig, Sabine Bartsch, Thomas Proisl. 2017. E-VIEW-alation – A large-scale evaluation study of association measures for collocation identification. In *Electronic lexicography in the 21st century. Proceedings of the eLex 2017 conference, Leiden, The Netherlands*.

Fauconnier, Gilles & Mark Turner. 1996. Blending as a central process of grammar. In Adele E. Goldberg (ed.), *Conceptual Structure, Discourse and Language*, 113–130. Stanford, CA: CSLI Publications.

Fauconnier, Gilles & Mark Turner. 2002. *The Way We Think: Conceptual Blending and the Mind's Hidden Complexities*. New York: Basic Books.

Felfe, Marc, Dagobert Höllein & Klaus Welke (eds.). *Regelbasierte Konstruktionsgrammatik: Musterbasiertheit vs. Idiomatizität*. Berlin/Boston: De Gruyter, 2024.

Fillmore, Charles J. 1968. The case for case. In Emmon Bach & Robert T. Harms (eds.), *Universals in Linguistic Theory*, 0–88. New York: Holt, Rinehart & Winston.

Fillmore, Charles J. 1985. Syntactic intrusions and the notion of grammatical construction. *Berkeley Linguistic Society* 11, 73–86.

Fillmore, Charles J. 1988. The Mechanisms of "Construction Grammar." In Shelley Axmaker, Annie Jassier & Helen Singmaster (eds.), *General Session and Parasession on Grammaticalization*, 35–55. Berkeley: Berkeley Linguistics Society.

Fillmore, Charles J. 2007. Valency issues in FrameNet. In Thomas Herbst & Katrin Götz-Votteler (eds.), *Valency. Theoretical, Descriptive and Cognitive Issues*, 129–160. Berlin/New York: Mouton de Gruyter.

Fillmore, Charles J. 2014. Frames, constructions and FrameNet. In Thomas Herbst, Hans-Jörg Schmid & Susen Faulhaber (eds.), *Constructions – Collocations – Patterns*, 121–166. Berlin: de Gruyter Mouton.

Fillmore, Charles J., Christopher R. Johnson & Miriam R. L. Petruck. 2003. Background to FrameNet. *International Journal of Lexicography* 16(3), 236–250.

Fillmore, Charles J., Russell R. Lee-Goldman & Russell Rhomieux. 2012. The FrameNet constructicon. In Ivan A. Sag & Hans C. Boas (eds.), *Sign-Based Construction Grammar*, 309–372. Stanford: CSLI.

Fillmore, Charles J., Paul Kay & Mary Catherine O'Connor. 1988. Regularity and idiomaticity in grammatical constructions: The case of *let alone*. *Language* 64(3), 501–538.

Fischer, Kerstin & Anatol Stefanowitsch. 2006. Konstruktionsgrammatik: Ein Überblick. In Kerstin Fischer & Anatol Stefanowitsch (eds.), *Konstruktionsgrammatik: Von der Anwendung zur Theorie*, 3–17. Tübingen: Stauffenburg.

Gilquin, Gaëtanelle. 2007. To err is not all: What corpus and elicitation can reveal about the use of collocation by learners. *Zeitschrift für Anglistik und Amerikanistik* 55(3), 273–291.

Gilquin, Gaëtanelle. 2022. Constructing learner speech: On the use of spoken data in Applied Construction Grammar. In Hans. C. Boas (ed.), *Directions for Pedagogical Construction Grammar: Learning and teaching (with) constructions*, 73–96. Berlin/Boston: Mouton de Gruyter.

Gilquin, Gaëtanelle. 2023. Causative constructions in process: How do they come into existence in learner writing? *Yearbook of the German Cognitive Linguistics Association* 11, 105–120.

Givón, Thomas. 1979. *On Understanding Grammar*. New York: Academic Press.

Gläser, Rosemarie. 1990. *Phraseologie der englischen Sprache*. Leipzig: Enzyklopädie.

Goldberg, Adele E. 1995. *Constructions: A Construction Grammar Approach to Argument Structure*. Chicago: Chicago University Press.

Goldberg, Adele E. 2006. *Constructions at Work: The Nature of Generalization in Language*. Oxford/New York: Oxford University Press.

Goldberg, Adele E. 2019. *Explain Me This: Creativity, Competition, and the Partial Productivity of Constructions*. Princeton/Oxford: Princeton University Press.

Goldberg, Adele E. & Thomas Herbst. 2021. The *nice-of-you* construction and its fragments. *Linguistics* 59(1), 285–318.

Goldberg, Adele E. & Ray Jackendoff. 2004. The English resultative as a family of constructions. *Language* 80(3), 532–568.

References   291

Granger, Sylviane & Magali Paquot. 2008. Disentangling the phraseological web. In Sylviane Granger & Fanny Meunier (eds.), *Phraseology: An Interdisciplinary Perspective*, 27–49. Amsterdam/Philadelphia: Benjamins.

Greenbaum, Sidney. 1969. *Studies in English Adverbial Usage*. London: Longman.

Greenbaum, Sidney. 1974. Some verb-intensifier collocations in American and British English. *American Speech* 49(1/2), 79–89.

Greenbaum, Sidney & Randolph Quirk. 1970. *Elicitation Experiments in English: Linguistic Studies in Use and Attitude*. London: Longman.

Gregory, Michelle L. and Laura A. Michaelis. 2001. Topicalization and left-dislocation: A functional opposition revisited. *Journal of Pragmatics* 33: 1665–1706.

Gries, Stefan Th. 2005. Syntactic priming: A corpus-based approach *Journal of Psycholinguistic Research* 34: 365–399.

Gries, Stefan Th. 2008. Phraseology and linguistic theory: A brief survey. In Sylviane Granger & Fanny Meunier (eds.), *Phraseology: An interdisciplinary perspective*, 3–25. Amsterdam/Philadelphia: Benjamins.

Gries, Stefan Th. & Anatol Stefanowitsch. 2004. Extending collostructional analysis: A corpus-based perspective on 'alternations.' *International Journal of Corpus Linguistics* 9(1), 97–129.

Gries, Stefan Th. & Stefanie Wulff. 2005. Do foreign learners have constructions? Evidence from priming, sorting, and corpora. *Annual Review of Cognitive Linguistics* 3, 182–200.

Habermann, Mechthild. 2023. The German *geschweige denn* construction. *Yearbook of the German Cognitive Linguistics Association* 11, 151–174.

Haegeman, Liliane. 1991. *Introduction to Government and Binding Theory*. Oxford/UK/Cambridge/US: Routledge.

Halliday, Michael A.K. 1967-8. Notes on transitivity and theme in English. *Journal of Linguistics*. 3(1) Part 1: 37–81, 3(2) Part 2: 199–244, 4(2) Part 3: 179–215.

Halliday, Michael A.K. 1970. Language structure and language function. In John Lyons (ed.), *New Horizons in Linguistics*, 140–165. Harmondsworth: Penguin.

Halliday, Michael A.K. 1994. *An Introduction to Functional Grammar*. 2nd edition. London: Arnold.

Halliday, Michael A.K. & Ruquaya Hasan. 1976. *Cohesion in English* (Longman Linguistics Library). London: Longman.

Hampe, Beate & Doris Schönefeld. 2003. Creative syntax: Iconic principles within the symbolic. In Wolfgang G. Müller & Olga Fischer (eds.), *From Sign to Signing*, 243–261. Amsterdam/Philadelphia: Benjamins.

Hanks, Patrick. 2000. Do word meanings exist? *Computers and the Humanities* 34 (1/2), 205–215.

Hausmann, Franz Josef. 1984. Wortschatzlernen ist Kollokationslernen. *Praxis des neusprachlichen Unterrichts*, 31, 394–406.

Hausmann, Franz Josef. 1985. Kollokationen im deutschen Wörterbuch: Ein Beitrag zur Theorie des lexikographischen Beispiels. In Henning Bergenholtz & Joachim Mugdan (eds.), *Lexikographie und Grammatik*, 118–129. Tübingen: Niemeyer.

Hausmann, Franz Josef. 2007. Die Kollokationen im Rahmen der Phraseologie: Systematische und historische Darstellung. *Zeitschrift für Anglistik und Amerikanistik* 55(3), 217–235.

Helbig, Gerhard & Wolfgang Schenkel. 1973. *Wörterbuch zur Valenz und Distribution deutscher Verben*. (2nd edition). Leipzig: Verlag Enzyklopädie.

Herbst, Thomas. 1983. *Untersuchungen zur Valenz englischer Adjektive und ihrer Nominalisierungen*. Tübingen: Narr.

Herbst, Thomas. 1984. Adjective complementation: A valency approach to making EFL dictionaries. *Applied Linguistics* V(1), 1–11.

Herbst, Thomas. 1996. What are collocations: *Sandy beaches* or *false teeth? English Studies* 77(4), 379–393.

Herbst, Thomas. 2005. Englische Grammatik ist nicht so kompliziert: Pro Minimalismus, Lücke und Polysemie – Kontra Prototypik und Semantik in grammatischer Terminologie. In Thomas Herbst (ed.), *Linguistische Dimensionen des Fremdsprachenunterrichts*, 11–28. Würzburg: Königshausen & Neumann.

Herbst, Thomas. 2010. *English Linguistics: A Coursebook for Students of English*. Berlin/New York: De Gruyter Mouton.

Herbst, Thomas. 2011a. The status of generalizations: Valency and argument structure constructions. *Zeitschrift für Anglistik und Amerikanistik* 59(4): 347–367.

Herbst, Thomas. 2011b. Choosing sandy beaches – collocations, probabemes and the idiom principle. In Thomas Herbst, Susen Faulhaber & Peter Uhrig (eds.), *The Phraseological View of Language: A Tribute to John Sinclair*, 27–57, Berlin/Boston: De Gruyter Mouton.

Herbst, Thomas. 2013. Von Fledermäusen, die auch Schläger sind, und von Gerundien, die es besser nicht gäbe. In Christoph Bürgel & Dirk Siepmann (eds), *Sprachwissenschaft – Fremdsprachendidaktik: Neue Impulse*, 57–76. Baltmansweiler: Schneider Verlag Hohengehren.

Herbst, Thomas. 2014a. Idiosyncrasies and generalizations: Argument structure, semantic roles and the valency realization principle. *Yearbook of the German Cognitive Linguistics Association* 2, 253–289.

Herbst, Thomas. 2014b. The valency approach to argument structure constructions. In Thomas Herbst, Hans-Jörg Schmid & Susen Faulhaber (eds.), *Constructions – Collocations – Patterns*, 167–216. Berlin, Boston: de Gruyter Mouton.

Herbst, Thomas. 2015. Why Construction Grammar catches the worm and corpus data can drive you crazy: Accounting for idiomatic and non-idiomatic idiomaticity. *Journal of Social Sciences* 11(3), 91–110.

Herbst, Thomas. 2016. Foreign language learning is construction learning: Principles of Pedagogic Construction Grammar. In Sabine De Knop & Gaëtanelle Gilquin (eds.), *Applied Construction Grammar*, 21–51. Berlin/Boston: de Gruyter Mouton.

Herbst, Thomas. 2016a. Foreign language learning is construction learning – what else? Moving towards Pedagogical Construction Grammar. In Sabine de Knop & Gaêtanelle Gilquin (eds.), *Applied Construction Grammar*, 21–51. Berlin/Boston: De Gruyter Mouton.

Herbst, Thomas. 2016b. Wörterbuch war gestern. Programm für ein unifiziertes Konstruktikon. In Stefan Schierholz, Rufus Hjalmar Gouws, Zita Hollós & Werner Wolski (eds.), *Wörterbuchforschung und Lexikographie*, 169–206. Berlin/Boston: De Gruyter.

Herbst, Thomas. 2018a. Menschliche Sprache: Ein Netzwerk aus Mustern genannt Konstruktionen. In Rudolf Freiburg (ed.), *Sprachwelten*, 105–127. Erlangen: FAU University Press.

Herbst, Thomas. 2018b. Is language a collostructicon? A proposal for looking at valency, argument structure and other constructions. In Pascual Cantos-Gomez & Moises Almela Sanchez (eds.). *Lexical Collocation Analysis: Advances and Applications*, 1–22. Cham: Springer.

Herbst, Thomas. 2019. Constructicons – A new type of reference work? *Lexicographica* 35(1), 3–14.

Herbst, Thomas. 2020a. Constructions, generalizations, and the unpredictability of language. *Constructions and Frames* 12(1): 56–96. [reprinted in Tiago Timponi Torrent, Ely Edison da Silva Matos & Natália Sathler Sigiliano (eds), 2022. *Construction Grammar across Borders*. Amsterdam/Philadelphia: Benjamins, 55–94.]

References   293

Herbst, Thomas. 2020b. Dependency and valency approaches. In Bas Aarts, Jill Bowie, & Gergana Popova (eds.), *The Oxford Handbook of English Grammar* (Oxford Handbooks in Linguistics), 124–152. Oxford/New York: Oxford University Press.

Herbst, Thomas. 2022. Frame elements, argument roles and word meaning – three sides of the same coin? In Kristian Blensenius (ed.), *Valency and Constructions*, 59–99. Göteborg: Meijerbergs institut for svensk etymologisk forskning.

Herbst, Thomas, David Heath, Ian F. Roe & Dieter Götz. 2004. *A Valency Dictionary of English: A Corpus-Based Analysis of the Complementation Patterns of English Verbs, Nouns and Adjectives*. Berlin/New York: Mouton de Gruyter.

Herbst, Thomas & Thomas Hoffmann. 2018. Construction Grammar for students: A Constructionist Approach to Syntactic Analysis (CASA). *Yearbook of the German Cognitive Linguistics Association* 6, 197–218.

Herbst, Thomas & Peter Uhrig. 2009–. *Erlangen Valency Patternbank. A corpus-based research tool for work on valency and argument structure constructions*. 2009. http://www.patternbank.fau.de

Herbst, Thomas & Peter Uhrig. 2020. The issue of specifying slots in argument structure constructions in terms of form and meaning. *Belgian Journal of Linguistics* 34, 135–147.

Herbst, Thomas & Susen Schüller. 2008. *Introduction to Syntactic Analysis: A Valency Approach*. Tübingen: Narr.

Hilpert, Martin. 2008. *Germanic Future Constructions: A Usage-Based Approach to Language Change*. Amsterdam/Philadelphia: Benjamins.

Hilpert 2019. *Construction Grammar and its Application to English*. Second edition. Edinburgh: Edinburgh University Press.

Hilpert, Martin. 2020. Constructional Approaches. In Bas Aarts, Jill Bowie & Gergana Popova (eds.), *The Oxford Handbook of English Grammar*, 106–123. Oxford/New York: Oxford University Press.

Hoffmann, Thomas. 2017. Multimodal constructs – multimodal constructions? The role of constructions in the working memory. *Linguistics Vanguard* 3,1.

Hoffmann, Thomas. 2018. Creativity and construction grammar: Cognitive and psychological issues. *Zeitschrift für Anglistik und Amerikanistik* 66(3), 259–276.

Hoffmann, Thomas. 2019a. *English Comparative Correlatives: Diachronic and Synchronic Variation at the Lexicon-Syntax Interface*. Cambridge: Cambridge University Press.

Hoffmann, Thomas. 2019b. Language and creativity: A construction grammar approach to linguistic creativity. *Linguistics Vanguard* 5(1), 1–8.

Hoffmann, Thomas. 2020. Construction Grammar and creativity: Evolution, psychology and cognitive science. *Cognitive Semiotics* 13(1), 1–11.

Hoffmann, Thomas. 2021a. Multimodal Construction Grammar: From multimodal constructs to multimodal constructions. In Xu Wen & John R. Taylor (eds.), *The Routledge Handbook of Cognitive Linguistics*. New York: Routledge, 78–92.

Hoffmann, Thomas. 2021b. *The Cognitive Foundation of Post-colonial Englishes: Construction Grammar as the Cognitive Theory for the Dynamic Model*. (Cambridge Elements in World Englishes). Cambridge: Cambridge University Press.

Hoffmann, Thomas. 2022a. Constructionist approaches to creativity. *Yearbook of the German Cognitive Linguistics Association* 10, 259–284.

Hoffmann, Thomas. 2022b. *Construction Grammar: The Structure of English*. (Cambridge Textbooks in Linguistics.) Cambridge: Cambridge University Press.

Hoffmann, Thomas. 2023. Constructicon in Progress: A short introduction to the constructionist approach to syntactic analysis (CASA). *Yearbook of the German Cognitive Linguistics Association* 11, 7–22.

Hoffmann, Thomas, Thomas Brunner & Jakob Horsch. 2020. English comparative correlative constructions: A usage-based account. *Open Linguistics* 6, 196–215.

Hoffmann, Thomas & Thomas Herbst. Forthc. *Identifying and combining English constructions – some challenges facing a Construction Grammar approach to syntactic analysis.*

Hoffmann, Thomas, Jakob Horsch & Thomas Brunner. 2019. The More Data, The Better: A Usage-based Account of the English Comparative Correlative Construction. *Cognitive Linguistics* 30(1), 1–36.

Hoffmann, Thomas & Graeme Trousdale (eds). 2013. *The Oxford Handbook of Construction Grammar.* Oxford: Oxford University Press.

Hollmann, Willem. 2014. Word classes: Towards a more comprehensive usage-based account. In Nikolas Gisborne & Willem B. Hollmann (eds.), *Theory and Data in Cognitive Linguistics.* Amsterdam: Benjamins, 211–238.

Huddleston, Rodney & Geoffrey K. Pullum. 2002. *The Cambridge Grammar of the English Language.* Cambridge: Cambridge University Press.

Hudson, Richard. 1984. *Word Grammar.* Oxford: Blackwell.

Imo, Wolfgang. 2015. Interactional construction grammar. *Linguistics Vanguard* 2015. 1(1), 69–77.

Jackendoff, Ray. 2002. *Foundations of Language: Brain, Meaning, Grammar, Evolution.* Oxford: Oxford University Press.

Jurafsky, Dan. 2003. Probabilistic modeling in psycholinguistics: Linguistic comprehension and production. In Rens Bod, Jennifer Hay & Stefanie Jannedy, (eds.), *Probabilistic Linguistics*, 39–95/96. Cambridge & MA & London: MIT Press.

Jurafsky, Daniel & James H. Martin. 2023. Vector Semantics and Embeddings. *Speech and Language Processing* (draft). https://web.stanford.edu/~jurafsky/slp3/6.pdf

Kaltenböck, Günther. 2020. Information structuring. In Bas Aarts, Jill Bowie & Gergana Popova (eds.), *The Oxford Handbook of English Grammar*, 461–482. Oxford/New York: Oxford University Press.

Keizer, Evelien. 2007. *The English Noun Phrase.* Cambridge/New York: Cambridge University Press.

Keizer, Evelien. 2020. Noun Phrases. In Bas Aarts, Jill Bowie & Gergana Popova (eds.), *The Oxford Handbook of English Grammar*, 335–357. Oxford/New York: Oxford University Press.

Kibrik, Andrej A. 2019. Rethinking agreement: Cognition-to-form mapping. *Cognitive Linguistics* 30(1), 37–83.

Kim, Jong-Bok & Laura Michaelis. 2020. *Syntactic Constructions in English.* Cambridge: Cambridge University Press.

Kiparsky, Paul & Carol Kiparsky. 1971. Fact. In Danny D. Steinberg & Leon A. Jakobovits (eds.), *Semantics: An Interdisciplinary Reader in Philosophy, Linguistics and Psychology*, 345–369. Cambridge: Cambridge University Press.

Klotz, Michael & Thomas Herbst. 2016. *English Dictionaries: A Linguistic Introduction.* Berlin: Erich Schmidt Verlag.

Knop, Sabine de & Gaëtanelle Gilquin. 2016. *Applied Construction Grammar.* Berlin/Boston: De Gruyter Mouton.

Krug, Manfred. 2000. *Emerging English Modals: A Corpus-Based Study of Grammaticalization.* Berlin/New York: Mouton de Gruyter.

Lakoff, George. 1987. *Women, Fire and Dangerous Things: What Categories Reveal about the Mind.* Chicago: Chicago University Press.

Lambrecht, Knut. 1994. *Information Structure and Sentence Form: Topic, Focus, and the Mental Representations of Discourse Referents.* Cambridge: Cambridge University Press.

Lambrecht, Knud. 2001. Dislocation. In Martin Haspelmath, Ekkehard König, Wulf Oesterreicher & Wolfgang Raible (eds.), *Language Typology and Language Universals: An International Handbook*, Vol. 2, 1050–1078. Berlin/New York: de Gruyter.

Langacker, Ronald W. 1987. *Foundations of Cognitive Grammar. Vol. 1 Theoretical Prerequisites.* Stanford: Stanford University Press.

Langacker, Ronald W. 1991. *Foundations of Cognitive Grammar. Vol. 2 Descriptive Application.* Stanford: Stanford University Press.

Langacker, Ronald W. 2003/2009. Constructions in Cognitive Grammar. In Ronald W. Langacker (ed.), *Investigations in Cognitive Grammar*, 1–39, Berlin/New York: Mouton de Gruyter. (originally in *English Linguistics* 20, 41–83)

Langacker, Ronald W. 2008a. *Cognitive Grammar: A Basic Introduction.* Oxford / New York: Oxford University Press.

Langacker, Ronald W. 2008b. The relevance of Cognitive Grammar for language pedagogy. In Sabine de Knop & Teun Rycker (eds.), *Cognitive Approaches to Pedagogical Grammar*, 7–35. Berlin: de Gruyter.

Langacker, Ronald W. 2020. Trees, assemblies, chains and windows. *Constructions and Frames* 12(1), 8–55.

Lapesa, Gabriella & Stefan Evert. 2014. A large scale evaluation of distributional semantic models: Parameters, interactions and model selection. *Transactions of the Association for Computational Linguistics* 2, 531–545.

Lea, Diana. 2007. Making a collocations dictionary. *Zeitschrift für Anglistik und Amerikanistik* 55(3), 261–271.

Leech, Geoffrey N. 1971. *Meaning and the English Verb.* London: Longman.

Leech, Geoffrey N. 1981. *Semantics.* Second edition. Harmondsworth: Penguin.

Leech, Geoffrey N. 1983. *Principles of Pragmatics.* London/New York: Longman.

Leech, Geoffrey N. & Jan Svartvik. 1975. *A Communicative Grammar of English.* London: Longman.

Leino, Jakko. 2013. Information structure. In Thomas Hoffmann & Graeme Trousdale, (eds.), *The Oxford Handbook of Construction Grammar*, 329–344. Oxford: Oxford University Press.

Lieven, Elena. 2014. First-language learning from a usage-based approach. In Thomas Herbst, Hans-Jörg Schmid, & Susen Faulhaber (eds.), *Constructions – Collocations – Patterns*, 9–32. Berlin/Boston: De Gruyter Mouton.

Lohndahl, Terje & Liliane Haegeman. 2020. Generative approaches. In Bas Aarts, Jill Bowie & Gergana Popova (eds.), *The Oxford Handbook of English Grammar*, 153–179. Oxford: Oxford University Press.

Lyngfelt, Benjamin, Lars Borin, Kyoko Ohara & Tiago Timponi Torrent (eds.). 2018. *Constructicography: Constructicon Development across Languages.* Amsterdam/Philadelphia: Benjamins.

MacWhinney, Brian. 2000. *The CHILDES Project: Tools for Analyzing Talk.* 3rd edn. Mahwah, NJ: Lawrence Erlbaum Associates.

Makkai, Adam. 1972. *Idiom Structure in English.* The Hague: Mouton.

Matthews, Peter. 1981. *Syntax.* Cambridge: Cambridge University Press.

Matthews, Peter. 2007. The scope of valency in grammar. In Thomas Herbst & Katrin Götz-Votteler (eds.), *Valency. Theoretical, Descriptive and Cognitive Issues*, 3–14. Berlin/New York: Mouton de Gruyter.

Michaelis, Laura A. 2013. Sign-Based Construction Grammar. In Thomas Hoffmann and Graeme Trousdale (eds.), *The Oxford Handbook of Construction Grammar*, 133–152. Oxford: Oxford University Press.

Minsky, Marvin. 1975. A framework for representing knowledge. In P. Winston (ed.), *The Psychology of Computer Vision*, 211–277. New York: McGraw-Hill.

Müller, Stefan. 2023. *Grammatical Theory: From Transformational Grammar to Constraint-based Approaches.* (Textbooks in Language Sciences 1). Berlin: Language Science Press.

Nesselhauf, Nadja. 2005. *Collocations in a Learner Corpus.* Amsterdam: Benjamins.

OED online. https://www.oed.com

Palmer, Frank R. 1971. *Grammar.* Harmondsworth: Penguin.

Palmer, Frank R. 1981. *Semantics.* Second edition. Cambridge: Cambridge University Press.

Patel, Malin, Armine Garibyan, Elodie Winckel & Stephanie Evert. 2023. A reference constructicon as a database. *Yearbook of the German Cognitive Linguistics Association* 11, 175–202.

Patten, Amanda & Florent Perek. 2019. Towards an English constructicon using patterns and frames. *International Journal of Corpus Linguistics* 24, 356–386.

Perek, Florent. 2015. *Argument Structure in Usage-Based Construction Grammar.* Amsterdam/Philadelphia: Benjamins.

Petruck, Miriam R. L. 1996. Frame semantics. In Jef Verschueren, Jan-Ola Östman, Jan Blommaert & Chris Bulcaen (eds.), *Handbook of Pragmatics*, 1–11. Amsterdam/Philadelphia: Benjamins.

Quirk, Randolph, Sidney Greenbaum, Geoffrey Leech & Jan Svartvik. 1985. *A Comprehensive Grammar of the English Language.* London: Longman.

Radden, Günter & René Dirven. 2007. *Cognitive English Grammar.* Amsterdam/Philadelphia: Benjamins.

Radford, Andrew. 1988. *Transformational Grammar: A First Course.* Cambridge: Cambridge University Press.

Radford, Andrew. 1993. Head-hunting: On the trail of the nominal Janus. In Greville B. Corbett, Norman M. Fraser & Scott McClashen (eds.), *Heads in Grammatical Theory*, 73–113. Cambridge: Cambridge University Press.

Rezac, Milan. 2006. On tough-movement. In Cedric Boeckx (ed.), *Minimalist Essays*, 288–325. Amsterdam/Philadelphia: Benjamins.

Rothweiler, Monika & Jörg Meibauer. 1999. Das Lexikon im Spracherwerb – Ein Überblick. In Jörg Meibauer & Monika Rothweiler (eds.), *Das Lexikon im Spracherwerb*, 9–31. Tübingen/Basel: Francke.

Sag, Ivan A. 2010. English filler-gap constructions. *Language* 86(3), 486–545.

Sanchez-Stockhammer, Christina. 2018. *English Compounds and their Spelling.* Cambridge: Cambridge University Press.

Sanchez-Stockhammer, Christina & Peter Uhrig. 2023. "I'm gonna get totally and utterly X-ed." Constructing drunkenness. *Yearbook of the German Cognitive Linguistics Association* 11, 121–150.

Schank, Roger C. & Robert P. Abelson. 1977. *Scripts, Plans, Goals, and Understanding: An Inquiry Into Human Knowledge Structures.* Hillsdale/NJ: Erlbaum.

Schmid, Hans-Jörg. 2000. *English Abstract Nouns as Conceptual Shells. From Corpus to Cognition*: Berlin/New York: Mouton de Gruyter.

Schmid, Hans-Jörg. 2003. Collocation: hard to pin down, but bloody useful. *Zeitschrift für Anglistik und Amerikanistik* 51(3), 235–258.

Schmid, Hans-Jörg. 2005. *Englische Morphologie und Wortbildung. Eine Einführung.* Berlin: Schmidt.

Schmid, Hans-Jörg. 2011. *English Morphology and Word-formation. An Introduction.* Berlin: Schmidt.

Schmid, Hans-Jörg. 2017. A framework for understanding entrenchment and its psychological foundations. In Hans-Jörg Schmid (ed.), *Entrenchment and the Psychology of Language Learning: How We Reorganize and Adapt Linguistic Knowledge*, 9–36. Boston: APA & Walter de Gruyter.

References   297

Schmid, Hans-Jörg. 2020. *The Dynamics of the Linguistic System: Usage, Conventionalization and Entrenchment*. Oxford: Oxford University Press.

Schönefeld, Doris. 2006. From conceptualization to linguistic expression: Where languages diversify. In Stefan Th. Gries & Anatol Stefanowitsch (eds.), *Corpora in Cognitive Linguistics: The Syntax-Lexis Interface*, 297–344. Berlin/New York: De Gruyter Mouton.

Schumacher, Helmut, Jacqueline Kubczak, Renate Schmidt & Vera de Ruiter. 2004. *VALBU – Valenzwörterbuch deutscher Verben*. Tübingen: Narr.

Siepmann, Dirk. 2007. Wortschatz und Grammatik: Zusammenbringen, was zusammengehört. *Beiträge zur Fremdsprachenvermittlung* 46, 59–80.

Sinclair, John McH. 2004. *Trust the Text*. London/New York: Routledge.

Sinclair, John McH. 2008. The phrase, the whole phrase and nothing but the phrase. In Sylviane Granger & Fanny Meunier (eds.), *Phraseology: An Interdisciplinary Perspective*, 407–410. Amsterdam/Philadelphia: Benjamins.

Sinclair, John McH. 1991. *Corpus, Concordance, Collocation*. Oxford/New York: Oxford University Press.

Sinclair, John McH. & Anna Mauranen. 2006. *Linear Unit Grammar: Integrating Speech and Writing*. Amsterdam/Philadelphia.

Sommerer, Lotte. 2018. *Article Emergence in Old English: A Constructionist Perspective*. Berlin/Boston: De Gruyter.

Steels, Luc. 2013. Fluid Construction Grammar. In Thomas Hoffmann & Graeme Trousdale (eds.), *The Oxford Handbook of Construction Grammar*, 153–167. Oxford: Oxford University Press.

Steen, Francis & Mark Turner. 2013. Multimodal construction grammar. In Mike Borkent, Barbara Dancygier & Jennifer Hinnell (eds.), *Language and the Creative Mind*, 255–274. Stanford, CA: CSLI Publications.

Stefanowitsch, Anatol. 2003. The English imperative: A construction-based approach. Unpublished manuscript, Universität Bremen.

Stefanowitsch, Anatol. 2011a. Argument structure: Item-based or distributed? *Zeitschrift für Anglistik und Amerikanistik* 59(4): 369–386.

Stefanowitsch, Anatol. 2011b. Keine Grammatik ohne Konstruktionen: Ein logisch-ökonomisches Argument für die Konstruktionsgrammatik. In Stefan Engelberg, Anke Holler & Kristel Proost (eds.), *Sprachliches Wissen zwischen Lexikon und Grammatik*, 181–210. Berlin/Boston: De Gruyter.

Stefanowitsch, Anatol. 2014. Collostructional analysis: A case study of the English *into*-causative. In Thomas Herbst, Hans-Jörg Schmid & Susen Faulhaber (eds.), *Constructions, Colocations, Patterns*, 216–238. Berlin/Boston: De Gruyter Mouton.

Stefanowitsch, Anatol. 2018. The goal-bias revisited: a collostructional approach. *Yearbook of the German Cognitive Linguistics Association* 6, 143–166.

Stefanowitsch, Anatol & Stefan Th. Gries. 2003. Collostructions: Investigating the interaction of words and constructions. *International Journal of Corpus Linguistics* 8(2), 209–243.

Stefanowitsch, Anatol & Ada Rohde. 2004. The goal bias in the encoding of motion events. In Günter Radden & Klaus-Uwe Panther (eds.), *Studies in Linguistic Motivation*, 249–268. Berlin & New York: Mouton de Gruyter.

Street, James & Ewa Dąbrowska. 2014. Lexically specific knowledge and individual differences in adult native speakers' processing of the English passive. *Applied Psycholinguistics* 35, 97–118.

Taylor, John R. 1989. *Linguistic Categorization*. Oxford/New York: Oxford University Press.

Tesnière, Lucien. 1959/2015. *Elements of Structural Syntax*. (Trans.) Timothy Osborne & Sylvain Kahane. Amsterdam/Philadelphia: Benjamins.

Tomasello, Michael. 1992. *First Verbs*. Cambridge/New York: Cambridge University Press.

Tomasello, Michael. 2003. *Constructing a Language*. Cambridge/MA/London: Harvard University Press.

Traugott, Elisabeth Closs. 2008. Grammaticalization, constructions and the incremental development of language: Suggestions from the development of degree modifiers in English. In Regine Eckardt, Gerhard Jäger & Tonjes Veenstra (eds.), *Variation, Selection, Development: Probing the Evolutionary Model of Language Change*, 219–250. Berlin/New York: Mouton de Gruyter.

Traugott, Elizabeth Closs. 2015. Toward a coherent account of grammatical constructionalization. In Jóhanna Barðdal, Elena Smirnova, Lotte Sommerer & Spike Gildea (eds.), *Diachronic Construction Grammar*, 51–79. Amsterdam: John Benjamins.

Turner, Mark. 2018. The role of creativity in multimodal Construction Grammar. *Zeitschrift für Anglistik und Amerikanistik* 66(3), 357–370.

Turner, Mark & Gilles Fauconnier. 1999. A mechanism of creativity. *Poetics Today* 20(3), 397–418.

Tyler, Andrea E. 2012. *Cognitive Linguistics and Second Language Learning: Theoretical Basics and Experimental Evidence*. New York/London: Routledge.

Tyler, Andrea E., Lourdes Ortega, Mariko Uno & Hae In Park (eds.). 2018. *Usage-inspired L2 Instruction*. Amsterdam/Philadelphia: Benjamins.

Uhrig, Peter. 2015. Why the Principle of No Synonymy is overrated. *Zeitschrift für Anglistik und Amerikanistik* 66(3), 323–337.

Uhrig, Peter. 2018. *Subjects in English: From Valency Grammar to a Constructionist Treatment of Non-Canonical Subjects*. Berlin/Boston: De Gruyter Mouton.

Uhrig, Peter. 2020. Multimodal research in linguistics. *Zeitschrift für Anglistik und Amerikanistik* 68(4), 345–349.

Uhrig, Peter. 2021. *Large-Scale Multimodal Corpus Linguistics – The Big Data Turn*. Habilitationsschrift Friedrich-Alexander-Universität Erlangen-Nürnberg (unpublished ms.).

Uhrig, Peter, Susen Faulhaber, Ewa Dąbrowska & Thomas Herbst. 2022. L2-words that go together – more on collocation and learner language. In Hans C. Boas (ed.), *Directions for Pedagogical Construction Grammar*, 97–119, Berlin/Boston: De Gruyter Mouton.

Ungerer, Friedrich and Hans-Jörg Schmid. 2006. *An Introduction to Cognitive Linguistics*. Second edition. London: Routledge.

Van Trijp, Remi. 2014. Cognitive vs. generative Construction Grammar: The case of coercion and argument structure. *Cognitive Linguistics* 26(4), 613–632.

Welke, Klaus. 2011. *Valenzgrammatik des Deutschen: Eine Einführung*. Berlin/New York: De Gruyter.

Welke, Klaus. 2019. *Konstruktionsgrammatik des Deutschen: Ein sprachgebrauchsbezogener Ansatz*. Berlin/Boston: De Gruyter.

Wells, John C. 2006. *English Intonation: An Introduction*. Cambridge: Cambridge University Press.

Wittgenstein, Ludwig. 1953. *Philosophical Investigations*. Oxford: Blackwell.

Ziem, Alexander. 2008. Frame-Semantik und Diskursanalyse: Skizze einer kognitionswissenschaftlich inspirierten Methode zur Analyse gesellschaftlichen Wissens. In Ingo H. Warnke & Jürgen Spitzmüller (eds.), *Methoden der Diskurslinguistik: Sprachwissenschaftliche Zugänge zur transtextuellen Ebene. Methoden*, 89–116. Berlin /New York: De Gruyter.

Ziem, Alexander & Alexander Lasch. 2013. *Konstruktionsgrammatik: Konzepte und Grundlagen gebrauchsorientierter Ansätze*. Berlin/Boston: De Gruyter.

Ziem, Alexander & Tim Feldmüller. 2023. Dimensions of constructional meanings in the German Constructicon: Why collo-profiles matter. *Yearbook of the German Cognitive Linguistics Association* 11, 203–226.

Constructicon

www.constructicon.de: *The CASA-ConstruCtiCon of the English Language.*

Corpora and other sources

BNC British National Corpus. Distributed by Oxford University Computing Service on behalf of the BNC Consortium.

Childes Elena Lieven & Jeannette Goh: *CHILDES English Thomas Corpus* https://childes.talkbank.org/access/Eng-UK/Thomas.html

MacWhinney, Brian. 2000. *The CHILDES Project: Tools for analyzing talk.* 3rd edn. Mahwah, NJ: Lawrence Erlbaum Associates.

COCA *Corpus of Contemporary English*, Mark Davies https://www.english-corpora.org/coca/

MOVIES *Movies 1930s–2018* (200 million words) https://www.english-corpora.org

NOW *News on the Web* (over 15 billion words) https://www.english-corpora.org

TV *TV corpus* (over 325 million words) https://www.english-corpora.org

NYT *New York Times* https://www.nytimes.com

Appendixes

APPENDIX I

List of argument and other semantic roles

The numbers in the following table refer to the figures in which the roles are described.

Role	Figures
ABILITY	5.36
ACTION	5.16 5.32 5.33 5.34 5.36 5.37 5.41 5.42
ÆFFECTED	5.3 5.5 5.6 5.7 5.8 5.15 5.16 5.24 5.25
ÆFFECTED-ATTRIBUTEE	5.12 5.14
ÆFFECTED-THEME	5.10
ÆFFECTOR	5.3 5.5 5.6 5.7 5.8 5.10 5.12 5.14 5.15 5.16 5.17 5.18 5.19 5.20 5.21 5.22 5.23 5.24 5.25 5.34 5.35 5.37 5.41
ÆFFECTOR-THEME	5.9
AGENT	5.39
ATTITUDE	5.33 5.34 5.37
ATTRIBUTE	5.11 5.12 5.28 5.31 5.36 5.37 5.38 5.39 5.40
ATTRIBUTTEE	5.11 5.13 5.29 5.32 5.36 5.37 5.38 5.39 5.40
BENEFICIARY	5.40
CATAPHOR	5.38 5.39 5.40 5.41 5.42
CAUSE	5.35
DEGREE OF DIFFICULTY	5.26
DESIRED-THING	5.23 5.24
DIRECTION	5.9 5.10
EMOTION	5.21
EVALUATION	5.32 5.41 5.42
FOCUS/TOPIC	5.18
GENERAL ISSUE	5.17
GOAL	5.9 5.10 5.19
GOAL-STATE	5.15
PARTNER	5.20 5.27 5.29
PATH	5.9 5.10
POTENTIAL-ÆFFECTOR	5.32 5.36
RECIPIENT	5.3 5.7 5.8 5.19
REFERENT	5.17
RESULT	5.13 5.14

SOURCE	5.9 5.10
SOURCE-STATE	5.15
SPECIFC ISSUE	5.18
STATE	5.35
SUBSTITUTE	5.25
TARGET	5.22
UNDERGOER	5.4 5.35
UNDERGOER-AFFECTED	5.33

APPENDIX II

Index of constructions

The following numbers refer to the sections in which the various constructions are discussed.

II.1 Sentence type cxns

DECLARATIVE-QUESTION CXN (DECQ)	3.3.2
DECLARATIVE-QUESTION-FRAGMENT CXNS	3.4
DECLARATIVE-STATEMENT CXN (DECS)	3.3.2
DECS-FRAGMENT CXN WITH PARTIAL REALIZATION OF PREDICATE	3.4
DECS-FRAGMENT CXN WITHOUT EXPRESSED SUBJECT REFERRING TO SPEAKER	3.4
EVALUATIVE-DECS-FRAGMENT CXN WITHOUT *IT* AND *BE*	3.4
EXCLAMATIVE CXN (EXCL)	3.3.4
IMPERATIVE-COMMAND CXN (IMP)	3.3.3
IMPERATIVE-COMMAND CXN (POSITIVE)	3.3.3
IMPERSONAL-DECS-FRAGMENT CXN WITHOUT *IT*	3.4
IMPERATIVE-COMMAND CONSTRUCTION (NEGATIVE) CXN (NIMP)	3.3.3
POSITIVE-*YOU*-IMPERATIVE-COMMAND CXN	3.3.3
SHORT-QUESTION CXNS	3.4
WH-NONSUBJECT-QUESTION CXN (WHQU)	3.3.2
WH-SUBJECT-QUESTION CXN (WHQU)	3.3.2
YES/NO-QUESTION CXN (YNQU)	3.3.2

II.2 Modal, aspect, tense and voice constructions

BE-ABOUT-TO-V CXN	4.3.4
BE-GOING-TO-V CXN	4.3.3.2
DO-SUPPORT CXN	4.9
FIRST-AND-THIRD-PERSON-SINGULAR-PAST-TENSE CXN (*HE-WAS* CXN)	4.3.2.1
FIRST-PERSON-PRESENT-TENSE CXN (*I-AM* CXN)	4.3.2.1
GENERAL-PAST-TENSE-CXN (2ND PERSON SG AND ALL PLURALS) (*YOU-WERE* CXN)	4.3.2.1
GENERAL-PRESENT-TENSE CXN (2ND PERSON SG AND ALL PLURALS) (*YOU-ARE* CXN)	4.3.2.1
MODAL CXNS	4.2.3
NEGATION	4.9
PASSIVE CXN	4.6
PERFECTIVE CXN	4.5

Appendix II. Index of constructions

PROGRESSIVE CXN	4.4
SUBJUNCTIVE	4.8
THIRD-PERSON-PRESENT-TENSE CXN (*SHE-IS* CXN)	4.3.2.1
USED-TO-V CXN	4.3.4
WILL CXN	4.3.3.1

II.3 Argument structure constructions

*ABLE*_{ETC}-TO-INFINITIVE CXN	5.10.5.5
ABOUT-GENERAL-ISSUE CXN	5.7.3
ADJECTIVAL-*ABOUT*-TOPIC-AREA CXN	5.10.3
ADJECTIVAL-*AT*-CAUSER CXN	5.10.3
ADJECTIVAL-*ON*-GOAL CXN	5.10.3
ADJECTIVAL-*THAT*-CAUSER CXN	5.10.4
ADJECTIVAL-*TO*-RECIPIENT/GOAL CXN:	5.10.3
ADJECTIVAL-*WH*-TOPIC/AREA CXN	5.10.4
ADJECTIVAL-*WITH*-PARTNER CXN	5.10.3
Æ FFECTED+*FOR*-DESIRED-THING CXN	5.7.7
AT-CHANGE-OF-STATE CXN	5.7.2
*BRAVE*_{ETC}-TO-INFINITIVE CXN	5.10.5.3
CAUSED-CHANGE-RESULTATIVE CXNS	5.6.3
CAUSED-MOTION CXN	5.5.1
CONATIVE CXN	5.7.6
*DIFFICULT*_{ETC}-TO-INFINITIVE CXN	5.10.5.1
DITRANSITIVE CXN (VARIOUS SUBTYPES)	5.1.3.3 5.4.2
EXCHANGE-*X-FOR-Y* CXN	5.7.7
FOR-DESIRED-THING CXN	5.7.7
IMPERSONAL-EVALUATION CXN	5.10.6.5
IMPORTANT-FOR-BENEFICARY cxn	5.10.6.3
IMPORTANT-FOR-EVENT CXN	5.10.6.2
INTO-CAUSATIVE CXN	5.7.2
INTRANSITIVE CXN	5.3
IT-THAT CXN	5.10.6.1
*LIKELY*_{ETC}-TO-INFINITIVE CXN	5.10.5.5
MEDIOPASSIVE CXN	5.8.4
MONOTRANSITIVE CXN (VARIOUS SUBTYPES)	5.4.1
NICE-OF-YOU CXN	5.10.6.4
NOMINAL-*FOR*-GOAL CXN	5.11
NOMINAL-*THAT*-CLAUSE CXN	5.11
NOMINAL-*TO*-RECIPIENT CXN	5.11
NOMINAL-*WH*-CLAUSE CXNS	5.11
NOMINAL-WH-TO-INFINITIVE CXNS	5.11
NOMINAL-*WITH*-PARTNER CXN:	5.11
OBJECT-ATTRIBUTE CXNS	5.6.2

ON-SPECIFC-ISSUE CXN	5.7.3
RESULTATIVE CXN	5.6.3
SELF-CHANGE-RESULTATIVE CXNS	5.6.3
SELF-MOTION CXN	5.5.1
SURPRISED$_{ETC}$-*TO*-INFINITIVE CXN	5.10.5.4
SUBJECT-ATTRIBUTE CXNS	5.6.1
THEY-ARE-WILLING-TO-PAY CXN	5.10.5.2
TO-RECIPIENT/GOAL CXN	5.7.4
WILLING$_{ETC}$-*TO*-INFINITIVE CXN	5.10.5.2
WITH-EMOTION CXN	5.7.5
WITH-PARTNER CXN	5.7.4

II.4   Noun phrase constructions

DEFINITE-1ST-PERSON-ACCUSATIVE-PLURAL CXN	6.4.3
DEFINITE-1ST-PERSON-ACCUSATIVE-SINGULAR CXN	6.4.3
DEFINITE-1ST-PERSON-NOMINATIVE-PLURAL CXN	6.4.3
DEFINITE-1ST-PERSON-PLURAL-REFLEXIVE CXN	6.4.3
DEFINITE-1ST-PERSON-SINGULAR-REFLEXIVE CXN	6.4.3
DEFINITE-2ND -PERSON-CXN	6.4.3
DEFINITE-2ND-PERSON-PLURAL-REFLEXIVE CXN	6.4.3
DEFINITE-2ND-PERSON-SINGULAR-REFLEXIVE CXN	6.4.3
DEFINITE-3RD-PERSON-ACCUSATIVE-PLURAL CXN	6.4.3
DEFINITE-3RD-PERSON-ACCUSATIVE-SINGULAR CXN	6.4.3
DEFINITE-3RD-PERSON-ACCUSATIVE-SINGULAR CXN	6.4.3
DEFINITE-3RD-PERSON-CXN	6.4.3
DEFINITE-3RD-PERSON-NOMINATIVE-PLURAL CXN	6.4.3
DEFINITE-3RD-PERSON-NOMINATIVE-SINGULAR CXN	6.4.3
DEFINITE-3RD-PERSON-NOMINATIVE-SINGULAR CXN	6.4.3
DEFINITE-3RD-PERSON-PLURAL-REFLEXIVE	6.4.3
DEFINITE-3RD-PERSON-SINGULAR-REFLEXIVE CXN	6.4.3
DEFINITE-3RD-PERSON-SINGULAR-REFLEXIVE CXN	6.4.3
DEFINITE-3RD-PERSON-SINGULAR-CXN	6.4.3
DEFINITE-1ST-PERSON-NOMINATIVE-SINGULAR CXN	6.4.3
DEFINITE-PLURAL-NP CXN	6.4.1
DEFINITE-SINGULAR-NP CXN	6.4.1
DEMONSTRATIVE-PLURAL-NP CXN	6.5
DEMONSTRATIVE-SINGULAR-NP CXN	6.5
DISCONTINUOUS-MODIFIER-OF-NOUN CXNS	6.10.2.3

308 A Construction Grammar of the English Language

EACH-OTHER CXN	6.3.3
FIRST-NAME-NP CXN	6.9
FULL-NAME-NP CXN	6.9
GENERAL-POSTMODIFIER-OF-NOUN CXN	6.10.2.2
GENERAL-QUANTIFIER-MASS-NP CXN	6.6.2
GENERAL-QUANTIFIER-PLURAL-NP CXN	6.6.2
GENERAL-QUANTITATIVE-SINGULAR-COUNT-NP CXN	6.6.2
GENITIVE-NP CXN	6.4.5
INDEFINITE-SINGULAR-COUNT-NP CXN	6.3
INDEFINITE-PLURAL-COUNT-NP CXN	6.3
LAST-NAME-NP CXN	6.8
MASS-NP CXN	6.3 6.8
NUMERICAL-PLURAL-NP CXN	6.6.1
NUMERICAL-SINGULAR-NP CXN	6.6.1
ONE-ANOTHER CXN	6.5.1
PREDICATIVE-POSSESSIVE CXN	6.3.4
PREMODIFIER-OF-NOUN CXN	6.10.2.1
PERSONAL-NAME CXNS	6.9
PERSONAL-PRONOUN CXN	6.4.2
POSSESSIVE-NP CXN	6.4.5
RANKING-NP CXNS	6.7
RECIPROCAL-NP CXN	6.4.4
REFLEXIVE-NP CXN	6.4.3
TITLE-FIRST-NAME-NP CXN	6.9
TITLE-FULL-NAME-NP CXN	6.9
TITLE-LAST-NAME-NP CXN	6.9
VALENCY-RELATED-POSTMODIFIER-OF-NOUN CXN	6.10.2.2
WH-NP CXNS	6.8

II.5   Adjective constructions

ADJECTIVE CXN	7.1.2
AS-AS CXN	7.4.3
COMPARATIVE CXN	7.4.1
DISCONTINUOUS-MODIFIER-OF-ADJECTIVE CXN	7.2.1.3
GENERAL-POSTMODIFIER-OF-ADJECTIVE CXNS	7.2.1.2
MORE-THAN-COMPARISON CXN (TYPE 1)	7.4.2
MORE-THAN-COMPARISON CXN (TYPE 2)	7.4.2
MORE-THAN-COMPARISON CXN (TYPE 3)	7.4.2

MOST-/LEAST-CXN	7.2.2
PREMODIFIER-OF-ADJECTIVE CXN	7.2.1.1
SUPERLATIVE CXN	7.2.2

II.6 Adjunct constructions

ADJUNCT CXN	8.8.2
AT-POINT-OF-LOCATION CXN	13.2.4.1
BENEFICIARY CXN	8.4
COMMENT CXNS	8.5
COMPARISON CXNS	8.4
CONDITION CXNS	8.4
CONTRAST CXN	8.4
INSTRUMENT/MEANS CXNS	8.3
LIKELIHOOD CXNS	8.5
MANNER	8.3
POINT-IN-TIME CXNS	8.2.3
POINT-OF-LOCATION CXN	8.2.2
PURPOSE CXNS	8.4
REASON CXNS	8.4
REPLACEMENT CXNS	8.4
ROLE CXN	8.4
SCOPE CXNS	8.6
STRUCTURING CXNS	8.6
TIME-DURATION CXNS	8.2.3
TIME-FREQUENCY CXNS	8.2.3
TIME-SEQUENCE CXNS	8.2.3
TIME-SPAN CXNS	8.2.3
VOCATIVE CXN	8.8.6

II.7 Other constructions

ADDITIVE-COORDINATION CXN	9.2.3
AFFIRMATIVE-TAG CXN	12.3
ALTERNATIVE-COORDINATION CXN	9.2.4
ASYNDETIC-COORDINATION CXN	9.2.3
COMPARATIVE-CORRELATIVE CXN	11.5.3
CONTROVERSIAL-TAG CXN	12.3

EXISTENTIAL-*THERE* CXN	12.4.1
FOCUS-NP CXN	10.3
GIVE-UP-MONOTRANSITIVE-VERB-PARTICLE CXN	11.3.1
GOD-KNOWS-WHAT CXN	11.5.2
HYPOTHETICAL-CONDITION CXN	9.4.4
INDIRECT SPEECH CXN	12.2.3
IT-CLEFT CXN	10.3
LEFT-DISLOCATION CXN	10.3
LET-ALONE CXN	11.5.1
PUT-UP-WITH-VERB-PARTICLE CXN	11.3.2
QUOTATIVE CXN	12.2.1
REALISTIC-CONDITION CXN	9.4.4
REFERENCE-TO-SOURCE CXN	12.2.2
RIGHT-DISLOCATION CXN	10.3
TAKE-OFF-SELF-MOTION-VERB-PARTICLE CXN	11.3.1
THE-EARLY-BIRD-CATCHES-THE-WORM CXN	11.2
THE-TWO-OF-THEM CXN	1.3.5
THE-X-ER-THE-Y-ER CXN (COMPARATIVE-CORRELATIVE CXN)	11.5.3
TOPICALIZATION CXN	10.3
UNREALISTIC-CONDITION CXN	9.4.4
WH-CLEFT CXN	10.3

Index

1st person 47, 52–54, 56, 57, 143
2nd person 47, 52–54, 57, 143
3rd person 25, 49, 52, 55–57, 143, 240, 259

A

A Grammar of Contemporary English
CGEL 3, 9, 26–27, 32, 39, 42–43, 49, 59, 70, 80, 95, 130, 138, 159, 161, 169, 182, 184–185, 191, 195, 209, 211, 223, 237, 244, 246, 249, 251, 252, 266, 273
Aarts, B. 27, 49, 182, 244, 246, 248
Aarts, F. 80–81, 95, 138, 156, 159, 167, 208–209
Aarts, J. 80–81, 95, 138, 156, 159, 167, 208–209
Abelson 206
ABILITY 122
abstraction 5, 8, 73–77, 84, 91, 95, 156, 215–216, 240
accusative 23, 25, 143–144
ACTION 101, 119–122, 127, 223
ACTION DISCUSSED 227
active 46–48, 64–66, 89, 108–112, 203, 271
additive coordination 193–195
adjective 23–24, 62, 65, 114–128, 130, 155, 162–175, 181, 186, 226, 240, 244, 249, 253, 260, 268–270, 272
ADJECTIVAL-VALENCY CXN 113, 116
adjunct 38, 159, 184–191, 249, 256–257, 260, 262–263, 271–273, 276, 280, 282, 284
ADJUNCT CXN 186–187, 278, 282–283
adverb 23, 25, 49, 72, 162–176, 195, 202, 245–250, 252, 256, 260–261, 265, 269–270, 272
adverbial 26, 28, 185, 191
ÆFFECTED 64, 75–76, 79, 82, 86–91, 93, 96, 98, 101, 106–113, 203, 217, 220–221, 271
ÆFFECTED-ATTRIBUTEE 99
ÆFFECTED-THEME 94, 219
ÆFFECTOR 64, 75, 79, 86–91, 93–95, 97, 99–109, 111, 113, 120–122, 126–127, 164, 203, 217, 219–221, 223, 271, 276
ÆFFECTOR-THEME 93
AFFECTED-ATTRIBUTE 97
agent 27, 29, 32, 72, 80, 85–86, 90, 93

Aktionsart 179
Allerton 239
Altenberg 10
alternative coordination 194–195
Ambridge 57, 74, 133
anchor 53, 147, 246
apodosis 228
argument (versus adjunct) 191
article 39, 137, 141–143, 160, 252–253, 258, 268–270
as 233, 264
aspect 35, 61–64, 66, 176, 178
asyndetic coordination 193–195, 297
ATTITUDE 120–122
Attr 81–82, 96–99, 113, 115–116, 164, 177, 188, 209–210, 235, 256, 260, 279–280, 282, 285
ATTRIBUTE 96–97, 114–116, 124–125, 163–164, 166–167, 169, 171–172
ATTRIBUTEE 96, 98, 114–116, 118–119, 124–125, 163–164, 168–169, 171–172, 174, 229
attributive (use) 23, 62, 65, 114, 165, 235, 244
AUTHORITY 227

B

Bauer, E.M. 40, 218,
Bauer, L. 15
BE-going-to-V 59–60, 220
Behrens 2, 73, 80
BENEFICIARY 64, 125, 180, 183
Bierwiaczonek 1, 137–138
blending 16–17, 112, 156, 166, 189, 192, 276–277, 285
Boas 1, 21, 74, 97, 98, 131
Booij 6
boundedness 142
Boyd 244
Bresnan 94
Brown 20, 204, 206
Brunner 228–229
Burgschmidt 15
Buysschaert 273
Bybee 2, 6–7, 19, 54, 60, 276

C

Cambridge Grammar of the English Language CAMG 3, 9, 22, 26–27, 49, 59, 80, 130, 138, 159, 161, 246, 248
canonical 217, 218, 266

Cappelle 226, 267
CARDINAL 9
cardinal number/numeral 8, 24, 148, 161
case 23, 111, 131, 143, 255–256, 265
case grammar 70, 111, 130–131
Casenhiser 13
CATAPHOR 124–127
CAUSE 121
cause 199
CAUSED-MOTION (CXN) 71, 75, 93–94, 97, 113
CAUSER 72, 80, 117, 199
change of location 189–190
change of state 71, 96–97, 100–101
Chomsky 3, 11, 108, 118, 216
chunk 8, 13, 19, 45, 73, 215–231, 248
CIRCUMSTANTIAL INFORMATION 186
Clark, E. 15
Clark, H.E. 15
co-headedness 138
cognitive 3, 17–19, 21, 29, 32–33, 42–43, 53, 57, 71, 74, 80, 104, 114, 130, 135, 159–160, 172, 175, 182–183, 188, 191–192, 203–204, 231, 236, 239–240, 244–245, 250, 252–253, 275–276, 285
Cognitive Grammar 2, 32, 136–137
cohesion 202
Colleman 74
collo-profile 8, 78–79, 218
collocation 3, 8, 10–11, 20, 50, 169, 215, 224–225, 284
comment 33, 181, 211, 233
comparative (cxn) 170–175, 240
COMPARATIVE-CORRELATIVE CXN 10, 227–230, 251
comparison 170–175
complement 26, 28, 39, 65, 70, 81–82, 130–131, 155, 159, 187, 191, 246
compositionality 6–7, 67, 216, 224
comprehension 45, 268
conative 105–106
conceptual blending 16–17, 155, 276, 285
concord 27, 33, 35, 112, 142
CONDITION 196, 200
condition 68, 180, 184, 196, 199–201
conjunction 23–24, 225–226, 245–248, 263
CONNECTEE 196–200

connection (cxn) 195–197, 202
CONNECTOR 195–197, 200, 202, 226, 246, 262–263
constraint 21, 37, 75, 212, 214
construal 61, 76, 94, 106, 114, 127, 135, 140, 203–204
construct 4, 15–18, 42, 51, 67, 112–113, 153, 157, 189, 212, 217, 275, 277–285
constructicon 5–6, 14, 18, 21, 74–75, 100, 108, 129, 160, 191, 225, 230, 250, 277, 285
construction grid 18, 42, 48, 51, 54, 58, 62, 64, 66–67, 98, 112–113, 116, 157–159, 165, 186–187, 221–222, 231–232, 249–250, 252, 258, 263–264, 277–285
constructional space 12, 239, 241–242, 254
contextual anchor 115, 119, 120– 122, 148–151, 163, 171–173, 227, 247
contextual anchor 53, 147
contextually optional 83
contrast 23, 33, 141, 198, 266
COORDINATEE 194–197, 279, 283, 284
coordination 16–18, 27, 34, 173, 192–198, 202, 226, 275, 277, 279, 283–284
COORDINATOR 194–195, 283, 284
corpus 10, 13, 20, 30–31, 43, 45, 71, 215, 224, 229, 239
count noun 23, 132, 139–141, 150, 160, 242, 255
Cowie 218
Croft 11, 37, 73–74, 87, 129, 203, 211, 216, 225, 230, 236, 253
Cruse 11, 37, 216–217, 225, 230, 236

D
Dąbrowksa 2, 5, 10, 13, 275–276
dative 23
De Knop 1, 21
Deacon 11
DECLARATIVE-QUESTION cxn 34, 42
DECLARATIVE-STATEMENT cxn 33–34, 41–42, 50–51, 57–58, 62, 64, 66, 112–113, 184, 186–187, 208, 222, 230, 232, 234, 265, 270–273, 278–285
definite
  definite reference 139
  definite-reciprocal 161
  definite-referential 143
  definite-reflexive 161
DEGREE OF DIFFICULTY 112
DEMONSTRATIVE 148

demonstrative 23–24, 137, 142, 147–148, 161, 242, 250, 252–253, 256–257
dependency grammar 130, 187
DESIRED THING 107, 183, 208
determinative 23, 26, 159, 161
determiner 10, 23, 26, 82, 138, 158–159, 161, 172, 228, 231, 250, 256–258
determiner phrase 138
Diamond 16, 275
Diessel 5, 74, 240–242
direct object 28, 271
DIRECTION 93–94, 105, 219, 222
Dirven 49, 118, 137, 142, 239
discontinuous modifier 156–157, 159, 167
discourse 13, 41, 134, 136–137, 197–201, 204–206, 212–213
distributional semantics 242
DITRANSITIVE (CXN) 2, 15, 72, 74–80, 83–84, 88–91, 94–95, 108, 113, 191, 232, 242, 267, 271
dividing line 9, 11, 20, 175, 216, 222
do-support cxn 16, 35, 37, 68–69, 259, 275, 280
Dugas 226

E
Ellis 2, 21, 57
Elman 241
EMOTION 105
emotion 23, 31, 104–105, 203, 263
encoding idioms 224
end weight 210
entrenchment 13–16, 32, 45, 144, 155, 188–189, 191, 230, 275, 285
Esser 27
EVALUATION 119, 126, 127
evaluative 41, 127, 154
Evert 10, 242
exception 17, 53, 80, 108, 185, 190, 193, 216, 226, 251
EXCLAMATIVE cxn 39
expectation 60, 103, 268–270
EXPERIENCER 87

F
familiarity 110
family 138, 148, 154, 182, 236
family resemblance 250
Fauconnier 16–17, 112, 276
Feldmüller 21

Fillmore 1–2, 4, 9–10, 21, 26, 28, 70, 75, 83, 111, 131, 185, 206, 216, 224–226, 228, 230, 252
Fischer 2
fixed 2, 7, 17, 175, 215, 228, 268
Fluid Construction Grammar 4, 21
FOCUS 209, 210
focus 32, 61–62, 102, 204, 206–211
Ford 94
form-meaning pairing 2–5, 11, 16, 18–19, 30, 71, 129, 138, 225, 248, 267–268, 275, 277, 285
fragment 39–42, 53, 126, 184, 218, 272
frame 19, 110–111, 127, 185, 206
frame element 110, 185
FrameNet 4, 21, 83, 93, 112, 130–131
frequency 5, 8, 10, 31, 44–45, 67, 78–79, 162, 188, 191, 217–218, 222, 224, 227, 230, 267, 285
future time 58–60, 90, 200

G
GENERAL ISSUE 101–102
GENERAL QUANTIFIER cxn 149–151, 258
generative 3, 11, 20, 26, 70, 108, 118, 216, 267
genitive 6, 23, 127, 143, 146–147, 161, 205, 240, 255–256
Gilquin 1, 21, 225
give up 219–220
given 60, 73, 204, 206, 272
Givón 43
goal 60, 72, 76–77, 92, 94–95, 103, 106, 108, 112, 116–117, 128–129, 190
GOAL 93, 94, 103, 113
GOAL-STATE 100–101
Goldberg 2, 5, 10–13, 15, 19, 21, 37, 40–41, 53, 70–76, 78, 80–81, 88, 90, 94, 97–98, 110, 125–126, 130–131, 176, 185, 212, 224, 240–242, 244, 268
gradable 166
gradient 49, 182–183, 217, 222, 225
grammaticalization 60, 220
Granger 217
Greenbaum 3, 224, 273
Gregory 212
Gries 13, 21, 36, 74, 94, 101, 216
ground 137
grouping 135–136, 243

H
Habermann 216
Haegeman 67, 188

Index

Halliday 28, 75, 182, 202, 204, 206
Hampe 17
Hanks 240
Hausmann 10
Helbig 130
Herbst 2–3, 8–10,12, 15–17, 21, 26–27,
    33, 40, 43, 53–54, 59, 70, 73, 75,
    78–81, 83, 88, 93–95, 111, 116, 118,
    125–126, 130–131, 138, 155, 159, 167,
    184–185, 190, 209, 216, 218, 224, 227,
    239, 242, 246, 248, 267, 271, 274,
    276, 280–281
here 236, 248–249, 261
Hilpert 2, 50, 59, 206, 209–212, 268
Hoffmann 2, 6–7, 10, 16–17, 19, 31, 33,
    37, 39–40, 51–53, 55, 57, 60–62, 66,
    75, 78, 81, 108–109, 133, 138, 142–143,
    167, 170, 204, 208–212, 218, 225,
    228–230, 271, 275–276, 279–281, 285
Horsch 228–229
Huddleston 3, 246
hypothetical condition 200

I

idiom 3, 7–8, 11, 215–219, 221–231,
    241, 284
idiom principle 20, 110, 215–216
idiosyncratic 8, 10, 68, 77, 225,
    229–230, 243, 252
IMPERATIVE-COMMAND cxn
    (negative) 38, 279
IMPERATIVE-COMMAND cxn
    (positive) 37, 279
impersonal (cxn) 40–41, 60, 118,
    123–129, 236–237
indefinite 6, 23–24, 82–83, 85,
    134–139, 141–142, 157–158, 160,
    205–206, 258
indefinite reference 134–137, 141
indirect object 28, 78, 90, 271
indirect speech 46, 234
infinitive 4, 25, 27–28, 45, 48–52, 68,
    88, 91, 117–126, 128, 130, 156, 167,
    195, 226, 248, 251, 259–260, 262, 270
information structure 87, 109–110,
    203–214, 266, 270
INSTRUMENT 104–105, 111, 179
INSTRUMENT/MEANS 179
intention reading 204
interjection 23
interrogative 33–37, 39, 51, 69, 152,
    228, 251–252, 259, 263, 270

into-causative cxn 100–101
intonation 19, 34, 41, 207–208
INTRANSITIVE CXN 86, 279
inversion 201, 274
it 124–127
it-cleft cxn 208–211, 214
item-related(ness) 76–79, 108, 128,
    156, 165, 253, 258
item-specific(ity) 20, 80, 104, 160,
    250, 258

J

Jackendoff 97, 204, 206, 229
joint attention 204–205
Jurafsky 45, 242
juxtaposition 275–276

K

Kaltenböck 204
Kay 2, 9–10, 216, 224–230, 252
Keizer 138
Kibrik 53
Kim 209–210
Kiparsky 126
Klotz 10

L

Lakoff 2, 238
Lambrecht 204, 206, 209, 211–212,
    214
Langacker 1–3, 11–12, 14, 16, 20–21,
    23, 28, 32, 43, 49, 94, 130, 133–137,
    139–140, 142, 153, 182, 189, 192,
    215–216, 236, 239–240, 246, 248, 253,
    267
Lapesa 242
Lea 10
Lee-Goldman 21
Leech 3, 42, 61, 204, 273
left-dislocation (cxn) 211–213
Leino 204, 206, 214
lemma 6, 135, 239–240, 242
lexicogrammatical continuum 11
lexicogrammatical space 11
Lieven 2, 13, 57, 74, 132, 215, 276
ligature 8, 231, 248
likelihood 181
Lohndahl 67
low level (of abstraction) 73, 76, 80,
    216
Lyngfelt 21

M

Mackin 218
MacWhinney 14, 30
Makkai 224
manner 179, 185, 187, 189, 249, 272
Martin 242
mass noun 23, 138–140, 149–151, 160
Matthews 4, 138
McCaig 218
meaning potential 239–240, 243, 255
meaning *see* form-meaning pairing
    2–5, 11, 16, 18–19, 30, 71, 129, 138,
    225, 248, 267–268, 275, 277, 285
mediopassive 76, 111–112, 119
Meibauer 132
mental space 176, 185
metaphor 17, 74, 91, 105, 110, 134, 178,
    187, 203, 236, 242, 261, 267
Michaelis 1, 209–210, 212
Minsky 206
modal cxn 18, 50, 51, 64
modal(s) (cxn) 18, 25, 27, 33, 35,
    44–51, 53, 57, 59, 64, 66, 68, 80,
    88–89, 121–123, 181, 186–187, 231,
    234, 259–260, 270, 274, 278–279,
    284–285
monotransitive (cxn) 4, 16, 18–19,
    83–91, 106, 109, 203, 208, 220–222,
    233, 275, 278, 282
more-comparative cxn 173
MORE-THAN CXN 171–174
MOST/LEAST CXN 168–169, 171, 182
mover 92–93
Müller 21

N

name 152–154, 207, 279
Nesselhauf 224
network 2, 5, 12, 37, 128–129, 183,
    239–263, 268
new 206–213, 278
nominal 32, 78, 113, 126–129, 132–161
nominative 23, 143
non-derivational 108
noun 4, 8, 15, 62, 79–80, 114, 127–128,
    138–161, 165, 168–170, 173–174, 177,
    244–246, 249–250, 252, 255, 260
noun phrase 10, 18–19, 23–24, 26, 28,
    32–33, 82, 85, 88, 109, 129–130,
    132–161, 191, 226, 229, 236, 246–248,
    252, 268–271
NP cxn 18

null instantiation 83
NUMBER 149
number 8, 23–25, 27, 33, 54, 139, 143, 148–151, 154, 235, 255, 257
numeral 24, 26, 161, 253, 257–258

O
O'Connor 2, 9–10, 216, 224–230, 252
Obj 79, 88– 91, 94, 97, 99, 101, 107–108, 113, 116, 172, 186–187, 209, 217, 221, 223, 232, 278–279, 281–285
object 18–19, 22, 26, 28, 70, 72, 78–79, 81–82, 84–91, 96–109, 116, 118, 123, 133–134, 164, 168, 195, 233, 267, 270–271, 278
Obj$_{pp}$ 93–94, 101–108, 281–283
OBJECT-ATTRIBUTE CXN 97, 116, 164, 285
OED 127, 219
operator (verb) 34–36, 42, 51, 68, 234–235, 274
optional 25, 83, 185, 191
or-coordination 17–18
ORDINAL 151

P
Palmer 217, 242, 268
Paquot 217
participant 32, 64, 75–78, 87, 94, 106, 110–111, 130, 206, 259, 271
particle 68, 82, 132, 218–223, 233, 245–250, 261–262, 264
PARTNER 103–104, 115–116, 127
passive 64–66, 108–112, 271, 283
PAST-TENSE CXN 47, 51–57, 58, 62–63, 66
Patel 21
path 92–94, 185, 190, 219
PATH 93, 94
patient 29, 64, 72, 87, 90
Patten 21
Perek 21, 106
PERFECTIVE CXN 63–64, 232
PERSONAL NAME CXN
Petruck 111
phraseological unit 217
plural 6, 8, 23, 33, 52–54, 57, 67, 141–143, 148–150, 240, 242–244, 255
point in time 60, 90, 178, 187–189, 248
point of location 92, 177, 184–185, 188–189, 247–248
polysemy 108, 241–242
possessive pronoun 146, 161, 256

POSSESSOR 146
POSSESSUM 146
postmodifier (cxn) 116–117, 127–128, 138–139, 158–160, 166–167, 184, 186, 190
POTENTIAL ÆFFECTOR 120, 122
pragmatic (meaning/information) 19–20, 31, 37, 41, 210, 214, 216, 225
pre-emption 14–15, 74–75
pre-head 137, 159–161
PRED 34–39, 42, 51, 58, 62, 64, 66, 72, 113, 186, 222, 232, 278–285
predicative possessive cxn 147
predicative use 165
PRED$_{REST}$ 35–36, 38–39, 42, 113
premodifier (cxn) 25–26, 146, 154–155, 157–160, 165–168, 227, 244, 247, 249, 252, 256, 260, 262–263, 268–270, 272
preposition 4, 24, 26, 62, 72, 82, 84, 99–109, 116, 118, 123, 130, 133, 155, 166–167, 176–177, 183, 195, 219, 222–223, 244–248, 261–262
present-tense (cxn) 46–47, 52–58, 63–64, 66–67, 112, 232, 280. 283–285
presupposition 120
principle of no synonymy 212
processing effort 265–270
production 45, 191, 224
PROGRESSIVE CXN 60, 62, 285
pronoun 8, 23–24, 26, 77, 132, 137, 143–146, 152, 160–161, 172, 205, 209, 211–213, 223, 235, 250, 255–256, 265
proper noun 23, 132, 138–140, 153, 160, 255
PROPOSITION 186
protasis 228
prototype 43, 88, 97, 104, 140, 216, 245, 252–253
proverb 216–217
PSEUDO-CLEFT CXN 152, 209, 251
Pullum 3, 246
purpose 4, 180, 183, 187, 199
put up with 223

Q
quantifier 138–139, 149–151, 161, 166, 174, 232, 250, 252, 257–258
QUANTIFIER 150–151, 172–173
quasi-modal 121–123
question 4, 13, 16, 20, 32, 34–36, 39, 41–42, 49–51, 152, 184, 207–208, 251, 263, 265, 274–275
Quirk 3, 26, 224, 273

quotative (cxn) 232–233
quote 232–233

R
Radden 49, 118, 137, 142, 239
Radford 138
Radical Construction Grammar (Radical CxG) 129
ranking (cxn) 151, 161
realistic condition 201
REASON 180, 199
RECIPIENT 64, 72, 74, 76–77, 79, 82, 88–91, 94–95, 103, 108, 113, 116, 127–128
RECIPIENT-GOAL 103
reciprocal pronouns 145–146, 161, 256
recurrent 191, 215, 248
reference 58–60, 133–143, 147, 154, 163, 204–206, 209, 247, 255–258
REFERENT 148, 149, 150, 151, 173
reflexive pronoun 144–145, 161
reification 135–136
replacement 107
reporting clause 232–234
RESULT 98, 99
rheme 87, 204, 206, 211, 237
Rhomieux 21
right-dislocation (cxn) 211–213
role 71–82, 84, 86–89, 94–98, 102–111, 113, 116, 123, 127, 129–131, 146, 163, 181, 190, 196, 203, 223, 238, 262
Rothweiler 132

S
Sag 152, 212
Sanchez-Stockhammer 216, 239
Schank 206
Scheibman 19
Schenkel 130
Schmid 7, 14, 16–17, 206, 216, 224
Schönefeld 17, 225
Schüller 26, 33
Schumacher 130
scope-construction 182
SELF-MOTION CONSTRUCTION 93, 190, 218–219, 222
semantic coherence principle 76
semi-fixed 215
sentence-type construction 30–42
sequence 198
Siepmann 21
Sign-based Construction Grammar 4, 21

Index   315

Sinclair 10, 14, 20, 110, 202, 215–216
singular 23, 25, 33, 52–57, 141–143, 150–151, 157–158, 206
so 263
Sommerer 138
SOURCE 93–94, 190
SOURCE-STATE 101
SPECIFIC ISSUE 101–102
STATE 121, 187
Steels 1
Stefanowitsch 2, 11, 36, 38, 92, 101, 131, 268
STIMULUS 87
stranded preposition 109
structural(ism) 30, 47, 55, 138, 185, 232, 268
structuring construction 182, 273
SUBJ 18, 34–39, 42, 51, 58, 62, 64, 66, 113, 186–187, 209–210, 217, 222, 232, 278–285
Subj 18, 79, 81–86, 88–91, 93–94, 96–99, 101–108, 112–113, 115, 164, 172, 186–187, 221–223, 232, 278–285
SUBJECT-ATTRIBUTE CXN 96, 113, 164, 279–281
SUBSTITUTE 108
superimposition 257–276
superlative constructions 168–169, 171–172
Svartvik 3, 234, 273
syndetic 192–197, 262, 283
Szczerbinski 13

T
tag 234–235
TARGET 105–106
Taylor 43, 244
Tesnière 130, 187
that-clause 88, 123–124, 128–129
theory of mind 204
there, existential there 235–236
THING 134–137

THING DISLIKED 123
THING INDICATED 247
Thomas corpus 13–14, 30, 43, 49, 71, 204, 206
time 51–60, 178–179
  TIME-DURATION 178–179
  TIME-FREQUENCY 178–179
  TIME-SEQUENCE 178–179
  TIME-SPAN 178–179
title construction 152–154
Tobin 226
Tomasello 2, 13, 15, 31–32, 57, 73–74, 204, 215
tone 192, 207, 272
TOPIC 211–213
TOPIC-AREA 82, 99, 117
topicalization 211–214
Torrent 21
transitional probability 45, 222
transparent 218–219, 224
Traugott 60, 187
Trousdale 2
Turner 16–17, 112, 276
Tyler 21

U
Uhrig 10, 19, 85, 93, 94, 118, 184, 190, 212, 216, 237, 267, 276
uncount noun 23, 132, 225, 255
UNDERGOER 86, 120–121, 203
unrealistic condition 68
usage conditions 37, 41–42, 52–53, 57, 184, 212, 268, 273

V
V-EN 63–66, 232, 283
V-ING 61, 62, 222, 285
valency 70, 74–84, 104, 115–116, 128, 130–131, 187
Valency Dictionary of English 83, 124, 130
Van Trijp 33

V_{BASE} 37, 38, 51, 54–55, 57, 64–65, 113, 278, 283
vector 242
verb 24–25, 43–69, 74–80, 259–260, 270
verb-particle 218–223
V_M 50–51, 64, 113, 283
vocative 38, 191
V_T 54–58, 62, 64, 66, 113, 222, 232, 279–284
V_{TM} 34–37, 39, 42, 51, 58, 62, 64, 66, 113, 186–187, 222, 232, 278–285

W
weather verbs 236–237
Welke 98, 131
Wells 207
wh-clause 117, 128, 167, 211, 237, 251
wh-cleft 209–211, 263
WH-NONSUBJECT-QUESTION CXN 36, 64
WH-SUBJECT QUESTION CXN 36
wh-to-infinitive 128
wh-word 162, 234, 251–252
Wittgenstein 182
word 2, 4, 6–8, 10–11, 239–264
word class 22–25, 82, 113–114, 128–129, 160–161, 195, 240, 243–264
WORD CXN 17
word order 34, 57, 81, 189, 196, 208, 214, 219, 233, 265–274
Wulff 21

Y
YES-NO-QUESTION CXN 18, 35, 42, 51, 58, 113
Yule 20, 204, 206

Z
zero 52
Ziem 2, 21, 111